WEST RIDERS BEST

1966: Before, Then & After

ROB VANSTONE

West Riders Best – 1966: Before, Then & After
by Rob Vanstone

First Printing – July 2009

Copyright © 2009
Rob Vanstone

Published by
The Leader-Post Carrier Foundation Inc.
c/o The Leader-Post Ltd.
1964 Park Street
P.O. Box 2020
Regina, Saskatchewan Canada S4P 3G4

Library and Archives Canada Cataloguing in Publication
Vanstone, Rob, 1964-
        West Riders best : 1966: before, then & after / Rob Vanstone.

ISBN 978-1-897010-60-0

        1. Saskatchewan Roughriders (Football team)--History. 2. Football players--Saskatchewan--Biography. 3. Grey Cup (Football)--History.
I. Leader-Post Carrier Foundation Inc II. Title.

GV948.3.S37V36 2009   796.335'6409712445   C2009-903708-4

Cover and page design by Brian Danchuk, Brian Danchuk Design, Regina
Page formatting by Iona Glabus

Designed, Printed and Produced in Canada by:
Centax Books, a division of PrintWest Communications Ltd.
Publishing Director: Dan Marce
Publishing Coordinator: Iona Glabus
1150 Eighth Avenue, Regina, Saskatchewan, Canada S4R 1C9
(306) 525-2304   FAX: (306) 757-2439
centax@printwest.com   www.centaxbooks.com

Supporting Community and Education

At the time of publication of this 1966 Roughriders tribute book, the Leader-Post Foundation had awarded more than $250,000 in educational scholarships over its 25 years of existence. The foundation has donated and/or committed to a $100,000 donation to the Hospitals of Regina expansion program, earmarked for a library in the birthing area of the Regina General Hospital.

In addition to raising scholarship funds, this tribute to the Roughriders' 1966 championship team will provide a legacy to the first-ever Roughrider Grey Cup champions.

The Leader-Post Foundation would also like to thank the Saskatchewan Sports Hall of Fame and Museum (SSHFM) and the Saskatchewan Lotteries Trust for their generous financial support under the terms of the Sport History Project Grant. It would also like to acknowledge the technical assistance offered by SSHFM staff and members of the SSHFM's Sport History Project Committee in preparing this publication.

Thank you for purchasing this book and for helping those we assist in their educational endeavors.

Photo Credits:

This project would not have been complete without the following who have contributed and lent their photographs for our use:

Saskatchewan Sports Hall of Fame and Museum (SSHFM)
The Leader-Post
Heenan Studios and the late Gord Heenan
Solilo Studios, John, Ken and Bruce Solilo
West's Studios
The Vancouver Sun
The Vancouver Province
The Shaw family
The StarPhoenix
The Lancaster family
The Edmonton Journal
The Willie Jacobs family
Joseph Dojack
Cover photo courtesy of *Vancouver Sun*
Back cover photo courtesy of Don Webb

DEDICATION

To my father, Alan Vanstone, who limited his reading to science fiction — although I hope he would have made an exception in this case.

To my mother, Helen Mather, who was so excited about this project that she framed the outline.

To my beautiful wife, Chryssoula Filippakopoulos, who allowed me to write the book of my dreams — even when I took my files on vacation, intruding upon her precious carry-on space in the process.

And to the 1966 Saskatchewan Roughriders. When I was growing up, you were my heroes. Now I am proud to call you friends. It is an honour to tell your story.

TABLE OF CONTENTS

AUTHOR BIOGRAPHY

Rob Vanstone — *the Leader-Post's* Sports Editor and sports columnist — was born in Regina and grew up following the Saskatchewan Roughriders. He has been working full-time at *the Leader-Post* since 1987 and has covered the Roughriders on a regular basis since 1996. As a spectator or reporter, Vanstone has been in attendance for the Roughriders' Grey Cup appearances in 1976, 1989, 1997 and 2007. His first airplane trip, at the age of eight, was to Winnipeg for the 1972 Western Conference final — which the Roughriders won 27-24 on the strength of a patented Ron Lancaster comeback.

In 2008, Vanstone covered the Summer Olympic Games in Beijing for Canwest News Service, and will also be part of the newspaper chain's team for the 2010 Winter Olympic Games in Vancouver and Whistler, B.C. Vanstone is a graduate of Massey School, Campbell Collegiate and the University of Regina's School of Journalism and Communications. Vanstone and his wife, Chryssoula Filippakopoulos, were married in 1999.

Rob Vanstone *holding the 1966 Grey Cup football caught by Alan Ford (see page 163)* | Photo courtesy of *Leader-Post*

Photo courtesy of Don Webb

SASKATCHEWAN ROUGHRIDERS – 1966 GREY CUP CHAMPIONS

1ST ROW: Don MacDonald (President), Tom Beynon, Al Benecick, Clyde Brock, Ken Reed, Ron Atchison, Ted Urness, Jack Abendschan, Ed McQuarters

2ND ROW: Eagle Keys (head coach), Gord Barwell, Dale West, Alan Ford, Galen Wahlmeier, Gil Petmanis, Cliff Shaw, Wayne Shaw, Jim Worden, Ken Preston (general manager)

3RD ROW: Jack Gotta (assistant coach), Moe Levesque, Wally Dempsey, Garner Ekstran, Reg Whitehouse, Mike Ringer, Hugh Campbell, Ted Dushinski, Henry Dorsch, Jim Duncan (assistant coach)

4TH ROW: Dale Laird (equipment manager), Gene Wlasiuk, Bruce Bennett, Ron Lancaster, Paul Dudley, Ed Buchanan, Larry Dumelie, George Reed, Bob Kosid, Sandy Archer (trainer)

PROLOGUE

"Somewhere, sometime, somebody might write a history of the Saskatchewan Roughriders. If it is far in the future when the 1966 season is re-told, readers won't believe it. It will be classed as a fiction piece because no game, no sport or no team would believably have all the happenings of the 1966 Saskatchewan Roughriders."

— **Laurie Artiss, *Leader-Post*, September 1966.**

Forty years had elapsed since the Saskatchewan Roughriders' Grey Cup championship of 1966, but in one respect, nothing had changed. Nobody wanted to leave the room.

Ron Lancaster, for one, had sat in his stall at Vancouver's Empire Stadium on Nov. 26, 1966, soaking in the aftermath of the Roughriders' ice-breaking Grey Cup victory. "There probably isn't a much better feeling than to be in the locker room after winning a game," Lancaster reflected. "It's almost like a relief that the season's over, and it went the way you wanted it to, because that doesn't happen very often where everything goes your way. It was just nice to sit around and enjoy it."

They enjoyed it again in July of 2006, when the Roughriders staged a 40th-anniversary reunion of their first-ever

Hugh Campbell and Ron Lancaster *1966 Grey Cup |*
Photo courtesy of *Vancouver Sun*

championship edition. The much-anticipated event concluded with a breakfast at the Hotel Saskatchewan Radisson Plaza.

"When the gathering came to an end, grown men could not hold back their tears," defensive lineman Ed McQuarters said. "The four-day reunion was over. Many players stood around, prolonging the event. Some wept openly, shook hands, and embraced each other. Wives were clinging to each other, weeping as they said goodbye. It appeared that every other person in the room had a camera, and the cameras were being put to good use."

McQuarters and his wife, Bunny, sat at a table that morning with Roughriders president and chief executive officer Jim Hopson, who had played a key role in organizing the reunion. For the most part, it was a celebration. But the final few hours — the precious time spent at breakfast — were bittersweet.

"That morning, I remember seeing guys like Hugh Campbell — who is usually a quiet, reserved guy — get emotional," Hopson said of the reunion. "It was something to see. There was a recognition among the guys in that room that there were some people they probably wouldn't see again because of travel or because of people passing away. It's sad, but it's a fact of life."

Indeed, four members of the 1966 Roughriders who were alive at the time of the reunion would be gone by 2008 – Lancaster, offensive lineman Reg Whitehouse, tight end Jim Worden and trainer Sandy Archer. Neither Whitehouse nor Worden attended the reunion, but Lancaster and Archer revelled in the occasion. "Sandy was in his glory at the reunion – holding court, smoking a cigarette and telling stories," Hopson said. "George Reed was laughing so hard he was almost crying, and those were probably the same stories Sandy told 50 years ago."

Had anything changed over these 40 years? Appearances, for starters. The hair was grey, or less abundant. Some players walked with limps — an enduring souvenir of time spent playing the unforgiving and often brutal game of Canadian professional football. In some cases, there were notable differences in weight — but not necessarily in the direction one might have expected. Linemen Jack Abendschan, Tom Beynon and Don Gerhardt looked more like defensive backs. All in their early 60s, they appeared to be at least 10 years younger.

The reunion brought out the kid in everyone. For four days in the summer of 2006, they were the 1966 Saskatchewan Roughriders once again. They heard the applause. They signed autographs for reverential fans. And they were together.

"It was really interesting seeing the joy on the faces of the guys, with their teammates, family members and kids here," Hopson said. "It was interesting to see how much they reverted back to being 25. You're talking about guys who were by and large in their 60s, or even their 70s, and you're watching them be kids again. It was remarkable how much they'd go back to being teammates, with all the kidding and ribbing. Here we are, 40 years later. They've all raised families and done a lot of things in their lives since then, but they're still juicing each other about 40 years ago. It was like 40 years didn't pass."

Hugh Campbell was typically a step ahead of everyone during his phenomenally successful career as a Canadian Football League receiver, coach and executive. Naturally, the intuitive Campbell knew what to expect well in advance of the 1966 Roughriders' gathering, having attended in May of 2005 a reunion of the Whitworth College football team, which he had coached before assuming the Edmonton Eskimos' reins. The same dynamic was at work during the football reunions in Regina and Spokane, Wash.

"It's about a group of people who had a moment in time that keeps this bond forever," Campbell said as the 1966 reunion neared. "That's why they're all back, and the ones who can't come are wishing they were there. The thing that everybody is always amazed at — like when we went back to Saskatchewan [for a 25-year reunion in 1991] — is that it only takes about 15 minutes and everybody's acting like they did when we played. They're being silly and saying the same jokes. There's something in your brain. It's all in there, but you haven't brought it out for so long. Once you get it warmed up, your behaviour is the same. You're not going to go out and steal a car or anything, but you're just as likely to behave however you behaved back then. There's no bullshit.

"If you go to a high school reunion or an office-building reunion, then everybody's trying to impress people with how distinguished they are, and with how they have a nice car or something. You go to a football reunion and nobody's trying to act above or different than how they acted before, because there are no secrets on a football team. Within the locker room, everybody knows. So when you go back to a reunion of that group, it's instantaneous. You know which guy you'd want to have babysit your kids or, in this day and age, your grandkids."

Nobody had a grander time at the reunion than Ed McQuarters. "Ed is a guy I have a tremendous amount of time and respect for," Hopson said of his friend and former Roughriders teammate. "He's a quiet guy and a reserved guy, but at the reunion, Ed just seemed to come alive. He was electric that weekend. He had actually stayed home from his high school reunion to be part of our reunion. When I think of memories from the reunion, I think of Ed."

McQuarters could not stop thinking of the reunion from the moment it was announced. "I immediately got butterflies in the pit of my stomach," he said. "Forty years had passed since

Ed McQuarters *40 years later* | Photo courtesy of *Leader-Post*

all of us teammates had been together. I was worried that I wouldn't remember everybody's names, and I experienced even more anxiety that perhaps I might not remember the names of their wives. As reunion week got closer, I became preoccupied with thoughts of seeing a group of men that I grew to love during our playing days together. Sure, winning brings a team closer together than if the team is not winning, but that fact was just a small reason for my feelings toward this special group."

McQuarters arrived in Regina midway through the 1966 season after being released by the National Football League's St. Louis Cardinals, in whose training camp he had encountered racism. He immediately found a home in Saskatchewan, where he was one of the few black players on the team, and never left.

Many members of the 1966 Roughriders point to McQuarters as the difference-maker in that landmark season — quite the compliment, considering the esteemed company he kept. In 1966, Lancaster was named the Western Conference's outstanding player, Reed enjoyed one of 11 seasons in which he rushed for at least 1,000 yards, and Campbell caught 17 touchdown passes (a CFL single-season record at the time). But it was McQuarters who solidified the defence. His fumble return for a touchdown in the latter stages of a 1966 playoff game in Winnipeg cemented Saskatchewan's first Grey Cup berth since 1951. McQuarters and his defensive cohorts proceeded to stifle the potent Ottawa offence for most of the 1966 league final, which ended with Saskatchewan winning 29-14.

Years later, McQuarters confided that he did not enjoy football, but he loved the people. He played in four Grey Cups, earned distinction as the CFL's outstanding defensive player in 1967, and was eventually enshrined in the Canadian Football Hall of Fame. He raised a family and was a respected employee at SaskPower for more than 30 years. With all that to his name, McQuarters referred to four days in July of 2006 as one of the most important periods in his life.

"Every once in a while, an event of outstanding proportions happens," he said. "Forty years later, it was happening again. As the days grew nearer to the event, I was like a kid on Christmas Eve — excited and looking forward to a visit from Santa. Finally, reunion week arrived. Immediately, I could hear Bob Kosid laughing before I even stepped into the Telegraph Room at Casino Regina on the first day of events. The first former teammate I saw was Jack Abendschan, then Don Gerhardt, then Clyde Brock. As I greeted and embraced all in attendance, I realized that I could recall all their names. Greeting their wives, I also realized that I could recall all their names, too. Everyone looked good! I thought, 'Wow! We're back together again.'"

There was not a happier guy in the room that day than Ed McQuarters.

I had not met Ed McQuarters until January of 2006, at which point he floored me.

He was one of the last people I expected to interview for this project. At best, I had hoped for grudging co-operation, and perhaps an obligatory quote or two from this pivotal player. Given his invaluable contributions during the 1966 season, McQuarters had to be represented in some depth. But how? I envisioned having to lean on others for substantive material pertaining to McQuarters. This is a man, I was told, who eschewed the limelight and was not enamoured of the interview process. Nonetheless, I attempted to contact him while preparing a *Leader-Post* series that would commemorate the 40th anniversary of the Roughriders' long-awaited triumph — the 1966 Grey Cup.

I had a home address, but not a telephone number, for McQuarters. So I wrote him a short letter, explaining my project. I asked him to contact me if he was amenable to an interview. The letter was mailed without an abundance of optimism. A few days later, I arrived in the newsroom to find the good name of "Ed McQuarters" in my e-mail account. He could not have responded more promptly or cordially. He offered to visit the *Leader-Post* to be interviewed. For more than two hours, I was spellbound as McQuarters told his life story. As this dignified and thoughtful gentleman spoke so expansively with eloquence, passion and candor, I thought, "Maybe I've got something here." At that point, I began thinking in terms of a project that was even more ambitious than an already substantial five-part newspaper series. Could there be a book in this? The conversation with McQuarters altered the scope of my research. I began to conduct more extensive interviews with members of the 1966 Roughriders. The mindset: "I will write this as a newspaper series but research it as though I were preparing a book, just in case."

Between December of 2005 and June of 2006, virtually every living member of the 1966 Roughriders was contacted. Only in rare instances, such as when I attempted to reach an ailing Jim Worden in the spring of 2006, was it impractical to conduct an interview. By then, the 1966 Grey Cup was an obsession. The 40th-anniversary reunion was looming, and I was already looking beyond that to the possibility of celebrating the 1966 Roughriders in greater depth. The interviews continued for nearly three years after the reunion, extending far beyond the players. Close to 100 people were interviewed, many of them on multiple occasions.

This book, once a pipe dream, is the satisfaction of a lingering curiosity about the 1966 Roughriders. As one who was

Dave Ridgway *Victory is oh so sweet!* |
Photo courtesy of *Leader-Post*

born in 1964, I did not have first-hand recollection of watching that team play — although a football loving mother assures me I frequented Taylor Field during that championship season. Mom also recalls I was lodged in front of a neighbour's television on the afternoon of Nov. 26, 1966, when the franchise won its first championship since the inception of the Regina Rugby Club in 1910.

They would not win the Grey Cup again until Nov. 26, 1989 — 23 years to the day after the Roughriders had upset Ottawa at Empire Stadium. In 1989, I witnessed Dave Ridgway's game-winning, last-second field goal from a seat in the upper extremities of Toronto's SkyDome (now Rogers Centre). By then, technology had advanced to the point where almost everyone owned a VCR. Thousands of Roughriders fans videotaped the 1989 classic, in which Saskatchewan defeated the Hamilton Tiger-Cats 43-40. For anyone who craved more footage, a commemorative video was quickly produced.

The Grey Cup victory of 2007, an event I covered for the *Leader-Post*, was widely recorded by fans and exhaustively reported by the media. Within a year of the Roughriders' 23-19 championship victory over the Winnipeg Blue Bombers, CKRM's Rod Pedersen had released a book about the 2007 season. Meanwhile, I kept pecking away at the 1966 retrospective, hoping to further an understanding and appreciation of Saskatchewan's first Grey Cup team. The running joke in the newsroom became: "If Rod Pedersen can write the 2007 book in less than a year, why are we waiting more than 40 years for 1966?"

Although the events of 1966 were the impetus for the research, the project quickly evolved into something of considerably greater dimension than one game, or one season. This book strives to tell the story of several eras in the lives of a diverse, beloved and colourful cast of characters — beginning with the evolution of the team in the early 1950s. How was the 1966 team formed? Why did that team win that year? Why weren't there several more Grey Cup titles? And what became of those who played for the 1966 Roughriders?

The stories of their lives, which provide the foundation for this book, are alternately poignant, humorous, revealing, nostalgic, tragic, deeply personal and, despite the passage of time, surprisingly fresh — even to the participants themselves. It has been the highlight of my career to write about these men. I hope you enjoy getting to know them as much as I did.

CHAPTER 1 | "OUR TEAM IS RED-HOT"

Dale West's surname was appropriate to the occasion. He was at Taylor Field when the Saskatchewan Roughriders won the West in 1951. At the time, he was 10 years old and attending his first pro football game. "My dad took me to Regina and we saw Saskatchewan defeat Edmonton to go to the Grey Cup in 1951," said the Cabri-born West, who grew up in Saskatoon. "The next time they were in a Grey Cup, I was playing in it."

Fifteen years later, West registered a key interception to help Saskatchewan earn a 29-14 Grey Cup victory over the Ottawa Rough Riders at Empire Stadium in Vancouver. By then, West was an established Canadian Football League star. In 1951, by contrast, a wide-eyed West watched the climax of a long-weekend home playoff set against the Edmonton Eskimos. West and his father were sitting in the northwest corner of Taylor Field, 15 rows up. As has been the case throughout their history, the Roughriders did it the hard way. Edmonton posted a 15-11 home-field victory, holding the visitors to two first downs, to open the best-of-three Western Interprovincial Football Union final. The series then moved to Regina for games on Nov. 10 and, if necessary, Nov. 12.

Saskatchewan forced a deciding game by winning 12-5. Two days later, 12,463 people were shoehorned into Taylor Field, which at the time had a capacity of 8,700. The last available seat at the stadium was occupied by 1 p.m., a half-hour before the much-anticipated kickoff. At one end of the field, the Lions Band was providing pre-game entertainment, as was the Roughriders' Symphony Five on the opposite side.

Since the conclusion of Game 2, the field had been covered with four tons of straw and 350 pieces of old canvas. Fans and players braved the chilly conditions during a game in which points, it seemed, would be at a premium. Saskatchewan assumed quarter leads of 6-0, 7-0 and 8-0 as a prelude to a wild final period, which would include two touchdowns by each team. Saskatchewan went ahead to stay when quarterback Glenn Dobbs — a charismatic figure who had instantly captured the imagination of the Roughriders' fans during his first (and finest) season in Regina — scored from one yard out to give his team a 19-12 lead. The Roughriders staved off an Edmonton rally to win 19-18.

At that point, the excitement was only beginning. Youngsters invaded the Roughriders' dressing room and shook hands with the victorious players. Clair Warner, in his 32nd year of serving the team in a volunteer capacity, sat back, smiled, and savoured the spectacle. "We may lose some equipment today," Warner told the *Leader-Post*, which had delayed the publication of its Monday edition so it could document the deciding game. "I don't care. The kids are welcome to it. I'm satisfied."

Clair Warner |
Photo courtesy of SSHFM

The Saskatchewan players would not be satisfied until they had adhered to football tradition by throwing the triumphant head coach, in this case Harry (Blackjack) Smith,

Glenn Dobbs (*left*) **and Harry Smith** |
Photo courtesy of SSHFM

into the shower. Smith had the presence of mind to discard his trousers before being saturated. "You were wonderful," Smith told his players as they hauled him toward the shower. "There may have been better football games than that one today, but nobody ever played as hard as you did. I'm proud of you all. You're my boys!"

Meanwhile, frenzied fans were uprooting the uprights and carrying them out of the stadium — "over the helpless grins of Regina policemen," according to a *Leader-Post* report. "If there were wooden goal posts, down they came," said Marge Smith, who attended the game. "It was just a normal thing back then."

Led by the Symphony Five, several hundred fans paraded downtown to city hall, with the goal posts in tow, chanting, "Our team is red-hot!" The throng moved to the Hotel Saskatchewan, and then back to city hall, where the band played the team's theme song, "On Roughriders." By that time, the ranks of revellers had swelled to more than 1,000.

Eventually, one member of the giddy group suggested that the goal posts — or what remained of them — should be presented to Dobbs. The idea quickly received widespread assent. The parade continued down Albert Street, to 13th Avenue, to Dobbs' residence on the 2100-block Montague Street. One problem: Neither Dobbs nor his wife had yet returned home. However, a babysitter brought out Dobbs' two sons — Glenn Jr., 6, and Johnny, 3 — to greet the crowd. That acknowledgement did not placate some diehards in the group, who refused to leave the premises until there was a sighting of Dobbs.

"The goal posts, still huge pieces of timber, despite the chunks that had been torn from them, were a little unwieldy, so someone borrowed an axe and proceeded to reduce the posts to more comfortable size," the *Leader-Post* reported. "Then they were erected in front of the Dobbs' residence and decorated with the Rider colours and signs reading 'Thanks Dobber' and 'Hi Dobber.' "

The return of Dobbs elicited a roar among the 100 fans who greeted him. He got out of the car, thanked the crowd, said good night to his sons, and accompanied Mrs. Dobbs to a dinner at the Assiniboia Club. The dinner was hosted by Roughriders president Bob Kramer.

Kramer presided over a Roughriders team which aggressively pursued American players who elevated the club's fortunes in 1951 and would contribute in the years to follow. Most notably, there was the successful courtship with Dobbs, a first-round draft pick of the National Football League's Chicago Cardinals. Dobbs had been a Heisman Trophy candidate and All-American at Tulsa University.

After graduating from Tulsa, Dobbs spent four seasons in the old All-America Football Conference, earning most-valuable-player honours with the 1946 Brooklyn Dodgers (yes, there was also a football team by that name). He went on to excel with the AAFC's Los Angeles Dons, who folded after the 1949 season. The 6-foot-4 passer remained involved with football in 1950 as a radio commentator on Oklahoma A&M college games.

Around the same time, Roughriders supporters Don MacDonald and Charlie Hay were conducting business with an engineering firm in Tulsa. On one business trip, MacDonald — who would eventually become the first Roughriders president to celebrate a Grey Cup victory — got a tip that Dobbs was available. MacDonald did not have time to put out feelers to Dobbs, so he suggested that Hay do so on a subsequent trip. Sure enough, Dobbs expressed interest. That provided the impetus for Roughriders board member Jack Rowand to fly to Tulsa at his own expense and conduct week-long contract negotiations.

Don MacDonald |

There was only one snag. Dobbs would not be available until 1951 because he was obligated to fulfil his broadcast contract. In any event, the Roughriders eventually got their man, who had also been wooed by the NFL's Chicago Bears and their legendary coach, George (Papa Bear) Halas. "I was going to sign with the Riders or the Bears," Dobbs recalled in 1998. "I asked Mr. Halas if he could match the offer. He didn't come up to my expectations so I told him, 'I'm signing with Saskatchewan.' He wished me good luck. I turned around and shook hands with the guys on the Roughriders' board and that was it. It worked out beautifully. I enjoyed my time up there."

The association was mutually enjoyable from the outset. Dobbs was introduced to Regina, which then had 71,319 inhabitants, on a frigid Feb. 25 afternoon in 1951 — and was immediately ushered to a Quarterback Club gathering at the Grand Theatre, where newly appointed head coach Harry (Blackjack) Smith was also introduced. "I remember thinking, 'That'll be nice. There won't be too many people,' " Dobbs said. "Wouldn't you know it? The darned place was packed and the lineup outside was a block long."

The Quarterback Club was packed a half-hour before Dobbs was to arrive. In typically accommodating fashion, he proceeded outside and met hundreds of freezing fans, who braved a blizzard and minus-30 temperatures. He also made a lasting impression during another offseason visit. The fence outside Taylor Field needed painting, so Dobbs chipped in — enabling the fans to enjoy what was quite literally a brush with greatness.

"My second time up there, everyone got a paint brush," Dobbs said. "The whole team showed up. I've never seen so many people. We painted the whole stadium in one day. We didn't do a bad job, either. Before, I had played in Brooklyn and Los Angeles. You'd see people at the games, especially in California. There would be 50 or 100 kids lining up for autographs. You'd see them, but you'd never see them again. In Regina, you knew those people. You knew everybody. You'd call everybody by their first name. It was wonderful. It was a blessing. It was the greatest part of my career."

During the magical season of 1951, Dobbs piloted the Roughriders to their first-ever first-place finish in the Western Interprovincial Football Union. He threw 28 touchdown passes — a franchise record, equalled by Ron Lancaster in 1966 — in 14 regular-season games and averaged 44.2 yards per punt. Twenty of his 90 punts produced single points.

Dobbs was productive like nobody Roughriders fans had ever seen at football's pivotal position, despite being 31 when he made his debut in Saskatchewan. But Dobbs' remarkable appeal transcended statistics — including his dimensions (6-foot-4 and 215 pounds). He was congenial, obliging, Hollywood handsome, and charismatic.

Glenn Dobbs | Photo courtesy of SSHFM

The quarterback's popularity quickly soared, as did sales of Dobber jeans and Dobber shirts. Several cars had licence plates which read "Dobberville." The Regina post office received letters addressed to "Dobberville, Saskatchewan," and, naturally, so did the man himself. "Those were great times," Dobbs reflected. "We used to go to church with the people and visit their homes and their schools. Little kids would come to the door, wanting autographs. We'd say, 'Sure, come on in!' We were the hard-workingest bunch of guys you ever saw."

That attitude — along with the recruitment of top-calibre Americans such as Dobbs, receivers Jack Russell and Jack Nix, two-way lineman Martin Ruby and centre Red Ettinger — helped the 1951 Roughriders finish with an 8-6 record. Oddly enough, one of the losses spawned a Roughriders tradition. On Labour Day weekend, the Roughriders faced the Winnipeg Blue Bombers before a record crowd of 12,028. In the fourth quarter, Bombers quarterback Indian Jack Jacobs came off the bench to throw three touchdown passes and engineer a 24-22 Winnipeg victory. That was the first memorable Roughriders-Bombers game in what has become a series of Labour Day Classics.

The 1951 Roughriders went on to post an identical regular-season record as Edmonton and Winnipeg. A tiebreaking formula based on points for and against worked in Saskatchewan's favour. Next stop: Edmonton.

Taylor Field *Sellout in the 1950s* | Photo courtesy of SSHFM

Three gruelling games against Edmonton propelled Saskatchewan into the Grey Cup against Ottawa. The adulation over Dobbs reached its peak. As the fans celebrated his presence, the iconic quarterback reciprocated.

"It's the fans," he told reporters on Nov. 12, 1951. "The people up here have been terrific. I played college football and had a turn at the pro game. I was in Los Angeles a long time and nobody cared much about the footballers off the field. I came up here and every door was open to me. The other boys who came up [from the United States] will say the same thing. We had to win. The fans deserved it!"

The Roughriders' loyalists suitably celebrated their team's first appearance in the national final since 1934, when they had lost for the seventh time in as many trips to the big game. "I don't care what happens in the Grey Cup," one fan said in the presence of the *Leader-Post's* Tom (Scotty) Melville. "It will be an anticlimax. I'm satisfied. I'M HAPPY!" So were the bean-counters at Canadian Pacific Railway. The company was deluged by inquiries from fans who wanted to travel to Toronto via train for the Grey Cup.

The Rider Special was to leave the Queen City early in the afternoon of Nov. 21 and arrive in Toronto 48 hours later — one day before the game. The base rate for the return trip was $54.15, with sleeping accommodations costing extra. Two baggage cars on the Special were set aside for dancing and other entertainment.

Meanwhile, floats were being designed and built for the formal Grey Cup parade. One of the floats was to contain 15,000 miniature loaves of bread, which were to be distributed to onlookers who lined the streets of Toronto. The Roughriders' float displayed a giant football and a key. "It's been a long long time since 1934," read the message on the float. "The Dobber holds the key." The floats would be pulled by Saskatchewan draft horses, which were conveniently at a livestock show in Toronto.

Myrtle Bainbridge, an 18-year-old student from Balfour Tech, was also to be part of the eastward-bound Saskatchewan contingent. She had been named Miss Saskatchewan Roughrider during the first home playoff game, thereby ensuring that she would travel to Toronto for the Miss Grey Cup pageant. As it turned out, Bainbridge would have plenty of company en route to Toronto. The response to the Rider Special was so overwhelming that a second train was required. "This is great, but it's giving us a headache," marvelled Tommy McLeod, the chairman of Regina's Grey Cup committee. "Now we have to double what we had planned to do. There'll be two more baggage cars for dancing and whoop-de-do, and there'll have to be another hillbilly orchestra. Still, it's a thing that doesn't happen every day and we'll do our utmost to look after everybody."

The team boarded a train on the Monday of Grey Cup week, two days after a Quarterback Club rally at the Regina Armoury attracted 3,000 well-wishers. Roughriders fans, nearly 500 strong, boarded the Rider Special on Nov. 21. Two rail-liners, dubbed the "Green" and "White" trains, departed within 20 minutes of one another. Another 150 people embarked that week via Trans-Canada Airlines, a precursor to Air Canada.

"Football fever in usually staid Regina has never been higher and there was no hiding the whooping crowd of Toronto-bound fans and the hundreds more that packed the station to see them off," Trevor Lloyd wrote in the *Leader-Post*. "It was the noisiest, gayest and most colourful crowd that Regina has seen in many a year but only an example of a bigger and better show that fans hope to put on when their Roughriders return with the Grey Cup."

Two days later, the passengers disembarked in Toronto, led by two bands — the Hungry and Thirsty Fours. "The noise was so terrific that the steady grinding from the drills working on Toronto's new multi-million-dollar subway in front of the Union Station was drowned out," *Leader-Post* scribe Harvey Dryden reported. "Big, white, 10-gallon hats were everywhere and it wasn't long before the Roughriders crowd completely took over the lobby of the Royal York hotel. It was like a great big carnival with everybody having a good time." The welcoming committee at Union Station included Roughriders players, many of whom were present to greet their wives or girlfriends. Dobbs, as always, was a magnetic presence. A procession of fans approached him to wish him good luck in the Grey Cup, to be played on a Saturday afternoon at Varsity Stadium.

Good luck? That was a foreign concept to the Roughriders as the 1951 Grey Cup loomed. Entering the 1951 final, the Roughriders had played in seven Grey Cups, losing each time. The combined score: 181-27.

The Roughriders came agonizingly close to reaching their eighth Grey Cup in 1949 when they opposed the Calgary Stampeders in the two-game, total-points Western Interprovincial Football League final. Calgary won 18-12 in Game 1 at Taylor Field. The game concluded when Saskatchewan was stopped on Calgary's one-yard line. The Roughriders then travelled to Calgary, needing to win Game 2 by at least seven points to advance to their first Grey Cup since 1934. Saskatchewan won the series finale 9-4, but Calgary captured the two-game set, 22-21.

In the waning minutes of Game 2, the Roughriders had two opportunities to kick the winning field goal. Buck Rogers was called upon to attempt the first kick. "It was a lead-pipe cinch, right in front," recalled Roy Wright, a member of the 1949 Roughriders. "It was almost like a convert. Buck Rogers lined up for the field goal and kicked it right into the line. Les Lear was Calgary's playing coach at the time and he got called for offside, so we got another chance." And Riders head coach Fred Grant called upon another kicker. "This time, Del Wardien — who was a tremendous football player — kicked it," Wright said. "Well, if he doesn't kick it right into the line ... We didn't get to go to the Grey Cup."

That would change two years later.

As the 1951 Grey Cup approached, Dobbs was hampered by a severe charleyhorse and three broken ribs — injuries that were concealed or downplayed in advance of the game.

It got worse. Jack Russell, the all-star receiver, had injured a knee on the last play of the deciding game against Edmonton and would not be able to participate in the Grey Cup. Martin Ruby (who had a shoulder injury) and Red Ettinger (bruised ribs) were able to play, but only with the aid of Novocaine. Exacerbating the problem, fullback Bob Sandberg — a product of Hibbing, Minn., who had played in the WIFU as a non-import on the grounds that he had lived in Winnipeg for four straight years — would be designated as an import by the Canadian Rugby Union. Therefore, he could not play in the Grey Cup because the

Roughriders would have exceeded the import quota with him in the lineup. The offensive backfield was hampered even further by ankle injuries to Al Bodine and Del Wardien.

Come game time, the Roughriders assumed a 2-0 lead on back-to-back punt singles by Dobbs, only to have Ottawa respond with 20 consecutive points before a record crowd of 27,326 — which, according to a *Leader-Post* headline, helped make "Staid Toronto gay for football final." Saskatchewan rallied with five-point touchdowns by Jack Nix and Sully Glasser, with Ettinger converting both majors, but it was too late. Ottawa won, 21-14.

In the Roughriders' dressing room after the game, the sobbing of one player was clearly audible. Mickey Maguire was despondent after fumbling away two punts. His miscues had led to an Ottawa touchdown and single. The second fumble, in the latter stages, was particularly crucial as Saskatchewan desperately needed possession of the football.

Dobbs sat down in the stall next to Maguire and offered words of consolation. "Look, kid, you didn't lose that ball game for us," Dobbs told him. "We all lost it — the guys in the backfield and the guys in the line. We all did something wrong. I did a lot of things that were wrong. I threw a lot of passes that were pretty poor. No one man ever lost a game, just as no one man ever won it. Cut it out. Do you hear me? Cut it out. Forget those fumbles. You're all right."

Dobbs then ruffled Maguire's hair and returned to his allotted space in the dressing room, ever the epitome of class, regardless of the circumstances.

Back in Regina, a gigantic headline — TOUGH LUCK! — adorned the front page of the *Leader-Post*. Tough luck, indeed.

"In the Grey Cup, Glenn was pretty much playing on one foot," recalled Bob Pelling, who caught three of Dobbs' passes in that game. "He was hurting a whole lot, but he played well and it was close." Head coach Harry Smith noted that the general spate of injuries also hurt the Roughriders' chances. "We just didn't have the manpower to go around," he told the press after the game. "If we had suited a full club, I'm sure we would have taken it."

The Roughriders had little choice but to ponder some hypotheticals. What if Dobbs had been healthy? What if his favourite target, Russell, had been available? What if . . .? "We would have kicked the tar out of Ottawa if we had been at full strength," team president Bob Kramer said.

Saskatchewan did celebrate one notable victory while in Toronto. Myrtle Bainbridge was named Miss Grey Cup. The female influence was also noted the day after the Grey Cup, when three Saskatchewan ladies obtained a small pail and decorated it with green-and-white ribbons, constructing a makeshift trophy. They proceeded to board a Regina-bound train at Union Station. At every stop during the westward trek, the fans chanted, "Look, we got the Grey Cup," while parading around the station platforms. As the train approached Sudbury, Ont., some of the female passengers organized a square dance. Those plans changed upon arrival, however, when a Western polka broke out during a 15-minute station stop. Eventually, the trains slowed to a halt on Regina's South Railway Street, after which goal posts were carried around downtown Regina. Five men had returned home with a section of the Varsity Stadium uprights. "Ottawa fans tried to steal it from us in Toronto, so we checked it at the station," one of the men explained. "We brought it back in the baggage car."

The team returned from Toronto three days after the game. Fans flocked to the train station to welcome home the runners-up. Supporters lined the streets as the Roughriders were transported in special cars from the train station to Regina's primary hockey facility, Exhibition Stadium, where more than 5,000 well-wishers were waiting. The welcoming committee included Premier Tommy Douglas, who told the team: "Don't feel too badly if you had a little trouble with Ottawa. I've had some trouble with Ottawa myself."

As always, the loudest applause was reserved for the revered quarterback. "I'm sorry we haven't won the Grey Cup," Dobbs told the boisterous gathering. "We should have it and the only reason we haven't got it is because we left everything in that strenuous Edmonton series. None of us Americans ever expected a welcome like this."

Dobbs was serenaded by one of the Grey Cup week's most popular songs, which included the lyrics, "We don't give a darn for all the rest of Canada. We're from Dobberville." The spirit inside the Stadium masked the fact that the Roughriders' Grey Cup slate had dropped to 0-and-8.

But, for a change, the Roughriders were actually a viable opponent in a Grey Cup. That fact was not lost on the people who packed Exhibition Stadium. "Thanks from the bottom of my heart," president Bob Kramer told the crowd. "I sincerely hope you'll back us again next year when we go out after that Cup."

Little did Kramer, or anyone else, suspect that "next year" was 15 years away.

CHAPTER 2 # "THE TOUGHEST THING I'VE EVER HAD TO DO"

As the 1952 season dawned, football fans across the country knew about Dobberville. But few people had heard of two actual Saskatchewan communities, named Fielding and Mullingar. Ron Atchison, who had ties to both burgs, was hardly familiar to fans himself.

That would eventually change. Over 17 seasons as a Roughriders defensive lineman, Atchison would earn all-star honours and help Saskatchewan win its first-ever Grey Cup. He would eventually be enshrined in the Canadian Football Hall of Fame. Nobody — not even Atchison — envisioned that in the spring of 1952.

Atchison did not receive a formal invitation to the Roughriders' training camp after completing his junior eligibility in 1949 with the Saskatoon Hilltops, for whom he played his first three seasons of organized football. In fact, he sat out the 1950 and 1951 seasons while driving a pickup and delivery truck for Marshall Wells Co., in Saskatoon. The Hilltops saw something in Atchison, a strapping youngster with unrefined talent and a voracious appetite for on-field combat. Cliff McClocklin, who had watched Atchison play for the Hilltops, was so impressed that he kept imploring him to try out for the Roughriders, even during his hiatus from football.

"On that advice, I came down and just walked into camp and told them that I was a Hilltopper and wanted to try out," Atchison said. "They accepted me and I played for the next 17 years ... I was just a walk-on. You never know who's going to walk on, right?" The Roughriders sized up Atchison and opted to give him a look. "I just told them my story — that I was a Hilltopper and that I was now too old for the Hilltops," he continued. "I said the Hilltops had suggested I come down here and try out. They said, 'Oh, you're welcome. Come on in.' They treated me 100 per cent." Despite having doubts about his lack of experience, he ended up making the team.

Only a few years earlier, any kind of football career was unimaginable for Atchison, who spent time in four different communities before joining the Roughriders. He was born in Mullingar, just north of North Battleford (to where the family eventually moved). "My family lived on this farm and my father got sick and he was hospitalized and so my mom took us to North Battleford, where he was in hospital," Atchison recalled. "My parents parted there [and separated]. Then we moved to Saskatoon and that's where I got into a group of bad guys and did everything. They went to a reform school."

Atchison could have followed the same path, if not for some fortunate timing. "The only thing that saved me was one day we were at the riding stable and this little short guy came up and wanted to know if someone would be interested in herding sheep," he said, rewinding to 1942. "I told him I was. I made arrangements with my mom. She said, 'Yes. Take him, take him.' So I went out there."

At 12, Atchison began herding sheep in Fielding, which is between North Battleford and Saskatoon. Initially, Atchison worked on Charlie Neumeier's farm for three months. The nomadic youngster soon became a full-time farmhand. "I left school when I was about 14 or 15," Atchison said. "They didn't know where I was. I just walked out. I don't think anybody looked too hard. I became a farm boy and that's really what changed my life. Charlie was a bachelor then and he didn't drink or smoke or swear, so he was a hell of a good influence. I know what it would have been like if he hadn't been the type of man that he was. The other three guys, they all smartened up, but it wasn't until after they did a year in jail. They went to jail when I went out to Charlie's. Otherwise, I would have been with them. They became pretty good citizens."

That description certainly did not apply when Atchison first associated with the troublesome trio. "The guys who I was in Saskatoon with were about three years older than me," he said. "They would pick on somebody and then they would tell me to kick his ass. They called me Farmer because I was off the farm. They would pick a fight with some guy and they would get into a talk with him. Then they would tell me, 'Kick his ass, Farms,' so I would commence to fight with him. I never got beat. I was as tough as nails and I liked to fight."

Atchison had developed his pugilistic skills under the tutelage of his grandfather, Tom Martin, who had been in the British navy. "He was the one who actually first taught me how to hold my dukes up and how to guard myself. He was the father of my mother, so he lived with us for several years," said Atchison, who ended up using his farm wages to help buy his mother a house in Saskatoon.

She would not occupy the residence for very long. She died of cancer when Atchison was 18. At that point, Atchison moved back to Saskatoon and into the home he had bought. He also reconnected with a friend who had gone on to play for the Hilltops. The friend enticed Atchison to join the team as well. Three years later, he would also walk on with the Roughriders and meet player-coach Glenn Dobbs.

"I was lucky with the timing," Atchison said in a 1985 interview with Arnie Tiefenbach of the *Leader-Post*. "The team that went to the Grey Cup in 1951 had kind of disintegrated, so they were rebuilding when I got there. Teams only carried eight Americans in those days, so they needed Canadians. I guess Dobbs had seen something in me that he thought could be worked into a football player."

It took work, along with some veteran guidance from fellow defensive lineman Mario DeMarco. "He was an old pro and I guess you might say he was a little bit lazy," Atchison told Tiefenbach with a smile. "Every time he had the chance, he'd come up to me on the bench and say, 'Atch, take my place.' There was only one coach then and he'd be so busy with other things, he wouldn't even notice. Mario actually gave me more playing time than the coach did! You'd never get away with that nowadays."

Another rookie Canadian on the 1952 Roughriders was offensive lineman Reg Whitehouse. The Montreal-born Whitehouse also entertained overtures from the Ottawa Rough Riders, along with a scholarship offer from Florida State University, after starring in junior football with

Ron Atchison |

the Notre Dame de Grace Maple Leafs. According to *Rider Pride*, a team history by Garry Andrews and Bob Calder, Ottawa had offered Whitehouse $300 more per season. However, Dobbs convinced Antonia Whitehouse that her son — who was only 19 at the time — was best suited for Saskatchewan. "Mrs. Whitehouse," Dobbs is quoted as saying in *Rider Pride*, "we wouldn't invite anyone to try out for our club who isn't the kind of person we'd invite to our own church."

There was no joy in Dobberville as the Roughriders languished in 1952. Although Dobbs remained a popular figure, the team's results did not engender as much excitement as his presence. The optimism of 1951 soon dissipated.

Reg Whitehouse |

Dobbs was back, but the circumstances were discernibly different. The quarterback's right leg, injured during training camp, impeded his performance throughout what would be a disappointing season. The team won only three games after selling a club-record 7,200 season tickets. The absence of Dobbs' favourite targets did not aid the Roughriders' cause. Jack Nix had joined the United States Marine Corps. Jack Russell was injured for the entire season. Red Ettinger, Jack Wedley and Bob Sandberg had also departed. By season's end, Dobbs and Martin Ruby were the only big-name Americans from 1951 who remained with the Green and White.

There was one other difference of note from the division-championship season. Dobbs had succeeded Harry (Blackjack) Smith as head coach. According to Roy Wright, who was the backup quarterback to Dobbs in 1951, the Roughriders' regression was largely attributable to management's decision to dump Smith.

"I didn't agree with it," recalled Wright, who returned punts and played halfback during his swan-song season of 1952. "He certainly deserved another kick at the cat, being that he took us there in his first year. [The 1952 season] was a disappointment. It was because of the replacements in coaching and playing. We had a dandy start [defeating the Edmonton Eskimos 25-5 in the regular-season opener] and then it started to go all downhill. It looked like it could work, but it was a letdown."

Those sentiments were shared by halfback Bob Pelling. "Dobbs was a heck of an athlete," Pelling said. "He came back in '52 and he was a bad coach. Most guys who are good athletes are perfectionists and they expect everyone else to be that way. Everybody had to be that good ... I really thought it was a bad year for Dobbs. He didn't bring in the ballplayers we needed. There was nothing new. Blackjack would get guys riled up and make them do something better, which Dobbs didn't do ... It took a special coach to do things. No question, it was [Smith's] work that took the team in '51 to the Grey Cup. I thought he'd do a better job and look for players the next year. When he was gone, it just seemed to fall apart. Dobbs just didn't have what Blackjack had."

Dobbs threw 14 touchdown passes — half as many as in the previous season — and did not handle the punting, ceding those duties to Butch Avinger. After rushing for seven majors in 1951, Dobbs did not score a touchdown the following season. "They had Dobbs coach and play," Wright said. "That's a tall order. It's tough to play and organize who's in on offence and defence. You lose the outside-looking-in on the various aspects of the game."

Through it all, Dobbs never lost his electric personality. "Oh, he was a great guy," Wright remembered. "There was nothing wrong with Glenn. He was maybe a little over his prime."

Frank Filchock | *Photo courtesy of* SSHFM

Dobbs was a newcomer to the CFL in the early 1950s, but he was 31 when he joined the Roughriders. His Canadian football career would conclude in 1953, when the Roughriders rallied to post an 8-7-1 record. Dobbs led Saskatchewan in touchdown passes, with nine, that season. But head coach Frank Filchock — who passed for a team-high 925 yards — also saw significant playing time at quarterback. So did a youngster named Frank Tripucka.

Tripucka's introduction to Regina — which took place well before he joined the Roughriders — was not pleasant. "I got married the day before graduating [in 1949] and we decided to go to Lake Louise," the former Notre Dame Fighting Irish star said.

"We were a little past Calgary. We were going through this town and I had a breakdown in my car. They got a mechanic and they fixed it and I went on my way. I never thought any more about Regina until four years later when [wife] Randy and I are getting off the plane and I said, 'Does this look familiar?' We got in the car and we're going to the hotel and I said, 'Does this look familiar to you?' She said, 'Yeah, we were here four years ago.' That's God's honest truth. Who the hell ever knew we were going back there?"

Initially, Tripucka's second visit to Regina was not any more enjoyable than his first. "I went up there with my wife and, at that time, we had three kids," said Tripucka, who is from Bloomfield, N.J. "I said, 'What the hell are we getting into?' The plane landed at the airport, which was just outside of town. I took one look at it and went, 'Holy God. What am I doing?' There was nothing but wheat fields, just flat as a pancake." Tripucka quickly warmed up to Regina, even though warming up could be difficult, given the climate. He enjoyed playing in Saskatchewan "except for the weather. Oh, Jesus. Half the time, you had to wear sneakers with cleats in them. Right after Labour Day, you could expect frozen ground. It was like playing on cement. Of course, the wind would drive you nuts, too, but you had to put up with it. The money was good, so you can't complain about the money."

Those were the days when Canadian teams could offer import players salaries that were comparable to, and often in excess of, wages paid by American-based squads. "I was with the Chicago Cardinals and we were going no place fast," Tripucka said. "All of a sudden, I get a call from Regina. I didn't even know where the hell it was. The guy says, 'How would you like to come to Regina and be the quarterback for the Roughriders?' So I said, 'Well, how much money are you paying?' I tell ya, they doubled the salary of what I was making in Chicago, so I said, 'Well, I'll be there!' I ended up spending six years there."

Canadian professional football was also alluring for American players such as University of Alabama stars Bobby Marlow and John Wozniak, erstwhile Cleveland Browns playmakers Mac Speedie and Ken Carpenter, former University of Indiana centre Mel Becket, New York Giants alumnus Mario DeMarco (who arrived in Saskatchewan via the Edmonton Eskimos), ex-Dallas Texans halfback Stan Williams and Baylor product Larry Isbell.

"If you were a halfway-decent American, they loved it," Tripucka said in reference to the rabid Roughriders fans. "Those people went crazy for football up there. Oh, they packed them in. We did a lot of throwing. They went crazy over the Americans. As long as you produced, that was it. They didn't care. If you got beat, you got beat, but they loved those Americans. You had all kinds of training in high school and college and then on into pro football, whereas the Canadian kids didn't have that luxury."

The influx of imports aided the restoration of the Roughriders' respectability, as they posted 10-victory

Frank Tripucka |
Photo courtesy of SSHFM

seasons in 1954, 1955 and 1956. "Everything was about getting into the playoffs," Tripucka said. "The funny thing about it is that the Canadian people didn't even worry about winning it. All they wanted to do was be in it, which was easy for the players — because otherwise, if you didn't win it, you'd end up getting fired. All they wanted to do was be in it, so we made it each time. We never did win it."

Saskatchewan lost to the Winnipeg Blue Bombers in two agonizingly close two-game, total-point playoff series in 1954 and 1955 before finally upending the Bombers in the opening round of the 1956 postseason. The Roughriders then collided with Jackie Parker, Normie Kwong, Johnny Bright and the Eskimos, who won the best-of-three Western final, 2-1. Saskatchewan won the opener at home, 23-22, before the series moved to Edmonton. The Eskimos won 20-12 and 51-7 at home before defeating the Montreal Alouettes in the Grey Cup for the third consecutive year.

Despite the lopsided loss to Edmonton, the 1956 season was not over for some of the most prominent Roughriders. The East-West Shrine All-Star Game in Vancouver beckoned. The nine participants from Saskatchewan included Tripucka, offensive lineman Reg Whitehouse, defensive end Gord Sturtridge and centre Mel Becket. Defensive tackle Ray Syrnyk and guard Mario DeMarco, both of whom had enjoyed strong 1956 seasons, were among the spectators at Vancouver's Empire Stadium as the Western all-stars blanked the East 35-0. Tripucka outshone his opposite number, Montreal quarterback Sam (The Rifle) Etcheverry, by throwing touchdown passes to Jackie Parker and Bud Grant. Whitehouse figured in the scoring on Dec. 8, 1956, kicking five converts.

Before leaving Regina, Reg Whitehouse had an uncomfortable conversation with his wife, the former Joanne Baird — Miss Grey Cup 1953. "When we left Regina to go to the all-star game, I said, 'I've got a funny feeling about this thing. I'd rather you not come,' " Whitehouse recalled. Tripucka also had reservations about making the excursion, but for different reasons.

Late in the 1956 season, Tripucka's family had returned to New Jersey. He had remained in Regina to fulfil his obligations to the Roughriders and, dutifully, also consented to play in the all-star game. Tripucka's teammates urged him to return to Regina with them after the all-star contest, but the star quarterback had misgivings. "I was out there [in Western Canada] for two weeks without my family and I started missing them, so rather than go back to Regina, I said, 'I'm going to go home,' " Tripucka said. "I said goodbye to those guys at the airport and they got on the plane to go back to Regina."

Tripucka later boarded a flight from Vancouver to Toronto, where he was to connect to New York. "In Toronto, one of the airline people comes running up to me and says, 'Did you know anybody on that plane that was going from Vancouver to Regina?' " he recalled. "I said, 'I knew five different people.' He said, 'The plane hasn't been found.' " Back in New Jersey, Randy Tripucka fielded a telephone call from someone who thought her well-known husband had been aboard the ill-fated flight. "A reporter called me and said something and realized that I didn't know what he was talking about," Mrs. Tripucka said. "He fudged it over so well that I didn't think anything about it. I said, 'No, he's coming home.' Maybe a couple of hours later, someone else called because he landed in New York." The final leg of the flight was emotional for Tripucka. "I was lucky, let's put it that way," he said. "God was good to me."

The passengers on Trans-Canada Airlines Flight 810 were not as fortunate. While over the Rocky Mountains, the North Star aircraft encountered a problem with one of its four engines and crashed into 8,200-foot Mount Slesse, near Chilliwack, B.C., on the evening of Dec. 9, 1956. Four Saskatchewan players — Becket, DeMarco, Sturtridge and Syrnyk — were among 62 people killed, as were Sturtridge's wife (Mildred), Roughriders director Harold McElroy (who attended all the team's games, home and away) and Calvin Jones of the Winnipeg Blue Bombers. Jones was to have flown out in the morning, but he slept in and took the later, fateful flight. At the time, it was the worst disaster in the history of Canadian aviation.

"It was a hell of a shock because you're not going to see those guys again," said Sandy Archer, who was the Roughriders' trainer from 1951 to 1980. "For a day or two, you thought, 'Well, they've crashed on a mountain. They'll find it. Maybe there's a lot of people alive.' " Back in Regina, anxious residents waited for news and prayed for word of survivors. "People were in a state of disbelief and shock, and heads were held low as the citizens of this city stared at the sidewalk as they walked around downtown, many with tears in their eyes," long-time Roughriders fan John Lynch said.

The Sturtridges had left their three children (Valerie, 6, Vicki, 5, and 15-month-old Gordon) with a babysitter. The babysitter phoned Atchison's residence the morning after the crash. Atchison was entrusted with the responsibility of informing the children that their parents were missing. "It's the toughest thing I've ever had to do," Atchison told Dave Komosky of the *StarPhoenix* in 1987. The children were eventually raised in B.C. by Sturtridge's parents.

To this day, Richard and Bess Eisler pass a home on 17th Avenue in Regina and think of the Sturtridges. They were two doors down from the Eislers, who still reside in the house they purchased in 1955. Bess used to babysit the Sturtridges' children. Gord Sturtridge often dropped by and sat on the Eislers' deck. "When Gord was selected an all-star in '56, I bought him a big bottle of whisky, tied a big, green ribbon on it, and took it over," Richard Eisler remembered before his wife added, "and he came over and had a drink from it with you." Not long after that, the Sturtridges made their fateful trip to Vancouver. "The crash was horrifying, especially for the people who knew them," said Bess Eisler, whom Gordon Sturtridge referred to as Peaches. "It was a very sad time for the whole city."

As devastating as the accident was, Whitehouse felt blessed to have been spared. He had taken an earlier flight. "Reg always took the first plane out," his wife said. "He wanted the others to do the same thing." The Whitehouses spent the next half-century knowing how close they had come to being on that aircraft. "The morning I was leaving, Reg cancelled my ticket on that flight," his wife remembered. "He had a feeling." The premonition saved the couple's lives. "If I'd have asked my wife to come to the all-star game in Vancouver, we would have caught the plane that took the bunch of them," said the veteran lineman, who completed a 15-year playing career with the 1966 Roughriders. "We had been married a year.

I had to turn her down on something like that. That could have been the end of the story right there."

Their son, Timber Whitehouse, shared the story 52 years later. "Dad told her, 'You are not getting on that flight,'" Timber said. "She was quite annoyed, but he was not going to let her go. Something told him. He could not explain it. It was simply a feeling in his gut and he felt a compelling need to act on it. If he could have replayed it, he would have demanded that no one take that flight. It haunted him for quite a while. It was extremely emotional for him because some of his best friends in his life were on that flight."

Ron Atchison, who had then completed his fifth season with the Roughriders, had similar feelings of bereavement and relief. "I was selected to go on that trip, but I had an injury on my foot," Atchison said. "I had an ankle problem that needed to be operated on, so when they went to B.C., I was here getting the ankle fixed. I've been a lucky kind of guy, you know? I should have been with them, for all intents and purposes. I couldn't get it out of my mind forever because of how close I was."

The Roughriders retired the uniform numbers of Becket (40), DeMarco (55), Syrnyk (56) and Sturtridge (73). The Becket-DeMarco Memorial Trophy was established to annually recognize the top lineman in the West.

Mario DeMarco |
Photo courtesy of Gord Heenan, Heenan Studios

Mel Becket |
Photo courtesy of Gord Heenan, Heenan Studios

Gord Sturtridge |
Photo courtesy of SSHFM

Ray Syrnyk |
Photo courtesy of SSHFM

CHAPTER **3** # "WHAT THE HELL HAPPENED, LEN?"

The Roughriders were left reeling in every respect by the 1956 airplane crash that claimed four Saskatchewan players — Mario DeMarco, Gord Sturtridge, Mel Becket and Ray Syrnyk. "We had four starting ballplayers who were suddenly gone," trainer Sandy Archer said in 2005. "That's a fair part of a team. Today, they dress 40 players and they've got about 20 guys hanging around. Back then, we'd dress 32 players and we'd have maybe one or two guys around. It was a big difference in the cost to the team, so we didn't have many guys. Losing those four guys made a big difference and it hurt a lot." The hurt paled in comparison to the sadness over the deaths of DeMarco, Sturtridge, Becket and Syrnyk, and their absences were noted on the football field. The 1957 Roughriders won only three games, a result the team's executive deemed unpalatable.

Frank Filchock, who had coached the Roughriders since 1953, was terminated shortly after the 1957 season. "We have one losing year and I'm fired," Filchock told the *Leader-Post*. An intensive search for a new head coach began. Various names were tossed around, in print and on coffee row, as possible successors. However, the most famous name of all slipped under the radar for two months following Filchock's ouster.

In mid-January of 1958, the *Leader-Post* reported that the Roughriders' head-coaching job had been offered to National Football League legend Sammy Baugh. While with the Washington Redskins, Slingin' Sammy had revolutionized the passing game. The Roughriders' executive, led by first-year president Sam Taylor, hoped that Baugh would generate a comparable level of excitement in Saskatchewan. Baugh, who was the head football coach at Hardin-Simmons University in Abilene, Texas when he was wooed by the

Roughriders, told the *Abilene Reporter News* that Saskatchewan had offered him a three-year contract "for the most money I'll ever be offered in coaching."

Baugh had two years remaining on his contract at Hardin-Simmons, but school officials had granted him permission to leave if the Saskatchewan offer proved irresistible. However, Baugh decided at the 11th hour to remain at the university. With Baugh poised to leave for Saskatchewan, Hardin-Simmons administrators and school alumni had gone on an all-out offensive to retain Baugh. He opted to stay when a five-year contract extension was offered. "Baugh is as fine a person as I've ever met," Taylor told the *Leader-Post*. "He would have been a natural with the Riders but they like him so well in West Texas that they simply wouldn't let him go."

The search continued, but not for much longer. A week after Baugh declined the offer, the Roughriders' president — the son of Neil J. (Piffles) Taylor, after whom Taylor Field had been named — introduced George Terlep as the head coach. Terlep had been the Hamilton Tiger-Cats' backfield coach in 1957, when they won the Grey Cup. Upon hiring Terlep, the Roughriders thought their football-operations side was set for 1958. They were mistaken.

In late March, Riders manager Dean Griffing — the job description of "general manager" was not yet used by the team — announced he was leaving for Tucson, Ariz., to become the GM of a team in a fledgling football loop. Griffing left after four seasons as the Riders' manager. He was also familiar to fans who followed the team from 1936 to 1942, a period in which he coached and perennially earned all-star honours at centre. Griffing's second extended stint with the Roughriders ended because the Tucson job offered the promise of more security (falsely, as it turned out). Once again, the Roughriders were looking to address a void. Applications were invited.

Three weeks later, the Roughriders appointed a new manager — but he was hardly new to the team or the province. Although Ken Preston was raised in Portland, Ont., and played at Queen's University in Kingston, Ont., he was closely associated with football in Regina. After graduating from Queen's with a commerce degree, Preston moved to Regina in 1940 to accept a job with the treasury department. He also made his pro football debut with the Roughriders that season. At one point, it appeared that Saskatchewan would be a pitstop for Preston, who moved to Winnipeg and played for the Blue Bombers in 1941 after being transferred to Manitoba by the treasury department. The next three years were spent in the armed forces before he joined the Ottawa Rough Riders in 1945.

Ken Preston *as a player* |
Photo courtesy of SSHFM

The allure of a head-coaching position brought Preston back to Regina in 1946. He abandoned coaching during the 1947 season, when Fred Grant took over, but remained with the team for one more season as a quarterback and linebacker. Then it was off to the real world. In 1949, Preston bought a company that manufactured paper boxes and then concentrated on business endeavours. However, football was not entirely out of his blood. Preston remained involved with the sport by coaching the Regina Junior Bombers in 1950 and 1951. He went on to become a Western Interprovincial Football Union official and a part-time manager of the Roughriders. Those duties were expanded when the team's president — who liked the ultimately successful candidate's mix of business and football experience — encouraged Preston to think outside the box.

"When Sam Taylor asked me in 1958 to take over as general manager, I said I thought I could do all that was required in half a day," Preston said in a 1985 interview with Arnie Tiefenbach of the *Leader-Post*. "So that's what I did, and I spent the other half-day over at my paper-box plant. Of course, I was paid for half a day, too!" The famously frugal Preston would not have had it any other way. After a while, though, Preston decided to devote his full attention to football and divested himself of the paper-box company. "When he first started, they weren't doing that well," said Bill Preston, Ken's son. "That was one of the reasons he quit [the box-making]. My father didn't like doing anything mediocre." With Preston in charge and George Terlep coaching, the Roughriders would improve on their dismal 1957 showing by posting a 7-7-2 record and finishing third in the West. But that would be as good as it got under Terlep.

When the 1959 Roughriders convened for training camp, quarterback Frank Tripucka was gone — traded to the Ottawa Rough Riders for five players. Tripucka was initially replaced by Don Allard and Bob Brodhead. Allard completed only 45.3 per cent of his passes, with six touchdowns and 21 interceptions. Brodhead served up interceptions with the same frequency, being picked off 15 times while throwing only four touchdown passes. One two-game stretch was particularly painful. After suffering a 55-0 loss to the host Edmonton Eskimos in the third regular-season game, the Roughriders returned home and absorbed a 61-8 evisceration at the hands of the Winnipeg Blue Bombers.

Saskatchewan lost again in Edmonton on Oct. 3, 1959, falling 44-15 to drop to 0-10. Welcome to Canadian professional football, Al Benecick. The latter defeat in Edmonton came in his first game with the Roughriders. "Afterwards, we were at the airport," said Benecick, who would become a Hall of Fame offensive lineman. "It was embarrassing. The president back then [Sam Taylor] said, 'Ah, let's have a drink,' and he bought us drinks. I felt like a little kid. I was crying. I was so pissed off. I said, 'What

Al Benecick |

the hell did I do?' And I had signed for a year. I said, 'Holy Christmas, what did I get into here?' "

Benecick was summoned to replace two-way lineman Jim Marshall, who would go on to become an NFL star with the Minnesota Vikings. Marshall also earned a degree of notoriety for returning a fumble in the wrong direction in a 1964 game. Such a play would have been ideal for the 1959 Roughriders' highlight reel, if there had been such a thing. What a season. "It was awful," said Benecick, who was activated after Marshall strained his back. "Instead of drinking one beer after the game, you drank three or four. Sad to say ... And they weren't victory beers, you know? It was, 'Dear Lord, please help us. Something's got to give.' "

Benecick was accustomed to more success at Syracuse University, where he blocked for the legendary Jim Brown. "Jim was just a darn good athlete," Benecick said. "He was a better lacrosse player than football player." Brown made an immediate impact in the NFL, starring with the Cleveland Browns. Benecick's introduction to pro football was not nearly as pleasant. He signed with the Philadelphia Eagles, but that would be the highlight of his time in Pennsylvania. Benecick played in some exhibition games with the Eagles, but it occurred to him that life might be better in Saskatchewan.

Before that futile season, Terlep had invited Benecick to play in Canada, but Benecick was drawn initially to Philadelphia. When that situation soured, he called the Roughriders and said, "I'll be leaving. I don't like what's going on." Little did he know that the final seven games of a dismal CFL season awaited him. Nor did Benecick suspect that, by the time he arrived in Regina, Terlep would be gone.

Terlep was deposed by the winless Roughriders on Sept. 30, 1959, after the team's record descended to 0-9 (by which time Saskatchewan had been outscored by an astounding 334-93). "It's hard to believe that my ability can disappear in one year," Terlep said, echoing comments Frank Filchock had made after his own dismissal nearly two years earlier. Terlep felt the lack of Canadian talent contributed to the Roughriders' failings and his firing, which followed his refusal to comply with the board's request that he resign. "The Riders were handicapped because few Canadian players have been developed or brought in over the past half-dozen years," he said. "I did what I could with what I inherited." Terlep also sounded an ominous note about the team's future. "Saskatchewan is in a rather precarious position in regard to football," the 36-year-old coach said. "I suppose in some ways it has always been that way."

With Terlep gone, the Roughriders' brain trust summoned a familiar face — that of Frank Tripucka. "The Tripper" was reacquired from Ottawa in a cash deal, but strictly as a coach. His quarterbacking days were over — or so everyone thought. Tripucka made his head-coaching debut in a 44-15 loss to Edmonton, but only after voicing concerns to the Roughriders' executive about Terlep's situation. "I said, 'Hey, wait a minute. George Terlep's a good friend of mine — another Notre Dame guy, you know,' " Tripucka recalled. "I said, 'I don't want to go taking somebody else's job.' Terlep got ahold of me and we had lunch together. He said, 'Don't worry about it. I'll go home and I'll find a job. You go ahead and take it.' " Terlep promptly joined Ottawa, becoming the Rough Riders' backfield coach. Tripucka would coach the Roughriders to their only official victory of that sad season — a 15-14 conquest of the host B.C. Lions on Oct. 5, 1959.

Tripucka would soon be utilized in another, more familiar, capacity due to an acute shortage of arms. Bob Brodhead's release led to the elevation of the equally ineffectual Don Allard to the starting quarterback's role. Allard suffered a shoulder separation in the season's 14th game, a 45-6 home-field loss to B.C. His understudy, Ron Adam, aggravated an ankle injury in the same game. That left the Roughriders with only one healthy signal-caller, Jack Urness, and he was virtually bereft of professional experience. The Regina-born Urness — whose brother, Ted, would later star for the Roughriders — suffered a nasty gash to a leg during the very same Edmonton game. As a result, the Roughriders turned to their fourth "quarterback" of the game — receiver Jack Hill. He threw two passes. Both were intercepted.

Faced with a paucity of pivots, the Roughriders contacted the league office and sought permission to dress Tripucka. He was ineligible because teams could not add imports to the roster beyond Oct. 1 (the day Tripucka was hired). Commissioner Sydney Halter granted permission after Ottawa and all the Western clubs consented. Nary an objection was raised, because Saskatchewan's final two games could not influence the standings in any way. The games went ahead, albeit with the Bombers and Eskimos guaranteed victories by forfeit.

"We agreed on allowing Tripucka to play," Eskimos head coach Eagle Keys said. "This being what you might call a nothing game, we gave our consent because we want to see the Riders make a game of it. Any team would be seriously handicapped if it didn't have a top-notch quarterback to call upon." Edmonton proceeded to win 20-19 at Taylor Field. Tripucka, who had replaced Ron Adam in the second quarter, threw an interception in the final minute. "Who should take the blame — the coach or the quarterback?" Tripucka quipped after the game. To conclude the season, the Roughriders journeyed to Winnipeg for what became a unique game in franchise history.

The 1959 season was punctuated in suitably bizarre fashion when the Roughriders won, yet lost. The scoreboard read "Saskatchewan 37, Winnipeg 30," but an asterisk was applied to the CFL statistics. Winnipeg won by virtue of the forfeiture, but the game statistics were declared official by Halter. That was good news for Ferd Burket, who established a single-game franchise record by scoring five touchdowns (on four runs and one reception). Also of note, Winnipeg's Ernie Pitts caught his 15th and 16th touchdown passes, setting a single-season league record (breaking the mark set the previous year by Saskatchewan's Jack Hill). Pitts' record endured until 1966, when Saskatchewan's Hugh Campbell made 17 scoring grabs. Such prosperity seemed incomprehensible during the darkest days of 1959.

The 1960 season was not much better, even though the Roughriders doubled their victory total (going 2-12-2). The Roughriders had hoped that Tripucka would return as head coach for that season, but he had other intentions. "The kids were getting to school age and I wanted them to go to school [in the United States], so that straightened that out real quick," he said. The Roughriders ended up turning to another star player, Ken Carpenter,

Bob Kramer (left) and his son Don *circa 1963* |
Photo courtesy of Kramer Tractor archives

who was handed the head-coaching reins in 1960. That was a short-lived tenure, as was the custom with the Roughriders in those days. Carpenter resigned after the 1960 season and joined the Denver Broncos of the upstart American Football League — whose ranks would include general manager Dean Griffing, head coach Frank Filchock and, at quarterback, Frank Tripucka.

After finishing dead-last in 1959 and 1960, it was feared that the Roughriders franchise would be dead, period. Attendance had plummeted. Four-digit totals were as routine as the defeats. As a result, the Roughriders were saddled with a $78,000 deficit. In a crisis situation, Bob Kramer — under whose presidency the Roughriders had reached the Grey Cup in 1951 — returned to the helm. Kramer and an army of volunteers embarked on an ambitious save-the-team campaign, the objective being to sell 10,000 season tickets.

As the fans responded to the call over the winter, the perennial question was raised: Who would be the coach?

The Roughriders' brass opted for a known commodity — at least in American gridiron circles — by appointing Steve Owen as head coach. The National Football League warhorse had coached the New York Giants from 1930 to 1953, guiding them to league titles in 1934 and 1938. Owen was in his 60s when he was courted by Saskatchewan. He helped to restore a measure of respectability by coaching the Roughriders to records of 5-10-1 (in 1961) and 8-7-1 (1962).

Although the Roughriders improved in 1962, that season did include one of the low points in team history — a 67-21 loss to the host Hamilton Tiger-Cats. The Roughriders surrendered a league-record 10 touchdown passes (including eight by Joe Zuger) two days after beginning an Eastern swing with a 29-21 victory over Ottawa. "We came into the locker room afterwards and the press comes up to Steve Owen and says, 'What happened? You're supposed to be a defensive coach!' " defensive end Garner Ekstran remembered. "Steve said, 'If I hadn't been a [bleeping] genius, it would have been 100-0!' That was Steve. The next time we played in Hamilton [two years later], Larry Dumelie went to

Hugh Campbell and said, 'Would you like to see where they beat me for a touchdown the last time we were here?' Hugh said, 'Yeah,' so Dumelie started pointing all over the field, going, 'Here ... here ... here ... here ...' "

After the 1962 season, Owen was named coach-of-the-year, only to resign shortly thereafter without vehement objections from the Roughriders' management committee. Owen, who had suffered a heart attack during his tenure with the Roughriders, died on May 17, 1964, at age 66. Two years later, he was inducted into the Pro Football Hall of Fame.

Anyone who dealt with Owen during his two-year tenure in Saskatchewan had some anecdotes to spin. That included John Badham, who was the play-by-play man for radio broadcasts. "We had a guy down on the field because we were always trying to get information when somebody would get hurt," Badham said. "There was a little dugout and Mal Isaac was down there and we'd communicate back and forth. Somebody would get hurt and he'd walk over and see Sandy Archer and Sandy would say, 'He'll be back. His leg's broken in half,' and all that. The old coach, Stout Steve Owen, was there one game. One of the players got hurt, so Mal walks by the bench to where Sandy Archer was working on the guy. Steve just reaches back, puts his arm around him, and says, 'What the hell? What down is that over there? What yardage is that over there?' Mal looked at him and said something. Steve turned and looked at him and said, 'Who the hell are you?' "

Nobody has enjoyed telling Steve Owen stories more than Dale West, whose introductory CFL season was also that of the colourful field boss. "Stout Steve was a classic," West remembered. "Steve had forgotten a lot of football, but he still knew more than anyone else. We used to call him the Old Man. He was a fantastic person."

The speedy West was a flanker with the Roughriders before moving to the defensive backfield in 1963. He scored his first CFL touchdown on a long pass from Bob Ptacek in 1962. It was an eye-catching play — except to Owen, whose vision was failing. "I came back to the bench and I was proud as hell," West said. "Steve was looking at the other end of the field, saying to [assistant coach] Len Younce, 'What the hell happened, Len?' How to deflate an ego! I expected a pat on the back and I got, 'What the hell happened, Len?' "

Steve Owen *circa 1961* | Photo courtesy of SSHFM

CHAPTER 4 | # "LOGICAL CAME IN THIRD"

Perhaps head coach Steve Owen missed Dale West's first CFL touchdown because of the rookie's blinding speed — which was evident well before he suited up for the Roughriders. In 1959, West completed the 100-yard dash in a record 9.8 seconds at the Saskatchewan High Schools Athletic Association track and field championships. That standard is forever etched in the record book, being that the finish line is now 100 metres away. West's prowess as a sprinter was such that he attended the Canadian trials for the Pan American Games in 1959. He was named an alternate by virtue of finishing fourth over 100 yards.

"I got to be a damned good alternate," quipped West, who also assumed that role in another sport at which he excelled — speed skating. West competed in the Canadian trials for the 1960 Winter Olympic Games. In fact, he was the leader after the first day, having covered 500 metres in brisk fashion, only to be surpassed in the days to come. Once again, West was named an alternate, but did not travel to Squaw Valley, Calif., for the Olympics. "That was the first time women were involved [in speed skating] in the Winter Olympics," West recalled. "Canada decided that they were going to send a four-person team. Ordinarily, I would have gone, but they decided they were going to send two men and two women. Canada split the team. It was fair. Stuff happens. It wasn't that big a deal. I wasn't that upset because at that particular time, I knew I was going to go south, anyway."

The University of Arizona beckoned, thanks to West's proficiency in yet a third sport — football. While playing for Saskatoon's Bedford Road Collegiate in 1958, West rushed for 1,434 yards and scored 134 points. The following season, it was off to Tucson, where fellow Saskatchewanians and future Roughriders teammates Ted Urness and Larry Dumelie were already part of the football program. Former Roughriders manager Dean Griffing was principally responsible for Urness and Dumelie receiving football scholarships to Arizona. Griffing was no longer in the Roughriders' employ by the time West embarked for Arizona, but the trail had been blazed two years earlier.

"Arizona was really a different kind of experience," West reflected. "There were 125 guys on scholarship, and the heat — it was something! We started practice about 6:30 in the morning. The first day, by eight o'clock in the morning, it would be 105 or 108 degrees. The nice folks, of course, had watered the field the night before, so the steam would come up. Almost everybody just wilted the first day. You couldn't drink water. No, no, no! That made you soft. In Texas and the southeast that year, several players died from heat exhaustion, and the NCAA came out and said, 'You've got to give them a drink of water every 45 minutes.' I had long talks with myself about, 'What are you doing here?' You'd put your head down in the huddle and your helmet would fill up with sweat, so that when you stood up straight you got a bath afterwards. It was ridiculously hot, but I got used to it."

West spent two years at Arizona, where he saw limited duty at running back. He left Arizona after his sophomore year and returned to Saskatoon. "I decided when I was home for the summer that, 'Well, I'll check this football out up here,' and it worked out that they still wanted me here," he said. "I thought, 'It's time to get back to Canada.' "

The University of Saskatchewan Huskies' brain trust concurred. West spent the 1961 season with the Huskies' resurrected football program while being monitored by the Roughriders, who owned his rights due to the CFL territorial-protection provision that was in effect at the time. In the spring of 1962, the 21-year-old West was visited by Roughriders assistant coach Len Younce. "Training camp had already started," West said. "He came up to Saskatoon and took me out for lunch and wined and dined me across from the university and invited me down. I came down on the rail-liner with all the folks who were protesting during the doctors' strike. I missed most of two-a-days. I think I was only there for about two or three days of two-a-days. That was when Stout Steve took me aside and said, 'I don't know what this 12th player does, but you're him.' "

Owen was more accustomed to strategizing with 11 men a side, as was the case in the NFL. Like some American coaches of the day, Owen embraced an offensive scheme in which the more conventional 11 players were emphasized, with the 12th man splitting far wide and generally staying out of the way. However, West's speed made him practically impossible to ignore. As a rookie in 1962, he made 13 receptions for 306 yards — an average of 23.5 yards per catch — and three touchdowns. He also spent some time in the defensive backfield. "In hindsight, I sure wish that I knew that I was going to start all 16 games that year," West said. "I might have picked up more than the $3,500 that I got."

West caught three more scoring passes in 1963, despite making only five receptions — on which he averaged a stratospheric 34.8 yards. He caught twice as many passes while playing on defence with the 1963 Roughriders, leading the CFL in interceptions (with 10) while making a seamless transition to safety under new head coach Bob Shaw. At training camp in 1963, Shaw took note of West's athleticism and prescribed increased duty in the secondary. The move was applauded in the *Leader-Post* by columnist John Robertson, who had this to say about West in the Oct. 18, 1963 edition: "Game in and game out, he has been a tower of strength on pass defence. He is known as the club's centre fielder. It didn't take the speed merchants on opposing clubs long to find out they couldn't outrun or outleap him. He has made mistakes, but the thing that impresses you most about him is that at 22 he's going to get even better."

Although he would also be named a Western Conference all-star in 1964 and 1965, the 1963 season was West's best from a statistical standpoint. He was decorated as the Western Conference's outstanding Canadian that year, losing out to Ottawa quarterback Russ Jackson for league honours. West was recognized after returning his 10 interceptions for 226 yards, including a touchdown. "One of the reasons that I was able to get so many interceptions was the fact that the quarterbacks didn't judge my speed correctly and didn't anticipate my closing speed," he said. "As well, there weren't as many quarterbacks with guns for arms and this gave me a better chance of closing on the ball. Plus, there

Dale West | Photo courtesy of Gord Heenan, Heenan Studios

was an awful lot of luck involved, because even after they had seen that I could close quickly, either they didn't believe it or they were just stubborn."

At first, it was difficult for West to believe that he was playing for the Roughriders. He was not far-removed from a time, in the mid-1950s, when Roughriders stars Reg Whitehouse and Larry Isbell had visited his boys' club at St. Thomas-Wesley United Church in Saskatoon. At that point, who could have imagined that West and Whitehouse would eventually become teammates? The significance of simply being a Roughrider was appreciated by West.

"There is a uniqueness to growing up in Saskatchewan and being able to play with the Saskatchewan Roughriders," he reflected. "I don't know if the feeling would exist in any other province. It is such a part of our culture, our *raison d'etre*, that we're football fans. To actually play in Taylor Field and follow in the footsteps of Glenn Dobbs and Sully Glasser and Tare Rennebohm and Mel Becket and Mario DeMarco and Gord Sturtridge and Paul Anderson and all the folks who came before, it's kind of a special feeling."

West's introduction to Canadian professional football, up close and personal, came in 1951 when he watched Glenn Dobbs quarterback the Roughriders to victory in the Western final amid the bedlam at Taylor Field. Dobbs' presence also left an imprint on Larry Dumelie and ignited his passion for football.

In the early 1950s, while Dumelie and his brother Gil were attending Regina's Campion College, they headed over to the stadium to watch a Roughriders game. "And there was Glenn Dobbs and the boys," Larry Dumelie recalled. "That was just so impressive to see that. That's sort of where I made up my mind I wanted to play the game."

As Dumelie continued to follow the Roughriders, he became an admirer of bruising Bobby Marlow, who meted out on-field punishment while excelling at fullback and linebacker. "I saw him hit a couple of guys and I thought, 'Boy, this looks like a lot of fun,' " Dumelie said. "He stuck in my mind as the kind of player that I would have liked to have been. Of course, there's no feeling like running with the ball. The first time I ran with the ball and had all these guys tackling me and getting away from them and running into them, it was just a special feeling — unlike anything I've ever felt." Dumelie progressed to the point where he eventually joined West in the Roughriders' defensive backfield. Despite being only 5-foot-10 and 190 pounds, Dumelie hit opposing ball-carriers with a fury and an impact that belied his modest physical stature.

Like West, Dumelie was a small-town boy. He spent some of his formative years near that noted football incubator, Fir Mountain, which is — or was — in proximity to the southern Saskatchewan community of Assiniboia. "I was born in LaFleche because Fir Mountain didn't have a hospital," Dumelie said in 2006. "The closest hospital was in LaFleche. After Fir Mountain disappeared, my folks moved to LaFleche, so it sort of became the centre of the family, but the family farm is still operating. My younger brother runs it. Fir Mountain disappeared. The railroad is gone. The elevators are gone. There was a hotel. There were three restaurants. There was a garage. There was a curling rink and a theatre and schools, and that's all gone. Everything is gone — just buried. But that's happened to a lot of towns in Saskatchewan, unfortunately. There were probably a couple of hundred people there. We didn't live in the town. We were on the farm."

It wasn't a well-established farm system, at least in terms of formal football instruction. "I remember the first time I played football," Dumelie said. "We played soccer in the schoolyard and we made up our own rules. One of the rules we had was that you could pick up the ball and run with it, so that was my first time playing football. I think we played tackle, too. We didn't worry about it. We were rough-and-tumble kids out in the schoolyard."

Finishing school was conducted in Regina. "When I went to Campion, Gil and I had never seen a football game," Dumelie said. "We had never seen a football. We didn't have a clue. We said, 'Well, we'll go out for the football team. What do we do?' The coach said, 'You're farm boys, so you play on the line and just don't let anybody between you.' " It was an unlikely line of work for Larry Dumelie, considering that he was 150 pounds at the time. Nonetheless, he was a lineman, and the wheels were in motion for a career in football. One key player was Fred Wagman, who would become the Roughriders' president in the 1990s. Wagman took note of Dumelie's aptitude for football and its physical elements, suggesting that he try out for the Regina Rams junior team.

Dumelie spent the 1955 and 1956 seasons with the Rams, primarily at fullback, before accepting a football scholarship to play at the University of Arizona. It was there that he

Larry Dumelie |

began playing defence more extensively. He saw another side of the ball and, ultimately, of humanity when introduced to racism that was prevalent in the United States at the time. When the Arizona team travelled to Lubbock, Texas to play Texas Tech, the visiting team's black players were forced to stay at a different hotel. "It blew me away," Dumelie said. "The team put up a little bit of a fuss about it but, in the final analysis, we still went ahead with it. That would be 1958 or so. We had about six black guys on our team. They just accepted it. It was part of the world. They didn't make an issue out of it. I guess they could have, but they all knew that's the way it was. Unless you were an activist, you just went along with it. That was life."

After three seasons at Arizona, Dumelie became a Roughrider, and thus began an eight-year stint with the team. In 1964 — Dumelie's best year, in his own estimation — he registered six of his 13 career interceptions. Not only that, he levelled Montreal Alouettes star running back George Dixon. "That hit on Dixon, it pretty much finished his career and it pretty near finished mine, too," Dumelie said. "I was never quite the same after that. I had about a 40-yard run at him. I was playing the corner, so I dropped back to cover the pass, and they threw one of those floaters. The ball arrived just a split-second before I did. He didn't even get his head down and I got him with a helmet-to-helmet shot. His knee blew out, but my neck was never the same. I went down and he went down. It was a great hit, but I'd like to take it back because it wasn't good for either one of us."

The Roughriders' Arizona connection also included Ted Urness — a future Hall of Fame offensive lineman. Along with Dumelie, Urness embarked for and enrolled in the University of Arizona in 1957. Their foray to the United States was orchestrated by Dean Griffing, who was the Roughriders' manager at the time. "Dean was an American and he followed the Rams and the Hilltops," Urness recalled. "He thought maybe we had a little bit of potential to play professionally. He said, 'Why don't you guys consider going to college in the United States?' I'd never been over the border. I was 20 years old." Griffing had set up interviews for Dumelie and Urness at five American schools, so they started driving southward in January of 1957.

They stopped at the University of Montana in Bozeman, and carried on to Boulder, Colo., where the University of Colorado is situated. The next stop was Tucson, home of the University of Arizona. Urness and Dumelie quickly warmed to their new environment. "When you're in Arizona in 1957 and it's 25 or 30 below in Saskatchewan ...," Urness said with a chuckle. "These two dummies were walking around for a week at the University of Arizona. They showed us everything. We were saying, 'This is where we've got to go.' You didn't have to be too smart."

While wending their way back to Saskatchewan, Urness and Dumelie visited the campuses of Fresno State and Washington State, but the tours were a formality. Arizona was interested. Urness and Dumelie liked the program, the weather and the opportunity. "For a couple of hobos out of Regina, it was pretty impressive, so we were pretty excited," Urness said. "It was the weather that basically drove our decision. But Dean Griffing was pretty much the guy who put Larry and I in college. It was pretty unusual in those days. It's more common now ... I really have to thank the Americans because they took us on with full scholarships."

The Regina-born Urness was well-schooled in football as far back as he can remember. His Preeceville-born father, Al, played for the Roughriders from 1926 to 1932 — tasting defeat in the Grey Cup in each of his final five seasons. Ted's uncle, Fred Goodman, was also a Roughrider in that era (1929-33). And while Ted was at Arizona, his brother Jack was a quarterback with the Roughriders, in 1958 and 1959. Considering the extensive family ties to the Roughriders, Ted's objective was to some day play for the team himself. The stint in Arizona was an important step toward that goal.

While in Tucson, Urness and Dumelie experienced the dog days of summer — literally. "We were really hillbillies or hayshakers or whatever you want to call it," Urness said. "We didn't have any money, but they provided us everything [as per the terms of the scholarship]. I think we got $10 a month for laundry. We used to work in the offseason at the dog track in Tucson. In the evenings, Larry and I would go four, five or six times a week to the dog track, as did Dale West. We got paid $6 a night and we'd lead the dogs around. In each race, you'd load them up into the chute. You'd trot down to the finish line and then you'd have the race. Then you pick the dogs up and lead them back and congratulate the winners. That was a big revenue stream for us. After, we'd go and get beer for 20 cents or whatever it was. That was how we supplemented our extracurricular activity."

One fine day, the income was supplemented to an extent that neither Urness nor Dumelie could believe. "I'll never forget this," Urness began. "Larry Dumelie was kind of a gambler. He'd always be a couple of days ahead with who was running in the dog races. There was one dog favoured for this race, called Logical. This one night, we were all working and one of the guys who wasn't working placed a $2 bet for everybody. I think there were 10 of us, so we put $20 on the nose on a longshot dog — a big, gangly young thing. Larry got to lead Logical, which was the favourite.

"You walk these dogs around the track, one behind the other. Larry got to this loading chute. It's kind of like a racetrack. They've got these doors that come up and you get behind your dog and pick his ass up and you throw him into the chute, and you hold his ass in there and they lower the gate. Well, we were at the loading dock and we were loading these dogs. Up goes the gate, and Larry shoves the favourite in backwards. He's got it by the throat and it's trying to get out. Nobody else can see it. There's a big commotion. We realize that he has just loaded the favourite backwards. Sure as hell, the dog comes out backwards, head over heels.

"Logical came in third, and our dog won. We made 80-some dollars each. It was unreal. That's the first and only race I've ever seen fixed in my life. They would have killed us. Nobody said anything. We were terrified. We thought we'd all lose our jobs. We made $86, and we got paid $6 a night. That was like two weeks' work. We kind of chuckled a little bit. We said our odds had improved pretty dramatically because we had loaded the thing backwards. I feel sorry for the people who put money on him."

Money was also a reason Urness decided to sign with the Roughriders — not that he needed much enticing, considering the family's connection to the team. Coming out of college, he was drafted by the Denver Broncos, who were then approaching their second season in the fledgling American Football League. Griffing was the Broncos' general manager at the time. "I didn't even try to negotiate a contract with them," Urness said. "I'd made my mind up that I was going to come back to Saskatchewan. Ken Preston came down and offered me a contract in February

Ted Urness | Photo courtesy of Gord Heenan, Heenan Studios

of 1961 to play for the Roughriders. As I recall, he offered me a $1,000 signing bonus plus a contract — and $1,000 in 1961, to a kid just graduating from university and getting ready to get married, was like Fort Knox. I signed a one-year contract." Urness was paid between $6,000 and $7,000 per annum. "That was a lot of money then," he said. "That was more than I could earn at a job full time. I wanted to come home. I don't think I could have done much better, even in Denver at the time."

Urness did not require any introduction to the Roughriders, of course, but professional football itself was a novelty. At the outset, Urness was primarily deployed as a guard, although he did see some action at tackle and centre. At the latter position, he would eventually become one of Canadian football's all-time greats. That was something Urness aspired to, but could hardly envision, in the early 1960s. "All of a sudden, I was a Saskatchewan Roughrider," he said. "From sandlot football to playing for Scott Collegiate for a couple of years and then going to the Regina Rams — yeah, it was pretty exciting following the Roughriders. To be a Roughrider, it was always a dream. I never thought it would turn out the way it did. It was a wonderful time."

CHAPTER 5 # "YOU PRODUCE OR YOU GET OUT"

Had circumstances been different, Wayne Shaw's graduating class would have consisted of Wayne Shaw — period. "They were not going to have a Grade 12 in Bladworth High School because I was the only one in Grade 12," Shaw said, rewinding to 1956. "They said, 'We're not going to have Grade 12 here just for you. You've got to go to Davidson.' " Shaw, who grew up on a farm between Davidson and Bladworth, opted instead to complete high school in another small Saskatchewan community — Wilcox.

Shaw selected Notre Dame College with designs on furthering his hockey career. Enrollment at Notre Dame would, in fact, contribute to his advancement in athletics, but not as envisioned. "I had never played organized football before Grade 12," said Shaw, who was more involved in hockey, baseball, and track and field. "At recess in Bladworth High School, there were farm boys from everywhere and we would play football without equipment. We would rip our shirts, and our mother would be all upset."

Some of those pickup games included two of Shaw's four brothers — Doug (who was precisely one year older than Wayne) and Dennis (two years younger). "One day, I hit Dennis and hurt him," Shaw said. "Dennis was on Doug's team, and Doug got mad and came over and smacked me on the side of the head and broke his finger. He went to Davidson to get his finger fixed. Then he came back and said, 'Man, you've got a hard head!' "

That head would soon be shaved. "My mother and dad drove me down to Wilcox," Shaw remembered. "As soon as Father Murray saw me, he said, 'You've got to get a haircut.' I had an ordinary haircut, but I had to get a brush cut." That was his first brush with greatness in the form of Monsignor Athol Murray, who had founded the southern Saskatchewan residential school in 1927.

Notre Dame was renowned as a hockey factory, and that was part of the allure for Shaw. His introduction to football in a more serious vein resulted from an informal game held in Wilcox. Shaw derived so much enjoyment from a touch football game that he ended up trying out for the Notre Dame Hounds gridders. Little did Shaw know that he would be a football player for the next 16 years, including 12 with the Roughriders.

Shaw's introduction to football was anything but auspicious. As a neophyte, it was obvious that he required more work. An additional indoctrination was prescribed by the Hounds' quarterback. "Stewie McNiven said to Cy MacDonald, the coach: 'Wayne needs to get more practise as the fullback, because he hasn't played before,'" Shaw said. "He'd run me up and down the field. I was in good shape, but I'd never played football before." Suddenly, Shaw was playing football considerably longer than most of his classmates. In addition to participating in the daily 90-minute practice, he would spend a supplementary hour with McNiven. "Football exercise is different than hockey or baseball," Shaw noted. "When I played baseball and hockey, we never did stops and starts, running up and down the field. We would practise football for an hour and a half. I would take a handoff for five or 10 yards, run down the field, and so on. After two or three practices, I said, 'That's it. I'm not doing this anymore.' I was practising for 2½ hours. Everyone else was practising for an hour and a half. I said, 'OK, that's it. I quit!'"

The hierarchy at Notre Dame was not pleased. "They said, 'OK, you've got to work in the kitchen,'" he recalled. "They had me for a couple of days doing the worst jobs in the kitchen, like cleaning the pots and pans. So, after two days, I said, 'OK, I'll play football.'" And play he did. As a Grade 12 rookie at Notre Dame, Shaw was primarily an offensive and defensive end. His aptitude for football, particularly on defence, was quickly noted.

Shaw also made a seamless transition to the classrooms of Notre Dame, sporting a Grade 12 average exceeding 90 per cent. He was so impressed by the environment at Notre Dame that he remained enrolled there for 1½ years following graduation from high school. Notre Dame's arts program was affiliated with the University of Ottawa, so Shaw's studies were concentrated in that discipline. He also honed his football skills with a travelling Hounds team that played exhibition games against the Regina Rams, Saskatoon Hilltops, and the like.

Beyond Grade 12, Shaw developed a greater relationship with and appreciation for Athol Murray. "The first big thing that I learned from Father Murray was that the really great books were the old ones, not the brand-new ones," said Shaw, who eventually operated his own bookstore. "Father Murray would get up and spout Plato, Aristotle and Socrates. He was in love with the old philosophers … Father Murray was an enthusiastic guy. He would be ranting and raving about all of this stuff — not like a normal teacher. He'd get excited about something and he'd go running upstairs or running into his office. He always had a cigarette. He'd have two cigarettes going sometimes because he'd get excited and light up another cigarette."

Shaw also had multiple things on the go by the fall of 1958. Along with serving on Notre Dame's student council and tending to his studies, he was managing an outdoor rink and a student canteen. He was so busy with myriad responsibilities that his marks descended to

B's and C's. The workload became unsustainable. Shaw needed a respite. He decided to leave Notre Dame shortly before Christmas of 1958, with the intent of returning the following autumn after having divested himself of all the extra responsibilities.

That plan, like his intention of becoming an elite hockey player, never came to fruition. In 1959, Shaw enrolled at the University of Saskatchewan — which had just resuscitated its football program — and began playing in the junior ranks with the Hilltops. Shaw's successes over two years with the Hilltops attracted the attention of the Roughriders. As a result, he became part of the influx of Saskatchewan-born talent that joined the Roughriders in the early 1960s — an infusion that also included Dale West, Larry Dumelie and Ted Urness.

As was the case with Urness, Shaw became a Roughrider in 1961. According to Shaw, the comparisons ended there. "When I went to Regina in '61, I was treated like a fourth-class citizen," Shaw said. "First-class citizens were American veterans. Second-class citizens were Canadian veterans. Third-class citizens were American rookies. Fourth-class citizens were Canadian rookies. Ted Urness and I started in '61. He made six grand and I made two. You know why? He came back from Arizona. And did you know that I was a starter before he was? I started my first year as outside linebacker and made $2,000. And Ted made six grand because he'd been an American [collegiate player]. In '63, I made an all-star team and I started making more money and I was treated like a second-class citizen, let's say."

Shaw quickly became a first-class linebacker, even though he was hardly a textbook tackler. He was renowned for an unconventional, but effective, tackling technique that resulted in the nickname "Clamps." Once Shaw got his hands on a ball-carrier, that typically signalled the conclusion of the play. The first priority was to shed the blocker, which Shaw did routinely but not in adherence to the coaching manual. "I'd use his momentum to get rid of him, because I couldn't get under him," Shaw noted. "I always figured that I'm 210 or 215 pounds. If a 240-pound guard gets a four-yard run at me, and if we meet straight ahead and I'm not lower than him, he's going to eliminate me. So I would grab them by the shoulder pads and use their momentum to get rid of them.

"This used to piss them all off. Even the coach would get pissed off. He'd say, 'Get your nose down in there,' but I couldn't play that way. [Roughriders defensive lineman] Garner Ekstran was only about 210 or 215. If he wasn't down real low, he had no hope, but he was strong like a bull. I couldn't get down that low. We played a different way. It's just the way it was from working on the farm. I had very strong legs and strong arms."

Shaw also had a strong supporter in Eagle Keys, who served as the Roughriders' head coach from 1965 to 1970. "We used to have a guest coach from North Dakota," Shaw said. "He became a friend of mine. He used to tell me, 'The first time I was in camp, I told Eagle that he should cut Shaw and cut Atch because their technique was no good.' " Keys was not prepared to part company with Shaw or venerable defensive lineman Ron Atchison. "Eagle said, 'Well, they may not have the technique but they get the job done,' " Shaw said.

Although Shaw quickly impressed the Roughriders' coaches, he did not receive wider recognition until a 1963 game against the Winnipeg Blue Bombers, whose star running back was the legendary Lincoln Locomotive. "I made my first all-star team because I tackled the great Leo Lewis," Shaw said. "[Winnipeg media luminaries] Jack Wells and Jack Matheson said, 'Where the hell did this farm boy come from? He's tackling the great Leo Lewis!' It was just because I could use my arms and get rid of the blockers and get into the action. If I had put my nose down underneath like they used to tell me to do, Leo Lewis would have been gone for 10 yards before I got rid of the guard. After a while, the coaches said, 'OK, if you can do it that way, fine.' "

"Clamps" earned Western Conference all-star recognition for the first of six times in 1963, when Bob Shaw (no relation) was the Roughriders' head coach. "Bob Shaw gave us all a hard time, many times," Wayne Shaw said. "My older brother Al and I went into the service-station business in about 1963. One day in practice at Campion College, we're having a scrimmage and somebody else goes in for me. I'm standing on the sideline and some guy comes up from behind and starts talking to me about a car. Bob Shaw saw me talking and gave me hell. I shouldn't have been doing it, but a fan comes up behind you ... When we practised, the fans used to be everywhere."

Wayne Shaw *putting the "Clamps" on a Montreal Alouettes ball-carrier* | Photo courtesy of SSHFM

Bob Shaw was everywhere — or so it seemed — during a lengthy football career as a player and coach. Shaw was an eyewitness to some momentous events in football and world history before replacing Steve Owen as the Roughriders' field boss in 1963. By that time, Shaw had already coached some players who went on to become Pro Football Hall of Famers, drawing upon the influences of some notable mentors — including Paul Brown and Earl (Curly) Lambeau. They helped to mould Shaw into a player who left an enduring imprint on the National Football League's record book. But some of his most important contributions transcended football.

Shortly after the Japanese attacked Pearl Harbor on Dec. 7, 1941, Shaw joined the United States Army and served in the Second World War. He enlisted after helping the Ohio State Buckeyes win a national championship and earning All-American honours as a junior while playing for Paul Brown. Not long after getting married, Shaw was off to Europe with the 104th Infantry. "I had a pretty good job while I was there," he said. "I had weapons training and I also went through intelligence and reconnaissance school. Due to my training, they made me the regimental commander's personal bodyguard."

The 6-foot-4, 226-pound Shaw returned to the United States in 1945 to take amphibious training in preparation for a climactic invasion of Japan. "We were going to go and take it out," he said. "We were about ready to go when the war ended. They dropped the bomb, so I didn't have to go over there." Shaw was soon discharged, clearing the way for him to resume his football career — this time in the professional ranks. He spent the 1945 NFL season with the Cleveland Rams, who moved to Los Angeles the following year. He was out of football for the 1947 and 1948 seasons while recovering from a neck injury, but returned to the Rams in 1949.

Shaw's finest year — and his finest day — came in 1950 after he was dealt to the Chicago Cardinals, who were coached by Lambeau. That season, Shaw averaged 20.2 yards on his 48 receptions, 12 of which went for touchdowns. Five of the touchdown receptions were amassed on one memorable day — Oct. 2, 1950 — in a 55-13 victory over the Baltimore Colts. "I had caught four touchdown passes and someone called down from the press box and told Curly that I was tied with the record," Shaw said. "So he sent me back in and they threw me another touchdown pass." Jim Hardy threw all five scoring passes, which covered 40, 17, 18, 29 and eight yards. Hardy also threw a sixth touchdown pass that day, and an apparent seventh was dropped.

Shaw still owns a share of the NFL single-game touchdown-receptions record, which was eventually tied by Kellen Winslow of the San Diego Chargers (in 1981) and Jerry Rice of the San Francisco 49ers (1990).

At 29, Shaw figured to have a few more productive years in the NFL, only to be derailed by a contract dispute with the Cardinals. Hearing of this, Les Lear — a former Rams teammate who was coaching Calgary — invited Shaw to play in Canada. As a Stampeder, he led the West in scoring in 1951 and 1952. In the latter season, Shaw produced 110 points — a record that stood until 1958 when the Roughriders' Jack Hill, who was Tripucka's favourite receiver, piled up 145 points while moonlighting as a kicker.

After retiring as a player in 1953, Shaw completed his education degree at Otterbein College in his hometown of Westerville, Ohio. He then went into teaching — but not in the conventional sense. He embarked on a coaching career that continued until the 1980s, making every effort to emulate his mentor from Ohio State. "Paul Brown was a super coach," Shaw said. "I patterned my coaching after him and his way." Among other things, Brown prided himself on organization and discipline.

As a coach, Shaw quickly ascended to the NFL, serving as an assistant to Weeb Ewbank with Baltimore. As the Colts' pass-offence and receivers coach, Shaw became well-acquainted with quarterback Johnny Unitas. "John was just an ordinary guy who had talent and knew how to use it," Shaw said. "He knew his job and went about it."

Unitas was at his best on Dec. 28, 1958, when the Colts met the New York Giants in the NFL's championship game. The final was decided in overtime when Alan Ameche accessed a gaping hole for a one-yard touchdown run that gave the Colts a 23-17 victory. That game, which triggered a surge in the NFL's popularity, is often described as the greatest in league history.

"It never entered our minds that people would be talking about that game 50 years later," Shaw said of the classic contest, which was held at Yankee Stadium and savoured by a national television audience. "It was a great game, but I didn't think of it as an end-all." Colts fans felt differently, as evidenced by the explosive reaction when the team landed in Baltimore. "The excitement and commotion came when we got home," he recalled. "We were on a bus. The airport was flooded with people and we couldn't get out. They were trying to crawl on the bus and the whole nine yards."

Nearly 50 years later, it came to light that Shaw's involvement in the 1958 classic was especially noteworthy for his actions in the week leading up to the game. At the behest of Colts owner Carroll Rosenbloom, Shaw — who was also an advance scout for the team — watched the Giants' practices from the roof of an apartment building overlooking Yankee Stadium. "He asked me to go up, and I went up for the week before the game and observed them," Shaw said. "I remember getting caught by the building manager, and I told him I was a reporter and I was writing a story that I spied on the club."

Although Shaw is proud to have been part of a landmark event in NFL history, he "certainly had a concern" about snooping on an opponent's practice. He was worried that he would never coach again if he was caught.

Rosenbloom was so determined to gather some intelligence that Shaw was promised a job for life if the plan was exposed. With the owner's backing, Shaw headed for New York and found a rooftop vantage point. "It helped in this regard: They didn't do anything different, and that's a good thing to know when you're playing a team," he said. "It just reconfirmed that they were doing what they were doing all year long."

The lack of variation irked Giants legend Frank Gifford, who referenced Shaw in a book about the 1958 final, *The Glory Game.* "Apparently, Rosenbloom wanted to win the game that badly — for a lot of reasons," Gifford wrote. "Supposedly Shaw reported that we didn't appear to be working on anything new. But it didn't take a rocket scientist to figure that out.

We hardly ever did anything different on offence, and never on defence. In fact, we hadn't changed anything since the regular-season game in November when we'd beaten them. They didn't need Shaw. They just needed some film from our first game."

Nearly a half-century later, New England Patriots head coach Bill Belichick was fined $500,000 by the NFL after one of his team's video assistants was caught taping the New York Jets' defensive signals during a game in 2007. The incident was quickly dubbed Spygate. "Well, he did it a little bit differently, didn't he?" a chuckling Shaw said of Belichick. "I did it first-hand. He did it with cameras."

Although Shaw and Rosenbloom had talked about long-term employment, it didn't turn out that way. "I left after that year because of the raise they wanted to give me, and I went out to the San Francisco 49ers," Shaw said. "That ended my relationship with Rosenbloom." What kind of raise was he offered? "Ha ha ha," Shaw responded. "It was $400. The problem was that the line coach got $800 because he had two kids and I only had one, and that was their explanation."

After a stint with the 49ers, Shaw accepted the head-coaching position at New Mexico Military Institute. While coaching at the junior college in Roswell, N.M., Shaw started a quarterback named Roger Staubach, who went on to play for Navy, win the Heisman Trophy in 1963, and star for the Dallas Cowboys before being enshrined in the Pro Football Hall of Fame.

Staubach was full of promise — and doubts — when he arrived in Roswell for the 1960 season. The Cincinnati-born quarterback was wondering whether to play college football closer to home, but aspired to join the United States Naval Academy. He enrolled at New Mexico Military Institute to improve his English grade and facilitate an easier transition into the Naval Academy.

In one season under Shaw, Staubach improved his comprehension of a pro-style offence. Shaw also helped Staubach, who was primarily a running quarterback in high school, refine his passing techniques. "He was a fine coach and introduced me to the wide-open, pro-set offence," Staubach wrote in his autobiography, *First Down, Lifetime To Go*. "Coach Shaw helped me in other ways, too. He knew I was homesick so he used some reverse psychology. He started telling me I had to help the other guys on the team who were homesick. It worked. I relaxed. Shaw took a bunch of guys who had never played together and put together a 9-1 record. I hit over 60 per cent of my passes. I had finally become a passer."

Staubach also used his right arm to great effect as a relief pitcher with New Mexico Military Institute's baseball team. However, his primary contributions to the team were in the outfield — he was a third-team junior college All-American — and at the plate (where he batted .320). "He was a great baseball player," said Shaw, who also coached Staubach on the basketball team in Roswell. "He was a centre-fielder and he had great jump on the ball. I think he could have played pro baseball."

After three years as the football coach, basketball coach and athletic director at New Mexico Military Institute, Shaw was ready to return to pro football. The Roughriders just happened to be in search of a field boss following the departure of 1962 CFL coach-of-the-year Steve Owen.

Roughriders president Bob Kramer introduced Shaw to the team's directors on Jan. 18, 1963. Although a coach's job security is traditionally tenuous, that was especially true in Saskatchewan. Shaw became the Roughriders' sixth head coach in a seven-year span. Despite the team's tendency to ashcan head coaches, Shaw was entirely amenable to a one-year contract. "If I can't do the job for you in one season, then I don't deserve to hold the position any longer," Shaw said when his appointment was announced.

Shaw's predecessor was an easygoing gent who often interrupted team meetings to spin yarns about

Trainer **Sandy Archer**, **Jim Copeland**, **Neil Habig** (behind Copeland), **Bob Ptacek**, **Hinckley Archer** (behind Ptacek), **Bill Clarke** (standing), all to the left of head coach **Bob Shaw** | Photo courtesy of SSHFM

his lengthy tenure with the New York Giants. Owen's replacement was not as popular with the players. Shaw did not dispute the characterization of him as a tough, demanding coach. "Oh, I was," Shaw said. "There's an old saying that you're a pro and you're paid to produce. You produce or you get out. That's always been a philosophy."

Media types found Shaw to be more amiable. The *Leader-Post*'s John Robertson described Shaw as "a reporter's dream" and lauded the incoming coach for his co-operative, candid nature. Shaw's pull-no-punches attitude was evidenced by his appraisal of the 1962 Roughriders, having critiqued film of a team that finished with an 8-7-1 record. "I thought they were extremely fortunate, from what I've seen," Shaw told the newspaper. "Mind you, they played some outstanding football, but too many times they left a lot to be desired. There were too many vital errors, made too often. All I can say is that the club must have had tremendous desire to go as far as it did."

For the Roughriders to go further, Shaw realized that improvement on offence was imperative. Yes, the Roughriders had Ray Purdin — who scored 14 touchdowns in 1962 — but, aside from him, there was little in the way of potency. That explained why Saskatchewan averaged a modest 16.8 points per game in its final season under Steve Owen.

Entering the 1963 season, a premier pass-catcher was on Shaw's wish list. And although Bob Ptacek had a decent year in 1962, throwing for 2,317 yards and 15 touchdowns, Shaw told a "Meet The Coaches" gathering at Regina's Trianon Ballroom that he was looking for improvement at quarterback. Who that quarterback would be remained open to speculation well into 1963.

CHAPTER 6 | # "HE'LL GET KILLED"

The Roughriders' decision to fire head coach George Terlep in 1959 paid off in ways that nobody could have envisioned at the time of his ouster. Terlep, remember, was dumped by the Roughriders in 1959 after their record plummeted to 0-9. The Ottawa Rough Riders promptly hired Terlep as their backfield coach. By 1960, he had been promoted by Ottawa to the role of general manager. In that capacity, Terlep recruited a young man who would become a legendary figure in Roughriders and CFL history — Ron Lancaster.

One day, Terlep received a phone call from Bill Edwards, who was then the head football coach at Wittenberg College (now Wittenberg University). Before arriving at the Springfield, Ohio campus, Edwards had been the head coach at Vanderbilt University, where Terlep was his backfield coach. That connection was re-established when Edwards called Terlep to suggest that the 5-foot-9¾ Lancaster, who was graduating as Wittenberg's starting quarterback, would be a nice fit for Canadian football. Edwards also conveyed that sentiment to Lancaster.

"Coming out of school, it was the first year of the American Football League," Lancaster recalled.

Ron Lancaster *in college* |
Photo courtesy of Wittenberg University

"I heard from some of those teams about signing contracts there. Coach Edwards advised me to stay away from that league because they were signing everybody. They were giving a lot of guys no-cut contracts. He thought I should go and play football. I was planning on playing baseball." In fact, baseball was in his sights even after he made a deal with Ottawa. If his stint in the nation's capital had been abbreviated, he would have tried out for the Washington Senators.

Lancaster, who played shortstop for Wittenberg, had earlier worked out for four major-league teams — the Pittsburgh Pirates, Philadelphia Phillies, Detroit Tigers and Cleveland Indians. The session with the Indians took place before a game against the Baltimore Orioles. "This coach is hitting me ground balls between pitches," Lancaster recounted. "I'd field them and throw them to first base. The coach hollers, 'Cut it loose! Throw the damn ball!' Woody Held, who was playing third base for Cleveland at that time, walked over and said, 'Hey, kid, they just want to see how strong your arm is. They don't give a shit if you throw it up in the second tier.' "

Held's message resonated with Lancaster. "The next ball they hit me, I picked it up and let it go. When it went over the first baseman's head, it was still rising. It hit about 12 rows up. The coach hollers, 'Now that's the way to throw the damn thing!' I figured, 'I can throw it up there all day.' I'll never forget that workout. I had a lot of fun playing baseball." But football eventually won out. Lancaster figured he could always return to baseball if a pro football career did not materialize.

Terlep had been impressed by game film Edwards had shipped to Ottawa. With that in mind, Terlep embarked for Springfield to visit Lancaster. The meeting was amicable, and Lancaster decided to become a Rough Rider.

In Lancaster, Ottawa landed a quarterback who had guided Wittenberg to a 25-8-1 record over four seasons. By the fifth game of his freshman year, he was the starter. In his sophomore year, Wittenberg won a conference title. He was named an Ohio Athletic Conference all-star as a senior while also being honoured as his team's most valuable player. Lancaster was much like his school, in that success was attained despite modest dimensions. Wittenberg's student population hovered around 2,200 when he arrived in 1956 from his hometown of Clairton, Pa., which is 30 kilometres south of Pittsburgh. He was actually born in nearby Fairchance, but the family soon moved to Clairton.

George Terlep |
Photo courtesy of SSHFM

Growing up, Lancaster had aspirations of quarterbacking the Pittsburgh Steelers or playing shortstop for the Pirates. The oldest of Elmer and Dorothy Lancaster's 10 children, Ron lived with his family in a three-bedroom, two-storey rowhouse. "Upstairs, there were three bedrooms. You do the math with 12 people," said Bill Lancaster, one of Ron's three brothers. The Lancasters lived in a project — government housing for low-income families, with a rent of $65 per month — that stretched for 84 blocks, with six dwellings per block. Most of those families had connections to U.S. Steel's Clairton mill, where Elmer typically worked 16-hour days, six days per week. He spent 36 years at the steel mill, his salary peaking at $17,000 per year. "One time I asked, 'Dad, why did we never have a car?' " Bill said. "He said, 'We didn't need one. If it's a nice day, I can walk a mile and a half to the steel mill. If it's cold out, I can take the bus.' That was the way it was."

Sports quickly became a way of life for Ron Lancaster, both at the organized and pickup levels. The sandlots and football fields of Clairton were a second home. "Ronnie was a quarterback at 10 years old," Bill Lancaster said. "My mother tells the story where he came home and said, 'They've got me at some position called quarterback. I don't know what to do, but that's where they put me.' " And that is where he stayed. Ron Lancaster ended up playing for the Clairton High Bears, starting at quarterback as a junior and senior, while also playing defensive back and punting left-footed. Bill Lancaster attended Friday night high school football games that attracted overflow crowds of 10,000 in football-mad western Pennsylvania — also the origin of football legends such as Johnny Unitas, Joe Namath and Mike Ditka.

Ron Lancaster proceeded to enrol at Wittenberg, which he attended on an academic scholarship, and quickly impressed head coach Bill Edwards. "I was sold on the idea that if football was good for the big man, then why not the little man, too?" Edwards recalled in a 1979 interview with the *Leader-Post*. "We knew we couldn't get the big ones, anyway. They'd go to Ohio or Michigan." Lancaster did wind up in Ohio, but his destination did not even remotely resemble Ohio State University. "I got him when he was around 165 pounds," Edwards said. "A lot of schools wouldn't look at him because of that, but I was thinking a few years ahead — say, when he was a junior."

That timetable was soon amended. "Bob Rosencrans was our quarterback when Ron came," Dave Maurer, who was Wittenberg's backfield coach when Lancaster arrived, told the *Leader-Post*'s Dave Senick in 1979. "It didn't take Bill and I long to realize that we should get Lancaster in right away." Some diplomacy was required. "Bill didn't want to shatter Rosencrans so he called him in one day and asked if he had seen the pro game on TV last Sunday," Maurer continued. "Y.A. Tittle and Charlie Conerly alternated at quarterback for the New York Giants. Bill told Rosey he thought it wasn't a bad idea for us to alternate. He told him Lancaster would start and he'd sit on the sidelines and analyse the other team. That way, he'd be able to come in and pick them apart. Rosey never did get back in the game and Lancaster had the starting job."

Such intuitiveness was one of the traits that would eventually get Edwards inducted into the College Football Hall of Fame. One of his closest collegiate coaching confidantes was Steve Belichick, who joined Edwards' staff at Vanderbilt in 1949. Their friendship flourished to the extent that a baby boy — William Steven Belichick — was named after both men in 1952. Bill Belichick later won three Super Bowls as head coach of the New England Patriots.

Another legendary coach, Frank Clair, was in charge when Lancaster signed for $8,500 with Rough Riders in 1960. Clair liked Lancaster's athleticism and deployed him in Ottawa's defensive backfield. A youngster named Peter Mansbridge was also impressed. "In 1960, I was only 12," said Mansbridge, who went on to become the chief correspondent for *The National* on CBC Television. "Me and my friends used to go out to Lansdowne Park and the Rough Riders would often be practising beside the stadium. The big deal would be to carry their helmet. You used to run over and ask them if you could carry the helmet and walk back to the dressing room. If you were really lucky, you could rip off one of the chinstraps and walk away with it. So, one day, there was this kid, Number 16." Ron Lancaster, meet Peter Mansbridge. "I got to carry his helmet," Mansbridge continued. "That was the impression someone can have on a small kid, so I kept my eye out for him. He was more of a defensive back than a quarterback at the beginning."

It was an auspicious beginning. In the second game of the 1960 season, Lancaster intercepted three passes, returning one for a touchdown. Lancaster also saw significant duty at quarterback, with the remainder of the playing time being given to Russ Jackson. Lancaster was especially effective in Game 2 of the Eastern Conference final against the Toronto Argonauts, throwing two long passes to Bobby Simpson to help Ottawa register a 21-20 come-from-behind victory, and a 54-41 victory in the two-game, total-point set. But Jackson started the 1960 Grey Cup and was the far busier of the Ottawa quarterbacks that day, helping the Rough Riders defeat the Eagle Keys-coached Edmonton Eskimos 16-6.

Lancaster and Jackson were also the Rough Riders' quarterbacks in 1961 and 1962. Although it was a luxury, the presence of two capable signal-callers also created some divisiveness. "I think it happens, no matter what," Jackson reflected. "If you're winning, everybody's sort of happy, but if you start to lose, it's, 'Well, so-and-so should have been playing.' I think the fans started to get divided in terms of who they wanted the coach to play. I always felt there was a lot of pressure to go in and perform immediately because if you didn't, you had the idea that maybe you'd be taken out. I think that rests in the back of your mind when you start a football game with another quarterback who is equal to you sitting on the bench."

"I was never too happy with that situation," Lancaster told *CFL Illustrated* in 1971. "The first year wasn't too bad because Russ got hurt. I had been playing defensive halfback but when Russ was hurt, I got the chance to play nine games in a row. I needed that experience. But 1962 was different. Things just weren't going right and neither Russ or I was happy with what we were doing. We lost eight of our last nine games and the atmosphere was murderous. I knew that the fans were split over Russ and myself and it was always in my mind that maybe the players on our own team were also split."

By 1963, the Canadian-born Jackson was Frank Clair's preferred pivot. Jackson's Canadian status — Lancaster was classified as an import at the time — factored into the equation. To remain in Ottawa, Lancaster had to earn a position as a defensive back. However, the Rough Riders' training-camp roster also included rookie Bob O'Billovich. "When O'Billovich came in and played defensive back, it just made the decision that much easier," Lancaster said. "It became apparent that for the good of the team, one of us [Lancaster or Jackson] had to go. In those days, the quarterback counted against the ratio so it was a no-brainer that I would be

Russ Jackson | Photo courtesy of *Leader-Post* archives

Ron Lancaster | Photo courtesy of *Leader-Post* archives

traded. I wondered where I was going to go. They didn't take me on their trip to the West — Edmonton and Vancouver — for their last preseason games so I knew something was up. I saw in the paper where Saskatchewan got the heck beat out of them — 40-0 — in a preseason game, so I figured, 'Sure enough, they're going to trade me out there,' and they did."

For "a broken helmet with no face mask," according to Lancaster, he became a Saskatchewan Roughrider. The compensation was actually $500. The deal included a proviso that Saskatchewan would not trade him to an Eastern Conference team unless it was back to Ottawa. The deal was beneficial for all concerned. "Obie had a nice career with Ottawa, Russ had a great career in Ottawa, and the trade to Saskatchewan was the best thing that could have happened for me in my career," Lancaster said. He could say that with the benefit of hindsight. Initially, he had reservations about being dispatched to Regina. "I wasn't too knocked out about it," he admitted. "I got off the airplane and nobody was there to meet me. It took a while to get used to. Someone was supposed to meet me there and take me to practice. I had to get a cab. The cabbie took me to Campion College." Once there, Lancaster met his new teammates, including a rookie fullback.

When a first down was required, George Reed almost always found the marker. It was a different scenario in the summer of 1963, when Reed drove to Regina from his home in Renton, Wash., for his first pro football training camp.

"Regina wasn't really clearly marked," Reed said. "Where the overpass is on Albert Street now, it used to be a four-way stop. I came to the four-way stop. I guess I had missed the sign saying 'Regina' and if there was a sign, it was very small. I was in Balgonie when I stopped for gas and I asked the guy how much farther I had to go to get to Regina. He said, 'Well, you've got about 11 miles to go back that way and you'll run into it.' "

Unlike Ron Lancaster, Reed arrived with at least some fanfare. Whereas the *Leader-Post*'s introductory mention of Lancaster was in the ninth paragraph of a story heralding the Roughriders' decision to release Chuck Gullickson, Dave Shaw and Ken Webster, Reed's signing was heralded with a photo of him in a Washington State uniform, along with a June 8, 1963 story headlined "New fullback joins Riders."

At one time, football was not Reed's forte. "Baseball probably was my first love," he said. "It was baseball, probably basketball and then football. Probably the thing that steered me away from baseball was, back in those days, they only gave partial scholarships for baseball. Football was a full scholarship, and I needed all the help I could get in order to go to university."

George Reed Sr., and his wife, Maggie, raised 12 children — six boys and six girls. The Reeds moved from Vicksburg, Miss., to Renton when George Jr. was three. "My father worked in the steel mill in Seattle, and he was also hustling on the side, picking up copper and that type of thing when he wasn't at his full-time job to make a little extra money," Reed recalled.

The younger Reed also held down multiple positions — on the football field. He was a running back and defensive back at Renton High School. After continuing with the sport at Washington State, Reed played running back and linebacker. He excelled as a junior and senior after recovering from a broken ankle that ruined his sophomore season. "You could hear the bone break all over the practice field," Washington State teammate Hugh Campbell said. "It was one of the scariest things. When that happened, the odds of George Reed being the all-time great were pretty slim. We didn't know if he'd come back and play the next year for us in college."

Reed not only played the next year (1961), he was named Washington State's most valuable player. He also served as one of the team's co-captains and earned most-inspirational-player honours. The 6-foot-0, 205-pounder punctuated his college career by appearing in two showcases for graduating seniors — the Hula Bowl and East-West Shrine Bowl. "In the East-West game, he made the first few tackles, because they had two really good fullbacks and they were short at linebacker," said Campbell, who was named most valuable player in that game. "The coach said, 'I know he can play defence. Let's put him over there for a while.' "

Double duty was nothing new for Reed. "I averaged 58 minutes a game when I was in university," he remembered. "I might have been a better linebacker than I was a running back. It created a toll. I never really thought about it then. I never wanted the coach to call me off the field, because it was normally a long run off the field and then he'd say, 'Go right back in.' "

The inexhaustible Reed attracted the attention of the British Columbia Lions, who secured his Canadian Football League rights. "At the time, they had Nub Beamer," Reed noted. "They thought that he was going to be their fullback for several more years, so they traded my rights to Saskatchewan. I don't know for what — maybe a dollar." Reed's initial reaction: "Where the hell is Saskatchewan?" Reed was soon visited by Roughriders general manager Ken Preston and assistant coach Len Younce. "We came to terms," Reed said, "and that's how I became a Roughrider."

A little coercion from defensive lineman Garner Ekstran didn't hurt. Ekstran had joined the Roughriders in 1961 after playing at Washington State. "I talked to Ken Preston until I didn't think he wanted to see me," Ekstran said. "I tried to get across to Preston that George was a hell of a running back. Those of us who played with him in college knew how good he was, but nobody else knew."

Imagine Ekstran's delight when he reported to training camp in 1963 and was reacquainted with Reed. "I came in a week late, as I used to do, and George came up to me and said, 'You son of a bitch.' I said, 'What's wrong?' He said, 'We've got six fullbacks in camp.' I said, 'Don't sweat it, George.' "

He sweated it, anyway. "I was kind of shell-shocked," Reed said. "We had the old pot-bellied stove in the dressing room and a couple of light bulbs hanging down. I had great equipment when I played at Washington State, so you looked at it [in Regina] and shook your head and said, 'What the hell did you get yourself into?' "

George Reed | Photo courtesy of *Leader-Post*

Reed's apprehensions were not eased by his introduction to the Roughriders' first-year head coach. "Bob Shaw told me that I was too small to play fullback for him and that I might catch on as a utility back," Reed said. "If I hadn't been so stubborn, I probably would have turned around and went back home and just went to the National Football League. I was just determined to show him that I could play football, and it wound up that way."

More than 40 years later, Shaw countered Reed's version of events. "Oh my goodness. Where in the hell did he get that idea?" an incredulous Shaw asked. "I told him he was too small? Oh, Christ. He was a powerhouse. He was a hell of a fullback. And he thought I said he was too small? I never believed that. Heavens, no."

Shaw thought enough of Reed that he named him a starter for the Roughriders' 1963 regular-season opener, supplanting Ferd Burket. "I just kept watching guys in front of me get cut," Reed said. "Then the night before we got ready to play Edmonton in the first game, I was instructed that I was the starting fullback."

Reed ended up rushing 16 times for a team-high 74 yards in a 19-16 victory over the host Eskimos. Reed's one-yard touchdown run in the fourth quarter provided the margin of victory. Reed's CFL debut was unabashedly praised by the *Leader-Post*'s John Robertson, who wrote: "If you saw rookie George Reed ripping up the middle through the Eskimo defences with the speed of an explosive halfback and the power of a Sherman tank, you must have applauded coach Bob Shaw's decision to let the Washington State product fall heir to the job."

The Roughriders' starting quarterback that day was Bob Ptacek. Ron Lancaster had just arrived in Regina after being traded westward by the Ottawa Rough Riders. "When I got there, they were more or less preparing for the game," Lancaster said. "I didn't get to know a lot of guys, but I got to know George because we both lived at the Kitchener Hotel. We all lived down there.

"George was a hard worker in practice. He hustled. He ran hard. He wasn't that big, but he had real good speed. He would be back returning kickoffs. That's kind of unusual [for a fullback]. He could do it all. He could catch. He could block. He could run. Little did you know that we had a guy who was going to set all those rushing records coming into camp — a guy who the National Football League said was too small."

NFL types were not overwhelmed with Hugh Campbell's measurables, either. The wiry flanker was not an imposing physical specimen. As a runner, Campbell was neither fluid nor fast. Even so, defensive backs found him virtually impossible to cover during his stellar collegiate career. NFL scouts had to take notice of that, so Campbell was selected by the San Francisco 49ers in the fourth round of the 1963 draft.

Campbell arrived at San Francisco's training camp with eye-popping credentials, having earned All-American honours in all three of his seasons at Washington State in Pullman, Wash. At the time, freshmen were not eligible to play on NCAA major-college varsity teams. He had joined Washington State after starring at quarterback at Los Gatos (Calif.) High School.

"He was kind of a scrawny, skinny little guy going out for football," former Washington State basketball coach Marv Harshman, who watched the football team's fall camp from the sideline in 1959, said in a 1990 interview with Les Donison of the *Leader-Post*. "Physically, he didn't look like he should be in college. He looked like a little high school kid." Harshman was soon impressed by Campbell's other attributes. "If I would have known about him, I probably wouldn't have recruited him as a basketball player, but I sure would have recruited him as a human being," said Harshman, a 1985 enshrinee into the Naismith Memorial Basketball Hall of Fame. "I wish he was one of my sons."

Unlike Harshman, Garner Ekstran was instantly wowed by Campbell. "It was obvious from Day 1 that Hugh could get open and he was going to catch every ball that was close," said Ekstran, a former Washington State teammate who joined the Roughriders in 1961. "If he could get a hand on it, he'd catch it. He had the ability to get open. He'd keep his body between the ball and the defender. Doing that, he'd get hit, but they weren't going to intercept it, either. You could tell he was going to be good when he was a sophomore."

As a sophomore, Campbell led the nation in receptions — with 66. He went on to establish school career records by catching 176 passes for 2,452 yards over three years at Washington State. The numbers were more impressive than Campbell's appearance. As one scouting report put it: "He's slow, looks awkward and has the general appearance of a tired young man looking for a place to sit down. Looks can be so deceiving." Were they ever.

"He could just do things on the football field that you wouldn't believe," said Reed, whose time at Washington State coincided with Campbell's. "If you just watched him warming up, you'd wonder how he was ever going to play. Then you'd throw a football his way and he could go get it. I never saw a quarterback overthrow him. Everybody said he didn't have good speed, but he had that football speed. Once that football was in the air, it was his. He did some amazing things. One time we were playing the University of Wyoming and he sprained both of his ankles in the first half. He told the trainer to get him a pair of tennis shoes. I don't know how many passes he caught [while wearing tennis shoes], but he tore them up in the second half. That's just the kind of player he was."

Despite glittering collegiate credentials, Campbell was among the 49ers' final cuts. At that point, the unofficial Saskatchewan chapter of the Washington State Alumni Association began lobbying the Roughriders' head coach on Campbell's behalf.

"George Reed and Garner Ekstran told me that they'd be watching films and Bob Shaw would keep saying in front of all the team, 'Does anybody know anywhere where there's somebody who can catch the ball? I don't care if he's fast, but I just need somebody,' " Campbell said. "So Garner went up to the guy and told him, 'Well, we did have a guy at Washington State who was pretty good.' "

There were two problems. The American Football League's Buffalo Bills were also interested, so Campbell had to be convinced that Canadian football was his best option. Reed and Ekstran helped in this regard. So did the fact that the Roughriders' contract offer was $12,000 higher than Buffalo's. The other obstacle: Campbell was on the Toronto Argonauts' negotiation list at the time of his release by San Francisco. It took a cagey move by Shaw for Toronto to relinquish Campbell's CFL rights. Campbell said the Roughriders' head coach offered this advice: "Tell them there's no way that you're going there, and I'll get you." Toronto dropped Campbell. Saskatchewan happily claimed him. He arrived in Regina on Sept. 18, 1963, after the Roughriders had played nine of their 16 regular-season games.

"Bob Shaw did come out to the airport to meet the plane," Campbell remembered. "He was nice and drove us to the hotel." Campbell figured a hotel would suffice. He did not see the need for anything but temporary accommodations. "I told my wife, 'Don't unpack too much,' " he said. "We came to Regina with a suitcase each. We each had a plate, a fork, a knife and a spoon, besides a few clothes and a cup or something. We thought, 'We're only going to be there five weeks. We'll take some stuff we can live on for five weeks.' Bob Shaw tried to get me to come without my wife. We were fairly newly married and that wasn't an option, so we both came."

Campbell was soon introduced to *Leader-Post* columnist John Robertson, whose trademark enthusiasm did not extend to the newest Roughriders receiver. Robertson's initial reaction: "If this guy is a split end, we'd better go back to the airport and meet the second section."

Robertson had more to say about his first impression of Campbell: "He looked like a kid who had just dropped in to borrow the barbells after getting sand kicked in his face at a Muscle Beach party. When I shook hands with him, I noticed his biceps protruded like a pigeon's kneecaps. He looked as if he'd been saving his meal money so he could afford to get his shoulder blades sharpened, and I could just envision trainer Sandy Archer putting in the order for the next week's pre-game steaks: 'Twenty rare, six medium, seven well-done and one ... intravenously.'"

Robertson conveyed his skepticism to Bob Shaw. The Roughriders' field boss responded more optimistically: "His college coach says not to judge him by appearances. From what I've read, he can really haul 'em in." Robertson remained unconvinced. "He'll get killed," the scribe told Shaw.

Hugh Campbell | Photo courtesy of *Leader-Post* archives

Reed knew better, given his past experiences with Campbell at Washington State. "It was exciting to see him," Reed said. "It was kind of interesting to listen to some of the ballplayers saying, 'Who's this guy? He can't run or anything.' And then all of a sudden they start getting into the passing drills and, of course, he caught everything that was thrown to him and they couldn't defend the guy. There was utter disbelief that he could be that good."

The Roughriders' offence couldn't have been much worse. Saskatchewan had gone two games without scoring a touchdown when Campbell touched down in Regina. The lack of production had also created a lack of certainty at quarterback.

CHAPTER **7** | # "THE LITTLE MIRACLE"

Midway through the 1963 CFL season, the Saskatchewan Roughriders were still searching for a quarterback who would remind people of Frank Tripucka — and that included Tripucka himself. Tripucka became part of the Roughriders' quarterbacking equation, again, when the offence stalled.

Bob Shaw had started Ron Lancaster for six consecutive games, the last of which was an 8-2 loss to the visiting B.C. Lions. Shaw shifted gears the following week against the host Calgary Stampeders. Lancaster was left behind in Regina when Shaw started newly acquired Lee Grosscup, whom the New York Giants had selected in the first round of the 1959 NFL draft. When the offence faltered under Grosscup's direction, Shaw turned to opening-day starter Bob Ptacek. Neither Grosscup nor Ptacek produced; Saskatchewan was held without a touchdown for the second successive game, tying Calgary 4-4.

The quarterback carousel continued to spin wildly as the Roughriders prepared for a Sept. 21 home date with Edmonton. Lancaster was once again in the picture, but so was Tripucka. When last seen in Regina, Tripucka had been a player-coach with the 1959 Roughriders — the worst team in franchise history. The subsequent three seasons were spent with the American Football League's Denver Broncos, with whom Tripucka — who threw the first touchdown pass in AFL history — enjoyed so much success that he was eventually inducted into the team's Ring of Fame. But by the time Tripucka resurfaced in Regina, he was nearing 36 and barely a facsimile of the quarterback who had starred for Saskatchewan during the 1950s.

"Tripucka was quoted as saying, 'I've only got 10 good throws left in me. Do you want me to use them up in one quarter?' " said Dale West, who was a sophomore receiver/safety with the 1963 Roughriders. "We really needed someone to step up. There was always an airlift." Tripucka landed on Sept. 20, 1963 at 1:26 a.m., after voluntarily retiring from the Broncos and being waived through the AFL. The Roughriders' next game was but 30 hours away. "I just hope they're not expecting miracles," Tripucka told the *Leader-Post*.

Shaw decided to start Lancaster against Edmonton — thereby bumping Grosscup — but soon deployed Tripucka. "When Ron could muster only one first down in the opening quarter, Tripucka did take over and more than a few fans were wondering not only whether Lancaster was through for the evening, but if he had just about run out the string as a Rider," the *Leader-Post*'s John Robertson wrote.

Shaw's decision to insert Tripucka appeared to be ingenious when his first three passes were completed, but the fourth was intercepted. Tripucka was picked off twice more before Shaw reverted to Lancaster to open the fourth quarter, with Saskatchewan trailing 4-1. Edmonton expanded the lead to 7-1 when Bill Mitchell kicked a 37-yard field goal. The Eskimos almost went ahead 8-1 on a Mike Lashuk punt into the end zone, but the Roughriders' Gene Wlasiuk returned the ball to the one-yard line.

"With the wind against them, all seemed lost for the Roughriders," Robertson wrote. At that point, it seemed reasonable to project that Saskatchewan would lament a third consecutive game without a touchdown. Lancaster had other ideas. He promptly marched

Frank Tripucka | Photo courtesy of Gord Heenan, Heenan Studios   **Ron Lancaster** | Photo courtesy of *Leader-Post*

the Roughriders 109 yards on 16 plays, two of which were successful third-and-one gambles on which he carried the ball himself. The drive concluded when Lancaster found Dale West from eight yards away for the tying touchdown. Reg Whitehouse's convert with 1:35 remaining provided the margin of victory.

Lancaster's touchdown pass seemed as improbable as the drive itself. After rolling out to the right on second-and-goal, he was confronted by a horde of Eskimos. "I could see West in the end zone but guys kept grabbing me," Lancaster told the *Leader-Post*. "I could hear coach Shaw yelling from the bench to throw the darn thing, but every time I raised my arm someone bumped into me. When I finally got it away, I was sure it was going to hit the goal post, but it missed by about a foot."

Lancaster bought himself some time on that play, and perhaps as a Roughrider as well. "That was, according to Shaw, his last chance," West said. "He'd better do something or he was on his way. Everyone liked Ronnie and had a lot of confidence in him." Shaw was not exuding confidence, however, and Tripucka received most of the playing time behind centre for the following three games — despite Lancaster's heroics against Edmonton.

Tripucka made what proved to be his final start Oct. 12, 1963 against the host B.C. Lions, who won 26-6. The *Leader-Post*'s account of the game was headlined: "SAME STORY, NO OFFENCE." So, once again, Shaw turned to Lancaster with the hope that he could spark the Roughriders' attack. Given a second chance — or a third chance, depending on your interpretation — Lancaster left no doubt that he was the best of several quarterbacks who auditioned for the Roughriders in 1963.

On the first play from scrimmage against the visiting Stampeders, Lancaster looked deep for West. The result: an 86-yard touchdown. Lancaster threw two more scoring passes, including his first to Hugh Campbell, while passing for 311 yards. Lancaster also threw deep to Campbell on the Roughriders' final possession, drawing a pass-interference penalty. George Reed rushed for five yards on the next play before Whitehouse, who had missed two converts earlier in the game, kicked a 26-yard field goal with 16 seconds remaining to lift Saskatchewan into a 33-33 tie.

Tripucka had also appeared in that game, going 3-for-3 and throwing a touchdown pass to Jack Gotta, but Lancaster's point had been made. John Robertson noted that Lancaster was "solidly entrenched" as the No. 1 quarterback. In the process, Lancaster had found a favourite receiver. "Hugh Campbell showed Rider fans why many experts considered him the top catcher in the U.S. college ranks that year," Robertson wrote. "He pulled in five tosses and three of them were nothing short of unbelievable."

The rapport between Lancaster and Campbell was also evident in the Roughriders' next game — a 32-20 road victory over the Montreal Alouettes. For the second straight week, Lancaster threw three touchdown passes. One of those majors was produced by Campbell, who made six receptions for 99 yards. "If Hugh Campbell isn't the closest thing to perfection as a pass receiver that this club has seen since the days of Stan Williams and Ken Carpenter, then I've missed my guess," Robertson wrote from Montreal. "The guy is admittedly slow-footed. In fact, he looks as if he's running ankle-deep in corn syrup. But he has the moves of Mandrake the Magician."

Campbell and Lancaster also clicked for six points three days later in a 44-28 loss to the host Toronto Argonauts in the regular-season finale. Despite playing in only seven games, Campbell was second among the Roughriders in catches (30) and receiving yards (426). Gotta's 34 receptions and 478 yards led the way. But the most significant statistic was the Roughriders' record (7-7-2), which placed them third in the Western Conference. Next on the itinerary was a playoff matchup with the second-seeded Calgary Stampeders (10-4-2).

Lancaster and Campbell collaborated on a touchdown pass for the fourth successive game in the opener of a two-game, total-points Western Conference semifinal. That was the extent of the Roughriders' highlight reel. Calgary won 35-9 at home, rendering the second game — to be played two days later at Taylor Field — a mere formality in the view of most observers.

"My parents used to come down from Saskatoon for our games," Dale West recalled. "Leading up to that game, it was raining and the weather wasn't great. We were talking on the phone and they said, 'We're not going to come down.' I said, 'Too bad. You're going to miss a hell of a game.' I had a feeling about it." That put him in the minority.

Football coaches are typically unwavering in their optimism, but Roughriders field boss Bob Shaw was also a realist. When asked 44 years later if he thought the Roughriders had a chance to oust Calgary after incurring a 26-point deficit in the opener, Shaw responded: "No, but we didn't give up. We had a team meeting. One of my players — a Canadian tackle named Bill Clarke — decided we should have a sleeper play."

The sleeper, since outlawed by the CFL, unfolded after Saskatchewan's opening play from scrimmage. The Roughriders' Ray Purdin ambled toward the sideline and off the field — or so the Stampeders' defence presumed. On the Saskatchewan sideline, the coaches were abuzz as they tried to ensure that Purdin was in position. As Saskatchewan snapped the ball on second down, Purdin was standing just inbounds. Stampeders defensive back Doug Elmore noticed Purdin at the last second and belatedly scrambled toward the

Bill Clarke | Photo courtesy of Gord Heenan, Heenan Studios

Ray Purdin | Photo courtesy of Gord Heenan, Heenan Studios

sideline. Purdin caught Lancaster's pass and sped 76 yards to paydirt. "By golly, it worked," Shaw recalled. "It started us off, boy."

The Stampeders were reeling from Saskatchewan's robust start. "When they came out with the sleeper play on the sidelines, we were pretty shook up," Stampeders linebacking legend Wayne Harris reflected. Frank Tripucka's convert of Purdin's touchdown pared the Stampeders' lead in the two-game set to 19 points. Calgary's advantage was eventually reduced to 10 points on the final play of the first half, when Lancaster found Dick Cohee for a one-yard touchdown pass, defying conventional wisdom and crossing up everyone who had anticipated a run. At that point, interest intensified in a Game 2 many thought was a formality. "At halftime, the stands filled up," West said. "A lot of people came. They were listening on the radio, heard that we were coming back, and they wanted to be involved in it. It was absolutely amazing."

Calgary opened the third quarter on a single by Larry Robinson, but Saskatchewan answered with back-to-back touchdown passes by Lancaster, who found Cohee and Ed Buchanan for majors. Entering the fourth quarter, Saskatchewan was ahead 42-39, and Taylor Field was a madhouse. The excitement was tempered, albeit temporarily, by a Calgary rally. Robinson's convert of an Earl Lunsford touchdown gave the Stampeders a 46-42 lead. Later, Robinson attempted a field goal from the Roughriders' 23-yard line, only to settle for a single that put Calgary up 47-42.

After Robinson's third of four misses on the day, Saskatchewan scrimmaged the ball on its 25-yard line with slightly more than three minutes remaining. Lancaster promptly hit Cohee for 44 yards before throwing deep for Campbell. The ball was not caught, but Elmore was called for pass interference on the Stampeders' 10-yard line. Reed ran for a touchdown on the next play to put the Roughriders ahead 48-47, but the convert attempt failed.

Calgary assumed possession with two minutes left and meticulously marched the football into Saskatchewan territory. On the final play, Robinson lined up for a potential series-winning field goal from the 35-yard line. The kick went just wide and was fielded by Saskatchewan's Gene Wlasiuk, who punted the ball out of the end zone to avert a single that would have created a tie. Wlasiuk's boot travelled to Saskatchewan's 40-yard line, where Robinson caught the ball and attempted to punt it back into the end zone. However,

Robinson's desperation kick in the face of pressure sailed out of bounds at the 25-yard line and the gun sounded. "A friend and I ran on to the field after the game, like everybody else, carrying a banner," said future Roughriders president Tom Shepherd, who was 20 at the time. "A cop started chasing after us. We ended up wrapping the banner around the cop."

"Hardly anybody could believe it," Bob Shaw remembered. "It was something else, I'll tell you. Golly, Ned ..." Five years earlier, Shaw had been involved in another classic contest. He was an assistant coach with the Baltimore Colts when they posted a 23-17 overtime victory over the New York Giants in the 1958 NFL championship game. Yet, when Shaw was asked if the 1958 thriller was unrivalled in his experience, he replied: "As far as I'm concerned, that Calgary playoff game at Regina was a hell of a game — coming back from 26 points. The world's championship game was a great one, too."

Lancaster, whom Shaw had twice relegated to backup status during the 1963 season, threw for 492 yards — then a Western Conference single-game record — as the Roughriders shocked Calgary. Five of Lancaster's passes went for touchdowns on Nov. 12, 1963, as he engineered one of the most improbable comebacks in football history. It was soon dubbed "The Little Miracle of Taylor Field."

"That one was a fluke," Lancaster said. "When we were down 26 points in '63 going into the second game of a total-point series, that's a fluke. You shouldn't win. But, on the other hand, if you're going to play the game, you don't play the game to lose, either. You play to win. Things happen. Sometimes you get lucky at it and sometimes you don't. That particular day, it was our day and we got it done."

Saskatchewan had registered a playoff victory for the first time since 1956. "It's one of those games you just can't believe," marvelled John Badham, a sportscaster with Regina's CKCK Radio at the time. "That might have been one of those turning points in the history of the team. The whole thing really caught fire. That comeback victory took the whole province by storm. It's hard to say when you start thinking about defining moments, but that could have been one of those moments where it really came together with the fans, the team and the town."

The electrifying conquest propelled Saskatchewan into the best-of-three Western Conference final against the B.C. Lions. After losing the opener 19-7 at Taylor Field, the Roughriders travelled to Vancouver and extended their season by winning 13-8 — with Lancaster finding Dick Cohee for the game-winning touchdown pass at 9:16 of the fourth quarter. The outcome had to be disconcerting to experts who had installed B.C. as a 16-point favourite.

In the deciding game, the Roughriders and Lions were to collide on Nov. 23, 1963, with a Grey Cup berth at stake. Early in the afternoon of Nov. 22, the Roughriders were on a team bus, travelling to Grouse Mountain during a sightseeing trip, when they learned that President John F. Kennedy had been assassinated in Dallas. "When the news about the shooting of the president came on the radio, it got quiet and remained that way," Lancaster said. With the world in mourning, the Roughriders-Lions showdown went ahead the following day as scheduled. NFL commissioner Pete Rozelle would regret his decision not to postpone games on the Sunday following the assassination; however, the Roughriders and Lions also squared off one day earlier. "There was talk about not playing, but it never got very far," Lancaster said. "We just went ahead and played — at least B.C. did. They beat us 36-1."

Even so, Bob Shaw felt compelled to applaud his players. "You guys gave me everything," he said during a postgame address. "I couldn't have asked for anything more. I'd just like to tell you that no matter what happens, I'm mighty proud of you people." The Roughriders' faithful felt the same way. The lopsided result did not deter an estimated 1,000 fans from welcoming home the team at the Regina airport — at 2 a.m.

By 1963, Garner Ekstran had found a home in Saskatchewan — receiving All-Canadian defensive end honours for the second successive season. Ekstran far exceeded his expectations, being that he initially viewed Saskatchewan as a one-year proposition. Ekstran, from Washington State University, joined the Roughriders on the recommendation of his college roommate, guard Ron Green. After Green signed with Saskatchewan, he asked Ekstran what his plans were for the 1961 football season. "I gave him a couple of ideas and he said, 'Why don't you go to Saskatchewan with me? We'll play one year and then leave. We'll go back to the NFL,' " Ekstran said. "It sounded like a good deal."

Ekstran would become a mainstay with the Roughriders, whereas Green never played in a game with

Garner Ekstran | Photo courtesy of SSHFM

Saskatchewan after being injured before his first pro training camp. Ekstran didn't expect his stay in Canada to be lengthy, either. "Then I found out that there was a clause in there that you had to play out your option, which meant you were going to be there the second year," he said. "If you played out your option, you took a 10-per-cent cut in wages. Of course, a rookie is going to get the 10-per-cent cut — there's no question about that — and they offered me a raise [as part of a new contract]. It doesn't take a genius to figure out that you'd better sign for another year. That contract also had an option on it. After that point, I never had a question. It was, 'I want to stay.' "

And stay he did, although he faced the prospect of leaving the team in October of 1962. Ekstran was a member of the National Guard, which meant he was on alert during the Cuban Missile Crisis. "I got a telegram or a letter saying that my company was on 48-hour notice and if we were activated, I was expected to be there," he remembered. "I didn't even think about it. If I had got the call, I would have gone, but I didn't get the call." Ultimately, Ekstran found his calling as a member of the Roughriders. "We were just going to play a year and come back down," he reflected. "Didn't work that way. Then after two or three years, you got to know all the guys and became good friends. We had a ball club that was improving. Why leave?"

The Roughriders began the 1964 campaign without a quarterback controversy. Ron Lancaster was the uncontested starter. In his first full season with Saskatchewan, he threw for 2,256 yards and a league-high 16 touchdowns, despite missing three games and most of a fourth with a broken rib.

The 1964 season was in its first month when rival head coaches began praising the Roughriders' passer. "Ron Lancaster provided that little bit extra the Riders needed to jell," Winnipeg Blue Bombers field boss Bud Grant said the day before his team lost 37-29 to Saskatchewan. "He has intelligence and experience — two essential ingredients in the makeup of a winning quarterback. Furthermore, he can pass more accurately on the run than any quarterback I've seen. It's uncanny."

Those sentiments were echoed three weeks later by the Edmonton Eskimos' head coach. "Lancaster knows his way around," Neill Armstrong told the *Leader-Post*. "They told me all over the league that he wasn't much of a pivot, but I'm glad I've kept an open mind on this. He's a real scrambler — next to impossible to catch when he starts dodging around in the backfield. It's a terror trying to keep those receivers covered three or four times longer than normal."

Armstrong's apprehensions were well-founded. The next day in Edmonton, Lancaster threw four touchdown passes as Saskatchewan won 56-8. Hugh Campbell — en route to his first 1,000-yard season — caught 10 passes for 146 yards and three majors. But arguably, Lancaster and Campbell weren't even the most dangerous Roughriders. Ed Buchanan ravaged the Eskimos' defence for 301 yards. The fleet halfback carried 19 times for 199 yards, including a 73-yard touchdown, and also caught three passes for 102 yards. A Roughrider would not again hit triple digits in rushing and receiving yards in the same game until 2006. That feat was accomplished by Kenton Keith, who subsequently spent one season with the NFL's Indianapolis Colts before signing with Hamilton.

Buchanan went on to enjoy one of the finest individual seasons in Roughriders history. He rushed for 1,390 yards in 1964 (a team record at the time) while averaging 7.8 yards per carry. The easygoing Californian was also a weapon in the passing attack, averaging 18.9 yards on 36 receptions. Along with 2,071 yards from scrimmage, Buchanan added a team-high 352 yards on 13 kickoff returns. All that for $1,000.

That was what it cost to claim Buchanan on waivers from Calgary during the 1963 season. After two seasons with Calgary, he was caught in a numbers game. The Stampeders' primary ball-carriers were CFL stars Lovell Coleman and Earl Lunsford. All-purpose back Jim Dillard was also in the mix. Hence, Buchanan was deemed expendable by Stampeders head coach Bobby Dobbs (whose brother, Glenn, had quarterbacked the Roughriders from 1951 to 1953). "That trade was the best thing that ever happened to me," Buchanan told the *Leader-Post* in 1964. "Dobbs wanted me to run over people. That's not my style."

Buchanan foreshadowed his brilliance of 1964 by scoring two touchdowns against his former Calgary comrades when the Roughriders won "The Little Miracle of Taylor Field." Although Ron Lancaster, George Reed and Hugh Campbell are often portrayed as the Roughriders' key

Ed Buchanan | Photo courtesy of *Leader-Post*

additions of 1963, Buchanan should not be overlooked. "He was so fast that when he was carrying the ball, I could hear him coming," Roughriders offensive tackle Clyde Brock said. "I could hear his speed, if that makes any kind of sense."

Defensive back Bob Kosid offers a contrasting description of Buchanan. "Some guys can run and it's like there's sweat flying off and there's saliva and they are making all kinds of noise," Kosid said. "Then there are guys who can run and it's like the way they make cars today. You can't even know when you turn on the ignition that the engine's on. It's silent. Those guys just went like the wind. Buchanan was like that. He could just absolutely fly."

While Buchanan was dodging would-be tacklers, Reed was punishing them. In 1964, the bruising fullback enjoyed his first of 11 1,000-yard rushing seasons, gaining 1,012 yards and scoring 10 touchdowns. Reed helped Saskatchewan register a league-high 45 touchdowns. One season earlier, the Roughriders' 28 majors had been the fewest in the nine-team league. A 9-7 regular-season record placed Saskatchewan third in the Western Conference in 1964. For the second consecutive year, the Roughriders were to face the second-ranked Stampeders (12-4) in a two-game total-points semifinal. Saskatchewan's offensive potency was evident in the opener, when Lancaster completed 28 of 35 passes for 376 yards to help his team win 34-25 at Taylor Field.

The Roughriders began Game 2 in auspicious fashion when Reed ran for a touchdown on the opening drive. But the host Stampeders scored the final 51 points, winning 51-6 and eliminating Saskatchewan. "Don't blame the defence," Lancaster told the *Leader-Post*'s John Robertson after going 8-for-24 with five interceptions. "They played their butts off, but we left them out on the field for about 50 minutes because we couldn't move the football."

Lancaster went on to say that he felt sorry for veteran Roughriders linemen Ron Atchison, Reg Whitehouse and Bill Clarke. Atchison and Whitehouse would return, but Clarke had just completed a 14-year career on the Roughriders' defensive line. "They don't have many more kicks at this thing," Lancaster lamented. "There'll be other years for me, and that eases the pain a little."

Shortly after the 1964 season, word circulated that the Toronto Argonauts were wooing Roughriders head coach Bob Shaw. In December of 1964, Shaw signed a three-year contract to coach the Argonauts, who offered him a healthy raise — a reported $20,000 per year, with a $5,000 annual bonus. Shaw had one year left on his contract with the Roughriders, having signed an extension following the 1963 season. "I've come to consider this place my home, and all of the fine people that I've met as my friends," he told the *Leader-Post*. "It's not easy to sever such ties, but sometimes it has to be done. I only hope the people will understand my reasons." Under Shaw, the Roughriders' offence had been rescued from dormancy after Lancaster, Reed, Campbell and Buchanan arrived in 1963. Key contributors such as offensive tackle Clyde Brock, tight end Jim Worden, defensive back Bob Kosid, defensive/ offensive back Henry Dorsch and receiver Gord Barwell came aboard in 1964. In those days, the head coach played a role in the recruiting process, along with general manager Ken Preston, so Shaw should share in the credit for the infusion of talent and its deployment.

Bob Kosid |

There was only one problem. Many of the Roughriders disliked playing for the demanding Shaw. Lancaster and Reed were foremost among the detractors.

CHAPTER 8 **"LOW KEY"**

At 26, Ron Lancaster was thinking about becoming a former Roughriders quarterback. "I had almost officially retired," he recalled. "I had applied for a high school football job down around Springfield, Ohio. If they would have made their mind up before basketball season ended, I would have taken the job and I wouldn't have come back."

Lancaster's disenchantment was largely attributable to a tenuous relationship with Bob Shaw, the Roughriders' head coach in 1963 and 1964. "We didn't see eye to eye on a whole lot," Lancaster said. "I didn't really enjoy playing those two years. Lana [the first of Ron and Bev Lancaster's three children] was going to be starting school. It was time to make some decisions, so I sort of decided to hang 'em up and get on with life and go coach."

Like Lancaster, George Reed had joined the Roughriders in 1963. "I played the second year and I had enough of Bob Shaw," Reed said. "I had already accepted a high school coaching job and I wasn't coming back. I don't think Ronnie was coming back to play the '65 year. The only reason we came back was simply that Eagle Keys was hired — and the rest is history."

Keys had joined the Roughriders' coaching staff in 1964 as an assistant to Shaw. When Shaw resigned following the 1964 CFL season to become the Argonauts' head coach, Keys was appointed his successor. One of his shrewdest moves leading up to the 1965 season was to phone Lancaster. "I don't think I necessarily talked him into playing, but I told him that he would be the quarterback and that we'd go from there," Keys remembered.

"That's all I wanted to hear," Lancaster said. "That meant a lot to me for him to tell me that. You don't play a very good football game when you're always worried about being pulled, because if you're worried about making mistakes you're going to make a ton of them.

You're going to make mistakes as it is, but there's no sense making more because of being concerned about it."

Lancaster signed a two-year contract in April of 1965, when he moved to Regina and purchased a home, but he did not feel a sense of entitlement. He merely wanted a demonstration of faith from his head coach. "Now, I know this: If I hadn't done the job and we hadn't won, he'd have replaced me, too, but that's the breaks," Lancaster said. "At least he had the confidence in me to tell me, 'OK, you'll be the starter. When you get yourself into trouble, you've got to get yourself out of it.' From then on, you take it and go with it. It'll either work or it won't. In my case, it did."

Shaw took issue with the perception that he was skeptical of Lancaster's ability. "How could I be? He was my quarterback," Shaw said. "He was the starting quarterback. There was never any backup for him at all that I remember."

There was a succession of quarterbacking candidates in 1963, when Lancaster joined the Roughriders. Lancaster accepted most of the snaps the following year. The understudy, Bob Ptacek, was summoned only when Lancaster was sidelined with a broken rib. "If I had thought he [Ptacek] was the better quarterback, I would have played him," Shaw said. "I think that was more on Ronnie's side than it was on mine. I respected Ronnie Lancaster. I appreciated what he did. Maybe he never thought I did, but I certainly did."

Even after Lancaster became the week-in, week-out starter, there was friction between the quarterback and his head coach. "We had our ups and downs, Ronnie and I," acknowledged Shaw, who felt confident the two could have overcome such differences had he returned in 1965. Lancaster had a different view. He was on the verge of retirement, as Reed also claimed to be. "They would have been back," Shaw countered. "They were pro football players. Maybe I was just too rough on them. It didn't hurt them any." When apprised of the concerns voiced by Lancaster and Reed, Shaw responded: "That's the way they thought of me, I guess. I can't help it."

Shaw does not dispute the contention that playing for him could be taxing. "My practices were tough," he said. "I was a disciplinarian and they knew it. I probably ruffled some feathers. They can say that I was a bastard and all that, but it doesn't really matter because we won some ball games and did a pretty good job … People all think I'm a bad guy, but I'm not. I'm just trying to do a job."

The transition from Shaw to Keys was quickly noted by the Roughriders players — and not just Lancaster and Reed. "There was a noticeable difference, is the best I can put it," receiver Hugh Campbell said. "I personally thought Shaw was fine. I was only there with him a year and a half. When I had Bob Shaw, I liked that he cut to the chase. It was not tactful the way he acted or what he said. He just blurted out whatever he blurted out. I was used to that. I had two high school coaches who were both very rough and tough. It didn't bother me.

"When Eagle came, he was more of a players' coach. We hit it right getting Eagle at that time, but he hit it right getting all of us at that time, because by then Ronnie had gained the confidence and could do a lot of the running of the offence. Eagle did a great job with

Ronnie in the office and then when we'd get to practice, he'd already told Ronnie what to do. Ronnie would go through the play list and almost every day he would skip one, just to make sure Eagle was awake. At the end, Ronnie would say, 'OK, that's it,' and Eagle would say, 'No, you forgot 29AO.' Then we'd run 29AO and everyone would laugh. We ran every play in each direction — sweep to the left, sweep to the right. We'd run every play, every day. That was just the way he coached. He said to me, 'Hughie, I don't know any other way to do it, except to just work at it.' So that's what we did. We worked at it."

And not just on the football field. "Eagle would be up in that little office of his on Hill Avenue and it seemed to me every time you walked in there, he was watching film," trainer Sandy Archer said. "The thing would be, 'Click, click, click, click,' back and forth, back and forth. He did it every day. It must have paid off."

Eagle Keys *during 1966 Grey Cup week* |
Photo courtesy of *Vancouver Sun*

Keys and Lancaster clicked as well. "I just enjoyed being around him," Lancaster said. "I liked him as a person. I enjoyed talking football with him. He taught me to watch films. He made me learn things. At the same time, he allowed me to play the game the way I knew how to play. He was the kind of guy who you wanted to win for. He was fun to be with. When it's all said and done, that meant a lot."

Players felt comfortable talking with Keys, but few of them really knew him. "He wouldn't communicate a lot," defensive lineman Ron Atchison said. "He talked strictly business. That wasn't only to me. That was to his own assistants. Eagle was very reclusive, you know. It would take a psychiatrist to figure out Eagle." Atchison did not say that disparagingly, noting that "Eagle was a wonderful guy."

"Eagle was by far the best coach I ever played for," linebacker Wayne Shaw added. "Before Eagle came along, the coaches all gave everybody hell all the time. That was the way coaching was for everybody. Just be a tough guy. But Eagle had this figured out."

Knute Rockne-style speeches were not Keys' forte. "Eagle was the last guy to ever give a pep talk," defensive back Bob Kosid said. "I would have fallen down on the floor and absolutely cracked up, along with a whole bunch of other people, if Eagle ever gave a pep talk. Eagle was — and I have to put capital letters on this — LOW KEY. Fortunately, that's probably the way we liked it. We didn't want any rah-rah stuff. Been there, done that."

John Badham, who covered the Roughriders for CKCK Radio, could attest to Keys' low-key style. The broadcaster quickly discovered that Keys was not the most engaging conversationalist with the media. "Eagle was too funny," Badham said. "He was so quiet. I remember distinctly walking into the old offices up in the exhibition grounds where the team practised and Eagle's sitting at his desk with his feet up, staring at the wall. Jack Gotta was sitting at one desk and Jimmy Duncan at the other. They were the assistant coaches. I walk in and say 'Hey Jim' and 'Hey Jocko.' I sat down in front of Eagle's desk and said, 'Hi Eagle.' " For a while, that was all that was said. "I sat there and sat there," Badham continued. "Finally, he looks over and says, 'Hello, Badham.' I said, 'What are you doing?' It almost felt like it was another hour. Finally, he says, 'I'm thinkin' ...' Jocko got up and he was laughing so hard he had to leave. Gotta and Duncan, they just took off. Eagle was quite a man, though."

Eagle Keys had quite a career even before he arrived in Saskatchewan. His involvement in Canadian football dated back to 1949, when he joined the Montreal Alouettes as a player and helped them win a Grey Cup that season. However, it was against Montreal that Keys had his most-celebrated game in uniform.

Keys was with the Edmonton Eskimos when they faced Montreal in the 1954 Grey Cup. The Eskimos' Jackie Parker scored the tying touchdown late in the fourth quarter when he recovered a Chuck Hunsinger fumble and sprinted 90 yards to pay dirt. Bob Dean kicked the convert that provided the margin of victory. "I hurt my leg in the first quarter," Keys recalled. "I didn't think I could get back on the field. [Eskimos head coach] Pop Ivy asked me if I could even get back on the field to centre the ball [on placements] because we didn't have a backup centre who was that consistent, so I said, 'I'll try to get on the field. I don't know whether I can make it or not.' I got on the field and I snapped the ball most of the time, but I didn't snap the ball for the last play that won the game."

Legend has it that Keys did snap that ball while playing with a broken leg. "It was a broken leg, yeah, but it wasn't broken in two," he pointed out. "It wasn't a crack."

Also according to lore, Keys hails from Turkey Neck Bend in Kentucky. That, too, is a fallacy. Keys is actually from nearby Tompkinsville. "Turkey Neck Bend was a little place in the river about seven miles from Tompkinsville," Keys told author Graham Kelly for his 2001 Roughriders history book, *Green Grit*. "People used to ask me where I was from and I'd say 'Tompkinsville.' And they'd ask, 'Where in the world is that?' I finally got to saying 'Tompkinsville is near Turkey Neck Bend' so they wouldn't ask me any more questions. I used it up here one time and the media picked it up."

The story was told many a time as Keys became a fixture in Canadian professional football. After concluding his playing career in the 1954 Cup classic, Keys turned to coaching. He was an Eskimos assistant coach before becoming the team's field boss in 1959. The Eskimos reached the Grey Cup in Keys' second season as head coach, losing to Ottawa. At the time, Ottawa's roster included a rookie quarterback, Ron Lancaster.

Edmonton finished second in the West in 1961, posting a respectable 10-5-1 record, before going 6-9-1 and 2-14-0. The two-win season was such an ordeal that the wives of

Eskimos players Don Getty and Oscar Kruger blasted Keys on a postgame radio show. Mrs. Getty and Mrs. Kruger maintained that Keys had lost the confidence of the Eskimos' players, that he had not properly utilized the talent at his disposal, and that he should be dismissed. "The last year in Edmonton wasn't fun," said defensive end/linebacker Ken Reed, who played for the Eskimos in 1963 and 1964 before joining the Roughriders in 1965. "A lot of the guys were getting long in the tooth who were stars. There was a lot of finger-pointing and a lot of turmoil. It was just a bad mix."

Eagle Keys (left) *and* ***Bob Shaw*** | Photo courtesy of SSHFM

Keys was soon fired, but he wasn't unemployed for long. Bob Shaw hired him as an assistant coach with Saskatchewan before the 1964 season. Although Keys was by then a seasoned CFL coach, it took him a while to adjust to the free-wheeling surroundings. "He came to me after a game in Edmonton when he was an assistant coach with Bob," Garner Ekstran said. "We beat Edmonton and he came and sat down in the stall next to me. He said, 'I can't believe any ball club acts like you guys act in the dressing room before a game and still goes out and wins.' I said, 'Get used to it. That's the way this team is.' Eagle was not a coach who was used to players before a game taping up a teammate's underwear and throwing it out the window. He couldn't believe it. The guys would go out and play a game after doing all that bullshit for two hours."

Keys quickly became a popular figure with the players, and management took notice. There was little surprise when Keys was named Saskatchewan's head coach on Dec. 30, 1964, signing a two-year contract. Eagle Keys' first full season as the Roughriders' field boss was hardly an unqualified success. Saskatchewan's 8-7-1 record that year was comparable to its 7-7-2 and 9-7-0 slates under Shaw.

However, it was a notable accomplishment for the Roughriders to finish above .500 in light of the fact that they were ravaged by injuries. Eleven players missed significant playing time in 1965. Tailback Ed Buchanan (broken leg), quarterback-turned-linebacker Bob Ptacek (severed Achilles tendon) and defensive tackle Ron Atchison (knee surgery) were sidelined for most of the season. "In the Rider camp, it is an unsettled state," the *Leader-Post*'s Laurie Artiss wrote in September. "This is nothing new. Before each game, Eagle Keys first counts noses. Then he asks all those present to stand. Those who don't fall down are then inserted in the lineup."

Despite the Roughriders' susceptibility to injuries, there was a healthy dose of offence. Hugh Campbell had another superlative season, catching 73 passes for a Western Conference-record 1,329 yards and 10 touchdowns. Ron Lancaster threw for 2,586 yards and 17 scores, prompting Hamilton Tiger-Cats defensive back Garney Henley to suggest that the Roughriders' No. 23 was better than any quarterback in the Eastern Conference, including Russ Jackson. And George Reed had what proved to be his best season as a Roughrider — which was saying something.

In 16 games, Reed gained 1,768 yards along the ground, becoming only the second CFLer to rush for a mile in a single season. Earl Lunsford of Calgary previously accomplished that feat in 1964, amassing 1,794 rushing yards. Reed enjoyed his finest day on Oct. 24, 1965, erupting for 268 yards in a 30-14 victory over the host B.C. Lions. His single-game total was a Western Conference record and second on the CFL's all-time list, behind Ron Stewart's 287 yard outburst with the 1960 Ottawa Rough Riders.

George Reed | Photo courtesy of SSHFM

"The only thing that stands out about that game is we went into the game knowing we had to win to have a shot at making the playoffs," Reed said of his 268-yard outing. "That was a very critical game for us. The guys blocked well and I seemed to be able to run the football and do things that we needed to do.

"I always played pretty well in B.C., too. I always had that little edge because B.C. used to have my rights. I knew a lot about B.C. I didn't know a lot about Regina when they traded my rights to Regina. I'm glad it worked out the way it did. It gave me a little extra incentive against them. More of my family from Seattle was able to come up and see me play. They would all pile into a couple of cars and they would drive up and spend the evening with me. After the game, I was able to spend a couple of hours with them before they headed back. It was always nice that way. We tried to give them a good show."

Gord Barwell added to the record collection at Vancouver's Empire Stadium when he caught a 102-yard touchdown pass from Lancaster. That would stand as the longest aerial in Roughriders history until Kent Austin and Jeff Fairholm collaborated for a 107-yarder in

1990. That long-distance major in Vancouver — which gave Barwell a single-game average per catch of 102 yards — was an example of Eagle Keys' ingenuity. "When I was in Edmonton, we came into Vancouver and hit the Lions on a similar kind of play," Keys told Laurie Artiss. "It went to [Tommy Joe] Coffey for a touchdown. This started me thinking about something similar on the plane trip out here."

Gord Barwell |
Photo courtesy of SSHFM

Barwell was flying as he sprinted down the right sideline on the Roughriders' opening play from scrimmage. Lions defensive back Bill Munsey was left far behind. Lancaster's deep throw was unerring. Covering 100 yards in brisk fashion was routine for Barwell, who had travelled that distance in under 10 seconds as a track and field star in his native Saskatoon. Barwell's speed also served him well in football. The junior Saskatoon Hilltops took notice, but they would have him for only one year. At 19, Barwell was invited to the Roughriders' training camp and made a quick and favourable impression. He dressed for six games in 1964 and all 16 the following season.

Barwell's coming-out party as a Roughrider was on Aug. 7, 1965. Although his statistics were modest — two receptions for 31 yards — his timing was impeccable. Barwell scored his first CFL touchdown on a third-down gamble, hooking up with Lancaster from nine yards away. Barwell also made a leaping, 20-yard catch to set up the game-winning touchdown by Campbell. That score gave Saskatchewan a 20-18 victory over the Stampeders, who squandered an 18-0 first-half lead.

Barwell did not score another touchdown until the 102-yarder in B.C. That six-pointer kick-started the Roughriders, who secured a playoff berth with a victory. Two weeks later, the Roughriders were destined for Winnipeg to play the Blue Bombers in the Western Conference semifinal.

By 1965, the two-game total-points semifinal format had been ashcanned in favour of a sudden-death affair. In the waning minutes, Lancaster had an opportunity to throw a second touchdown pass, and perhaps win the game. From the Blue Bombers' 10-yard line, Lancaster looked toward tight end Jim Worden in the end zone. The ball never got there. It hit an upright. "Everybody says, 'Well, if we hadn't hit the goal post ...,' " Lancaster reflected. "There was a defensive back that wasn't too far away. It would have been a race whether the ball had gotten to Worden or the defensive back had gotten to it first. Anyway, it didn't get there ... I guess I should have aimed it at the upright. Then I would have missed it."

Following the Bombers' 15-9 victory, *Leader-Post* columnist Laurie Artiss offered his thoughts on the pass to Worden. "A small controversy developed over that one," Artiss wrote. "Was Worden in the clear? Certainly he was when Lancaster threw the ball but defender Barrie Hansen was streaking toward the receiver when the ball hit the post. [Bombers head coach] Bud Grant said he wasn't worried on the play: 'I saw Hansen moving and thought he could have intercepted.' "

In keeping with the theme of the 1965 season, the Roughriders suffered a major injury during the playoff game in Winnipeg. Venerable offensive lineman Reg Whitehouse tore cartilage in a knee, fuelling speculation that he might retire after 14 years in Green and White. Artiss took the series of injuries into account when assessing the 1965 Roughriders: "Most football coaches in the country are wondering how Eagle Keys got this club this far in the first place."

One reason was that the Roughriders adhered to what became a maxim: "Let George Do It." Reed's 1,768-yard rushing season was saluted in mid-November when he became the first Roughrider to be named the CFL's outstanding player. In selfless fashion, Reed preferred to discuss his award within the context of a team. "I think it was significant from the standpoint that Saskatchewan was being put back on the map," Reed said. "I took it as an award for all the guys that I played with."

Although Reed was pleased to win the award, he succinctly outlined his priorities upon receiving the trophy: "Now we have to think of next year — and winning."

CHAPTER 9 # "DRUMMED OUT OF CAMP"

Perhaps it was gamesmanship. Maybe it was just a matter of being polite. It is conceivable that the remarks were carefully tailored for the audience. Or maybe, just maybe, Winnipeg Blue Bombers head coach Bud Grant was providing a candid — and prophetic — response in February of 1966 when he was asked what people could expect from that year's edition of the Saskatchewan Roughriders.

At a sports banquet in Saskatoon, Grant unreservedly praised a rival team in the CFL's Western Conference while also commending the league's reigning outstanding player, fellow head-table guest George Reed. "The Riders had the best offensive line in Canada," Grant said, "and they had the most complete football player in Reed, a fellow who could carry the ball, catch passes and block." Grant went on to declare that the percentages were with the Roughriders for the 1966 season, and that he feared Saskatchewan more than he did the Calgary Stampeders. That was quite a compliment, considering that Calgary had finished first in the West in 1965, posting a 12-4-0 record. Winnipeg (11-5-0) was a close second, followed by Saskatchewan (8-7-1). Despite a mediocre record, the Roughriders had thrown a scare into the Blue Bombers in the 1965 West semifinal, losing 15-9. The Bombers proceeded to outlast Calgary in the best-of-three West final, only to fall 22-17 to the Hamilton Tiger-Cats in the Grey Cup.

As the Roughriders prepared for the 1966 season, there was not a drastic difference in personnel. They would be heavily reliant upon talent stockpiled during the first half of the 1960s, with some refinements. The Roughriders were banking on better luck regarding injuries, which had plagued the team in 1965. As another season loomed, the Roughriders knew there would have to be a respite for trainer Sandy Archer — The Wizard of Gauze — if they were to break a habit of finishing third in their division.

The winter of 1966 also included sad news. Al Ritchie, a coach and manager with the Regina Roughriders in the 1920s and 1930s, died Feb. 21 at age 75. Ritchie had coached the Roughriders to Grey Cup berths from 1929 to 1932. He was also closely associated with the Regina Pats junior hockey team, which he had coached to Memorial Cup titles in 1925 and 1930. "Al Ritchie was the Knute Rockne of Canada," said Monsignor Athol Murray, a close friend and the founder of Notre Dame College in Wilcox. "We have had many greats in sport, but Al Ritchie was their peer." Western Football Conference president Don McPherson, also a long-time member of the Roughriders' executive, noted that Ritchie's death was "a sad blow to the Canadian sports fraternity." Hal Pawson of the *Edmonton Journal* offered this testimonial: "He gave Regina its Roughriders. So he didn't invent, or even start them. But they flowered in his care."

During Al Ritchie's tenure as the Roughriders' coach and manager, the team had customarily played before a few thousand fans. In his lifetime, he was able to see interest in the team grow exponentially. By 1965, the Roughriders were capable of attracting overflow crowds that pushed 18,000, hence the need for an expanded Taylor Field.

For the 1966 season, capacity had been increased to 17,989, thanks to a new concrete grandstand on the stadium's east side. The grandstand, 55 rows high, sat between the 35-yard lines and was flanked by bleachers that extended to the goal lines. Fifty-yard-line season tickets on the west side cost $42, with a peak rate of $40 in the new stands. There was another new feature for Roughriders games in 1966 — three Sunday afternoon dates. Sundays had previously been avoided in observance of the Sabbath. "Playing under lights is nice — and necessary — but traditionalists will still tell you football was a game to be played under the warming autumn sun," read an excerpt from a March 26, 1966 *Leader-Post* article.

The Roughriders' training camp roster, published in the *Leader-Post* on June 25, consisted of 53 names. All but one of those players stepped on to the field the following day for the team's first workout of 1966. The noticeable absentee was Ted Urness, a five-year veteran who was coming off his first season as an all-Canadian centre.

Urness and the Roughriders had conducted protracted negotiations throughout the 1965 season without being able to produce a signed agreement. Urness opted against reporting to the 1966 training camp until the contractual issue could be resolved, once and for all. After a five-day holdout, Urness signed a two-year deal. Upon reporting, Urness was pleased to see offensive-line cohort Reg Whitehouse. Nearing 33, he was back for a 15th season, looking to extend a consecutive-games streak of 240.

At the other end of the spectrum were the rookies — such as import offensive tackle Dick Pratt. He would be well-remembered long after his departure from the Roughriders' camp. "He was out of Kansas and he was a good football player," said Ron Lancaster, who knew as well as anyone that Pratt's Roughriders legacy had little to do with football. "They had a thing where after the meal and before the meeting, we would go in the other room and there was a piano in there and stuff. Pratt was good on the piano and the drums, so the guys would make him perform."

The rookie show was a staple at training camps throughout the CFL. Veterans customarily implored the newcomers to display their talent, or lack thereof. Many of the hopefuls were hopelessly out of tune, or devoid of skills beyond football. And then there was the ever-smiling Pratt. Sitting at the piano, Pratt served as an accompanist during other players' routines. But the real show-stopper was his performance on the drums. The *Leader-Post*'s Laurie Artiss reported that Pratt "literally brought down the house with his drum solos." Artiss also suggested that Pratt should be given five minutes to perform at halftime of the next Roughriders game.

Pratt was also impressing his teammates and coaches on the field. That was not altogether surprising, since he had opened holes for future NFL star Gale Sayers at the University of Kansas. The Roughriders' offensive line was tough to crack, but Pratt was holding his own. But the entertainer in him won out. Pratt opted for "exit, stage right." One week into July, as the Roughriders' intrasquad game loomed, he decided on a career change. "He decided he wasn't going to play football," Lancaster said. "He decided he was going to pursue music. He went and talked to the coach and he left." As Artiss put it: "You might say he was drummed out of camp."

The other highlight of the rookie show — dubbed the Rider Follies — was provided by rookie defensive end Don Gerhardt. Artiss observed that Gerhardt had the other players "rolling in the aisles" with his uncanny impersonation of the Roughriders' head coach.

"I can mimic people pretty well. I kind of have fun doing that," Gerhardt remembered. "Usually it's just in fun, but I did an imitation of Eagle Keys — his stare and his Kentucky accent — and kind of shuffled around on the stage. Guys just cried, they were laughing so hard, because I had him down really well. I had a cigarette drooping out of my mouth and I was asking questions of [assistant coach] Jim Duncan and all that kind of stuff.

"Eagle was really a bright man. He probably saw it as just giving him a hard time, one man to another, because I wasn't trying to denigrate him at all. I can remember some of the things I said. He could never remember Ken Reed's name. He *could* remember Ken Reed's nickname. For some reason, somebody had called him Walrus. Eagle couldn't get 'Walrus' out of his mouth. It was 'War-r-r-rlus.' He got it backwards. So I was doing the 'War-r-r-rlus' thing. As well, Eagle couldn't say 'Thud.' He would say, 'Wait for the *thuuuuud* of the punter and then you go downfield.' I said that, and guys were just crying. I didn't have anything else. That's what I thought of, so that's what I did, in a naive young guy's way. Anyway, it was a fun evening, but Ron Lancaster was absolutely sure I was a dead duck the next day. He thought I was going to get cut."

Gerhardt escaped the axe — and eventually discovered that Keys was not rankled by the impression. "A few days later, he kind of cracked a smile," Gerhardt said. "He was a very handsome guy when he'd smile, but he'd rarely give you just a little smile on the edge of his mouth. He gave me a couple of signals that it was OK with him. He always called me 'Gear-hardt,' so I'm pretty sure I got a little grin and a 'Gear-hardt.' "

Gerhardt, recruited from Concodia College in Moorhead, Minn., quickly became a factor on the defensive line. For that, the Roughriders could thank assistant coach Jack Gotta. He

Ken Preston *(left)* with **Alan Sangster** |
Photo courtesy of SSHFM

Hugh Campbell *Gluey Hughie does it again* |
Photo courtesy of SSHFM

was in the Fargo-Moorhead area the day after Gerhardt was bypassed in the 1966 National Football League draft. The Los Angeles Rams and Minnesota Vikings had shown interest, but Saskatchewan's offer was superior. "At that time, if you were out of a small school or if you were a lineman, you could probably make as much or more in Canada than in the States," Gerhardt said. "I'm glad I went up there. It was just wonderful. I just loved it."

Suffice to say that Gerhardt overcame the apprehensions of the first two days. Fears emanating from the rookie show were one thing. There was also his introduction to two of the Roughriders' fiercest linemen — Ron Atchison and Al Benecick. "Those two guys had lockers two or three spaces apart," Gerhardt said. "I walked into the locker room and there they both were. Benny came over to say 'Hi' to me. Atch didn't. I thought, 'What in the world did I get myself into?' They were two tough-looking warhorses. Good night ..."

The new and improved Taylor Field was unveiled to the masses on July 8, 1966, when the Roughriders' intrasquad game was played before an estimated 8,000 onlookers. For the record, the Green squad defeated the Whites 21-20.

Not surprisingly, Hugh Campbell was in fine form. The all-star flanker, who had hit the 1,000-yard mark in his first two full seasons with Saskatchewan, caught nine passes for 172 yards and one touchdown. The identity of Campbell's collaborator was more of a surprise. Rookie quarterback Tom Kennedy completed 15 of 19 passes for 221 yards, including touchdown passes to Campbell, Jesse Willis and Don Thompson. The Greens got two touchdowns from Ed Buchanan and a single major from Gil Petmanis.

Buchanan should have had three touchdowns, actually, but he dropped a perfectly thrown bomb from Lancaster after getting open by 10 yards. Following the game, Ron Atchison and Ted Urness jokingly presented the easygoing Buchanan with a large, open cardboard carton with handles taped to it. "They suggested he use it for those long passes when he is in the clear," the *Leader-Post*'s Laurie Artiss noted.

Kennedy's CFL career peaked in that intrasquad game. Four days later, he completed six of 19 passes, with two interceptions, in the Roughriders' preseason opener. Despite Kennedy's struggles, Saskatchewan was able to defeat the host Montreal Alouettes 23-17. The Roughriders set the tone on the opening play from scrimmage when Lancaster hit newly acquired halfback Paul Dudley for a 73-yard touchdown pass. Lancaster gave way to Kennedy after the first quarter.

Two nights later, the Roughriders resumed their gruelling exhibition schedule in Ottawa. The home team won 19-10. The big news: Roughriders defensive back Dale West suffered a dislocated shoulder that forced him to miss the beginning of the 1966 regular season. Lancaster handled most of the quarterbacking before being replaced by Kennedy late in the game. Kennedy was 1-for-5 for 20 yards in what turned out to be his Saskatchewan swan song. Shortly after the Ottawa game, he joined the Brooklyn Dodgers, who held his Intercontinental Football League rights and threatened to seek an injunction to ensure that he reported.

 With Kennedy out of the equation, the Roughriders were scrambling for another quarterback. Three days after arriving in Regina, Ed Buzzell suited up for the Roughriders' preseason finale and completed but five of 17 passes — although two of those passes resulted in touchdowns by Campbell.

The Roughriders' other signal-caller on that day was rookie Bruce Bennett, who was a first-team All-American high school quarterback as a senior in Valdosta, Ga., before enrolling at the University of Florida and becoming one of the NCAA's top defensive backs. Bennett went 3-for-5 while playing most of the first half. His most impressive effort, however, was a devastating block he applied — 50 yards downfield — on a long run by Jesse Willis. The play was negated by a penalty, but Bennett's effort left an impression.

As the exhibition season wound down, Keys offered his thoughts on the Roughriders' recruits. He singled out Dudley, who had bounced around the pro football ranks since 1962, as the "top newcomer." Bennett was likewise singled out for praise as a quarterback and defensive back. Not to be forgotten was noted impressionist Don Gerhardt. Keys cited him for his "outstanding potential."

But did the 1966 Roughriders have Grey Cup potential? That was one of the key questions as the regular season approached. The *Leader-Post* picked Saskatchewan to once again finish third in the West. On the newspaper's CFL preview page, it was written that the Roughriders' front-liners were of championship calibre, but that "inexperienced reserves could force them to scramble."

Paul Dudley, Bruce Bennett and Don Gerhardt were the key newcomers emanating from the United States. Fresh faces among the Canadians were defensive tackle Moe Levesque and receiver Gil Petmanis.

The Roughriders entered the 1966 campaign with an offence that appeared to be set. The offensive line — centre Ted Urness, guards Al Benecick and Jack Abendschan, and tackles Clyde Brock and Reg Whitehouse — was widely touted as the nation's best. Fullback George Reed was coming off a season in which he was named the league's outstanding player. Ed Buchanan and Paul Dudley were also gifted ball-carriers. And then there was quarterback Ron Lancaster, who was especially effective in partnership with flanker Hugh Campbell. Tight end Jim Worden was a key contributor as a pass-catcher and a blocker. Alan Ford and Gord Barwell were promising receivers.

Defensively, the Roughriders appeared to be solid, although there was some uncertainty on the line. In 1966, the Roughriders often employed five defensive linemen — with Ron Atchison, the indestructible middle guard, flanked by two tackles and two ends. Saskatchewan began the regular season with Ken Reed and Moe Levesque at the tackles, and Garner Ekstran and Don Gerhardt at the end positions.

The next line of defence included middle linebacker Wally Dempsey, who was preparing for his sophomore season, and two-time all-star Wayne Shaw. When necessary, the versatile Ken Reed could also fit into the linebacking equation. In the defensive backfield, the Roughriders had more ability than size — and, in some cases, experience. Bruce Bennett quickly claimed the starting safety's position, bumping three-time all-star Dale West. Bennett's arrival resulted in the transformation of West to a defensive halfback, although the three-time all-star would miss the beginning of the regular season with a dislocated shoulder. Defensive halfback Bob Kosid and cornerback Larry Dumelie were entrenched in their positions, barring injury. Also in the mix in the secondary were Henry Dorsch, Ted Dushinski and Gene Wlasiuk.

Wlasiuk was also familiar to Roughriders fans as a punt returner. It was a thankless task, because blocking was not permitted on punt returns, but Wlasiuk relished the role as much as he savoured his cigars. Ed Buchanan, Paul Dudley, Alan Ford and George Reed would handle the kickoff returns. When a placement attempt was required, guard Jack Abendschan quickly donned a kicking shoe after his obligations on offence were completed.

Abendschan's right foot was not utilized for punting, however, so someone would have to replace Martin Fabi, who had averaged 42.5 yards per boot — tops in the Western Conference — in 1965. Fabi had reached an impasse in negotiations with the Roughriders during the offseason. He refused to report unless his salary demands were met by penurious general manager Ken Preston. The Roughriders expected Fabi to report at some point, so they did not strenuously recruit a punter. Second-year homebrew Alan Ford, who had punted at the University of the Pacific, got the first opportunity to succeed Fabi.

Considering the makeup and evolution of the team, what was the prognosis from within? "I don't think we felt we were anything great," Lancaster recalled. "We were just like any other team going into camp. We were looking forward to the season. We felt we had a pretty good football team and, if we made the playoffs, then anything could happen."

Entering the 1966 season, the Roughriders had made the playoffs four consecutive years, after missing out four times in a five-year span. However, Saskatchewan had not finished higher than third while repeatedly qualifying for the postseason. As the Roughriders fine-tuned for another season opener, head coach Eagle Keys expected his team's fortunes to ascend. "We are further advanced this year than last season at this time," he told the *Leader-Post* in one of his less-guarded moments. "We have pretty good balance and I really think we have a good chance to win it all."

CHAPTER 10

"I ONLY HAVE EYES FOR HUGH"

Hugh Campbell's supposedly slow gait did not prevent him from exploding out of the gate. Campbell caught three of Ron Lancaster's five touchdown passes as the Saskatchewan Roughriders opened their 1966 regular season with a 40-13 victory over the host Edmonton Eskimos. Gluey Hughie, as he was known, terrorized the Eskimos' secondary on the same day that Edmonton head coach Neill Armstrong's less-than-effusive critique of the Roughriders' ace receiver appeared in a published report. "Hugh Campbell is slower than most receivers in this league," Armstrong said. "He needs extra time to work into the clear."

In self-deprecating fashion, Lancaster was able to illustrate the uncanny timing that he and Campbell possessed: "Hugh was a very slow receiver and I had a very slow delivery, so it made it work for both parties. By the time he got down there, it took me that long to get ready to throw." Their success was a by-product of countless hours spent on the infield at Regina Exhibition Track. "When you went to practice, Hugh always wanted to stay out there and catch passes and work on things," Lancaster said. "He was a big believer in stuff like that. Every quarterback likes to have a go-to guy and you can't help but have a go-to guy when he wants to stay out there and catch passes."

Like Lancaster, Campbell pointed toward the importance of developing a rapport. "We did things before and after practice," Gluey Hughie said. "Ronnie and I ran about every play in practice because in those days there wasn't a big scout squad like teams have now. We ran all the other team's plays, so we were still playing catch the whole practice. There were some years, because of finances and the way things were, when there wasn't a lot of competition at training camp. There was one year, in particular, where I didn't have anybody trying out against me in training camp. They put the money in the positions where they knew they were going to need somebody."

Ron Lancaster and **Hugh Campbell** pondering their next move. | Photo courtesy of SSHFM

Lancaster made a habit of looking for Campbell from the outset. In 1964 — their first full season together — Campbell caught 65 passes for 1,000 yards and 11 touchdowns. The following year, the Roughriders' flanker made 73 receptions for a Western Conference-record 1,329 yards, with 10 majors. At times, it seemed like Campbell was the Roughriders' only receiver. That contention is supported by the statistics. In a 1965 preseason game against the visiting Winnipeg Blue Bombers, the Roughriders completed seven passes — all to Campbell — for 99 yards. Campbell was the passing attack despite playing with a dislocated finger. "Hughie only needs one hand and a couple of fingers to catch the ball," Roughriders head coach Eagle Keys said after the 9-8 exhibition victory over Winnipeg.

When the Roughriders next faced Winnipeg, Campbell was again unstoppable. He caught eight Lancaster aerials for 206 yards in a 25-6 regular-season victory over the host Bombers on Aug. 25, 1965. The Roughriders' other receivers combined for three catches and 38 yards. Such outings prompted a wisecrack from Roughriders tight end Jim Worden. "He said my favourite song was, 'I Only Have Eyes For Hugh,'" Lancaster quipped.

Lancaster was especially inclined to look for Campbell when a crucial catch was required. "When we were in trouble, we would do that," the Roughriders quarterback said. "I'd go to him a lot because it was easy to do. He delivered. If somebody's going to deliver, you're going to go to him more. Working together as much as we did, we knew what each other was going to do. I could throw the ball and he would go get it. You'd always take a chance with him because he would go and knock the ball down if it wasn't well-thrown. Either he got it or nobody got it. He was reliable, dependable, durable and he just got the job done. We had a good thing going so we weren't going to mess it up."

Instead, Campbell messed up opposing defences, using whatever tactics were required to get open. "He fools you," Tex Coulter, a former Montreal Alouette, said in the *Montreal Star*. "Campbell is the master of all the tricks of pass receiving. His most questionable move is one of his best. When he is running stride for stride in front of a defender, he will often 'shove off.' This takes precise timing. Just as the ball approaches, Campbell slows slightly and raises his elbow nearest the defender. The resulting collision throws the defender off stride and helps Campbell to accelerate in the direction of the ball. This is why he catches many passes that appear momentarily to be overthrown. He is much more than just a faker with great hands. He is by far the best actor among pro receivers. Acting takes up where faking leaves off in the receiving art and consists of the total atmosphere the receiver creates." Coulter's opinion was even endorsed within the Roughriders' ranks. "Campbell was a great pass-catcher," veteran trainer Sandy Archer said. "He caught more balls than he should have caught because he had the little knack. He'd go up for the ball with the defensive back and, if you watched him closely, the one elbow would be sticking out. I watched it. The defensive guy would be running into the elbow. Well, you couldn't call Campbell for interference."

Pity the poor defensive backs. "I'm telling you, he'd come down on me and I had him covered, but when he broke, he'd separate," said the Blue Bombers' Ken Ploen, who was a quarterback and defensive back. "You can't anticipate his break, so he'd break and I'd break with him and there was the ball. Ronnie had anticipated where he was going and he threw the ball. I didn't even know it. What can you do? Nothing. You're going to tackle the guy after he catches it — or hope you're going to tackle him. You were never overly concerned that Campbell's speed was going to burn you. It was the moves he put on you or lulling you to sleep. He was a very sly, intelligent football player and a great receiver. He had super hands and, running patterns and things, he was probably as good as anybody."

In that respect, Campbell was similar to Raymond Berry, a star receiver with the NFL's Baltimore Colts in the 1950s and 1960s. Bob Shaw was eminently qualified to make the comparison. Shaw coached the Colts' receivers, Berry included, in the late 1950s and was also the Roughriders' field boss when Campbell arrived in Saskatchewan. "Raymond Berry wasn't a fast receiver. Neither was Hughie Campbell," Shaw said. "They were both possession receivers and pattern-runners — not fast, but good pattern-runners — and had great hands. They caught everything that was thrown at them."

Like Berry, Campbell was almost professorial in his approach to pass-catching. There was not a wasted step. Every move was purposeful. "Hugh wrote a thesis on the art of pass receiving and it was very well done," Lancaster said. "He had quotes from all the receivers. I think there were guys like Dante Lavelli and Raymond Berry in it. Berry would be the guy you would compare him to back then, or maybe a Steve Largent after that. Hugh didn't have a lot of speed, but all I know is this: When he caught the ball behind a defensive back, he always got to the end zone first, and the only guy who came close to beating him all the time was the official. The defensive backs couldn't catch him, but that official would run with him right down the field."

There was an example to that effect in the Roughriders' second regular-season game of 1966 — a 38-14 victory over Winnipeg. Campbell scorched the Blue Bombers for three more touchdown catches, putting him on pace for a single-season total of 48. The final touchdown came on a 42-yard bomb, with Campbell outrunning defensive back Dick Thornton and scoring untouched, to the delight of 20,009 generally satisfied customers. The gathering of 20,000-plus was easily a franchise record during a season in which sellouts became routine. The previous high of 18,360 had been established in 1964 against the B.C. Lions. New standards for attendance were inevitable after Taylor Field was expanded, but the early-season crowds exceeded expectations.

According to the initial blueprint, the new seats would enable the Roughriders to dispense with the tradition of allowing fans to sit on the sidelines. However, the insatiable appetite for tickets in 1966 led to the extension of the status quo. "The city splurged for a few stands this season and it was intended to do away with those sideline sitters who devoured players and pigskins," the *Leader-Post*'s Laurie Artiss noted after the Winnipeg game. "So, in the very first league contest, grass-stained gentry are back in their old squatting grounds as they filled the park to a nose-count of 20,009 — two thousand over seating capacity." The fans' proximity to the playing surface could lead to some interesting developments. "There was a little white fence all the way around the field," defensive back Dale West recalled. "We had 10 rows of people sitting between the out-of-bounds marker and the white fence. We played a game against B.C. in 1962 or 1963. I remember Willie Fleming was running toward the sideline and I tackled him and we went right to the fence. It was like the Red Sea parting. We never touched a person. Their feet were about three feet away from the sideline."

A visit from the Lions always seemed to be eventful. An especially memorable one involved B.C. quarterback Joe Kapp. "One time, Kapp starts to run," Saskatchewan defensive back Bob Kosid said. "Now the only thing between he and the end zone is me. It's right along the sideline on the west side of the stands. Back in those days, they let people sit along the sidelines, like picnickers. They'd have their sandwiches and whatever's in the Thermos. Well, I hit Kapp and he goes flying on to a blanket, and these little old women are hitting him on the helmet with their Thermoses. I remember him saying, 'Jesus Christ, I've got to get out of here!' It was absolutely hilarious. Don't come to Taylor Field, my friend."

Winnipeg quarterback Ken Ploen could relate to Kapp's experiences. "The fans used to be all around that field, sitting right up to the out-of-bounds mark," Ploen said. "You'd go down the field and if you ever got knocked out of bounds or close to it, you got mugged before you got back on the field. The fans were rabid, but good fans. It was a fun place to play in." The surroundings were not as enjoyable in the visitors' locker room. "This was before I came, but I heard a story about the old pot-bellied stove in the dressing room," Ploen said. "One of the players had gone in at halftime and it was a pretty chilly day. He sat his helmet on the pot-bellied stove. They got through with all their yik-yakking and reviewing what they were going to do and they were ready to go out for the second half. He grabbed his helmet and it had melted." While improving their record to 2-0, the Roughriders scorched Winnipeg for five touchdowns. Four of them came from conventional sources. Campbell scored three times and fullback George Reed added a 42-yard touchdown run. Saskatchewan's other major was provided by guard Al Benecick, of all people. "Benecick scored his first touchdown ever when he went 34 yards with a recovered fumble when Bomber punt-return man Billy Martin flubbed a running catch," the *Leader-Post*'s Laurie Artiss reported. "But Benecick, who usually leads the offensive interference, may have trouble convincing his teammates of blocking's value. He disdained at least five blockers to stomp all over would-be tackler Ed Ulmer nearing the goal line." After stomping all over their first two opponents, the Roughriders had a considerably tougher time in Week 3 against the B.C. Lions. Saskatchewan eked out a 16-14 victory when a 50-yard field-goal attempt by the Lions' Bill Mitchell fell short on the final play. The nail-biter was witnessed by another Taylor Field record crowd — 20,379.

Saskatchewan scored what proved to be the winning touchdown when Lancaster found Reed in the end zone from 13 yards away at 3:44 of the fourth quarter, giving Saskatchewan a 16-7 lead. Reed's major had been preceded by a 59-yard pass from Lancaster to halfback Paul Dudley. Afterward, head coach Eagle Keys noted that Dudley "could be the find of the year."

Finding him used to be the tough part. Dudley had travelled all over the place since graduating from the University of Arkansas Razorbacks football program — where his teammates had included Lance Alworth (who became a star receiver with the San Diego Chargers) and Wayne Harris (a future Hall of Fame linebacker with Calgary).

The Green Bay Packers took note of Dudley's ability and selected him in the fourth round of the 1961 NFL draft. However, the Packers were hardly in need of running backs due to the presence of legendary ball-carriers Jim Taylor and Paul Hornung, so Dudley was tested as a defensive back before being released. He quickly caught on with the New York Giants and rushed for 100 yards on 27 carries in 1962, when he added nine receptions for 112 yards and one touchdown. After the 1962 season, New York traded Dudley to the Philadelphia Eagles, for whom he barely played. Philadelphia released Dudley after the 1964 exhibition season, at which point he became even more nomadic.

The Oakland Raiders were interested in Dudley, but could not pursue him because San Diego held his American Football

Paul Dudley | Photo courtesy of *Leader-Post*

League rights (having selected him in the 29th round of the 1962 AFL draft). San Diego was not interested in summoning Dudley with any urgency, so he opted to try Canadian football. After being contacted by Calgary head coach Bobby Dobbs, Dudley began motoring northward. There was only one problem: Dudley's CFL rights were actually owned by the Montreal Alouettes, so he changed direction and headed for Quebec.

As it turned out, Montreal wanted Dudley only as insurance in case of injury. Following an abbreviated stay in Montreal, Dudley was told that his services were not required. Once again, he was facing a long drive — back toward Calgary. By the time Dudley arrived in Calgary, he was informed that Montreal had sold his CFL rights to the Edmonton Eskimos. As usual, Dudley was supposed to be injury insurance, but the Eskimos' backs remained healthy. By that time, Dudley's 1964 season was a write-off, anyway.

Jerry Williams, who had taken over from Dobbs as Calgary's head coach, invited Dudley back to the Stampeders' camp for 1965. This time, Dudley made the team and received some playing time, only to be dropped. Guess who called again? The Alouettes. Montreal was anticipating the retirement of star running back George Dixon — who was never the same after absorbing the crunching hit by Roughriders defensive back Larry Dumelie in 1964. Thinking that there was a void in the Alouettes' backfield, Dudley flew to Montreal — only to be ignored again. An understandably miffed Dudley ended up leaving the Alouettes.

Next stop: San Diego. Dudley was still on the Chargers' protected list, so he embarked for California. By now, it will not be at all surprising to learn that Dudley did not play after joining his new team. Dudley spent the subsequent offseason teaching school in Calgary, where Roughriders running back Ed Buchanan also resided during the winter. Buchanan suggested to Dudley that it would be wise to call Roughriders head coach Eagle Keys.

Dudley turned heads right away, catching a 73-yard touchdown pass from Ron Lancaster on the Roughriders' opening play of the exhibition season. In the process, Dudley quickly made a positive impression with Keys and his players. "Paul was a very friendly person and he got along well with everybody," Lancaster said. "He was just a good guy." Dudley clicked very quickly with Lancaster. The Roughriders quarterback would soon be the best man at Dudley's wedding.

Dudley quickly emerged as an important, albeit unsung, component of the offence. As a rusher, he was a complement to George Reed. Dudley was also incorporated into the passing game and utilized as a kick returner. On top of it all, he was a character.

"Dudley called me up all the time and asked if I could go golfing," defensive back Bob Kosid said. "Unfortunately I couldn't go. It was a Saturday morning and I had something I had to do. I was working at [radio station] CKRM, and I had fixed him up with an interview for the Monday with a company downstairs. This would give him a job and some fortification for the season. Anyway, he goes out to the Murray Golf Course and the next thing I know, it's Monday morning and he doesn't show up. I said, 'Why would you botch this opportunity?' He said, 'Well, it's a long story, Bobby, but on the second hole, I was standing there and the ball dropped down near me. I looked back up and here was a guy on the tee. I yelled something at him and he yelled something back to me, and I didn't quite like what I heard, so I ran back up the hill and punched him out.' Guess who it was? It was the guy he was going to have the interview with on Monday."

The Roughriders' fourth game of 1966 was expected to be a rout — and, sure enough, it was. But the anticipated winner ended up losing in lopsided fashion. Saskatchewan carried a 3-0 record into an Aug. 17 game against the winless Stampeders. Records were irrelevant, as it turned out, and Calgary won 26-1.

Calgary's offence was powered by two touchdown passes from Peter Liske to Terry Evanshen. Lancaster had a rare off day, going 8-for-17 with four interceptions. The recently acquired Jim McKean was called upon to punt 11 times, and one of his kicks was blocked. It was that kind of day for the Roughriders. "When they win, they win 'em big," the *Leader-Post*'s Laurie Artiss commented. "When they lose, it's a bomb."

The same description could have applied to the Roughriders' following game, against Edmonton. The Eskimos, who had lost 40-13 at home to Saskatchewan in the regular-season opener, figured to be easy prey for the riled-up Roughriders at Taylor Field. But once again the game did not unfold as projected. Edmonton ended up winning 18-17 despite a spirited and sudden Saskatchewan comeback. After recovering a fumble by the Eskimos' Randy Kerbow in the final minute, the Roughriders marched to paydirt in two plays — a 45-yard screen pass to George Reed, followed by Lancaster's 20-yard payoff pitch to Gord Barwell. The extra point, which would have tied the game, proved to be far from automatic. The snap by Ted Urness was high and Jack Abendschan's convert attempt was partially blocked.

The term "special teams" was a misnomer throughout the game for Saskatchewan. A high snap to Alan Ford by Galen Wahlmeier resulted in a partially blocked punt. McKean, who also punted for Saskatchewan against the Eskimos, was erratic when called upon. McKean had also struggled the previous week against Calgary. "[Punting] is probably the single biggest problem the Rider coaching staff faces at the moment," Laurie Artiss wrote. "Eagle Keys knew he would have some problems replacing Martin Fabi in this department but probably didn't know it would be as severe as it has been in the last two games."

There was one more problem. In the second half against Edmonton, Roughriders halfback Ed Buchanan was helped off the field. He was soon diagnosed with strained knee ligaments and forced to miss all but one of the remaining regular-season games. It was yet another blow for Buchanan, who had been sidelined for most of the 1965 season with a broken leg.

In Buchanan's absence, the Roughriders had to lean more heavily on Dudley, a fellow import halfback. Dudley and Reed provided Saskatchewan with an abundance of ball-carrying ability, but one component was missing. In those days, the offensive configuration included a fullback, plus left and right halfbacks. Who would replace the multi-talented Buchanan at left halfback?

CHAPTER **11** # "THAT IS A DEAD DUCK"

Alan Ford made his first appearance on Taylor Field as a self-described "terrible" trumpet player during halftime of a Roughriders game during the 1950s. Ford, a member of the Regina Lions Band, did not have an inkling that he would eventually join mainstays such as Ron Atchison and Reg Whitehouse on the Roughriders. "I was telling Atch when I made the team, 'I was in the band when you were standing out there,' " Ford said. "I remember thinking, 'God, those guys look big.' "

As a Roughrider, Ford earned the monicker Mr. Versatility for his ability to contribute at several positions. Ford was deployed at offensive halfback, receiver, defensive back or linebacker, depending on the circumstances. He also contributed as a punter and kickoff returner. Was he equally versatile as a musician? "No," Ford responded. "I only played the trumpet ... and I was awful."

In terms of football, Ford's skills were seldom trumpeted at the time. "I was pretty small," he recalled. "I sort of never looked at football as being an option." In fact, Ford attended the University of the Pacific in Stockton, Calif., on a basketball scholarship. Phil Dynan, who taught Ford at Regina's Central Collegiate, used his United States connections to help arrange the scholarship. So much for Ford's original inclination to play basketball for the University of Saskatchewan Huskies.

As a freshman at Pacific, Ford's collegiate football experience was limited to the school's house league. "When I was playing intramural football, one of the guys who was playing basketball with me said, 'I've never seen a guy kick like that. I'm going to talk to the football guys about you because their punter is leaving after this year.' So the punter left and they asked me to change scholarships from basketball to football and do the punting. I thought, 'That would be pretty good. I'll fly all over the place. It's Division 1 football, and all I've got to do is punt.' In the last game of my sophomore year, I played a little bit. In my last two years there, I played all the time. I didn't do the punting my senior year, when I played a number of positions."

Ford's ability was noted by the Roughriders, who made him a territorial protection along with fellow Central Gophers alumnus Don Thompson. While at Central, Ford was involved in multiple sports, so eventually playing several positions in one sport was in keeping with his inclination. "That's the way it was in those days," he said. "Everything wasn't so specialized. When one sport ended, you'd go on to the next sport. Nowadays, if you're a hockey player, you can't do much else because you go to summer hockey school. Back then, once hockey was over, the next thing was track, and then there would be football in the fall. School was really important in the development of athletes in the system. Now a lot of the development is done outside the school system. Back then, you'd compete in everything and represent the school.

"I always looked at it from the coaches' standpoint because that's what I wanted to do at that point. I was playing football, but I thought of myself as a teacher and coach. Coaching was a great outlet for me when football was over. I looked at more positions than the one I played. I felt like I could play any position on the field and not make a mistake. I might get beat, but mentally I could play every position. I knew what to do because that's how coaches

Alan Ford *eyes the first-down marker* | Photo courtesy of John Solilo, Solilo Studios

looked at it." (One time, Ford's versatility even extended to the role of emergency trainer. He ended up taping his teammates' ankles at the Autostade in Montreal after a cab driver accidentally took Sandy Archer to Jarry Park, delaying the long-serving trainer's arrival until after the opening kickoff.)

The coaches got a first look at Ford during training camp in 1965, when he was rudely introduced to defensive end Garner Ekstran. "The rookies practised two or three days and all of a sudden all the veterans showed up, and we were going to practise with them," Ford said. "Everybody's sitting around upstairs at the exhibition grounds and in comes Garner. A lot of the veterans are there, and they start making sounds like a cow. I knew that this guy had a lot of respect from everybody in the room. When he walked in, it was, 'Moo!' He'd show up on the road, walking through the airport, and invariably someone would go, 'Moo!' And you just knew Garner was there.

"Garner's trademark was his clothesline. He and Bill Baker probably had the two best clotheslines that I've ever experienced. Garner did that to me about three days into my rookie training camp. I'm a running back coming out of the backfield and thinking, 'This is easy. I'm going to run a 10-yard out.' I got about six yards and all of a sudden, I'm on my back. I'd never experienced that before. I knew I had to get up and get back to the huddle because you didn't want to be hurt with an Eagle Keys team. The next time I came out and he said, 'Hey, rookie, you take a pretty good clothesline,' then I knew that maybe I was OK with the veterans. I'm sure I left teeth-prints on his forearm. Mine were a long list of teeth that hit his forearm."

Ted Dushinski also cut his teeth at the Roughriders' training camp in 1965. The Saskatoon-born defensive back quickly made an impression. "Ted was one of the boys," Ford said. "He fit in that mould with Larry Dumelie, Hank Dorsch, Bob Kosid and Ted Provost. If you caught the pass, you knew you were getting hit, big-time. I worked against Ted [Dushinski] a lot in practice. In training camp, we'd always have the Green and White game, and a lot of scrimmages before we got to the Green and White game. Those guys just knocked the heck out of you. That's what I remember the most about Ted.

"Off the field, he was sort of Mr. Party. He was a nice guy and just had a great time. It was like life was just a bowl of cherries, but when he got on the football field — a lot like Atch — his personality just changed. They were tough players. When he came in from the Saskatoon Hilltops, Dorsch, Dumelie and Kosid were already there and established. It doesn't take very long when you've been around the game a little bit to know who fits in with your style of play and who doesn't. It wasn't five days into training camp and those kind of guys were going, 'OK, come on, Ted.' They'd take him different places or go, 'OK, let's go have a beer in the trees over at Luther College.' He just fit in and you knew he was going to be a player for a lot of years."

Ford made his first start for the Roughriders on Aug. 28, 1966 against the host B.C. Lions, rushing four times for 16 yards in a 30-29 Saskatchewan victory. Ford — playing left halfback in place of the injured Ed Buchanan — also contributed to the pass protection that enabled Ron Lancaster to complete 19 of 26 attempts for 361 yards.

This is hardly a news flash, but Hugh Campbell was Lancaster's favourite receiver. Campbell caught nine passes for 196 yards, including touchdown bombs of 73 and 43 yards. On the 73-yarder, Campbell caught the football near the Lions' 45-yard line and outran defenders Pokie Allen and Mack Burton to the end zone. "It may have exploded the myth, once and for all, that Hugh Campbell is slow afoot," the *Leader-Post's* Laurie Artiss wrote.

The 73-yard connection with Lancaster made Campbell the Roughriders' all-time receiving yardage leader — only three years after he joined the team. With slightly more than 3,200 yards, Campbell surpassed Ken Carpenter's career total of 3,157. Campbell was one of many exciting performers during a Sunday afternoon shootout at Vancouver's Empire Stadium. The teams combined for more than 1,000 yards of offence, with the Lions producing 507 — eight more than the visitors.

Saskatchewan scored the game's final points at 6:54 of the fourth quarter when Jack Abendschan kicked a 25-yard, go-ahead field goal. The Lions attempted to counter with a decisive three-pointer, but Dale West blocked Bill Mitchell's 35-yard attempt as time expired. West had an unimpeded path to the kicker after teammates Garner Ekstran and Moe Levesque opened a gaping hole up the middle. It was poetic justice for West, who had been assessed a questionable pass-interference penalty on the previous play. "I must have been involved in like 400 games, playing and coaching, since coming to Canada 18 years ago," Eagle Keys told the *Leader-Post*. "I can't honestly recall a more exciting game. That really must have been something for the fans to watch."

It was appropriate that Hugh Campbell caught nearly 200 yards worth of passes on a day when Jim Worden registered career single-game highs. Even when the bruising tight end enjoyed his finest day statistically, Campbell was in the spotlight. Worden caught seven passes for 125 yards — personal bests in both categories — in the nail-biter at Empire Stadium. Worden's final reception put Saskatchewan in position for a game-winning field goal by Jack Abendschan. Earlier, a key block by Worden had sprung George Reed for a 25-yard run that set up Saskatchewan's first touchdown — a 12-yard run by Paul Dudley.

Although Campbell boasted better totals in Vancouver, Worden could not convincingly argue that he was overlooked. But the irrepressible Worden might have tried, anyway. "He told coach Keys that he was going to put a rear-view mirror on his helmet because all he did was clear defensive backs out for Campbell to catch passes, and his neck was getting sore from running forward and turning his head backwards," Ron Lancaster said. "He was something special, but what do you expect from a Wittenberg graduate?"

Like Lancaster, Worden emanated from tiny Wittenberg College (now Wittenberg University) in Springfield, Ohio. Worden made his collegiate debut the year after Lancaster graduated. Over Worden's four years at Wittenberg, the team posted a 33-2-1 record. He was twice a first-team conference all-star during that span. Even though Worden was a product of an NCAA Division 3 school, he was invited to play in the Senior Bowl, an annual showcase for the top graduating collegians.

Unfortunately, Worden suffered a knee injury in a workout preceding the Senior Bowl. The lack of exposure against stars from larger universities could have contributed to the fact

Jim Worden | Photo courtesy of *Leader-Post* archives

that he lasted until the 14th round of the 1964 NFL draft, when he was claimed by the Dallas Cowboys. Dallas need not have bothered. By the time the Cowboys contacted Worden, he had already signed with Saskatchewan.

Worden quickly made a favourable impression at the Roughriders' 1964 training camp. "Jim Worden from Wittenberg could be the find of the year," Bob Shaw, then in his second year as Saskatchewan's head coach, told John Robertson of the *Leader-Post*. "He was the best small-college player in the U.S. last year."

Those credentials were fine and dandy, but Worden also had to prove himself to the Roughriders' veterans — especially defensive linemen Garner Ekstran and Bill Clarke. "Garner and Bill used to kill offensive ends," defensive back Dale West recalled. "They'd have smiles on their faces whenever a rookie offensive end would come up. He would have to go between them and they would hammer him. The test was if you could stand up to them in practice, you were tough enough to play in the CFL." When Worden stood up to them, the Roughriders knew he was a keeper.

The 6-foot-2, 225-pound Worden caught only 11 passes as a first-year Roughrider — but averaged 20.7 yards per reception while scoring two touchdowns. It was not a coincidence that in 1964 Saskatchewan had two running backs exceed the 1,000-yard milestone for the first (and only) time in franchise history. With Worden acting as an extension of the offensive line, Ed Buchanan amassed 1,390 rushing yards and George Reed added 1,012.

Worden's role in the passing attack was expanded in 1965, when he caught 26 passes for 433 yards — an average of 16.6 yards per reception — and three touchdowns. The Roughriders' road grader of a tight end also helped to clear paths through which George Reed rushed for a franchise-record 1,768 yards.

By 1966, Worden had earned a reputation as one of the league's toughest players — a robust presence in every situation. Worden had the same mentality off the field. He lived as hard as he played. "He was in the middle of everything," Lancaster said. "He was a unique person." Worden was often carousing until the wee hours of the morning. He was known to show up bleary-eyed at Roughriders practices. But come game time, there was never a concern about No. 72. As rough as he sometimes looked arriving at the field, he would be even rougher on the opposition. "I never worried about The Hog," West said. "He was always ready to play." The same applied to Worden's running mate, middle linebacker Wally Dempsey.

Wally Dempsey | Photo courtesy of *Leader-Post* archives

"Me and Wally Dempsey were the nemesis of Eagle Keys," Worden said in a 1995 interview. "We won't get into specifics, but he kept getting balder. Ask him about the milk truck some time. We bought it for $75." They milked it for all it was worth, and then some. "We'd pile all the guys into that truck, even though I don't think it was street legal, and go hunting or go to practice," Worden continued. "Eagle would look at the parking lot, see that truck, and know we were raising hell. We'd take it uptown. We'd take it all the way to Saskatoon. We toured all over the countryside and had a ball. One day, we took it south of town, took the plates off, and let 'em come and get it. We figured Wayne Shaw would come and get it. He's probably still driving it."

Clyde Brock was the driver on one infamous day when Worden was riding shotgun. Brock, the Roughriders' towering offensive tackle, supplied the wheels for a regularly scheduled hunting expedition. "It was a brand-new yellow Pontiac — a Bonneville," Brock remembered. "We were out shooting one day. I think there was Worden and Wally Dempsey and Moe Levesque.

"We had come over a rise and there were a bunch of ducks sitting out there. Worden was sitting right behind me. It was a hardtop and all the windows came down, so we rolled the windows down and we stopped on the crest of this hill. Worden had just bought a Browning .22 rifle with a scope on it. It was really a nice little gun. We were quite a ways away and he said, 'Hey, do you think I can hit one of those ducks down there?' We stopped on the top of the hill and he laid the gun out the window.

"I slid way over to the side and he said, 'That is a dead duck.' *BAM*! With the scope on it, he's looking right over the top of my side-view mirror, and he shot my mirror right off! When he's laying the gun there and looking out the scope, the barrel is right below the scope and it's pointing right at the mirror. I think it was Levesque sitting on the other side. He laughed so hard that he hit the door handle and fell out of the car. It was really funny. By the way, I don't think Worden ever paid me for that mirror."

Darrell Mudra was confident the Montreal Alouettes' Sept. 5, 1966 game at Taylor Field would not be a mirror image of their previous visit to Regina — a 20-1 preseason victory for Saskatchewan. "Tell 'em we'll be back here again and will beat their ears off," Mudra, the Alouettes' head coach, said lightheartedly after the July 22 game. Mudra was not so jocular after the Labour Day matchup with Saskatchewan, which won 44-0. The Roughriders' offensive catalysts were their triplets — Ron Lancaster (who completed 13 of 14 passes for 219 yards), Hugh Campbell (11 catches, 194 yards, and his third three-touchdown game in seven weeks) and George Reed (18 carries, 118 yards, three touchdowns).

"They were really ready for us in this one," Mudra understated. "If that team keeps playing like that, there won't be anything stopping them from going to the Grey Cup. Lancaster and Campbell were simply unbelievable." Within earshot of the media, Alouettes owner Ted Workman wailed: "Inhumane! Inhumane!"

Montreal had allowed just 41 points over its previous five games, only to surrender that many in three quarters against Saskatchewan. The Roughriders' passing game was virtually flawless, with Lancaster's only incompletion coming on a bomb to Campbell that was knocked down. Paul Dudley even got into the act, throwing a 28-yard touchdown pass to Campbell on a halfback option.

Amid all the commotion about Lancaster and Campbell, it was surprisingly easy to overlook Reed — even though he had rushed for more than a mile in 1965. The early stages of the 1966 season were most notable for the Saskatchewan air show, but Reed's performance against Montreal reminded people of how vital he was to the Roughriders' arsenal.

By the mid-1960s, Saskatchewan had established a balance on offence. Defences could not be excessively conscious of the run because of Campbell's telepathic relationship with Lancaster. Any team that was overly preoccupied with neutralizing Campbell was liable to be subjected to an unrelenting ground assault. "If the coach or the team was selfish in any way, I think George Reed could have made even more yards," Campbell said. "I could have caught more passes. But we were a team. The idea wasn't how many touchdowns I could catch or how many yards George could make. It was a team. Ronnie was very good at playing the hand he was dealt and he did what he had to do to win games."

The Roughriders' varied threats created a conundrum for rival coaches. Before Montreal visited Taylor Field on Labour Day, Mudra quipped that "I expect nine of our people are designed to stop Campbell and the other three will be on Reed."

Some days, Lancaster was virtually unerring in collaboration with Campbell. On other occasions, Lancaster chose to send Reed into the line, time after time, and the punishing fullback would wear down the defence. Lancaster's ball-handling skills also enabled him to use play-action passes to considerable effect. Therefore, the establishment of the run was fundamental to everything the Roughriders sought to achieve on offence.

"The heart of the team was George Reed," centre Ted Urness said. "We gave him the ball 30 times a game. He was absolutely devastating for the first eight to 10 yards. If he broke free of that and got downfield, that's when you could catch him. If you didn't block for him, he ran over you. If you didn't want that to happen, you made a hole."

A similar principle applied in relation to Lancaster. If you wanted to be a component of the Roughriders' high-octane offence, you had to execute — period. Nothing less was acceptable to the exacting Lancaster. "On the football field, the huddle was his domain," Reed said. "He controlled the huddle and everybody had respect for him. If somebody said they could do something, he believed that they could do it. If they didn't do it, then he got all over them. Guys learned very quickly that if you told him you could do something and you couldn't do it, he got very irritated about it and he wouldn't call you again, but he wouldn't put that same trust in you. Another thing was the way he could remember things. He would tuck plays away in his head and it could be the fourth quarter or the next time we played that team before he pulled that play out of his head to use it. He just knew."

Lancaster was renowned as a diagnostician, but it would be erroneous to describe him as strictly clinical in his approach. His preparation was fuelled by a fixation with winning. "I just like to compete," he said. "I don't care whether we're going to play Hearts, throw darts or whatever. I'm going to compete to win. That's the way I play."

That attitude was contagious. "If you were in an alley fight, you wanted him to be beside you because he never thought anybody could beat him," Reed said. "They might get the best of him today, but he never thought anybody could beat him and he always felt he had time to win the football game. His mental toughness and the respect that he would get on the field from other players is what made him so good. He had the ability, but what made him outstanding was that the guys would follow him. They'd walk right through a wall for him."

Lancaster possessed more latitude, in terms of decision-making, than quarterbacks typically enjoy today. He was entrusted with play-calling responsibilities throughout his tenure as Saskatchewan's starter, and many of the Roughriders' offensive accomplishments were the result of his audibles. What he lacked in physical attributes was more than counteracted by his intelligence. "The guy was short. He was not particularly fast. I wouldn't say he had a bazooka for an arm or anything else, but he was intelligent," former Winnipeg Blue Bombers quarterback and defensive back Ken Ploen said. "He could throw on the run. He utilized his talent very well. In my time we called all the plays. We didn't get the plays sent in to us and all this garbage. The guy was a complete football player."

The Roughriders, meanwhile, were evolving into a complete football team in their second season under Eagle Keys. "Bob Shaw did change the complexion of this team when he took over in 1963 from the late Steve Owen," the *Leader-Post*'s Laurie Artiss wrote while referencing Keys' predecessors. "They were a third-place team when Shaw took over and a third-place team when he left, but he did alter things from a defence-orientated squad to an attack-minded creation. Eagle Keys appears to have polished both. The offence is operating in an even more electrifying manner and the defence is quite capable of winning the odd game on their own — if the offence ever blows a fuse."

The Roughriders had exceeded projections by the seven-game mark, when they were averaging 26.6 points per game. Keys had cited a goal of 25 points per game as the season

Ron Lancaster *throws to* ***Bob Richardson*** *in 1976* | Photo courtesy of *Leader-Post*

loomed. "They have scored so many more points than any other club in the country that it's ridiculous," Artiss marvelled.

Winnipeg head coach Bud Grant was also laudatory in his assessment of the Roughriders, labelling them "the best football team in Canada. They possess an outstanding offence and strong defence, an expert coach, top-notch quarterback, and make few errors." Jack Matheson of the *Winnipeg Tribune* offered another glowing appraisal of the Roughriders: "There isn't much doubt they have the best team in the West, if not in the country, at the moment, and I don't know why they couldn't continue to have it for three months."

CHAPTER 12 | # "THAT'S TAYLOR FIELD?"

The Winnipeg Blue Bombers achieved the rare distinction of limiting Hugh Campbell to a mere two receptions. However, the Bombers were hardly in a mood to be congratulated following a Sept. 11, 1966 home game against the Roughriders. Both of Campbell's catches went for touchdowns. One of them was a game-winning 10-yarder with 1:04 remaining in the fourth quarter, giving Saskatchewan a 27-24 victory.

Ron Lancaster's ears proved to be as important as his throwing arm. Early in the game, Winnipeg's Barrie Hansen had chewed out defensive-backfield cohort Ken Danchuk, saying: "When it's second down, play 'em tight, not loose! They're looking for the first down, not the long one!" Lancaster filed it away, waiting for the ideal time to catch the Blue Bombers in a situation where they would be eager — too eager — to pounce on an intermediate-range pass. That moment arrived on the Roughriders' final possession. The drive began inauspiciously when a screen pass to Gord Barwell resulted in a loss of six yards. On second-and-16, Lancaster figured the Bombers would defend the area around the yardsticks — recalling the earlier exhortations of Hansen — and decided the situation was conducive to a long-gainer. Lancaster called for Campbell, Barwell and Jim Worden to hook up in first-down territory. As the Roughriders' quarterback had expected, the Bombers converged on those three receivers. Meanwhile, Alan Ford was breezing past Danchuk. The pass was underthrown, but Ford came back for the ball and made the reception for a 51-yard advance. Lancaster then found Worden for 14 yards before firing the game-winner to Campbell.

Once again, Campbell was the nemesis of Winnipeg's outstanding cornerback, Dick Thornton. In Week 2, Campbell had scorched Thornton for three touchdowns. Thornton was determined to avoid a recurrence. Leading up to the rematch, Thornton told the media he had been thinking of nothing but Campbell all week and was "geared up" to face him.

Thornton responded by registering one interception in the Sept. 11 game, but ended up lamenting the ending. He slipped and fell on the play that produced Campbell's decisive touchdown. The victory gave Saskatchewan a 6-2 record for the first time in its modern era. "They've won several — and lost a couple — in a manner which defies description," Laurie Artiss wrote in the *Leader-Post*.

The Roughriders-Bombers game included Jack Abendschan's 47-yard field goal — the longest in the CFL season to that point. Abendschan also attempted a 59-yarder with the wind, only to come up short.

Bob Shaw had gotten wind of Abendschan in 1964. At the time, Abendschan was a senior guard and placekicker at the University of New Mexico. Shaw was in his second, and final, year as Saskatchewan's head coach. Abendschan committed to the Roughriders after Shaw visited New Mexico to sell the promising lineman on Saskatchewan. By the time Abendschan suited up for the Roughriders in 1965, Shaw was coaching the Toronto Argonauts and Eagle Keys was Saskatchewan's field boss.

Abendschan was introduced to Saskatchewan in July of 1965. He was accompanied on the long northward drive by University of New Mexico teammate Wayne Tvrdik, who was also trying out for the Roughriders that summer. "I was driving a Studebaker Lark," Abendschan said. "We had it packed full of clothes and stuff. We kept checking the radio to see what language they were speaking in Canada. We didn't know if we were going to have interpreters. I just didn't look into it that much. When I was in Eunice, New Mexico and went to the University of New Mexico in Albuquerque, I didn't hardly know anything about Canadian football. We just never heard much about it. I didn't know anything about Canada, so everything was all new."

That included the cuisine. "When I went to a restaurant, I asked for some chips with my hamburger," Abendschan said. "They brought me out french fries and I was expecting potato chips. I never expected anything like that."

Nor did he expect to be practising in the infield of a horse-racing track. "It didn't matter, just as long as I could play football," he said. "That never bothered me the whole time I was up there. You've got to practise

Jack Abendschan | Photo courtesy of SSHFM

somewhere, right? It doesn't matter whether it's in the middle of a horse track or over at Campion College.

"Back then — this may sound trite — but we played for the love of the game. We didn't play for the money. We wanted to get paid well, but it's not like it is now. The equipment, the demands that they make now, we weren't used to that. Look at a guy like Ron Atchison. He was sitting over there, 900 years old. He was taped from his head to his toes, yet he's still going out there playing the game and wanting to win that Grey Cup. That's the way it was. Everybody just loved playing the game. You could still play football and get paid for it. Wow ... that was awesome."

The day after their 27-24 victory in Winnipeg, the Roughriders announced that defensive tackle Ed McQuarters had joined the team on a five-day trial. He had just been released by the St. Louis Cardinals, with whom he had spent the 1965 NFL season after graduating from the University of Oklahoma.

Many years earlier, McQuarters had thought his initial experience with football would be a short trial. "In the beginning, I hated it because my feet hurt," said McQuarters, recalling his formative years in Tulsa, Okla. "My legs hurt. Everything hurt. I thought, 'How can they like this if it hurts all the time?' "

McQuarters remained involved in the sport thanks to his older brother. "What really inspired me to keep going was Sam," he said. "I was on the junior team and he was on the senior team, the varsity team. A couple of times, he would stop to watch us after their practice was over. He'd come home and laugh at me, saying, 'You guys don't know what you're doing.' He's kibitzing me and putting me down and telling me I was never going to be as good as him. That inspired me to keep going, along with watching him, admiring him and wanting to be like him."

McQuarters began to take note of the degree to which football was benefiting him. "All of a sudden, I noticed my pants were starting to fit looser," he said. "My shirts were fitting looser. I said to myself, 'Hey, Ed, you're losing weight.' I was starting to tone up."

The improved musculature also helped McQuarters in another athletic pursuit. After football season at Booker T. Washington High School in Tulsa, McQuarters turned to wrestling. "I went out for the team there and started losing more weight," he said. "All of a sudden now, the girls are starting to pay attention to me. I was saying, 'Well, this is not too bad.' "

McQuarters quickly discovered that he had an aptitude for wrestling, winning three of four matches in his introductory high school tournament. But the match he lost resonated more than the victories: "I'll never forget the guy's name — Jack Brisco from Blackwell, Oklahoma." Brisco eventually became an immensely successful professional wrestler. He was equally formidable when the combat was unscripted, as evidenced by the fact that he won an NCAA wrestling championship while representing Oklahoma State. "This guy was just a god with the physique and everything," McQuarters said, reflecting on his high school match with Brisco. "I was really psyched out and scared before I got on the mat. Just the looks of this guy terrified me.

"I didn't do too bad in the first three-minute period, but then his strength and knowledge of wrestling and technique just got to me. He turned me every way but loose. I was trying my best, but the guy was much stronger. With about a minute to go, he pinned me. I was so humiliated. I said to myself as soon as the referee hit the mat, 'Ed, you will never get pinned again. You will never get humiliated like that in sports again. You will die before you will let it happen to you.' "

That resolve fuelled McQuarters. He enjoyed success in various athletic disciplines, becoming an Oklahoma high school wrestling champion — earning most-outstanding-wrestler honours at the state meet — and an all-city and all-state lineman in football. Branching off into track and field, he set a Tulsa shot-put record in Grade 12 while also making the Dean's Honor Roll.

The people at the University of Oklahoma took notice. McQuarters was college-bound — on a wrestling scholarship. After placing second in the heavyweight division at the 1962 Big Eight championships, he received permission to convert to a football scholarship. McQuarters helped Oklahoma win the 1962 and 1964 Big Eight football titles before progressing to the NFL — having been selected by the St. Louis Cardinals in the 18th round of the 1965 draft. (One round later, the Cardinals drafted a Utah State running back named Roy Shivers — a future Roughriders general manager.)

"In an exhibition game that year we played the Cleveland Browns," McQuarters said. "I was playing defensive tackle that particular game. The legendary Jim Brown took the handoff. I had a straight shot at him. Just as I braced myself for the impact, he put a shake-and-bake move on me and I tackled nothing but grass. I mean, I took a real dive into the turf! As I was getting up, I thought to myself, 'So, that's how the great Jim Brown became great.' "

As a rookie, McQuarters played in every exhibition game with the Cardinals before being used sparingly during the regular season. He was hoping to make constructive use of the year's experience in 1966, but his second NFL training camp became nightmarish due to what he cited as several episodes of racism.

"I can enjoy a joke with the best of them," McQuarters said. "If a joke's being cracked, I can laugh like anybody else, but when you're sitting in a dressing room or in a meeting and you've got some guys that you know are bigots and racists, and everybody knows it, you don't appreciate it.

"Yeah, we would have some of the black guys laugh along with the bigots and racists when these kind of jokes and remarks were being made, but I couldn't. I refused to do it and I wasn't going to do it. I know it got me in trouble with St. Louis. The coaches would be in these meetings and they'd hear this stuff, too. Everybody was having a great chuckle. Why should I laugh? I'm not going to. We know you're a bigot and a racist. I'm not going to laugh at you. You're a fool, really. People would look at me. All of a sudden, it would be,

'McQuarters is not laughing. He's too serious about things. He's not a team player.' I knew how they were feeling and how they'd get this opinion about me."

McQuarters felt the racism spilled over to the football field during training camp. He cited one episode in which a Cardinals offensive lineman delivered a cheap shot below the knees. "The coaches had to pull us apart," McQuarters said. "We were just being pulled apart and he kicked at me and he grazed my thigh. He said, 'You n.....' He just started to say it. He was *that* close to saying it. He caught himself.

"When I heard it, my whole body just went hot. I was red-hot for a couple of seconds. I said, 'Oh, God, thank you for letting him stop.' If he had said it to me, all these other players were going to hear this from this fool. I was so relieved. I wouldn't have done any more than I would normally do, and that's maybe swing at him or something.

"But I'm glad he didn't say it, because I've got to play with all these guys, white and black. To have him say something like that, that probably would have ripped our team apart. He was that close. That's as close as I've ever come to being called that to my face. I'll never forget that."

Nor will he forget a late-August 1966 exhibition game against the host Los Angeles Rams. "You remember Merlin Olsen and Deacon Jones?" McQuarters said of the Rams' Hall of Fame defensive linemen, who combined with Roosevelt Grier and Lamar Lundy to form a carnivorous front four. "We were warming up on the field. The Rams were at the other end. All of a sudden, the crowd just goes crazy. Someone said, 'Here comes the Fearsome Foursome.' Everybody started going crazy because they'd been killing people in regular-season games.

"I'm terrified. I had never seen such huge human beings. The arms looked like they hung down to their calves. The crowd was going crazy. They knew they were the thing in that stadium, and they walked like it. You talk about swagger. And here I am down at the other end, looking at those guys. The reason I was so terrified was, the week before, the coach decided to try me at offensive guard, because I had played some offensive lineman — not a lot — at Oklahoma and in high school. I'm thinking I might have to play some in L.A., and I'm going to have to face these huge individuals.

"Willis Crenshaw, a fullback at the time on the Cardinals, came up to me and said, 'Hey, Mac. Look at that. I've got to run fullback. Maybe I should fake being hurt or something.' We were laughing. We were expected to get kicked, which is what happened. We were down by two or three touchdowns in the third quarter.

"Pretty soon, one of the bigots on our team started acting up. He was getting kicked on the offensive line, because those defensive linemen on L.A. were just killing us, so he decided to start a fight. The officials broke it up. One of our coaches said, 'You know you're going to get kicked. Don't embarrass us by starting a fight.' One of the bigots did it again. This time the fight was serious. Guys were fighting, screaming and kicking. L.A.'s players ran on the field and the Cardinals' players ran on the field."

The Cardinals' coaches scurried on to the field to try to break up the melee. Two St. Louis players remained on the sidelines — McQuarters and defensive back Abe Woodson.

"I looked at Woodson. Woodson looked at me," McQuarters said. "He wasn't going to go out there and fight. He's an old pro. He's beyond that. But I knew I should have been out there in the fight, because all the other people were out there. I was not there for one reason."

McQuarters was not prepared to participate in a battle he felt had been precipitated by a teammate he identified as a bigot. "I said, 'I won't go out there for you. If lightning comes down and threatens to strike me, I'll let it strike me because I'm not going out there to fight because of that fool,' and I didn't," he said. "I just kind of looked at the coach and the coach looked at me. The game was over. We got beat by two or three touchdowns. We got back to our training camp facilities in Lake Forest, Illinois." McQuarters would not be referring to the Cardinals as "we" for much longer.

McQuarters was released shortly after the 32-14 loss to Los Angeles. "There was a knock at the door," he said. "Sure enough, it was, 'McQuarters, the coach wants to see you. Bring your playbook.' I felt so much better because I finally heard what I knew was coming. It was a relief. I was expecting it.

"So I sat down with the coach and he said there were some teams that were interested. He mentioned San Francisco, Minnesota and another team I can't remember. He said, 'We just don't have enough room for you. Sorry it didn't work out.' You know the true story, but they're not going to come out and say it. They're going to be diplomatic. So I was gone, but I knew why. Later that day, I finally got everything in my car to drive back to St. Louis to my apartment where my wife and two sons were. I waited for less than two days for some of those teams to call that the coaches said were interested in me."

The NFL clubs never called. It was their loss, according to former Cardinals teammate Dave Meggyesy. He lauded McQuarters in a controversial 1970 book, *Out Of Their League*. "Ed was one of the quickest defensive linemen I have ever seen anywhere in football," Meggyesy wrote. "But [Cardinals head coach] Charley Winner said he felt McQuarters didn't have the correct attitude on the field. Actually, McQuarters' attitude was beautiful: he refused to take any shit from the whites. He carried himself with great dignity and certainly had the respect of his black teammates. Ed refused to smile at the cracks about black football players which were customary in training camp ... In my opinion, and in the opinion of many other veterans, McQuarters would have been a great defensive tackle in the National Football League. But because he refused to demean himself, Winner cut him from the squad. When Ed was in camp, the coaches' complaints had nothing to do with his ability as a player, but his aloofness and his inability to 'laugh and joke along with the other players.'"

McQuarters was soon contacted by Roughriders general manager Ken Preston. Head coach Eagle Keys had also been advised of McQuarters' availability and attributes by a Cardinals assistant coach, Jim Champion.

After committing to join the Roughriders, McQuarters took the milk run to Saskatchewan, flying from St. Louis to Minneapolis to Winnipeg to Regina. "I felt comfortable because the people just made me feel OK about coming to Regina," he said. "As soon as I hit Winnipeg, *Bam*! When you mentioned the Roughriders, everybody knew about the Roughriders. People were talking to me and it was all good stuff.

"The guy came on the public-address system on the plane and he said, 'Now we are starting our approach to Regina, blah blah blah.' One of the stewardesses found out that I was coming to the Roughriders and she was from Regina. The other stewardess — who was calling me Ed by now — said, 'There's Taylor Field, where you're going to be playing.' I said, 'My high school stadium was bigger than that.' That was a big shocker. I was watching these games on TV and there were crowds of 35,000 and 40,000 and Grey Cup games with 45,000. I had never seen Taylor Field before. I said, *'That's* Taylor Field?' "

Regina's airport was of comparably modest dimensions. "I landed and got my bag," McQuarters continued. "I was looking around the airport and thinking, 'You know what? This is not as big as I thought,' but the people were so nice. Every time you mentioned the Roughriders, everybody would just go crazy. That made everything all OK. I kind of forgot about how small things were compared to what I was used to."

The Roughriders' newest addition was promptly greeted by assistant coach Jack Gotta. "He said, 'Let me take you to Taylor Field,' " McQuarters said. "At the time, we practised in the exhibition grounds and we'd take the bus from there to the games. We drove around and it was September. There were all these horses all over the place. I thought, 'This is kind of weird.' I'm trying to make sense out of all this. I'm used to where you play, you practise right there. Jack Gotta said, 'We have an apartment for you. I'll take you over there to talk to the people, and we'll take you by the coach's office.' "

Head coach Eagle Keys had a lair upstairs, above a small shopping mall on Hill Avenue — not within walking distance of Taylor Field. "I was just used to everything being in the same place," McQuarters said. "We get over there and everything's all over the place. Again, everything was so small. The place was kind of hot. There's little coaches' offices and everybody was nice. Of course, I met Eagle Keys and he talked so slowly. He was from Kentucky. I got used to all of this stuff. That's how I got here."

Ed McQuarters |
Photo courtesy of Leader-Post archives

CHAPTER **13** # "I AM NOT COMING BACK"

An interesting sidebar to the Roughriders' game against the Toronto Argonauts pertained to the visiting head coach, Bob Shaw, who had left Saskatchewan after two seasons as the Roughriders' field boss to assume control of the Argonauts' on-field product. Although the Roughriders had already played against Shaw — winning 28-9 in Toronto in 1965 — he had yet to visit Taylor Field since leaving Regina. That changed on Sept. 18, 1966.

"There is no middle-of-the-road in a person's reactions to Bob Shaw," the *Leader-Post*'s Laurie Artiss wrote as game day neared. "He has that type of personality. Even opposing football coaches, always hesitant to talk about fellow lodge members, will express opinions on Bob. Some will insist you move slower in rebuilding a team, you don't rip it asunder as Shaw had done. Others claim they would have done exactly the same thing — only quicker.

"Players who have performed under Shaw are always prompt to say the man knows football, the techniques and strategies. Then they will tell you they suffocated under his supreme ego and couldn't warm to his harsh treatment or terrible temper."

Any criticism has to be tempered by the positive aspects of Shaw's two-year stay. "Let's be realistic," Artiss continued. "Bob Shaw was good for Regina and he fulfilled a couple of promises. He vowed he would give Regina an exciting team to watch and that he would put people in the park. In those two respects, he exceeded beyond all expectations."

Artiss' conclusion: "Make no mistake, this is now Eagle Keys' team and he deserves credit for any success it has. But there can be a thank you for Bob Shaw who brought players such as Lancaster, Campbell and Reed to Regina during his regime."

But Shaw never had the luxury of deploying anyone like Ed McQuarters. Despite being 6-foot-1 and 255 pounds, the newly arrived Roughriders defensive tackle ran like a halfback. For his CFL debut, he was inflicted upon the Argonauts and registered one of the Roughriders' five sacks to help them win 23-7.

Saskatchewan's offensive line cleared the way for the home side to rush for 264 yards. Afterward, Argonauts defensive tackle Dave Still singled out centre Ted Urness, although not by name. "Who the heck is that Number 43?" Still asked. "Boy, did he drill me a few times. He's sure tough — real tough! In fact, their whole line is."

Meanwhile, George Reed was savouring the outcome. The Saskatchewan fullback had dented Toronto for 172 yards on 29 carries. In two games against Shaw — a coach he disliked — Reed had rushed for 340 yards, including a 168-yard effort in 1965.

The second reunion with Shaw had exacted a toll. Reed emerged from the game with a charley horse and a sore arm — injuries that did not heal in time for the Roughriders' annual twin-bill in Eastern Conference cities. Despite the discomfort, Reed made the trip.

"He played through pain," Ron Lancaster recalled. "He was always slow getting off the field anyway, but I remember one time that Ed Buchanan came into the huddle and said, 'Don't give George the ball. He's hurt.' I said, 'Bullshit. If he's hurt, he won't be in the game.' I gave him the ball and he went 32 yards for a touchdown, so he wasn't hurt too bad, was he?

"George and I and everyone in the locker room used to laugh and say, 'There's no sense getting hurt. You've got to play, anyway.' He didn't believe in not playing. George played through a lot of pain a lot of times, but in those days that was the name of the game. You didn't have a very big roster. Durability was such a trait. If you didn't have the durability, you weren't going to play — you just weren't — and they would get rid of you."

George Reed | Photo courtesy of John Solilo, Solilo Studios

Given his resume, Reed would have been forgiven for missing a game or three, and surely would not have ceded his starting spot. But the larger question was this: Would Reed have forgiven himself for not wearing the Green and White? The CFL's outstanding player for 1965 would not be out, standing, if at all possible.

"I always felt that if I could manage to get on the football field, that I would play and I wouldn't hurt the team by playing," Reed said. "It was kind of self-protection, I guess. I always felt that if I didn't give another running back a chance to show what he could do, he couldn't take my job. That's the way I approached training camp and everything else — that I had to fight for my job every day. I always felt that it was time to play. I felt that if they can hit it, I can tape it up, so let's play.

"Yeah, I had a lot of aches and so forth. I can remember one time that we played B.C. and I pulled a hamstring. It was probably the only time that I ever pulled a hamstring. I could hardly walk. Sandy Archer, the trainer, taped it up. He said, 'Just go out and jog and see what you can do.' So I went out there and I couldn't do much. I came back in and said, 'If you tape it this way, I think I can play.' He taped it the way I wanted it to be taped and I think I gained 142 or 145 yards in that game. They had to almost carry me off the field at the end of the game, but I played through that. I guess I could tolerate pain."

Over 13 seasons in Saskatchewan, Reed missed only five games — one in 1964 and four in 1970. "You name it, he had it, and he played," Archer marvelled. "He wasn't going to quit." But even for Reed, the pain could become intolerable. That was the situation he and the Roughriders faced as they prepared to embark for their annual Eastern Conference swing.

Other circumstances pained one of the Roughriders as the Eastern trip loomed. Offensive lineman Tom Beynon, who had been acquired from the Hamilton Tiger-Cats near midseason, was facing an agonizing decision. Would he have to leave the Roughriders so soon after arriving?

Hamilton had selected Beynon in the first round of the 1965 CFL draft. Having just completed an engineering degree at Queen's University in Kingston, Ont., Beynon enrolled in law school at the University of Western Ontario in London. The first year of law classes left him broke. To cover the costs of continued education, he tried pro football. When the Roughriders picked up Beynon, he inquired as to whether he could transfer to the University of Saskatchewan's law school. That application was denied. "What to do now?" Beynon wondered. "One year of law school completed, two to go, and not enough money saved from the summer jobs to complete the second year."

Beynon proceeded to meet with William Carrothers, dean of law at Western Ontario, and they figured out how many games he would have to play with Saskatchewan to earn enough money for Year 2 of law school. "While I loved football, my first goal was to complete my law education, and I was blinded by my passion to achieve that goal," Beynon reflected in writing 40 years later.

Carrothers and Beynon concluded that the 25-year-old lineman's football income would enable him to accumulate the sufficient funds by Sept. 24, when the Roughriders were to play in Hamilton. The arduous Eastern swing also included a game two days later against the Ottawa Rough Riders. Carrothers reached the following compromise with Beynon: He would be registered at Western Ontario for the fall semester and able to resume his law studies on the condition that he was in class Sept. 27 — the morning after the game in Ottawa. Beynon promptly embarked for Regina, fully anticipating an abbreviated stay.

Although Beynon was used primarily on special teams, he quickly developed a special attachment to Saskatchewan. "The Riders were in first place," he wrote. "All of the fabulous Rider fans in the province were certain that a Grey Cup would be on the mantle by Christmas. It was a dream come true, playing professional football, and playing for the first-place team in the Canadian West. It was a privilege to play with the star players that were not only household names in Saskatchewan, but throughout Canada.

"To put it in perspective, it was probably like being in Green Bay in their glory years, and we had Eagle Keys as our head coach. He was our Vince Lombardi. He was our rock. Jim Duncan and Jack Gotta were our assistant coaches. The three of them were a team within a team and they collectively made the players all play better to achieve the magical goal.

"Sitting with Dean Carrothers some weeks before, the decision seemed dead easy. It was a money decision. I had never been to Regina. There was no passion for the Saskatchewan Roughriders. I had never met a player. But now, some weeks later, things were different. Regina and Saskatchewan were a part of me, as were the greatest teammates in the world. The players and their families were all so good to me. I was like a brother or a son. I was family."

Beynon's excitement over playing in Saskatchewan was mitigated by the knowledge that he was to return to Western Ontario two months before the Grey Cup. "I became concerned about my ever-growing conflict and the script that I had written that I was now committed to act out," Beynon wrote. "You see, playing football in Canada is special. However, being a player on the Saskatchewan Roughriders was as good as it gets."

But the clock was ticking. On Sept. 19, Beynon and offensive-line cohort Jack Abendschan went for dinner and a few refreshments. "While I enjoyed the evening, my mind was in other places — namely, 'How could I continue to play for the Roughriders and go to law school?' " Beynon wrote. "It just didn't seem possible. Jack noticed something was different and commented a couple of times, 'What's wrong?' After the second or third time, I asked Jack if he could keep a secret. And after being assured that Jack would keep what I told him a secret, the story began."

Beynon's message was succinct and sombre: "Jack, when we go east this weekend, I am not coming back." Those words, followed by Beynon's explanation, shocked Abendschan. "Tom, you are crazy," he responded. "We are in first place in the West, we are going to the Grey Cup, and we are going to win it."

Beynon went on to experience a restless night. At practice the following day, Abendschan periodically shook his head at him. That evening, Abendschan and Beynon returned to the now-defunct Golden West nightclub on south Albert Street. "Around midnight, a well-dressed person that Jack knew came over and joined our table," Beynon remembered. "Jack introduced me to Mr. Harold Pick, a lawyer in Regina — a great fan of Saskatchewan, and a great fan of the Saskatchewan Roughriders."

After some small talk, Pick said to Beynon, "Oh, aren't you the kid from the east that didn't want to go to law school out here?" Beynon could feel his temperature rising. "Not likely," he growled at Pick. "I wanted to transfer to the law school in Saskatoon. However, they didn't think that the commute from Regina was something that a student could undertake and go to school and play football as well." More small talk ensued. Pick finished his drink, got up, and said to Beynon, "If you really want to try to get into the law school, be at my office at five o'clock this morning and we will talk about it." Pick gave

Beynon a business card and said good night. An astonished Beynon looked across the table at Abendschan. "Sounds like maybe you've got a friend that might be able to help you," Abendschan said with a knowing smile.

Beynon returned to his room at the La Salle Hotel — a popular haunt for the players in those days — and implored the night watchman to make sure he was awake by 4:30 a.m., which was only two hours away. A sleep-deprived Beynon arrived at Pick's law office at 4:50. Pick surfaced at the appointed time. Pick, a prominent member of the Law Society of Saskatchewan, told Beynon he would attempt to broker the transfer to the U of S. Beynon signed an agreement that specified he would travel to Saskatoon to attend as many law classes as possible during football season, and that a spotless attendance record would be maintained (except for illness) during the offseason.

A few hours later, Beynon left for football practice, still uncertain about his future with the Roughriders. "I closed my eyes and dreamed, 'Could it possibly happen? Could I stay in Saskatchewan and be on a Grey Cup team with such a great group of guys?' " he wondered.

As the workout ended, Pick approached the practice field and said to Beynon, "You're in. You've been accepted. Classes start tomorrow." Pick had talked to Otto Lang, dean of the U of S law school, who had considered the matter with the admissions committee before approving Beynon's application. "Jack was standing behind me with a grin from ear to ear," a grateful Beynon concluded. "He was the author of my good fortune."

Buoyed by the knowledge that his return to Eastern Canada would only be temporary, Tom Beynon boarded a Toronto-bound flight with his Roughriders teammates on Sept. 23, 1966. The following day, the Roughriders were to visit the Hamilton Tiger-Cats, before playing in Ottawa against the Rough Riders 48 hours later.

Trips east were taxing at the best of times. The timing of this excursion was especially unfortunate for the Roughriders, given the discomfort George Reed was enduring. Saskatchewan's star fullback entered the Hamilton game with a charley horse and a sore arm. Compounding matters, Reed suffered a leg injury on the opening play and carried the football only five times against the Tiger-Cats. The injury woes were exacerbated when guard Al Benecick suffered a sprained ankle and linebacker Wayne Shaw strained knee ligaments during the Roughriders' 29-7 loss at Ivor Wynne Stadium.

Next stop: Ottawa. Benecick's troublesome ankle forced him to miss his first game since 1961. To fill the void at guard, linebacker Ken Reed was employed on both sides of the ball during the first half against the Rough Riders. For the second half, linebacker Cliff Shaw was moved to guard, enabling Reed to concentrate on defence. Wayne Shaw, Cliff's older brother, played despite strained knee ligaments.

The Roughriders also transmitted an emergency call for a defensive tackle. Moe Levesque had injured his back in Hamilton, rendering him unavailable for the Ottawa game. Saskatchewan urgently summoned Buddy-Joe Eilers, who had been cut a week earlier. Eilers had resurfaced in the Continental Football League, trying out for the Brooklyn Dodgers.

When Eilers heard the Roughriders' plea, he flew back to Canada and landed in Ottawa four hours before the game.

The circumstances were aligned against Saskatchewan, which did not utilize George Reed until he was called upon for blocking purposes in the fourth quarter. In light of all the adversity, it was difficult to imagine the Roughriders beating Ottawa. As expected, the eastern Riders prevailed, 18-8. Despite the defeat, head coach Eagle Keys praised his players for their "grit and guts" and noted that "our guys played a courageous game." Saskatchewan was still within three points until late in the game, when Gene Gaines intercepted Lancaster. On the final play, Ottawa padded the score with a touchdown run by Bo Scott.

Saskatchewan's lone touchdown was courtesy of an 18-yard pass from Lancaster to Hugh Campbell. Gluey Hughie's 15th touchdown catch left him one shy of the CFL's single-season record, established by the Winnipeg Blue Bombers' Ernie Pitts in 1959.

Also worth noting, **statistically**, was an 85-yard rushing performance by third-year Roughrider Henry Dorsch. With Reed sidelined for most of the Ottawa game, Dorsch carried the ball 14 times. Two days earlier in Hamilton, Dorsch had gained 54 yards on six rushes.

Dorsch's ball-carrying ability, while infrequently tapped by the Roughriders, should not have come as a surprise. He was the leading rusher at the University of Tulsa in 1962 and 1963. Even so, Dorsch was handed the football only 11 times — he gained 55 yards — over the 1964 and 1965 CFL seasons.

Like teammate Alan Ford, Dorsch was appreciated for his versatility. Much of his time with the Roughriders was spent in the defensive secondary or at linebacker. Dorsch was accustomed to the workload, having played in the offensive and defensive backfields at Tulsa. While at the Oklahoma university, Dorsch got to know legendary Roughriders quarterback Glenn Dobbs. He was the athletic director when Dorsch arrived in Tulsa, but became the head coach in 1961 when his brother Bobby was named the Calgary Stampeders' field boss.

As the head coach at Tulsa, Glenn Dobbs installed a pass-oriented offence, as was expected from someone who had thrown a team-record 28 touchdown passes for Saskatchewan in 1951. "He was a great ambassador for football up here," Dorsch said. "He really promoted it and the fans loved him. He was a real personable guy. He'd get out there and talk to the people. On the field, he was the coach and he was a tough coach. I didn't talk to him that much about when he played in Saskatchewan. He was more concerned about me going to class."

The Weyburn-born Dorsch did not take a direct route to Tulsa. He played one season of junior football with the Regina Rams before enrolling at the University of Denver. "Denver was a hockey school, but when I got down there, all of a sudden I realized that, 'Hey, I'm just as good as these guys.'" Dorsch said. "I ended up being team captain my freshman year and then they dropped football. We had a line coach, Bo Bollinger. He was an All-American at Oklahoma. He took 10 members of that freshman class to Tulsa because Dobbs hired him.

I was the only one who graduated. You talk about tough. Dobbs used to say, 'You're not going to be as good as the teams you play, but we're going to out-condition them in the fourth quarter,' and we did win a lot of games that way."

Tulsa won despite playing some of the top teams in NCAA football. "Dobbs scheduled teams like Alabama, Georgia, Georgia Tech, Tennessee and Arkansas," Dorsch said. "We had one hell of a schedule. I still remember the first game against Tennessee in their stadium. It was a bleak, dismal day. Tennessee had what looked like a Roman forum and they ran the old single-wing — student body left, student body right. It was just like throwing Christians to the lions. We hung in there and they finally beat us, but it was brutal.

"I had never played in front of a crowd of 50,000 or 60,000 people. They introduced us and the crowd just went, 'BOOOO!' That's the last time I ever heard a crowd. It did intimidate me a bit, but that was the last time. Even in Taylor Field, the only thing I'd ever hear was when we came off the field. If we had scored a touchdown or shut them down, there would be the applause then, but I'd never, ever hear the crowd after that. You have to get that out of your mind."

Henry Dorsch | Photo courtesy of SSHFM

Other aspects of top-level NCAA competition are easier and more enjoyable to retain. While playing against Alabama, Dorsch intercepted Joe Namath, who went on to become a Super Bowl-winning quarterback with the New York Jets. Instead of gloating about the play, Dorsch notes that "Joe Namath, for a sophomore, was pretty polished." But he had every reason to relish the fact that Joe Namath, superstar, once threw an interception to Henry Dorsch from Weyburn, Saskatchewan.

CHAPTER 14 | # "WRECKING EVERYBODY'S HOUSE"

For anyone who craved anonymity, there were two excellent options: (1) Enter the Witness Protection Program; or, (2) Toil in obscurity as Ron Lancaster's backup. As the Saskatchewan Roughriders reached the October stretch run of their 1966 regular-season schedule, Lancaster had not missed a play in two years.

That all changed during the second quarter of an Oct. 2 home game against Winnipeg. As the Roughriders' quarterback was preparing to unload a long pass, he was trapped behind the line of scrimmage. Worse yet, Lancaster suffered a sprained right ankle and was forced to leave the game. With Lancaster shelved, Roughriders head coach Eagle Keys turned to Plan B — Plan BB, actually, given that Bruce Bennett was next in line.

Bennett was not strictly a quarterback. Although he took some repetitions behind centre during practices, most of his time was spent concentrating on the starting safety's duties. By making the safety the understudy at quarterback, the Roughriders were able to save an import roster spot — which was important in an era when CFL teams were allowed to dress only 32 players.

In Lancaster's absence, the Roughriders fared as well as could be expected against Winnipeg. They salvaged an 11-11 tie thanks to Jack Abendschan's 52-yard field goal at 7:45 of the fourth quarter. Earlier, Bennett was able to direct a touchdown drive, which culminated when he sneaked over from the one-yard line. The major was set up by a 71-yard run by George Reed.

"In the huddle, I think it was Reggie Whitehouse who said, 'Bruce, I know you're a rookie, but when they line up in a certain defence, you need to check off and give the ball to George on a certain play,' " Bennett recalled. "I said, 'OK.' Probably the next play, they line up in that defensive front. I checked off and gave the ball to George. George runs about 70 yards and they catch him. We come back and run the quarterback sneak and I score. After the game, one of the reporters said, 'George runs the ball 70 yards and you get it on the one-yard line and you run it in.' I said, 'Yeah. My high school coach always told me that when you get into scoring territory, always give the ball to your best back.' George just rolled over laughing. I couldn't pass that up."

The Roughriders couldn't pass, period, with Lancaster unavailable. All four of Bennett's passes fell incomplete. A series of running plays that produced three first downs put Saskatchewan in position for Abendschan's game-tying field goal. "I'm sure I didn't call all the plays that Ron did, but I had a few plays that I could call," said Bennett, who ran the option effectively against Winnipeg. "I was limited. They didn't want to harm anybody."

Bennett was anything but limited as a quarterback in the early 1960s. He quarterbacked Valdosta (Ga.) High School to undefeated records and state championships in his junior and senior years — earning high school All-American honours in Grade 12 while also playing in the defensive backfield. In Bennett's high school football finale, he was the victorious quarterback in the state championship game despite burning his right (throwing) hand in a kitchen accident at home the day before.

Bennett was courted by the University of Florida, where he played quarterback and safety on the freshman team. He made the varsity squad as a sophomore, starting at safety and backing up at quarterback. When Bennett was a junior, the NCAA enacted a platoon system that prevented players from seeing duty on both sides of the ball. The Florida coaches opted to keep Bennett at safety because of his success at that position, and because they had a sophomore quarterback named Steve Spurrier, who would win the Heisman Trophy in 1966.

Entrenched as a safety, Bennett was named an All-American in 1964 and 1965. Based on those glittering credentials, it was reasonable to expect National Football League and American Football League franchises to be salivating over him. However, his size (or lack thereof) was a deterrent. The most-enticing offer for the 5-foot-10, 175-pounder came from Saskatchewan. "The St. Louis Cardinals invited me up to play there, but the Roughriders offered me more money than the Cardinals did," Bennett said. "At the time, the exchange was weighted in

Bruce Bennett | Photo courtesy of *Leader-Post* archives favour of the Canadian dollar, so I figured I was making a lot more money by going to Canada. It was several thousand dollars in bonus and a little in the contract. It was like $12,000, and I thought, 'I'm stealing from them.' Times have changed a little bit."

The rare injury to Ron Lancaster incited panic among the Roughriders' faithful. "So many people were calling the football club office for information that head coach Eagle Keys fled the place in terror," the *Leader-Post's* Laurie Artiss reported. "Trainer Sandy Archer was busy fielding phone calls and several were from people suggesting salves, sure-cures and the latest heat treatments. The concern is appreciated, but let all know that Lancaster is receiving the best of medical treatment."

Lancaster's right ankle had been placed in a cast after the Winnipeg game. His chances of playing in an Oct. 8 home game against Calgary were listed as "real remote" by Keys. With Lancaster in plaster, Bennett received a crash course in quarterbacking, CFL style. Import Mike Ringer was activated to back up Bennett at quarterback and play in the defensive backfield. Bennett's safety position was to be filled by Dale West, who had been in and out of the lineup due to a dislocated shoulder.

Even without Lancaster, it appeared the Roughriders had a chance to win on home turf. They led 16-15 before Calgary head coach Jerry Williams opted to replace struggling quarterback Jerry Keeling with Peter Liske. Liske proceeded to complete 15 of 18 passes for 194 yards and three touchdowns in the fourth quarter, powering Calgary to a 35-18 victory.

Bennett completed seven of 11 passes for 29 yards, with one touchdown (on a short toss to tight end Jim Worden) and an interception. Ringer was 2-for-4 for 18 yards. "The Riders went without the major threat of the pass," Laurie Artiss wrote. "Oh, they still had the pass in their arsenal, but it was more of a pop-gun than a bomb. It was simply too much to expect Bruce Bennett to 'read' when he hadn't had too many spelling lessons. He played as well as many rookie pro quarterbacks and better than some, but it was glaringly evident the position is so difficult that nobody walks in as an immediate success."

Linebacker Wayne Shaw played a key role in both Roughriders touchdowns — the first of which came when he returned an interception 32 yards. He also recovered a Keeling fumble and lugged the football to the 11-yard line to put Saskatchewan in position for Worden's major. The Roughriders emerged from the game with a 7-5-1 record, which gave them a four-point cushion atop the Western Conference. Despite the first-place standing, a four-game winless skid (consisting of three losses and a tie) created cause for concern.

The condition of a key leader — Ron Lancaster — continued to be a piping-hot topic as the Roughriders prepared for an Oct. 15 game in Vancouver against the B.C. Lions. Lancaster provided reassurance in mid-week when he said the sprained ankle is "the best it has felt since the injury." By no means was it close to 100 per cent, but it was apparent that a limited Lancaster was vastly superior to an unscathed backup.

Once game day arrived, Lancaster was again accepting snaps from Ted Urness. Artiss noted that Lancaster was "operating gingerly — but not slowly — on the most-talked-about ankle since 19th-century ladies first revealed theirs." The Roughriders limped out of the gate

Wayne Shaw | Photo courtesy of *Leader-Post* archives

at Empire Stadium, incurring a 14-0 deficit before rallying to create a 14-14 tie. In the third quarter, Saskatchewan outgained the Lions 153 yards to zero, but its point production consisted of a rouge that gave the visitors a 15-14 lead. Saskatchewan expanded its advantage to 22-14 when Jack Abendschan converted Henry Dorsch's two-yard touchdown run at 1:54 of the fourth quarter. The Lions responded with a Bill Munsey scoring run that narrowed the gap to 22-20. Bill Mitchell missed the convert. It had been that kind of year for Mitchell — at least against Saskatchewan.

In Week 3 of the regular season, Saskatchewan won 16-14 at Taylor Field after Mitchell came up short on a 50-yard field-goal attempt with no time remaining. A 50-yarder is a difficult kick, but Mitchell owned the CFL record for longest field goal — having connected from 58 yards away in 1964 while with the Edmonton Eskimos. Mitchell also lined up for a potential game-winning field goal on Aug. 28 at Empire Stadium, only to have Dale West block a 35-yard attempt on the final play to preserve Saskatchewan's 30-29 lead.

Mitchell had a chance for redemption in the teams' third meeting of 1966. Joe Kapp marched the Lions 73 yards in 10 plays — the last of which was a quarterback keeper that put B.C. directly in front of the uprights. Mitchell was then called upon to attempt a 32-yarder. The kick, while close, curled wide of the right upright. Gene Wlasiuk fielded the football in the end zone and exhausted the remaining seconds before conceding a meaningless single. Saskatchewan won, 22-21.

"Those close to the care and feeding of Mitchell should make certain that no sharp instruments are left lying around loose lest the exasperated kicker chooses to end it all," Laurie Artiss wrote after the Roughriders completed a three-game season sweep of the Lions, who lost by a combined four points.

The bizarre scheduling of the day called for the Lions to return to action only two days after playing host to the Roughriders. Despite a lack of recuperative and preparatory time — and with a road trip complicating matters — the Lions defeated Calgary 13-9. Five points from Bill Mitchell were a key factor in the B.C. victory, which enabled Saskatchewan to clinch top spot in the West for the first time since 1951.

First place was significant to all concerned, but especially to the veteran Roughriders who had experienced tougher times. Defensive lineman Garner Ekstran, for example, had joined the team in 1961, when it finished with a 5-10-1 record.

"It meant so much for those who remained from those teams to be able to stick together and be part of the team that turned things around," Ekstran reflected. "We really saw the other end of it. Even in '61, as bad as we were, there were so many fans who sat on the grass right on the sidelines. That was a great feeling, knowing that fans appreciated what we were trying to do, anyway. One thing I always felt about the fans is that it didn't matter if we won or lost, as long as the other team got hurt playing you."

Ask anyone on the 1966 Roughriders why that team was successful and he will inevitably cite camaraderie as a contributing factor. "We used to say that the team that drinks together, wins together — and there's some truth in that," Ekstran said. "We'd take a drink once in a while. It was a team deal."

When the team convened after games, there was but one stipulation. "We had a rule — and I don't want to say it was a hard-and-fast rule — but the way the players understood it was that you had to make an appearance at the party, especially if you lost," Lancaster said. "Everyone had to go. You didn't have to stay, but you needed to make an appearance and say hello to everybody and then you could go on your way. That's a sign of a pretty good team, when guys were willing to do that."

The gatherings were initially held at a player's residence. "We did that for a few years before we started wrecking everybody's house," Lancaster said with a chuckle. "Then we figured out that we should just collect money from all the players at the beginning of the season. We used to have our parties at the Vagabond, I believe it was. That way, somebody's wife didn't have to order food and didn't have to go to all that extra work and we didn't have to worry about busting up somebody's house, but there were some great parties. We had one at our place one time. Ed Buchanan had his electric guitar down in the basement. My neighbours never heard so much noise."

Not all Roughriders parties resembled *Animal House*. "They weren't wild and crazy," defensive lineman Don Gerhardt remembered. "They were fun, and that's what built part of our team. We went to somebody's house and sat with each other and danced with each other and just had a ball. It was really cool. That doesn't happen anymore, anywhere. Small groups will break up and go out. We did it all together. It really was fun."

As lives and careers progressed, the fun times continued to resonate with the players. "When you get all done and you look back on your career, if you remember the practices, you're sick," Lancaster said. "Games? You're only going to remember one or two. But the thing you're going to remember is the fun you had with the guys in the locker room, on the buses, in the hotels, and the camaraderie. What made it even better with these guys is so many of us lived here in Regina and we got to be with one another year-round. We used to play a lot of basketball together and things like that and party in the wintertime. It was a good situation for everybody."

Some of the parties were hosted by the genial giant, Clyde Brock, who joined the Roughriders during the 1964 season. "When I came to Canada, they weighed me in and I was 263 pounds," the 6-foot-5 offensive tackle remembered. "I was probably one of the biggest players in Canada. Now, my goodness, you have running backs who are 263 pounds — although maybe not in Canada. Now, 263 pounds is very small for an offensive lineman. That was what I weighed when I first got there. That's not what I was when I left. That's another story."

Brock made his pro football debut in 1962 with the NFL's Dallas Cowboys, who were coached by the stoic Tom Landry. "I'm not going to say he was not very friendly, but players didn't get too friendly with him," Brock said. "If we were standing in the hall talking and the word came that Landry was coming, everyone would scurry into the rooms and shut the doors. There was a lot of respect for the man, but he didn't let

Clyde Brock | Photo courtesy of *Leader-Post* archives

himself get real attached or friendly with the ballplayers. Later on, things changed with his attitude towards players and with players' attitudes towards him. He mellowed out a little bit more, I think."

The towering Brock played under the future Hall of Fame coach for all of 1962 and for seven games in 1963, before finishing that season with the San Francisco 49ers. When Brock was released by San Francisco in 1964, 49ers line coach Bill (Tiger) Johnson contacted a friend — then-Roughriders head coach Bob Shaw — with a well-placed tip. Brock promptly received a call from Shaw, who extended an invitation to join the Roughriders. Brock was initially inclined to join the Houston Oilers, who held his American Football League rights. "I was supposed to meet Houston in Las Vegas, where they were playing an exhibition game, but I thought I'd go to Canada," Brock said. "I had never been to Canada and I wanted to see what it was like. I figured it would be kind of fun, so we threw everything in the car and took off."

Shaw wasted little time in finding a spot for Brock on the Roughriders' offensive line, which was developing into one of the CFL's best units. The following year, Brock was named a Western Conference all-star for the first of five consecutive seasons. However, accolades were not always received from his head coach. Eagle Keys, who succeeded Shaw in 1965, saw that

Brock had potential and size in abundance. "Eagle always felt that he had to put a fire under my butt or something like that," the four-time All-Canadian said. "He and I had a couple of real words — nothing serious at all. Eagle was a good coach. There was no problem at all." Nonetheless, Keys kept pushing Brock, who chuckles at one memory: "Hugh Campbell said one time, 'Clyde, you're the only guy Eagle threatens to cut every year, and you always make the all-star team.'"

When the CFL's 1966 all-star teams were announced late in the season, almost half the Roughriders' starters were decorated. Eleven Saskatchewan players — the most in franchise history — were league or Western Conference all-stars.

The All-Canadians from Saskatchewan were fullback George Reed, flanker Hugh Campbell, offensive linemen Ted Urness, Al Benecick and Clyde Brock, and tight end Jim Worden. Benecick was named an all-star offensive tackle even though he played guard. The West team included Roughriders representatives Ron Lancaster (quarterback), Jack Abendschan (in a tie for a guard position), Bob Kosid (defensive back), Wayne Shaw (linebacker) and Garner Ekstran (defensive end).

The topic of individual laurels generated considerable debate as the 1966 regular season drew to a close. One particularly intriguing question was: Who was the Roughriders' most outstanding player? Compelling cases could be made for Lancaster, Campbell and Reed — all of whom were once again enjoying superlative seasons.

Reed rushed for 1,409 yards in 1966 despite missing most of two games due to injuries. Without Reed to power the offence, Saskatchewan lost both those games — road dates with the Hamilton Tiger-Cats and Ottawa Rough Riders. Reed's productivity was comparable to that of 1965 when he was healthy.

Campbell, meanwhile, caught six touchdown passes over the first two games en route to leading the league in regular-season scoring. Late in the season, another popular question was whether Campbell would be able to establish a CFL single-season record for touchdown receptions. He had 15 scoring grabs — one shy of the record — with two weeks remaining in regular-season play. Of course, Campbell could not have enjoyed such a sensational season without Lancaster's passing and play-calling. When the regular season concluded, Lancaster was the league's leader in touchdown passes (28), completion percentage (60.0) and average gain per pass (9.8).

With two games remaining in the regular season, the league announced that Lancaster was the Western Conference's nominee for most outstanding player. His competition for the league's award was a former teammate — Ottawa quarterback Russ Jackson.

Who would win?

Who should win?

It all made for a spirited debate on Regina's coffee row.

CHAPTER **15** # "JUST A NICE PLACE TO LIVE"

Coffee row, as denizens of Regina's sporting community once knew it, disappeared long ago. The Roughriders will always generate plenty of discussion, but Regina is missing the central establishment to visit for the latest gossip or the liveliest discourse. In the 1960s, there was little debate as to the location of the conversation. The La Salle Hotel was always abuzz.

"That's where the guys used to meet," Roughriders guard Al Benecick recalled. "Guys used to meet there for lunch or after a game or go there for a beer, especially if there was a victory. That was the place in downtown where you went if you wanted to know what was going on football-wise. It was where all the gossip was. Now it's different. The whole damn downtown has changed."

Benecick still lives in downtown Regina, not too far from where he resided in the 1960s. "I was living at the Kitchener Hotel, which no longer exists," he said. "The manager and his wife were the nicest people you'd ever want to meet. We didn't play football on Sundays [until 1966]. Everything was closed on Sundays — bar-rooms, movies. Sunday was God's day. I always had an open invitation to go to their house for dinner. Not only that, the room was spic and span and it cost $30 per month. The bed was made. The room was vacuumed. The toilets were cleaned. What more can you ask for? It was so welcoming. It felt like home. Hell, I didn't even get that at home. Somebody taking care of you for $30 a month? God ... a dollar a day. Of course, we had quite a few of the boys staying there, aside from the ones who were married and stayed home."

Some of the landmarks remain in downtown Regina. The Hotel Saskatchewan is as stately as ever. The Old City Hall is now a place to shop and watch live theatre. But

Hamilton Street, where the La Salle Hotel once stood, is often tranquil. Simpsons department store and its window displays are but a memory. Until 1964, the *Leader-Post* and CKCK Radio were located on the east side of Hamilton Street, across from the La Salle Hotel.

"And there was Whistling Willie on the corner of 11th and Hamilton," Dale West said of Willie Greer, a former Regina police constable. "He made sure everyone obeyed the traffic rules and walked on the right side of the crosswalk when they were crossing the street. I don't know if he ever fined anybody, but he whistled a lot. At the La Salle, everybody knew you. You certainly didn't go there to hide from people. You could have 20 conversations in there. A lot of the ballplayers hung out there — plus, the La Salle had a good bar. It was always an interesting place to be, let's put it that way."

So was Taylor Field. In 1966, when the Roughriders had a home game, it was common for the stadium to house one out of every six people who were in Regina. "You could go from one side of town to the next in 10 minutes," said West's defensive-backfield cohort, Bob Kosid. "Just go down Albert Street. It was very small. It was very local. I remember when Whitmore Park was under construction. Now you go out there and you can be halfway to Moose Jaw before you know it. Back in those days, Regina was a town of about 110,000 people. It was very local, very colloquial. People were just good ol' folks."

Entertainment options were scarce by today's standards. The Centre of the Arts (now Conexus Arts Centre) was still a few years away from opening. Exhibition Stadium — which was considered antiquated even in the 1960s — was Regina's primary hockey arena and rock concert venue. Multi-screen movie theatres were unheard of in Regina, much like the concept of selling a stadium's naming rights to a corporation. Cable television would not arrive until 1978. Conversations were more direct, and often one-on-one. The Internet? E-mail? Text-messaging? Facebook? Cellular phones? iPods? BlackBerrys? Twitter? Who could have envisioned those in an era when coffee row was the popular place to gather or exchange information?

When was the last time the Roughriders' starting quarterback was listed in the telephone directory? "I was in the phone book all the while I was in Regina," said Ron Lancaster, who became a year-round resident in 1965, following two seasons with the Roughriders. "As soon as we bought a house there and moved to Emerald Park Road, we were in the phone book. Every now and then somebody would call at 2:30 or 3 in the morning. Bev had the phone on her side and she'd answer the phone. They'd always ask if I was there and she'd say, 'No, he went to work.' It was really never a problem."

Rob Bresciani can attest to that. "Ronnie's phone number was in the book, so I would call him," Bresciani, a member of the 1988 and 1989 Roughriders, said while flashing back to his childhood. "He would always come to the phone and sound interested in me. He would ask, 'What do you do?' He never once said, 'I'm busy.' I probably phoned him three or four times. He made you feel important. I'd say to him, 'You're my favourite player and I love the Riders.' He would ask if I played football, what position I played and how I was doing. Those are things you don't forget."

Rodger Milliken has a similar recollection. Milliken and his friends used to visit the south-end Regina homes of Lancaster, George Reed, Bob Kosid and Ed McQuarters to get autographs. "I think the wives were accustomed to young autograph seekers, as they just let us in," Milliken said. "Ed McQuarters answered the front door." As Milliken recalled, Lancaster would even throw passes to the youngsters on the front lawn.

Lancaster was as big a name as will ever inhabit the city. He quickly became a revered Roughrider but, to many people, he was simply a neighbour, a coach or a phys. ed teacher. "I never looked at it as any big deal," he said. "I went to work at teaching school just like everybody else went to their jobs. I just happened to play football on the side.

"People there were good people. Our kids enjoyed it there. I never was one where if you're losing, you didn't go out. We still went out to eat and we still went to the show and we still went downtown. I don't ever believe in hiding when you're not winning, because that has nothing to do with you as a person. That just happens to be something you do for a living, playing football. We always went out with the other players and their wives. We followed the kids, whether Lana was cheerleading or Bob and Ronnie were playing basketball or hockey or football or baseball. I coached some baseball, too. It was just a nice place to live."

This much has not changed: The Roughriders are still the major celebrities in town. In the 1960s, as in the 21st century, the players talked about life in the fishbowl. The levels of recognizability and scrutiny were high. "Wherever you went, you were under the microscope," Kosid said. "I remember listening to Eagle Keys describing what it was like to be the coach of the Saskatchewan Roughriders. He said you have 50,000 assistant coaches."

Life under the microscope had its drawbacks, as it does today, but there were also some perks to the prominence. "Let me give you an example," Kosid began. "I was at the Hotel Saskatchewan. I had too much to drink. I was driving down Albert Street towards home. A policeman pulls me over. I get out of the car and it happened to be icy. I landed on my butt, so I lay on my back, look up at him, and hand him my licence. He said, 'Come on, Bobby. I'll put you in the car. We're going to get you home.' Anywhere else, I'd have been in jail for six months. That was the bright side.

"We'd go to the Molson House, and you could get away with murder there, but then you had to leave. We'd celebrate our victories and/or defeats but, in the same sense of the word, the rest of the time you had to work within the community. I know I did. Because of the nature, I sort of liked it. I didn't take it as being a pain in the butt. I said, 'This is really nice.' I came from Chicago. I liked that peace and comfort of knowing that I could walk down any street in Regina and not be accosted or shot at."

Saskatchewan's final regular-season home game of 1966 was played on a Saturday night before 13,591 shivering spectators — or 13,592, if you count the canine component. The *Leader-Post* published a photograph of Hugh Campbell carrying a stray dog off the field. The caption: "Campbell can catch anything ... 16th touchdown and a dog."

The Roughriders had reached the dog days of the regular season, having clinched first place in the Western Conference with two games remaining before the playoffs. Securing top spot would mean a first-round bye. As a result, the team went almost a month — from Oct. 15 to Nov. 13 — without facing a situation where losing had dire consequences.

As the Roughriders refined their game for the playoffs, the main curiosity pertained to whether Campbell could establish a CFL single-season record for touchdown receptions. Gluey Hughie claimed a share of the record by making one scoring grab in a 33-21 loss to the visiting Edmonton Eskimos on Oct. 22, 1966.

The record-tying catch came with 1:19 remaining in the game, when Lancaster hit Campbell from eight yards away on third down. Lancaster re-entered the game after understudy Mike Ringer, who was inserted after the Eskimos put the game out of reach, had thrown incompletions on first and second downs. Campbell's 16th touchdown grab of the season — his first in 26 days — enabled him to catch Ernie Pitts, who set the record with the 1959 Winnipeg Blue Bombers.

Lancaster threw two other touchdown passes, to Alan Ford and Gord Barwell. That was pretty much the extent of the highlights for the Roughriders, who spotted Edmonton a 28-0 lead. "We were lousy," head coach Eagle Keys said after the game. "I guess it might be natural for that mental letdown after clinching first place. It wasn't until we got mad at ourselves, and a little ashamed, that we started playing some football."

There was one more game to play in the regular season — an Oct. 25 appointment with the host Calgary Stampeders. With one victory and one tie to show for their past six games, the Roughriders were in need of some good news. It arrived in the form of an advisory that halfback Ed Buchanan was being reactivated after being sidelined since Week 5 — save for the Labour Day game against Montreal — with strained knee ligaments. Lancaster quickly reincorporated Buchanan into the offence, hitting the speedster with six completions for 123 yards — including an 80-yard bomb that produced one of the Roughriders' three aerial touchdowns in their 28-26 victory. Lancaster also found Barwell and, yes, Campbell for majors.

Campbell made history at 8:17 of the first quarter, when he ran a hook pattern and went to his knees to snare a 13-yard Lancaster aerial. Just like that, Campbell had his league-record 17th touchdown catch. When asked about the achievement 40-plus years later, Campbell responded: "It wasn't really a big deal. Did that happen in '66?"

That was in keeping with Campbell's team-first philosophy. He derived greater satisfaction from the fact that Saskatchewan completed the 1966 regular season on a victorious note, thanks to Jack Abendschan's game-winning 11-yard field goal with 24 seconds remaining.

The Roughriders finished the 1966 regular season with a 9-6-1 record, along with some impressive individual numbers. Lancaster's 28 touchdown passes tied a franchise single-season record, established 15 years earlier by Glenn Dobbs. Reed rushed for 1,409 yards. Campbell caught 66 passes for 1,109 yards while scoring a league-best 102 points. With less fanfare, Gene Wlasiuk was the CFL's leading punt returner — averaging 5.8 yards on 84 returns.

While modest by today's standards, that average was noteworthy because blocking was not permitted on punt returns. Upon fielding the punt, the sitting duck of a returner was facing a one-against-12 predicament. The 5-foot-9, 165-pounder willingly accepted the role, along with the inevitable bruises.

What motivated someone to return punts without blocking? "Stupidity," Wlasiuk replied. "The truth is, I never gave it any special consideration. It was harder to be a running back because you had to follow your blocks. I never had to worry about blockers. They never got in your way. I had a different approach to returning punts. My approach was this: Catch the ball and look for a soft stomach. Everyone thought I was looking for a hole."

Gene Wlasiuk on one of his 524 punt returns as a Rider ... and without blocking | Photo courtesy of SSHFM

One day, Wlasiuk went the whole way. On Aug. 9, 1962, he returned a punt 67 yards for a touchdown — a remarkable feat when you consider the extent to which he was outnumbered — in a 33-7 loss to the host B.C. Lions. "I was named star-of-the-game," Wlasiuk noted. "That's how bad we played."

Wlasiuk returned 524 punts over eight seasons with the Roughriders. Only one of those returns went for a touchdown. "I can tell you exactly how it happened," he said. "Two guys converged on me. Everybody expected them to make the tackle. I managed to avoid them. A big hole opened. I went down the sidelines with everyone chasing me. The kicker was Bob Schloredt. He was chasing me. So was a fast receiver named Mack Burton. I went down the left sideline and literally stutter-stepped them. I hesitated and they kept running. I think Burton went by me three times. I'd slow down, they'd fly past me, and then I'd keep running. Nobody touched me. When I got to the end zone, I wasn't tired at all. It was a nice, slow jaunt."

After scoring the touchdown, Wlasiuk calmly jogged back to the Roughriders' bench, where he was congratulated by head coach Steve Owen. Wlasiuk did not keep the football. "In those days, you didn't do those sorts of things," he said. "You just played the game and went home. You were doing something you were supposed to do. Nobody kept the game ball. The game ball was probably worth more than you were getting paid."

Wlasiuk first earned an income from playing football in 1957, when he joined the Winnipeg Blue Bombers out of the junior ranks. He became a Roughrider in 1959. "I got traded for a helmet and a jockstrap," he said. "I'll be honest. I wasn't sure if it was waivers or a trade. It must have been a trade because waivers in those days were $50. They couldn't afford that, so they traded for me."

Wlasiuk joined a team that would win one game in 1959, and only two times the following year. After that, the Roughriders gradually improved to the point where they finished first in the Western Conference in 1966. "Through that whole era, there was more fun every year," Wlasiuk told the *Leader-Post*'s Arnie Tiefenbach in 1985. "There was no fun in '59 and '60. I mean, how could you have fun? You might have a good practice, but who feels like going into the locker room and joking when you're 1-and-15? It hurts when you lose."

Galen Wahlmeier was hurting for other reasons. During the regular-season finale in Calgary, he damaged ligaments in his left knee. Surgery was prescribed. His season was over. The timing was painful for Wahlmeier, who had endured some of the Roughriders' roughest seasons after joining the team in 1957 out of the University of Kansas. He missed the following season while serving in the United States Army, but returned in 1959 for the glorious one-win season.

By 1966, the Roughriders were a drastically different team. Wahlmeier played in all 16 regular-season games to help Saskatchewan finish atop the Western Conference for the first time since 1951. But then his season ended, abruptly, in a game that did not have an influence on the standings. For the Western Conference playoffs, Wahlmeier's roster spot was taken by Don Bahnuik.

Don Bahnuik |

Galen Wahlmeier |

The Canora product did not suit up for Saskatchewan during the 1966 season, but practised with the team while toiling on the taxi squad. He had spent the previous three seasons playing junior football for the Regina Rams.

"It was pure chance that I ever got a chance to play," said Bahnuik, a defensive lineman. "It was a matter of being in the right place at the right time. A former Roughrider, Pete Martin, was a sales representative for a company that provided supplies to schools. We were playing a high school football game adjacent to the parking lot. He finished with the principal and the caretaker and casually stopped by to watch the game."

Martin liked what he saw. He pushed for Bahnuik to receive an invitation to a spring camp for graduating high school players. The Roughriders, Rams and Saskatoon Hilltops staged the camp to evaluate elite Saskatchewan talent.

"I was a raw rookie," Bahnuik said. "In my first year, Grade 10, we played six-man football. In Grades 11 and 12, we played nine-man. I wasn't accustomed to playing in a 12-man game. I came to camp and, as you can imagine, it was very intimidating, and I was very inexperienced. One person who took notice of me was Paul Anderson, who was a junior coach at that time. He saw something and worked closely with me over the three days of camp. I guess I took the pointers and did well enough over the three days to be invited to the Rams' training camp. I made the Rams that fall. In my case, it was pure luck that someone spotted some talent. It was pretty raw talent at that time."

Bahnuik's talent was refined to the point that he attended the Roughriders' training camp in 1964 and 1965, only to be returned to the Rams. Bahnuik ascended to the pro ranks in 1966, but did not occupy a CFL roster spot until the playoffs. "It was a bit of a dream," he said of being with the Roughriders. "When you practise with them all season long, you ease into it over the course of the year. But I wasn't part of the games. I was just practising. Everyone hates practices and loves the games."

Suddenly, Bahnuik was preparing to play in the Western Conference final. Saskatchewan had a bye in the first round of the playoffs, when the Winnipeg Blue Bombers faced the Edmonton Eskimos in a sudden-death divisional semifinal. The Bombers' 16-8 victory propelled them into the best-of-three final against Saskatchewan. While preparing to make his CFL debut against the Bombers, Bahnuik was also keeping an eye on the fortunes of his previous team. Two days before the Roughriders faced Winnipeg in their playoff opener, the Rams opposed the Montreal-based Notre Dame de Grace Maple Leafs for the Canadian junior football title at Saskatoon's Gordie Howe Bowl.

The Rams were bidding to become Regina's third national junior champion. The Queen City had previously won in 1928 (when Al Ritchie coached the Regina Pats to victory) and 1938 (when the Paul Dojack-coached Regina Dales prevailed). Regina's 28-year drought ended when the Rams, under head coach Gordon Currie, defeated Notre Dame de Grace. The score: 29-14.

CHAPTER 16 # "REGINA ALL THE WAY"

The Regina Rams' triumph in the 1966 Canadian junior football final — then known as the Little Grey Cup — was a testament to the strength of amateur football in Saskatchewan. While not directly involved with the Rams' program, Roughriders general manager Ken Preston could take a bow. Upon taking over in 1958, Preston made a concentrated effort to ensure that the Roughriders supported grassroots football. From the outset, Preston recognized that homegrown talent was the lifeblood of any Canadian professional football team. That point was re-emphasized in 1959 when George Terlep, who had just been fired as the Roughriders' head coach, bemoaned a dearth of top-quality Canadians on the team — which was winless at the time of his dismissal.

The composition of the Roughriders changed in the early 1960s. There was an infusion of talented Saskatchewan-born players such as linebacker Wayne Shaw (from the Bladworth-Davidson area, via Notre Dame College), centre Ted Urness (Regina) and defensive backs Dale West (born in Cabri; raised in Saskatoon) and Larry Dumelie (Fir Mountain). Although those players did not bear Preston's stamp, he understood the importance of ensuring that they received opportunities to blossom into pro prospects.

Into the mid-1960s, the base of local players continued to expand. Receiver Gord Barwell, defensive back Ted Dushinski and linebacker Cliff Shaw joined the Green and White from the Hilltops. Weyburn-born Henry Dorsch became a Roughrider after playing running back and defensive back at the University of Tulsa. Regina-born Alan Ford progressed to the Roughriders after playing at the University of the Pacific in Stockton, Calif. Rams graduate Don Bahnuik, from Canora, spent the 1966 season on the Roughriders' taxi squad before being activated for the Western Conference playoffs. Moreover, many import players became year-round Saskatchewanians. As more players — regardless of their origins —

Ken Preston | Photo courtesy of *Leader-Post* archives

became ingrained in the community, the team was truly the *Saskatchewan* Roughriders.

"My dad felt a huge responsibility because the Roughriders were representing the whole province," said Rich Preston, Ken's son. "He took it real personally. People talk about Ron Lancaster and George Reed and Hugh Campbell and Ed McQuarters, but the key to the success they had was the character Canadians and the supporting cast — guys like Garner Ekstran, who was an undersized defensive lineman. He was also big on players from Saskatchewan. If he had to choose between this guy and that guy, he'd pick the guy from Saskatchewan. Who would he rather play for if he was going to play in the CFL?"

Ken Preston could have taken credit for the success, were he so inclined. From the outset, the modest Preston encouraged the players to live and work in Regina. Practices began at 5 p.m., so that players could hold down regular jobs while pursuing a career in football. The Roughriders' ability to maintain a core of players in the city, throughout the year, contributed to team chemistry. "He always wanted players to become part of the community and get jobs," said Bill Preston, Ken's elder son. "He would always say, 'Get a job and live off that salary, buy apartments or property, and make your money work for you.' He was a member of the Wascana Country Club. He got out there on weekends as much as he could. He had contacts and he used them to try to get the players jobs if they wanted them."

Given the modest remuneration the players received, a second source of income came in very handy. Most efforts to extract a healthy raise from Preston were futile. "His office looked on to Pasqua Street," Ekstran remembered. "I was up there negotiating a contract with him. He had a swivel chair and all of a sudden he would turn the chair. When that happened, you knew it was time to get out of his office and not say another word. You could sit there for another eight hours and he'd just look at Pasqua Street. As a team, we had a lot of laughs and great times. If nothing else, we'd laugh about what Preston had done to us the day before. Maybe he was the catalyst for making us a team."

While fiercely protective of the dollar, Preston made an effort to ensure that contract talks were amicable. "It used to be something else," former Roughriders receiver Jack Gotta, an assistant coach with the 1966 squad, told the *Leader-Post*'s Bob Hughes in 1978. "I couldn't believe it sometimes when I went in to negotiate a contract with Ken when I was playing in Regina. You'd walk in, ready to fight with him, and he'd say 'How's your family?' and, the next thing you knew, you'd signed for what he wanted."

Defensive lineman Ron Atchison had a similar view of his negotiations with Preston. "He was a hard guy to dislike," Atchison said. "He never called you down. He was always calm, cool and collected. You could call him a cheap prick and he wouldn't hold it against you. He had a quiet manner about him. He didn't give you too many reasons to dislike him, except he didn't pay you as much as you wanted, but that was his job. We were the poorest team in the league. He had no choice at all. He could only give what the team would allow him to give you. That wasn't his fault and you had to realize that."

It was a sobering realization for the players, whose salary increases were incremental at best. "We were not a highly paid team," Atchison said. "We couldn't do it. We didn't have the fans to cover that cost. We'd get maybe 15,000 at a game and go to Edmonton and they'd have 30,000. We were lucky to be in the bloody game at all. We were a poverty team, no doubt about it." But the team survived, and eventually thrived, under Preston's direction. "Being a businessman, he was a dollars-and-cents guy," Bill Preston said. "He knew how much he could spend. There weren't all the lotteries and fundraisers like they have nowadays. As a small-market team, it must have been tough to compete with Montreal and Toronto."

When Preston was in charge, the players' options were finite. They could sign for what he was offering or seek employment in another field. At that time, players did not have agents to act as intermediaries. Free agency was a foreign concept. The players possessed little leverage, if any. "You could say to a player, 'All we're going to give you is $7,500 for the season. Take it or leave it,' " trainer Sandy Archer said in 2005. "If you do that to a guy today and say, 'We're only going to give you $45,000,' the guy will say, 'No way. I'm going to another team.' It's a different environment now. He was always trying to save money for the football team whatever way he could."

The same approach applied outside football. "I never knew what an allowance was," a chuckling Bill Preston recalled. "There was no such thing. I got a job working for him when they had training camp at Campion College. I figured it would give me some money. It was a monthly wage. When it came time to get my first paycheque, my dad said, 'I can't pay you very much because you ate at the training table,' so he deducted that. I ended up with basically nothing. I made a little extra money washing cars for the players. It was a thrill for me to be around those guys."

Bill Preston was a Roughriders waterboy for two years. At the time, he was also becoming a quarterback of note with the Sheldon-Williams Spartans high school football team. During respites in Roughriders practices, he received pointers on passing from Ron Lancaster. To this day, Preston appreciates the time Lancaster took to provide tutelage. But most of the time, the younger Preston was not in close interaction with the players. "I'm afraid I probably took on my father's personality more than any of us," said Preston, who has two brothers and one sister. "I was shy. I enjoyed my job, but I didn't go out of my way to pester the guys. I stayed in the background and enjoyed the bickering and jokes that went on in the locker room. I just sat back and enjoyed it. It was like a reality show."

Football was an ongoing reality at the Preston household. During the offseason, the Roughriders' general manager would plot the schedule on behalf of the CFL, using a magnetic board. "Even in the winter, I don't think he took much time off," Bill Preston said of his father. "He would go down south scouting. One thing I always wondered was, 'How did he have any contacts?' He was in Canada and all the contacts would be in the States. For the life of me, I can't figure out how he knew these people or whether they contacted him. They never had a head scout. I just remember that it was him and the secretary and the coaches. It was a whole different era."

In Preston's era, the general manager was not in the limelight. Despite the crucial role he played in the organization, Preston was seldom front and centre. Whereas future Roughriders general managers like Jim Spavital, John Herrera, Alan Ford, Roy Shivers and Eric Tillman were often the focus of attention, Preston was delighted to cede the spotlight to the coaches and players. Preston was as understated as he was under-rated. "He was one of the guys in the background who made sure that everything was running smoothly," Bill Preston said. "He liked it that way."

"You had to live in Regina to understand and appreciate Ken Preston," Lancaster remembered. "He was a very sociable, outgoing, nice person outside the office. You wouldn't get that impression if you only saw him in the office. He was quiet. He didn't say very much. He looked after the money and he did a great job of that. He didn't really ever interfere with football. He wouldn't go in and tell Eagle Keys or any of those coaches what to do. He knew what his job was and he did it. He wasn't boisterous about it.

"If you really wanted to know what he was like, you had to see him outside the office. I curled one year down at the Wascana Winter Club and he was a member there. I saw him in a light that I'd never seen him in before. He was always laughing and having a good time and fit in very well with everybody. He was a good guy — he really was."

In his ninth season as the general manager, Ken Preston could finally savour a first-place finish. However, the Roughriders were not entering the playoffs with momentum. After beginning the 1966 season with a 7-2-0 record, they had only two victories and one tie to show for the final seven games.

Over the first half of the schedule, Saskatchewan had produced 213 points — 75 more than the opposition — but was outscored 180-138 during the final eight games. The second-place Winnipeg Blue Bombers, whom Saskatchewan was preparing to face in the best-of-three Western Conference final, were statistically superior during the stretch run. Winnipeg, with an 8-7-1 record, had four victories in each half of the season, but had outscored the opposition 150-118 over the final four games.

Even so, the Bombers fell 14-7 to Saskatchewan in the opener of the Western Conference final. Ed McQuarters led the Roughriders' defence in tackles, with nine. The *Leader-Post*'s Laurie Artiss noted that the "Bombers finally had to make offensive changes and double-teaming just to stop, or slow down, McQuarters." Artiss also observed that

Bombers quarterback Ken Ploen "was wearing McQuarters like a second suit of underwear most of the day."

But it could not be said with any certainty that McQuarters was Saskatchewan's best defensive player against Winnipeg, which surrendered only one touchdown — an 11-yard reception by Gord Barwell. Third-year Roughriders defensive halfback Bob Kosid enjoyed a sparkling game, registering two crucial interceptions.

With Saskatchewan leading 11-0 midway through the second quarter, Ploen threw deep to Bill Cooper. Near the goal line, Kosid leaped in front of the receiver and wrapped his hands around the ball. Cooper attempted to pull the pigskin away from Kosid as the players fell to the turf. Kosid won the battle for the ball — even though Grant maintained that simultaneous possession should have been called, giving Cooper the reception — and a promising Winnipeg drive was extinguished.

Closer to halftime, Kosid again intercepted Ploen and returned the ball 36 yards to the Bombers' 46-yard line, setting up Jack Abendschan's second field goal of the game. "Kosid's play all season has been the type that brings pleasure to his own coaches, admiration from the opposition, and general silence from the spectators," Laurie Artiss wrote. "It wasn't this way Sunday. He was sensational for all the world — at least the nation on TV — to see."

And to think that Kosid might easily have been Blue Bombers property. The Roughriders and Blue Bombers both took note of his exploits at the University of Kentucky and almost simultaneously laid claim to his CFL rights. The league eventually supported Roughriders general manager Ken Preston's contention that he was the first to place Kosid on a negotiation list. Kosid was an especially valuable commodity in that he was Canadian-born but American-trained. Although Kosid was born in Brandon, the family soon moved to Minneapolis. After Kosid finished Grade 9, there was another move — to Chicago, where he flourished as a high school player.

Bob Kosid | *Photo courtesy of Leader-Post archives*

"My greatest claim to fame there was that I was on an all-Illinois team and my picture was next to Dick Butkus," Kosid said of the legendary Chicago Bears linebacker.

Kosid's all-state status was noted by some of the finest university teams in the United States. He was contacted by more than 100 schools before he chose the University of Kentucky. At the time, one of Kentucky's assistant coaches was Don Shula, who went on to become a prominent field boss in the NFL. Shula visited the Kosid household on a recruiting mission. At Kentucky, Kosid was utilized at running back and in the defensive backfield. "It was like coming into heaven," he said of playing at the high-profile NCAA school. "I really thought, 'Oh, man, this is the way it was supposed to be in the first place.' I took it for what it was. It was a gift I'd been given. Everybody who was current at that particular time was aware of Kentucky. It got headlines in *Sports Illustrated*. You were supposed to live up to a tradition, so I lived up to it."

After Kosid graduated from Kentucky, he was courted by the American Football League's Oakland Raiders. "They were my favourite team," he recalled. "At the time, I had three things on my mind as far as making a decision. I had just gotten married and my wife was pregnant. I had a commission in the U.S. Army and the future there was Vietnam. In the AFL, I would probably have rode the bench for a little bit of time, which I wasn't really wanting to do. Of all the three choices, I wanted to play. I thought, 'Well, OK, here we go — no money, but I'm going to have fun. I'm going to play.' I had no idea about the team, but I knew I would make an impact. Rather than go off to Hanoi or something like that, I took the safest choice. It ultimately proved to be the right one."

The day after Saskatchewan defeated the visiting Blue Bombers, the Ottawa Rough Riders' Russ Jackson received the Schenley Award as the CFL's most outstanding player. Saskatchewan quarterback Ron Lancaster was the runner-up.

Jackson was also decorated as the league's outstanding Canadian. The Rough Riders' pivot won both awards for the second time, having previously accomplished that feat in 1963. Calgary Stampeders linebacker Wayne Harris was the other recipient of a major CFL award in 1966. He was named the top lineman for the second successive year.

The Roughriders' series-opening victory over Winnipeg numbed some of the pain that resulted from a variety of injuries. Halfback Paul Dudley was hospitalized with a severely bruised kidney. Defensive halfback Dale West suffered his fourth shoulder dislocation of the season. Centre Ted Urness, who collapsed en route to the dressing room after the game, was diagnosed with a mild concussion.

Urness played in Game 2 at Winnipeg Stadium. Dudley, however, was gone for what remained of the 1966 season. The Roughriders had the luxury of replacing him with veteran speedster Ed Buchanan, who had missed most of the season with strained knee ligaments. With West sidelined, Gene Wlasiuk reclaimed a starting spot at defensive halfback.

The Roughriders faced another challenge as Game 2 loomed. How would they get to Winnipeg? With Air Canada on strike, contingency plans were required. At first, it appeared the Roughriders would have to charter two small aircraft from TransAir. Eventually, a larger aircraft was secured and re-routed from Las Vegas, enabling the entire team to fly to Winnipeg together.

Head coach Eagle Keys provided some levity as the Roughriders scrambled to make flight arrangements. "Eagle was funny this way," said Henry Dorsch, a defensive halfback who also backed up fullback George Reed. "George didn't like flying and Eagle said, 'Air Canada's on strike so we're going to go with another airline, but they don't have big planes so we're going to split the team in two. Half of you will go out in the morning and half will go out in the afternoon. Who wants to go in the morning?' People put up their hands. Ted Urness was our centre and I think Moe Levesque was our backup centre. Moe puts up his hand and Ted puts up his hand and Eagle says, 'No, we can't send both centres on the same flight.' It got a real reaction out of George."

CHAPTER **17** # "GO, ED! GO, ED!"

Saskatchewan Roughriders head coach Eagle Keys was not given to bold proclamations, but as Game 2 of the 1966 Western Conference final loomed, he did have an emphatic message for the team's longest-serving employee, trainer Sandy Archer: "We're going to win this." The Roughriders had won the opener of the best-of-three series, prevailing 14-7 at Taylor Field. Another victory over Winnipeg would propel Saskatchewan into the Grey Cup for the first time since 1951. Despite the confidence exuded by the ordinarily low-key Keys, the Roughriders knew that wrapping up the series in hostile environs would not be easy.

The first quarter was scoreless at Winnipeg Stadium. With Saskatchewan leading 4-2 at halftime, fans should have been looking for a Zamboni. One of the few signs of life was a long pass from Ron Lancaster to Hugh Campbell that put Saskatchewan in position for an Alan Ford rouge 10:22 into the second quarter. For most of the third quarter, the game appeared to be slipping away from the Roughriders. Winnipeg led 12-4 as the final quarter loomed, thanks primarily to a 54-yard touchdown run by Dave Raimey. At that point, the Roughriders desperately needed someone to enliven the offence.

Over to you, Ed Buchanan.

Buchanan was easy to overlook in light of the Roughriders' myriad weapons. After two injury-plagued seasons, a break finally went in Buchanan's favour in the 14th minute of the third quarter in Winnipeg. Following two first-down runs by George Reed, Lancaster handed the ball to Buchanan, who ran an off-tackle play. Buchanan was untouched by the first line of defence before eluding Bombers cornerback Dick Thornton near midfield en route to a 73-yard touchdown. Jack Abendschan's convert reduced Winnipeg's lead to 12-11.

"Ed Buchanan's name has never really been mentioned in the same way you might say George Reed or Hughie Campbell," defensive back Bob Kosid said. "Yet, his contribution meant a great deal."

Buchanan was quick to credit tight end Jim Worden for the touchdown. "Jim told me at halftime that he had discovered a weak spot on the left side of the Winnipeg defensive line," Buchanan told the *Leader-Post*. "When I looked up, I saw Jim Worden ahead of me. I stopped for a second and he threw a beautiful block — just as he told me at halftime. Then I just kept on running." As Keys put it: "That was the big run that got us back in the game."

Saskatchewan went ahead 14-12 midway through the fourth quarter when Abendschan kicked a 44-yard field goal, moments after barely missing from the 47. However, the lead was tenuous. With just under five minutes remaining, quarterback Ken Ploen moved Winnipeg to Saskatchewan's 47-yard line. The restoration of Winnipeg's lead was a distinct possibility. Another first down and the Bombers would be in field-goal range. Given the Roughriders' lack of production

Ed Buchanan | Photo courtesy of SSHFM

on offence in Game 2, another Winnipeg touchdown could have been a game-clincher.

Just inside Saskatchewan territory, Ploen dropped back to pass, only to encounter Don Gerhardt and Ken Reed of the Roughriders. "We did kind of a scissors — a high-low — on him," said Gerhardt, who ended up knocking the football out of Ploen's right hand before he could attempt to pass. Ed McQuarters quickly scooped up the ball near midfield.

"I can remember laying upside down and backwards, looking back down the field, and McQuarters was running the other way like mad," Gerhardt said.

"When I saw Ed McQuarters with the ball, I thought, 'This is the fastest guy on the defence — as a lineman. It's in the right hands,' " Ken Reed added.

"He was not only good, he was fast," Ploen said of McQuarters. "The guy could move for a big man." Nobody was going to catch McQuarters as he motored toward the goal line. Roughriders equipment manager Dale Laird was closer to McQuarters than any of the Winnipeg players. "We were looking at the possibility of a Game 3 back in Regina, and then Ed recovered the fumble," Laird recalled. "I ran almost to the goal line with him along the sidelines, yelling, 'Go, Ed! Go, Ed!' "

The first person to greet McQuarters in the end zone was defensive back Ted Dushinski. "Ted jumped up on me and was screaming at the top of his lungs, 'Mac, I love you! I love you! Whatever you want, I'll buy it for you, man. I love you!' " McQuarters remembered. "That was the first time I heard the word 'love' used in my presence among a group of professional football players. As a result, I'm not afraid to use it relating to 'macho' events. Ted's expression will stick in my mind forever."

Abendschan's convert gave Saskatchewan a 21-12 lead with 3:59 left in the fourth quarter. McQuarters' touchdown provided a much-needed cushion for the Roughriders, who surrendered a touchdown pass from Ploen to Ken Nielsen with just under one minute remaining.

"Somebody has to step up at the right time and make the big play and that's what Ed did," Ron Lancaster

Ed McQuarters | Photo courtesy of *Leader-Post* archives

said. "That was the key to our football team in that era. We weren't the best team, but we played pretty darned well as a unit and people stepped up and made plays when they had to be made. There's probably no better example than that of Ed's."

As the final seconds ticked away in Winnipeg, trainer Sandy Archer reminded himself of Eagle Keys' prediction: "We're going to win this." At first, Archer was skeptical. He had been the trainer since 1951, when Saskatchewan lost 21-14 to the Ottawa Rough Riders in the Grey Cup — leaving the Roughriders at 0-for-8 in the national final. In the years to follow, Roughriders fans and employees had become accustomed to disappointment, even despair. "I thought, 'Geez, we'll never get to the Grey Cup,' " said Archer, who was the team's sole holdover from its previous Grey Cup appearance.

Garner Ekstran could relate to the frustration. He had joined the Roughriders in 1961 and quickly become a regular on the defensive line. Over Ekstran's first five CFL seasons, the Roughriders enjoyed moderate success — but nothing to rival what they accomplished in Winnipeg on Nov. 16, 1966. As Ekstran remembered: "I went into the dressing room after the game and thought, 'Shit, we've finally turned it around.' "

Eagle Keys was even quieter than usual amid the revelry after the Roughriders clinched the 1966 Western Conference title. "I'm all shook up right now," Keys told reporters shortly after the final gun. "I can't talk to you now."

Once the commotion abated, Keys made himself available to the media and praised halfback Ed Buchanan for being the difference. Buchanan had rushed for 125 yards on 16 carries, including a 73-yard touchdown scamper, as a replacement for the injured Paul Dudley. George Reed added 101 rushing yards.

Although the Roughriders' potent passing attack had produced most of the fireworks — and headlines — during the 1966 season, a formidable ground assault had been crucial against Winnipeg. In the deciding game, Ron Lancaster had completed only six of 14 passes for 74 yards, but the expert play-caller knew better than to deviate from a successful formula. Winnipeg was unable to stop Buchanan and Reed, so why get fancy?

Saskatchewan's victory over Winnipeg triggered a torrent of inquiries from Roughriders fans who were determined to get to Vancouver to watch their team's first Grey Cup appearance since 1951. The morning after the game, Wally Read was among the Canadian National Railway employees who dealt with customers when they visited or telephoned Regina's Union Station. "From eight o'clock in the morning until my shift was over at 5 p.m., I would pick up the phone and give information out," Read said. "The second I hung up, the phone would ring."

Saskatchewan fans celebrated again the day after the Western Conference final. The Roughriders' flight from Winnipeg was late in arriving at the Regina airport. But after a 15-year wait for another Grey Cup berth, what was another 50 minutes?

The victorious players and coaches were greeted by several hundred shivering spectators at 7:30 p.m., on the evening of Nov. 17. The loyalists passed the time during the delay by rehearsing the lyrics to various Roughriders fight songs — with which the team would be serenaded after its chartered aircraft landed.

Head coach Eagle Keys was first off the plane. He strode through a gauntlet of cheerleaders while the Regina Lions Junior A Band provided a musical salute. Keys led the team on to a specially constructed platform in front of the terminal. One by one, the players were introduced — with some of the loudest ovations being reserved for defensive linemen Ed McQuarters and Ron Atchison. McQuarters' fumble return for a touchdown in Game 2 of the conference final had pretty much secured Saskatchewan's long-awaited Grey Cup berth. Atchison was finally poised to play in a league final, in his 15th season with the Green and White.

After winning the West, the Roughriders had a strong suspicion as to whom they would be opposing in the Grey Cup, to be held Nov. 26 at Empire Stadium in Vancouver. However, Ottawa had yet to be confirmed as the Eastern Conference representative.

Ottawa, which had won the East's regular-season title, met the overmatched Hamilton Tiger-Cats in the conference final. Whereas the Western Conference used a best-of-three format to declare its champion, a two-game total-points final was played in the East.

The Rough Riders won the opener 30-1 in Hamilton on Nov. 13. Russ Jackson completed 21 of 28 passes for 309 yards. One week later, while Saskatchewan watched on television, the Eastern Riders won 42-16 to take the two-game set, 72-17. Once again, Jackson's passing was precise. He completed 13 of 20 passes for 262 yards. The tone was set four minutes into the game, when Jackson found Whit Tucker for a scoring bomb. Ottawa also made eight interceptions, setting a CFL single-game record for larceny.

Ottawa routed Hamilton despite being denied home-field advantage in the conference final. The Rough Riders' home facility, Lansdowne Park, was unavailable because it was being renovated as part of Canada's 1967 centennial project. As a result, Ottawa's "home" playoff game was held in Montreal — not that the venue had any influence on the outcome. Ottawa would have won handily if the final had been played in Togo.

Despite the lopsided nature of the Eastern Conference final, the Rough Riders did encounter plenty of adversity en route to the Grey Cup. Assistant coach Bill Smyth died as the Rough Riders prepared for the playoffs.

During the Rough Riders' bye week, which they earned by virtue of finishing first in the East's regular-season standings, Smyth was taken to hospital with an arterial blood clot. He died three days later of acute heart failure at age 44. His heart had been weakened during a childhood bout with rheumatic fever.

"We had no idea what we were going to be like [against Hamilton] because we had all been to the funeral earlier that week," recalled Jackson, whose team wore black armbands during the conference final in memory of Smyth. "Once we were on the field, from my point of view, we didn't dwell on it. Once we started to play and we were successful, it just snowballed. We just did everything right and Hamilton didn't do anything right."

The 6-foot-4, 250-pound Smyth had been on Frank Clair's coaching staff in Ottawa since 1956. "He was well-respected by the team," Rough Riders defensive back Bob O'Billovich said. "He was really Frank Clair's right-hand man. They had a tremendous chemistry. It was like cutting off one of his arms. It was a real downer."

Ron Lancaster, who spent his first three CFL seasons in Ottawa before being dealt to Saskatchewan in 1963, was well-acquainted with Smyth. "Great guy," Lancaster remembered. "He was a booming, boisterous, tough son of a gun. Man, he would get on you in practice and raise hell and scream at you, but the players loved him. He had a laugh that you could hear all over the city and a voice to match. When he got on you, he didn't mess around. He was really a good person. He was tough, but he was good."

Ottawa players were hoping to win the Grey Cup as a tribute to the late Bill Smyth. And who was going to derail them? The point spread for the Grey Cup fluctuated during the week leading up to the game, with Ottawa favoured to win by five to eight points, depending on the day and the identity of the visionary. "Maybe we were the favourites because we had bombed Hamilton in the two-game total-point," Jackson mused while referring to the one-sided Eastern Conference final.

Saskatchewan defensive tackle Ron Atchison did not sound concerned about the degree to which Ottawa dominated the Eastern final. If anything, Atchison reasoned, the result out

East worked to Saskatchewan's advantage. "That sort of thing's pretty tough to live up to," Atchison told the *Leader-Post* as the Roughriders prepared to embark for Vancouver.

Eagle Keys, meanwhile, was guardedly optimistic. "We had a pretty close game with Ottawa back a while in the season," Keys said, alluding to an 18-8 loss in Ottawa on Sept. 26. "We're pretty confident."

George Reed was also confident the Roughriders would win the first Grey Cup in franchise history. "I was more pissed off that nobody gave us a chance and wrote us off," Reed said. "That probably was on our minds more than anything. The attitude was, 'We'll show them how good we are and that we can play on the same field with Ottawa.' "

The sentiments expressed by Reed were virtually universal among the Roughriders. As game day drew closer, the Roughriders kept emphasizing — but not believing — how their chances of winning were being roundly discounted.

"When you've got a bunch of fellows together who are professionals and somebody doesn't give them their just respect, it grinds on people," defensive back Bruce Bennett said. "It certainly was a motivator for us to prove that we were the calibre of team that was deserving to be in the Grey Cup. It was just something, I think, where we felt we needed to earn our respect. People weren't saying anything bad about us. I think it was the things they were saying about how good these folks in the East were, so we were just tired of hearing that."

The Roughriders were not without ammunition. They had an elite quarterback in Ron Lancaster — the Western Conference's nominee for most outstanding player. Reed had won the league's outstanding-player award the previous season. Hugh Campbell had registered a league-record 17 touchdown catches, and a CFL-best 102 points, in 1966. The offence was also driven by an elite line.

Even so, Ottawa was heavily favoured. Russ Jackson's presence had to be a factor, being that he had recently been honoured as the CFL's outstanding player and outstanding Canadian for 1966. Not only that, Ottawa had posted a league-best 11-3 record — compared to Saskatchewan's 9-6-1 slate. "I think the most relevant thing would be that we were 9-6-1," defensive back Bob Kosid noted. "I don't think the rest of the world gave us much credit. Ottawa was going to win the thing. We were the underdogs. We sort of relished that."

Given the talent on the Roughriders, why was their record an unremarkable 9-6-1 heading into the playoffs? "I've thought about that a million times," Kosid said. "The only answer I can tell you is that in those days, the CFL was loaded. You've got Joe Kapp and an extremely talented group of B.C. Lions. Winnipeg wasn't really too far behind, with Kenny Ploen. After that initial three years where you were playing against those guys, along came the Calgary Stampeders and all of a sudden they're threatening you every time you turn around. I think the CFL flourished in talent and had a great amount of excellent, excellent football players. It was tough to win."

On their way to Vancouver | Photo courtesy of *Leader-Post*

Before leaving for Vancouver on a Tuesday morning, the Roughriders held indoor workouts at the Regina Armoury on Sunday and Monday "to get the boys accustomed to that warm weather again," Eagle Keys noted. The practices did not include centre Galen Wahlmeier (who was gone for the season with a knee injury) and halfback Paul Dudley (severely bruised kidney). Defensive back Dale West was a question mark due to a chronically dislocated shoulder. If available for the Grey Cup, West would replace rookie defensive lineman Don Bahnuik on the roster. There was some concern over all-star centre Ted Urness, who had yet to miss any duty despite collapsing en route to the dressing room after the first playoff game against Winnipeg. The *Leader-Post* reported that Urness was still experiencing severe headaches as a result of a mild concussion, yet he was cleared to fly to Vancouver and expected to play in the Grey Cup.

Roughriders fans, roughly 200 strong, headed to the Regina airport — again — on Nov. 22 to wish the team well as it departed for Vancouver. Although Air Canada was on strike, the Roughriders were able to charter a 102-seat, DC-7C aircraft. They boarded the Pacific Western Airlines plane and flew directly to Vancouver.

The eastern Riders, by contrast, had every reason to bemoan their flight arrangements. The Air Canada strike left Ottawa without an alternative that was anything short of gruelling. The initial itinerary called for Ottawa to charter a plane and fly non-stop to Vancouver. No such luck. The Rough Riders pulled out all the stops to eventually reach Vancouver — landing in Chicago and Seattle before finally reaching their destination. It was fitting, perhaps, for a team that was noted for its touchdowns.

CHAPTER 18 | # "A TRIP I WILL NEVER FORGET"

Roughriders fans emulated their team's offence by staging an aerial and ground assault, all with the intent of finding their way to the Grey Cup, via whatever means possible. By Tuesday of Grey Cup week, all available airplane and train space had disappeared. The first flight — a Pacific Western Airlines charter — left the tarmac Tuesday morning. Six charter flights, each carrying 102 passengers, departed for Vancouver that week — including an aircraft carrying VIPs and a group of handicapped Roughriders supporters, with accompanying physicians. The demand for airline tickets was so intense that a waiting list was required.

Meanwhile, between 500 and 600 fans were reserving seats on The Canadian — a westward-bound Canadian Pacific rail-liner that left Regina's Union Station each morning at 6:32. Two extra cars were required to accommodate the fans. Additionally, arrangements were made for two special Grey Cup trains, with 16 and 15 cars, to leave Thursday morning. Those Canadian National Railways trains were to stop in Saskatoon and pick up more Roughriders fans before heading to Vancouver.

Quantifying the number of fans who drove or took a bus to Vancouver is more difficult. The same applies to Roughriders supporters who resided outside Saskatchewan. This much is certain: There was a ravenous appetite for Grey Cup tickets, to the extent that the Roughriders established a ticket office in the Hotel Vancouver. Early in the week, more than 4,000 tickets had been sold at that outlet.

The departure of the hordes of fans is a story in itself. Lorne Harasen, a reporter at CKCK Radio, was dispatched to Union Station to do live cut-ins on Johnny Sandison's popular morning show. "First I watched, longingly, as a brewery truck backed up to one of the cars and unloaded a load," Harasen recalled. "Then another truck pulled up and unloaded hard stuff." For Roughriders fans, the week was all about cheers and booze.

Neil Sawatzky remembers it well. The Regina-born Sawatzky and his older brother, Allan, secured seats on one of the many Vancouver-bound chartered buses. "There was no stopping our dream of going to the big game," Neil Sawatzky said. "As teenagers, this was to be our great adventure — our chance of a lifetime.

"The day of the trip could not arrive soon enough. We loaded on to one of the many chartered buses departing from the STC depot in downtown Regina, along with other faithful fans we'd never met before. As the bus pulled away, there was an air of excitement and eager anticipation. When we reached the south end of town and began to turn west on to the Trans-Canada Highway, the overhead luggage shifted and the sound of many clinking bottles was all that was necessary for laughter to erupt and the non-stop merriment to begin. By the time we hit Moose Jaw, many stories had already been told and songs had been sung. The bus rolled into Calgary late at night, where the driver was forced to transfer the whole rowdy gang on to a clean bus due to the deplorable state of the on-board toilet. No problem. As the transfer was being made, the revellers gave each other rides around the Calgary bus depot on luggage carts, chanting, 'Go Riders Go!' "

The Regina Police Boys Band played an instrumental role in the departures. The band, which was to perform in the Grey Cup parade and at the game, left from Union Station. "The trip started in true Grey Cup celebration with the band leading fans through the downtown station, with us playing and the fans following, singing and partying," recalled Broadview's Peter Barry, who was then a 14-year-old Reginan. "After a sendoff from the downtown railroad station, we took the dayliner to Saskatoon, boarded the train late at night in Saskatoon, and then ventured on to Vancouver via the famous train and a trip I will never forget. Our band was about 60 boys from 18 and under, so, of course, we didn't all sleep, with the excitement and all. The walk down to the diner car the first morning was a true learning experience. The partying was going on non-stop — people sleeping on luggage racks, between cars, booze everywhere, card and poker games, impromptu musicians entertaining. It was one huge party like you had never seen."

Not since 1951, anyway. In advance of Saskatchewan's previous appearance in the championship game, roughly 500 fans had boarded the Rider Special for Toronto. Another 150, or thereabouts, flew to Toronto. By comparison, Vancouver was about to welcome several *thousand* Saskatchewan supporters.

"Every time there was a major stop, the band would hustle off the train, form up, and then lead the party-goers into the train station," Barry said. "We would play for 10 minutes or so and then lead everyone back on to the train. It all sounds pretty wild, but one thing that I vividly remember was that it was all done without getting out of hand. The whole idea was to have a good time, not to be destructive. The railroad was prepared for that. The cars that we were in had to be the oldest that they could find and suitable for a train full of drunks."

Not to be forgotten were the non-Saskatchewan fans. The Ottawa rooters traded good-natured barbs with the Saskatchewan supporters. "The train was filled with fans, many from Ottawa, and the boos and cheers that erupted each time Russ Jackson's or Ron Lancaster's name was shouted in the club car made for a wonderful, friendly rivalry," said former Broadview resident Ian McKay, now of Indian Head. "At Calgary, several Stampeders fans boarded, adorned in red underwear. Their only luggage seemed to comprise several 40-ounce bottles."

Back in Regina, the citizens readied themselves for the game. Special provisions were made — or at least considered — in light of the extraordinary circumstances. Two prominent department stores — Robert Simpson Regina Ltd. and T. Eaton Co. Ltd. — advocated an adjustment of shopping hours because the Grey Cup was to be played on Saturday afternoon, normally a peak period for shopping. The proposal, calling for Friday night opening and Saturday afternoon closing, was nixed by city council.

"Nobody will be doing any shopping," a spokesman for Regina's Mid-West Motors told the *Leader-Post*. "It doesn't make much sense to be open." Given the massive interest in the game, most Regina stores planned to make television sets and radios available to employees and an anticipated trickle of shoppers. In the meantime, the stores were struggling to keep stylish Rider Booster Bonnets in stock.

Although city council did not support the holiday proclamation, assent was provided for a taxpayer-funded float, to be part of the Grey Cup parade. City council earmarked $12,000 (roughly $80,000 in today's dollars) for Grey Cup festivities and promotions, including the distribution of miniature loaves of bread — with the message "Regina, bread basket of the world" emblazoned on the wrappers.

The city and the province were to be represented in the parade by two floats, the Regina Police Boys Band, the Regina Lions Junior A Band, the Roughriders cheerleaders, the Riderettes, and Miss Roughrider — Jo-Ann Martin of Regina, who was the runner-up to Toronto's Dale-Ann Young for Miss Grey Cup honours. The cheerleaders and Riderettes departed on two chartered Greyhound buses. The cheerleaders were accompanied by the ballboys — Mel Ottenbreit and Rick Laird — and waterboy Rich Preston (the 14-year-old son of general manager Ken Preston). "The girls smuggled us on to the bus," Rich Preston said with a chuckle. "Back in those days, they were too cheap to fly the waterboys out, so we went along with the cheerleaders. That was interesting. I didn't mind that 17-hour bus ride. The bad news is that you're taking a bus to Vancouver. The good news is that you're taking a bus to Vancouver with the cheerleaders."

The westward-bound Saskatchewan delegation also included the Rider Roller Rooters — a septet of fans in wheelchairs who boarded the VIP flight, accompanied by four escorts, on the Thursday evening prior to Grey Cup. The Roller Rooters financed the trip by staging a series of fundraisers, including a cabaret, variety night and fashion show. Public donations also made the trip feasible. "This is the answer to all my dreams," Eddie Davey, the group's leader, told the *Leader-Post*. Afflicted with cerebral palsy, Davey had been named the Roughriders' most avid fan in 1951. The prize was a trip to the Grey Cup, in which Saskatchewan lost 21-14 to Ottawa, but illness prevented Davey from travelling to Toronto to watch his team's first Grey Cup appearance since 1934. In 1966, planning for a possible trip had begun a month before the Grey Cup game. Once Saskatchewan qualified for the league final, the Rider Roller Rooters — Davey, Bob Bachman, Ken Lamb, Larry Ford,

Darlene McEwen, Delores St. Germaine and Gillis George — were informed that they would be watching the game from a ramp overlooking midfield at Vancouver's Empire Stadium.

Ray Guay was among some 400 people who left Regina's train station on Thursday morning at 1 o'clock. Unlike most of the travellers, Guay did not have to arrange for time off work. For him, it was work. The *Leader-Post* had assigned Guay to the Grey Cup train.

Guay's duties were not strictly reportorial. The newspaper gave him several hundred copies of a Grey Cup preview section, to be distributed at Vancouver hotels. As well, the *Leader-Post* had asked him to hand out the aforementioned miniature loaves of bread, as part of the "bread basket of the world" promotion. Guay, the *Leader-Post*'s assistant city editor at the time, reported that the two Grey Cup Specials would cost Canadian National Railways about $50,000, or more than $300,000 in today's dollars. He quoted a CNR spokesman saying that the revenues would "just about" cover the expenditures.

John Haggett, a 20-year-old Reginan, did not require much coercing to join a friend, Gord Clark, on the Grey Cup train. "Gord desperately wanted to go," said Haggett, who went on to enjoy a lengthy teaching career at Nipawin's L.P. Miller Comprehensive High School. "His seat was on one side of the stadium and mine was on the other." But they were side by side on the train. "We had an upper berth, too," Haggett said. "We must have really splurged." A young couple on the train could not afford a berth, leading to some discomfort. "They were riding coach, sitting up the whole way," Haggett recalled. "They said, 'We would do anything to lie down for an hour.' I told them we had an upper berth and they said, 'Can we borrow it for a while?' " That was not a problem for Haggett. Clark, however, was elsewhere on the train and knew nothing of the arrangement. "Poor Gord," Haggett said. "He got quite a surprise when he went back to take a nap, and there they were."

The train also included a passenger who needed some training, judging by his behaviour. "This guy spent a lot of time on his hands and knees, barking like a dog," Haggett said. "He would crawl along the floor of the train. He'd stop at a group and start panting and point to his mouth, begging for beer. They'd pour some beer down his throat and pat him on the head and send him on his way." By the time the train arrived in Vancouver, the travellers met a welcoming committee that included the B.C. Lions cheerleaders. "The dog-man watched the cheerleaders as long as he could before getting down on his hands and knees and grabbing one of them by the leg," Haggett said. "A couple of cops grabbed him and away he went. I didn't see him again until the game, when he had a beer in his hand, again."

The Roughriders beat the rush to Vancouver. Upon arriving on Tuesday of Grey Cup week, they were determined to remain as inconspicuous as possible, as decreed by Eagle Keys. "To leave himself the time he needs for preparation, and also to come close to as secret workouts as possible, Keys is switching his practice sites each day, without informing anybody," Laurie Artiss wrote in the *Leader-Post*.

The media had been told that the Roughriders would be using the B.C. Lions' dressing room and practice field. However, the Western Conference champions' first workout was held at Callister Park — ordinarily a soccer pitch — on Tuesday, only three hours after the team landed in Vancouver. "It was assumed they'd be back there Wednesday," Artiss wrote. "The players thought so, and so did the bus driver. But as he pulled away from the dressing room, Keys told the driver to take them to Central Park, a large open area with several football and soccer fields. He gave me that sly little smile and said, 'This should keep the news guys busy trying to find us.' "

Keys also ensured that the players were out of the loop — at least as far as accommodations were concerned. "We were so far away in Burnaby," defensive back Dale West said. "I never, ever did get downtown until after the game. We were very far away from everything. We practised in three different places." The media eventually caught up with the team and interviews were conducted following practice.

The routine was foreign to the Roughriders, but not to Keys. "You always do what you've done in previous years," he reflected. "With Pop Ivy, when I was playing in Edmonton, they were winning and we were going away and staying at a different place and so forth prior to the game, so I more or less carried on from there."

Keys also imposed a strict curfew, with nightly bed checks. That was in contrast to Ottawa field boss Frank Clair, who did not impose such restrictions until the night before the game, which was played on a Saturday. The Roughriders' situation led the players to concoct a nickname for their out-of-the-way lodgings — The Monastery.

"It didn't bother me, because that was kind of my mindset, anyway," guard Jack Abendschan said. "I liked to get away and just meditate and get ready and keep my mind on the game. I didn't want any distractions." Keys was only too happy to oblige. "Wait until Saturday night," he told the players. "You can have more fun AFTER you win the Grey Cup."

A notable exception was halfback Paul Dudley, who was sidelined with a severely bruised kidney. Despite the injury, Dudley joined the Roughriders en route to Vancouver. "Every day, Bruce Bennett and I would go by his room," Ron Lancaster said. "He'd just be waking up. Eagle took him out there and told him he had to come to the meetings and practices. We never saw him all week. He'd rent a car and he'd forget. We'd say, 'Where's your car today?' and he'd say, 'I have no idea.' He'd have to wait for the rental-car agency. He'd call and tell them he lost the car. They'd find it, call him, and he'd go pick it up. He was hiding from Eagle all week. That's what I remember about Paul Dudley in the Grey Cup. He enjoyed it more than any of us, because he didn't care about that game. He was such a good guy. He was hurt and couldn't play, so what was he going to do coming to practice? He wouldn't have been able to run. He might as well go and have a good time and, I'll say this, he did."

Another free-spirited Roughrider, tight end Jim Worden, ensured that there was some levity when he encountered Ottawa quarterback Russ Jackson — who had been named the CFL's outstanding player for 1966.

"A brewery put on a seafood lunch at the Bayshore Inn the day before the Grey Cup," Dale West said. "Both teams were there. Worden, in typical fashion, goes up to shake hands with Russ Jackson. Worden had a lobster claw in his jacket. You should have seen Jackson's face when he shook the lobster claw. Typical Worden."

As game day drew closer, Artiss was approached by the ever-jovial Roughriders assistant coach, Jack Gotta. "I got an idea," Gotta said. "Let's play Saturday for the name. Whoever loses has to change their name."

Meanwhile, Saskatchewan defensive tackle Ed McQuarters — a recent addition — could only shake his head and wonder: "Could somebody explain to me how two teams could have the same unusual name?"

Another thing these teams had in common was terrific quarterbacking. Lancaster was the runner-up to Jackson for the league's most prestigious individual award. During interviews leading up to the Grey Cup, Lancaster did not take issue with the voters' selection of Jackson. "There's been some talk that Russ and I are not good friends, but we don't share any ill feeling," Lancaster told reporters. "We like to play against each other, though." Jackson was hoping to defy tradition by winning the outstanding-player award and a Grey Cup in the same year. The CFL's top player had not gone on to win the championship since the award was first presented in 1953.

Lancaster and Jackson had shared in a Grey Cup championship with Ottawa in 1960. Jackson handled most of the quarterbacking that day as Ottawa registered a 16-6 victory over the Eskimos, who were coached by Eagle Keys. Lancaster did not enjoy a breakthrough as a CFL quarterback until 1963, when he was traded to Saskatchewan — and now here he was, preparing for a crucial game against his former teammates, including Jackson. "Everybody said it was Ronnie against Russ Jackson," the latter recalled. "I always laughed, because we were never on the field at the same time. Quarterback versus quarterback seems to be the way they like to tee them up."

Ottawa versus Saskatchewan did not appear to be much of a matchup, according to some analysts. The Eastern Riders were 7½-point favourites when Grey Cup week began. "I believe they should be," Roughriders receiver Hugh Campbell told The Canadian Press. "All we have to do is go out and get the job done, but Ottawa has beaten us twice this year [including the pre-season]. I hope this isn't proof of anything."

The media and oddsmakers were not alone in building up the Eastern Conference champions. Ottawa head coach Frank Clair was effusive in praising his team. "I've had three Grey Cup winners since coming to Canadian football as a coach but, without knowing how Saturday's game is going to turn out, I'll say the current Ottawa Rough Riders are definitely the best team I've had anything to do with," Clair wrote during Grey Cup week. "When I make that statement, I'm talking about a lifetime in football. For me, there's never been a team like this or a season to equal this one. Saturday's outcome can't change that."

Clair's opposite number, Eagle Keys, cautioned against conceding a victory to Ottawa. "Don't count us out," Keys told the media the day before the game. "We've got a good club and we're ready. We might surprise a lot of people."

CHAPTER 19 | # "I NEVER SAW THE PARADE"

Throughout the Friday of Grey Cup week and into Saturday morning, Roughriders fans descended on Vancouver. The day before the game, an estimated 2,000 Roughriders supporters arrived at the CNR depot. By the hour, fans from Regina, Saskatoon, Winnipeg and Edmonton — and everywhere in between — set foot on Vancouver soil, eager for immersion in the Grey Cup festival.

"If there was an Ottawa Rough Rider supporter in the city, he certainly wasn't anywhere near the railway station," the *Vancouver Province*'s Wilf Bennett reported, noting that fans wearing 'Love Those Esks' and 'Blue Bomber Booster' buttons suspended their loyalties. "It was Regina all the way — all day — as past loyalties and rivalries were forgotten in the big Western putsch," Bennett wrote.

As fans stepped off the trains, they were greeted by bands — including the Regina Police Boys Band — along with the B.C. Lions' cheerleaders, the Lionettes. It was impossible to miss a gigantic banner: "WELCOME TO FRIENDLY VANCOUVER."

Ottawa fans, while outnumbered, would not be outdone. In mid-week, a group of Rough Riders rooters exhausted the transcontinental train's supply of beer and liquor. The Panorama, which normally carried 20 dozen bottles of beer and ale plus about 230 small bottles of spirits, had to be restocked after pulling into Vancouver.

Of the 2,000 people who arrived on Friday, one-quarter spent the overnight hours in some of the CNR's 17 sleeping cars, near the train station. Another 36 reservations had been made for people who would sleep on yachts moored beside the Bayshore Inn.

"It was predetermined that we would spend the night on the train rather than stay in hotels," Peter Barry recalled. "The bar car was one or two cars down from our car and the party went 24 hours a day. One incident I remember was at two or three o'clock in the morning, when there was a hell of a commotion out on the platform. A gang of people from the train had found a piano and were bringing it back to put in the bar car for entertainment. They had the piano halfway up into the bar-car door and it fell — of course breaking. After a quick discussion, it was decided that they'd go get another, and off they went."

Pianos were in vogue during Grey Cup week. In fact, a group of Reginans had loaded a piano on to the club car at Union Station. "My first recollection of the trip was listening to a very irate conductor telling us that 'there is NO way that you guys are putting a piano in my club car,' " Gary Crone wrote in an e-mail. "Some of the 'crazies' at CKCK Radio at the time figured that a piano would fit quite nicely into our Grey Cup plans and had managed to procure a smaller version of a grand piano. A quick strategy meeting was held, and two of the group were dispatched to create a diversion closer to the front of the train to get the conductor's attention away from our task. It was not very difficult to create a diversion with a trainload of hyped-up, excited Riders fans. Once he headed away from us, we simply picked the piano up and carried it around to the end of the train. The club car was the last car. We quickly opened the door on the opposite side of the train [from the conductor] and, in no time, the piano was set up and waiting. The late Jerry Barber, a sales rep at Molson Brewery, had been appointed as the pianist of choice and off we went. Jerry was a very accomplished pianist and had a large repertoire of songs. I think it was when we were passing through Moose Jaw that the conductor made his way back to the club car — only to find a piano and Jerry Barber leading a jam-packed car in one of the many renditions of 'On Roughriders' that was to be played and sung on that memorable weekend. Our conductor friend finally got into the spirit of things and eventually got into the game of, 'Hey, can you play this for me?' It seems that the piano never stopped all the way to Vancouver. In fact, it didn't even stop when we arrived in Vancouver. It was decided that the easiest way to get the piano to the hotel would be to liberate one of those big four-wheel carts that was used to haul baggage to the trains. From the train station, a hardy group of volunteers pushed and pulled the cart, with Jerry proudly pounding out 'On Roughriders' on the piano all the way to the Hotel Vancouver. No question, Jerry Barber would have won the off-field player-of-the-game award!"

Shortly after arriving in Vancouver, Crone visited the Grey Cup Parade route. "I remember stopping at a fence at a construction site to peek through the cracks, expecting to see the foundation for a new building," he said. "Much to my surprise, arranged on the site were the Vancouver SWAT team, police dogs and horses." They were at the ready, just in case the parade got out of hand.

Before the Rough Riders and Roughriders could collide, the rough rioters engaged in battle. The Grey Cup Parade, intended as a celebration of Canadian professional football and its charms, turned into a destructive mob scene in downtown Vancouver.

The first indication of trouble came at 7:30 p.m. — one hour into the 90-minute parade, which was witnessed by some 150,000 people over a span of 20 blocks — when crowds surged on to the road and momentarily impeded the parade route at the intersection of Georgia and Granville streets. Police reinforcements were required to settle the disturbance. Some unruly parade-goers were arrested, including one truculent teenager who fought with no fewer than eight officers as they shoved him into a paddy wagon.

That was a prelude to four hours of chaos, as the focus shifted from floats (137 in all), marching bands, cheerleaders and ticker tape. As the crowd continued to congest Georgia Street, some young revellers shouted: "Down with the courthouse fence!" There were various attempts to attack the fence, none of which succeeded. Those who attempted to scale the fence were stymied by awaiting officers who rapped the intruders' knuckles with two-by-fours. However, the rowdies left their imprint in other ways. By 9:30 p.m., the disturbance ceased to be isolated during the first — and last — night-time Grey Cup Parade.

Bottles were thrown at police officers and spectators, who were also bowled over by the surging crowd. According to the *Vancouver Sun*, "many of the fallen pedestrians were used as stepping stones." This led one constable to marvel: "It's a miracle someone wasn't trampled to death."

Police attempted to clear the sidewalks around 10 p.m., but to no avail. An all-out riot had erupted. All available police officers were summoned, along with some members of the RCMP. Law-enforcement officials — backed by paddy wagons — lined up shoulder-to-shoulder, across Georgia near Howe Street. After the police turned on to Howe, a crowd gathered on Georgia Street, outside the Georgia and Devonshire hotels.

Grey Cup parade rioters | Photo courtesy of *Vancouver Sun*

Grey Cup parade rioters | Photo courtesy of *Vancouver Sun*

This time, the gathering was lighthearted — mischievous but not malicious. Some guests of the Devonshire climbed out hotel windows and stood on a canopy, bowing to the crowd. The merriment was short-lived. The Devonshire's flags were soon torn down, street signs were vandalized, and Grey Cup decorations — dislodged by crazies who climbed light poles — were strewn over the streets. Trash cans were emptied and thrown.

It got worse. A dispute broke out between the crowd — an estimated 4,000 people over a three-block area — on the street and hotel guests in rooms overlooking the street. Hotel patrons dumped water on the mob before hurling glasses and jugs from their rooms. In reprisal, bottles were fired from street level, aimed at the hotel windows.

After police intervened outside the hotels, arrests were made "at the rate of a dozen a minute," according to the *Sun*. The brigade also included fire trucks, due to the fact that a fire alarm had been pulled in the Georgia Hotel — the unofficial Roughriders headquarters, with 85 per cent of its rooms occupied by Saskatchewan fans. The mob encircled the trucks, leaving the firefighters to guard their equipment and await rescue by police intervention.

The fray escalated to the point where officers felt compelled to brandish nightsticks during one of the evening's three major confrontations. Armed with billy clubs, the police personnel attempted to clear the area in front of the hotels. Their task was severely complicated by a barrage of flying bottles. This battle raged for a half-hour, as bottles, rocks and eggs flew. As the bedlam continued, police dogs were deployed.

While this was transpiring, three Reginans — John Lynch, Bob McIntyre and future Roughriders president John Lipp — had just checked into the nearby Hotel Vancouver. "We were barely into the rooms when we heard incredible screaming and noises outside," Lynch recalled. "I looked out the window to see what appeared to be a riot forming. As we watched, it continued to get wilder. Lipp suggested that we go downstairs and investigate it to see how serious it was, and I agreed. When we got downstairs and stuck our noses out the door, we were swept away in a tide of humanity. I was knocked to the sidewalk and stepped on and kicked while Lipp was thrust from side to side by the angry crowd. It was scary. At the last moment, the cavalry arrived in the form of Vancouver's finest with their dog squad and they quickly dispersed the crowd and hauled off several of the more vocal rioters in the paddy wagon. Lipp and I changed our underwear when we got back to the room. I must admit, it was one of the most frightening moments of my life."

Regina's John Haggett and his friend, Gord Clark, received a shock shortly after being dropped off in downtown Vancouver. They had hoped to see the parade. "I'll never forget this," said Haggett, now of Nipawin. "There was a crowd up ahead — wall-to-wall people. We were walking down the street toward the parade when, all of a sudden, the whole crowd turned around at the same time and ran toward us. It was like a stampede. We started running, too, when they brought out the riot police, riot shields and dogs. I never saw the parade."

Members of the Regina Police Boys Band, who marched in the parade, were also swept into the melee. "There were quite a few ugly experiences for the band during the parade because we were a 'police' band," member Peter Barry recalled. "Drunks tried to take flags from kids. We took quite a few punches. Instruments were punched, causing injuries. We did nonetheless go downtown after the parade to see everything, and we sure did. We were right in the middle of the riots for a while. It was crazy."

The Ottawa Rough Riders took notice. Unlike the Western Roughriders, Ottawa was staying downtown — not far away from the ruckus. "Things were getting goofy," Ottawa defensive back Bob O'Billovich remembered. "I think somebody threw a TV out the window of our hotel. It wasn't a player. It was somebody in the hotel." Suddenly, "screen pass" had an entirely new meaning.

When order was restored, police had arrested 443 people. More than half of the violations — 251 — were for being drunk in a public place. Another 162 people were charged with unlawful assembly. The remainder of the charges were for obstructing police, possession of an offensive weapon, impaired driving, theft, willful damage, dangerous driving, being in a dwelling unlawfully, and against a minor who was deemed to be in possession of liquor. Vancouver hospitals reported that 37 people were treated for minor injuries. Police officers escaped, somehow, with nothing more than cuts. "The marvel of it all was that nobody was killed," read a portion of a *Vancouver Province* editorial.

While in opposition to the spirit of the occasion, the riot could hardly be termed a surprise. Three years earlier, when the Grey Cup had previously visited Vancouver, a donnybrook had broken out along Granville Street as a postscript to the parade, with 171 arrests resulting. "On that occasion, there was a period of time when crowd control was lost completely," Mayor Bill Rathie told the *Vancouver Sun*. "[In 1966] it was under control at all times. Police felt they could control it, which wasn't the case in 1963. On the previous occasion, there was a period of up to an hour when they figured it was completely out of hand."

Vancouver alderman Tom Campbell lauded the police for its handling of the 1966 lunacy, but feared a reprise in the hours that followed Saturday afternoon's Grey Cup game. "They've had a taste of blood," Campbell told the *Sun*. "All the punks in town will be downtown tonight." Campbell, too, lamented the fact that the parade was held on a Friday evening, as opposed to the conventional Saturday morning. "It was just an invitation to the hoodlums," he told the *Sun*. "It got all the troublemakers downtown." Campbell labelled the prolonged rumble as "a fiasco, a farce and a disaster."

In that day's edition of the *Sun*, an editorial decried the riot. "In no conceivable way ... can carnival lenience be used to excuse last night's deplorable mob behaviour. Like the Halloween riots, this was idiot violence looking for a reason to happen. Perhaps the timing of the parade, and a too-feverish effort to generate a whoopee spirit, contributed to this mass misbehaviour. But there can be no doubt that the will to riot was there, waiting to be touched off, and what happened was to Vancouver's shame."

The rest of the revelry was in good fun. Hotel lobbies and pubs were popular haunts for football fans of all ages and descriptions — although Roughriders loyalists appeared to be most conspicuous. A *Sun* headline labelled the host city as "Vancouver, Sask."

156 | *"I NEVER SAW THE PARADE"*

One temporary Vancouverite felt right at home. "The late Charlie Underhill was the unofficial host of the Roughriders," Gary Crone remembered. "Charlie Tickets, as he was known, was the manager of Gillies Agencies — the official agency for Roughrider game tickets. One of Charlie's specialties was running one of the best hospitality suites at Grey Cup celebrations. One night, Charlie and a group of us returned to the hotel to partake in some late-night libations. Charlie had already sent someone ahead to open up the suite, so when the security guy asked Charlie for his room key, naturally he didn't have it. A small discussion occurred and the security guy became rather obnoxious. What he didn't know was that Charlie had, at one point, been a professional wrestler. Charlie finally picked the guy up, turned him upside down, walked on to the elevator, hung the guy over the control panel, and calmly said, 'UP, please!' "

Not everyone was impressed by the rowdies. "My only Grey Cup disappointment really has been the Saskatchewan rooters who I confidently predicted would enliven a festival that was becoming a bit of a bore," the *Toronto Star*'s Jim Proudfoot wrote. "Alas, none of the imaginative goings-on I envisaged has materialized. Instead, a bunch of dowdy old dames and adenoidal hicks, all plastered, staggers from hotel to hotel, making life miserable for everybody and occasionally bellowing 'Yay, Riders!' to prove Lord knows what. This is a manifestation of Canadian culture and nationalist spirit? If Mao hears about it, he'll send over two canoes loaded with Chinese and armed with pea-shooters and conquer the country."

Ottawa was widely expected to conquer the Western Riders, and one CFL head coach — interviewed by Jim Taylor of the *Vancouver Sun* — was no exception. "It keeps coming back to defence," said the coach, quoted anonymously. "Whit Tucker is the best deep receiver in the East, and the Saskatchewan deep backs have had problems all year. They've been improving, though, and they weren't nearly as weak in the late stages as the overall record indicates. They've got more pass rush with Ed McQuarters there now and they've got an edge in field-goal kicking with Jack Abendschan. They're underdogs and should be, but don't ever sell them short. This could be the best Grey Cup in years."

Still, Taylor lamented the lack of fireworks leading up to the game. Neither team was inclined toward inflammatory statements. There wasn't any outward sign of enmity between the Grey Cup foes.

"The trouble with this Grey Cup is that everybody's wearing a white hat," Taylor lamented in print. "It's not that you can't tell the bad guys from the good guys. There just aren't any bad guys. Not a black hat to be hissed or a team to be hated. And what kind of Grey Cup is that?" Taylor bemoaned the absence of a controversial figure such as Hamilton defensive tackle Angelo Mosca. "So what have we got?" Taylor asked. "Two teams so much alike their names are practically the same. Two teams who are so sincere they ought to swap their uniforms for blue business suits."

The always-readable Taylor was just getting started. "From the East, we have the Ottawa Rough Riders — dedicated, strong, motivated. From the West, we have the Saskatchewan Roughriders — just as dedicated, just as strong, just as motivated. Maybe we should all pray for a tie. One team is coached by a nice, home-spun guy named Eagle Keys. The other is coached by a nice, scholarly guy named Frank Clair. One team's quarterback (Russ Jackson) beat the other team's quarterback (Ron Lancaster) in voting for Canada's most outstanding player. And they can't say enough nice things about each other. No controversy. No threats. No promises to murder the other guys. It is to yawn. For the first time in years, the game itself is going to have to sell the Grey Cup. There just isn't anything else. Mind you, that football is probably going to be the best in years. But all this goodness, this air of sweetness and light, just seems so out of place in a Grey Cup week. It's enough to make a dedicated fan stay sober."

Would the Grey Cup turn out to be an expectedly sobering experience for the Ottawa side? The Winnipeg Blue Bombers' head coach thought so. "One thing I remember was Bud Grant telling me that Saskatchewan was going to win," recalled Laurie Artiss, who covered the 1966 Roughriders for the *Leader-Post*. "I was asking or telling Bud Grant about seeing the differences in how Saskatchewan and Ottawa prepared for the game. Grant, who was not the most vocal person, said, 'That's why Saskatchewan is going to win.' "

Roughriders trainer Sandy Archer wasn't so certain. "We weren't even supposed to win," he said. "I know we weren't supposed to bet, but I remember seeing the Ottawa trainer before the game. He was an Englishman. He said, 'Hey, you want to put some money on the game?' I said, 'Sure.' I wasn't feeling that confident but, anyway, I took his money and got the guys to put in what they wanted to put in ... $20 or $30, which was a fair bit of money then."

There were fears that people were going to get soaked for other reasons. Field conditions were a concern. "We were practising before the Grey Cup, and it had been raining," Roughriders equipment manager Dale Laird said. "The Empire Stadium turf was pretty soggy. We couldn't practise on it, so we'd dress at Empire Stadium, board a bus and go to a high school field to practise. When we were coming back to Empire Stadium, Hastings Street was up high and you could see down into the stadium. I was sitting behind Reggie Whitehouse on the bus and Ron Atchison was right behind us. We could see the stadium crew out there, spreading stuff on the field to try to dry it up. The field lights were on as brightly as they would be on game day. Reggie said, 'Look at all the stadium lights on.' I said, 'They're trying to dry the field.' Reggie said, 'With the lights?' Atch heard that and roared with laughter. Atch bugged him about that every day — at the hotel, at meetings, at practice. Atch would go up to Reggie and ask, 'With the lights?' "

The Roughriders arrived at Empire Stadium in mid-morning on Sat., Nov. 26, readying themselves for a 1 p.m. kickoff. "Game preparation is different for each player — an extremely personal ritual," Saskatchewan defensive tackle Ed McQuarters reflected. Some of the Roughriders played cards. Others reviewed their assignments. A few of them smoked cigarettes. And tight end Jim Worden, as was pregame custom, threw up.

Defensive lineman Garner Ekstran's pregame message to himself was simple but emphatic: "Beat the guy across from you until he doesn't want to hit you anymore."

Finally, it was time for the teams to hit the soggy Empire Stadium turf. For some of the principals, the warm-ups were interrupted by interviews with CBC commentators Ernie Afaganis and Nobby Wirkowski. Ron Lancaster was the first player to face a microphone. "There's times when I get a little nervous," Lancaster told Afaganis. "There's not really any special way [to avoid the nerves]. I usually like to go into a ball game relaxed and feeling like, 'Well, OK, we're here. We're going to play.'"

Then it was over to Wirkowski, who asked Ottawa quarterback Russ Jackson if Saskatchewan had any deficiencies. "Certainly, I don't think they have any glaring weaknesses, as proven by winning the Western Conference," Jackson responded.

The Ottawa passer went on to say that he expected to encounter difficulty throwing deep against the Roughriders defenders. "They play standard football and they play it tough," Jackson told CBC. "I think their strength is along their front wall and their linebackers. They've got some terrific defensive corners and it helps them a great deal in containing wide stuff and putting the rush on when they want to."

The network proceeded to switch back to Afaganis, who was shown standing beside Eagle Keys. The Roughriders' head coach, while cordial, offered brief but telling responses.

Afaganis: "I don't know if you know it — you probably do — but everyone in the country has been picking you to lose."

Keys: "Well, Ernie, this is a situation you really like to be in. Really, it just gives the players a little more incentive to win."

Afaganis: "The players themselves don't believe all the things they read, I suppose."

Keys: "No, we think we have a real good chance to win."

CHAPTER 20

"THE FANS HAVE INVADED THE FIELD!"

The weather was appropriately grey on Grey Cup day. Beneath an overcast sky, the Roughriders' mood lightened as they prepared to face the Ottawa Rough Riders. "One of the first things that anybody ever says about my part in that game is about when I slipped and fell during the introductions," veteran guard Jack Abendschan lamented. "It had been raining and they had those planks on the field. It was still natural turf and the track was muddy. I was going to jump the mud puddle and land on the wood, and my cleats slipped on the wet wood and I fell right on my butt. That's what you call infamous."

Teammates called it hilarious. "We were uptight a little bit," George Reed said. "When Abendschan slipped, that loosened everybody up and everybody was just laughing. It really released a lot of tension."

Abendschan soon became the first Roughrider to touch the football during the Grey Cup game of Nov. 26, 1966. His opening kickoff travelled 63 yards before being fielded by Bo Scott on the two-yard line. He returned the kickoff 31 yards before Russ Jackson — the league's most outstanding player for 1966 — guided a high-powered offence on to the field. An offside penalty against defensive lineman Garner Ekstran on the opening play put Ottawa in a first-and-five situation. Jim Dillard's three-yard run was followed by Scott's two-yarder, and a first down. On the ensuing play, Saskatchewan was again early off the mark. "That showed how fired up I was," Ekstran said.

Another first-and-five situation left Jackson salivating at the possibilities. Instead of running the ball on first down, the Ottawa quarterback opted to deploy his most dangerous weapon — flanker Whit Tucker. Jackson rolled to his left, set up at Ottawa's 40-yard line, and fired a perfect spiral downfield. Tucker caught the ball in stride near the left hash marks at the Saskatchewan 30-yard line and outran defensive back Larry Dumelie to the end zone to complete the 61-yard play. Only 2:28 into the game, one of Ottawa's pet plays — The Arrow — had opened the scoring. The Arrow called for Tucker to fake a block, such as the one he would make on an end run, before bursting downfield.

"I don't know what I was thinking," defensive halfback Dale West said. "I decided to go up and punish someone. It had never happened before, so why start now? Dumelie got blamed for it on TV." In fact, Dumelie was hardly culpable. "I was covering the wide guy on the other side of the field," Dumelie recalled. "I came deep and I saw Tucker all alone and I tried to get over to cover him. Dale came up and let him go. It was just a mental error. I guess he was too excited."

Ottawa's Moe (The Toe) Racine was wide left on the conversion attempt. It would be that kind of day for the kickers, as foretold, perhaps, by Abendschan's mishap during the player introductions. Racine did respond with a solid kickoff, hoofing the ball 61 yards to Ed Buchanan, who motored 22 yards. The Roughriders' first offensive play was often a handoff to George Reed, but this time around head coach Eagle Keys had something else in mind. During a pre-game interview with CBC's Ernie Afaganis, Keys had hinted at an element of unconventionality. "I think coming out in the opening series of plays, you'll see something different," Keys said. "You can't tell us about it?" Afaganis asked. "Well, it'll be something different," Keys responded. "I haven't seen it this year in Canadian football."

Gord Barwell *catch for 46 yards* | Photo courtesy of *Vancouver Sun*

And for good reason. The Roughriders flanked three receivers — including Buchanan — to the right side of the field. On first down, Ron Lancaster threw a near-lateral to Buchanan, who was dropped for a loss of four. Whereas Ottawa had enjoyed two first-and-fives on its opening series, Saskatchewan was now faced with a second-and-14 predicament. What else could go wrong for the Roughriders in the early stages? One soggy offensive guard. Two offsides. A long touchdown. Their own opening play a failure. The oddsmakers, who favoured Ottawa by a touchdown or more, must have been feeling self-assured.

But not so fast. Undaunted, Lancaster sent Gord Barwell deep and hit him in stride for a 46-yard gain, down to the Ottawa 42-yard line. Two incompletions and a punt followed. Still, the Eastern Conference champions were now backed up to their four-yard line. Six plays, two first downs and two more Saskatchewan offside penalties later, Ottawa was second-and-five on its 26-yard line.

Jackson went to the air, looking for Ted Watkins, but he had been tripped by defensive back Ted Dushinski. The foul went undetected by the officials. With the receiver out of the picture, Dale West snared the pass at the Ottawa 50-yard line and sped down the right sideline. As he neared the end zone, there was only one defender to beat — Russ Jackson. He ended up knocking West out of bounds at the nine-yard line. "The highlight for me was the interception," West noted. "The regret for me was being tackled by a quarterback." Jackson merely delayed the Saskatchewan touchdown. After a three-yard run by Reed, Lancaster called for play action, selling the Ottawa defence on the run before finding a wide-open Jim Worden in the end zone.

Jim Worden *touchdown* |
Photo courtesy of *Vancouver Province*

The collaboration had featured two graduates of tiny Wittenberg College. What were the odds? "Not very good," a chuckling Lancaster said. "First off, they never knew there was a quarterback or a tight end from Wittenberg. That is kind of amazing to be able to do that, because that doesn't happen very often. I don't care if it's Notre Dame."

The teams were one point apart after Abendschan's convert gave Saskatchewan a 7-6 lead 10 minutes into the game. Ottawa answered with four rapid-fire first downs, the last of which came on Jackson's 18-yard connection with — who else? — Tucker. On first-and-10, Jackson shook off pressure from Ekstran (who had defeated two blockers) before looking over the middle for Jay Roberts, who caught the short pass before having the ball jarred loose by Wayne Shaw. Saskatchewan's Wally Dempsey pounced on the ball at his team's 33-yard line. The Ottawa threat was extinguished on the final play of the first quarter. Ottawa had eight first downs to Saskatchewan's two, but trailed 7-6.

To begin the second quarter, Saskatchewan moved 58 yards in six plays, among them a 13-yard toss to Hugh Campbell and a 23-yarder to Buchanan. The latter gain required contortions by Buchanan, who ran a "wheel" route down the left sideline. After a short diversion to the left, Buchanan headed deep and settled under a floater by Lancaster. Buchanan looked for the ball, which was directly above him. He leaned back, adjusted to the pass, made the catch, and stepped out of bounds at the Ottawa 19. From there, Lancaster resorted to a tried-and-true tactic — a pass to Campbell in the end zone — but an incompletion resulted.

On second down, Lancaster was expected to look toward Campbell once again. "The pass route, as I remember, would have been Hugh and Worden running the outs and I was running the corner route," the Roughriders' Alan Ford recounted. "When I broke in the middle of the zone, I didn't expect that the pass was going to come, because most of the time you're just clearing out on that route. When we ran that, most of the time that was to pick up the first down and Hughie would just settle on the sidelines. I was surprised it was coming towards me."

Actually, the pass was coming toward Ottawa defensive back Bob O'Billovich, who was positioned in front of Ford, just inside the end zone, to the right of the goal posts. "I reacted to it well, but when I went up to catch it, it just kind of went through my hands," O'Billovich said. "Al had slipped because I had cut in front of him. He was trying to get back to the ball because the ball had been thrown a little behind him and I was cutting in front of him from the other side. When I got my hands on the ball and I didn't squeeze it and catch it, he fell down and it just dropped into his lap. It was just one of those things that happens. It should have been a pick. Great for them and bad for us."

Alan Ford *touchdown off a Bob O'Billovich tipped ball |*
Photo courtesy of *Vancouver Sun*

CBC play-by-play announcer Fred Sgambati lauded Ford for a "tremendously alert play." Ford was tempered in his assessment. "It was probably the easiest catch of my life," he said. "Of course, I tell my son it wasn't. I tell him it was a one-handed, one-foot-in, falling-backwards catch. It just kind of popped up and it still had enough momentum that it came past Obie and I caught it." At 4:25 of the second quarter, Lancaster already had two touchdown passes, although the second was perilously close to becoming crucial for another reason. "No question, it should have been intercepted," Lancaster stated. "That's why he played defence."

O'Billovich's hands had been more reliable in the two-game Eastern final, during which he made an interception against Hamilton. Given another such opportunity in the Grey Cup, O'Billovich could only bemoan the outcome of the play: "That play in the end zone would have turned it right around." Ford attributed his good fortune to the nature of sport and the inevitability of breaks. "In most games, whether it's playoffs or the championship games, there's a few plays like that where if they went the other way, the game's probably completely different," Ford reflected. "In hockey, how many times do you see a guy miss a great opportunity at one end and, bing, they come back and 10 seconds later they score against you?"

Ottawa struck with a "bing" of its own 42 seconds after Ford's touchdown and Abendschan's convert had given the underdogs from Saskatchewan a 14-6 lead. On the opening play of Ottawa's next possession, Jackson scrambled to his left to avoid pressure and unloaded the ball just before he was hit. Once again, the target was Tucker, who had motored past Dale West after loping upfield during the early stages of the play. The Roughriders' defensive halfback had anticipated that Tucker would migrate in the direction of Jackson. "When a quarterback is in trouble, the receiver is supposed to go toward the line of scrimmage. Tucker didn't and I did," West said. "You make assumptions and it happened there. I feel badly about that."

Tucker caught the ball at Saskatchewan's 40-yard line, outran Ted Dushinski and a diving West, and crossed the goal line for an 85-yard touchdown. He then calmly flipped the ball to the nearest official. "Such are moments of greatness manufactured," CBC's Fred Sgambati said. Racine's convert reduced Saskatchewan's lead to 14-13 at 5:07 of the second quarter. By that point, West had set up one Saskatchewan touchdown with an interception, and been victimized on both Ottawa majors. "Football is like any other sport," West said. "It's a game of mistakes. They were a couple of glaring ones. There's no sense in saying it was anybody else's fault. Stuff happens. There's nothing that you can really do about it. I'm not particularly upset about it, but I live with the mistakes. When you're involved with sport, you have to accept that kind of thing. You don't have to like it. That's what happens. If nobody made a mistake, all the games would be 0-0."

The offences stalled after Tucker's 85-yarder. There was nary a first down on the next four offensive series — the last of which concluded with Ottawa's Bill Cline punting for a single that created a 14-14 tie at 10:41 of the second quarter. Saskatchewan answered with a 42-yard bomb from Lancaster to Worden, but that effort went for naught, as Abendschan's 42-yard field-goal attempt was wide right and returned out of the end zone.

Saskatchewan's lead had evaporated, courtesy of eight straight points by Ottawa, but the Western Conference champions were encouraged by the situation. After all, Ottawa was widely expected to enjoy a comfortable advantage at the 30-minute mark. Late in the first half, Ottawa had attempted to take the lead, only to have Saskatchewan defend the deep pass. Russ Jackson spotted a wide-open Ted Watkins, but the trajectory of the throw was altered by an onrushing Don Gerhardt. Jackson also directed another bomb toward Tucker, but the play was foiled by Larry Dumelie.

"I think we knew we had it in our hands at halftime," Saskatchewan guard Al Benecick said. "They were starting to weaken a bit." One of the reasons was a robust effort by linebacker Wayne Shaw. "I'm sitting at halftime thinking I've played a pretty good game," Shaw said. "I see Eagle Keys go up to Jack Abendschan and say, 'Jack, keep it up. You're playing a good game.' I don't know how Jack played, but I know he tripped coming out. I'm sitting there thinking that I did really well. Then Eagle comes over to me and says, 'Wayne, you can do a little better.' Well, in the second half I'm all mad at Eagle. It seems to me that, in sport, it's the old story about the 110 per cent. It's corny, but you have to use some psychology sometimes to get guys to give a little extra effort. Eagle had it figured out."

Meanwhile, on the Empire Stadium turf, the halftime show was in progress. The theme: A salute to Canada's centennial, to be commemorated in 1967. The festivities at the 1966 Grey Cup included 100 people dressed as candles. Millions watched across the country, with CBC boasting that its telecast was "in colour." The statistics, meanwhile, were in black and white. Most notably, there were Tucker's three receptions for 164 yards and two long touchdowns. Hugh Campbell, by comparison, had been held in check. After catching a league-record 17 touchdown passes in the regular season, Gluey Hughie merely had a 13-yard reception to show for the first half of the Grey Cup. George Reed, another big gun on offence, had just seven carries for 31 yards, along with Saskatchewan's only first down rushing.

"All I told them at the half was that they were doing a fine job," Keys told reporters afterward. "I felt that we were starting to move in the second quarter, and that if we could keep the score down in the third quarter when Ottawa had the wind, that we would win."

In the second half, it quickly became evident that Saskatchewan would re-emphasize its ground game. Reed carried the ball on Saskatchewan's first three offensive plays, gaining nine, three and five yards. He rushed nine times for 46 yards in the third quarter, yet the stalemate continued. There was a potential game-changing play early in the quarter, when Ottawa's Mike Blum picked off Lancaster in Saskatchewan territory. However, the interception was negated because Blum was flagged for interfering with Worden — a call the Rough Riders questioned.

Nobody could question the Saskatchewan defence, which kept Ottawa hemmed in. On one occasion, Bill Cline was forced to punt from his end zone. Saskatchewan ended up with prime field position, scrimmaging the ball at the Ottawa 38-yard line, but was unable to capitalize. Abendschan attempted another field goal, from the 36, but the kick fell short. The Rough Riders were again uncomfortably close to their end zone. On first down from the three-yard line, Garner Ekstran dropped Jim Dillard for a loss of one. A four-yard run by Ron Stewart was followed by another Cline punt. Gene Wlasiuk fielded the 36-yard boot on Ottawa's 42 and barged straight ahead for 10 yards — a notable feat in an era when blocking on punt returns was forbidden.

From the 32, Lancaster turned to Reed, who began the drive with runs of five, four and three yards, the latter coming on a third-down gamble. On first down from the 20, Lancaster threw incomplete to Campbell in the end zone. An offside penalty to Ottawa, which jumped early after Lancaster changed his cadence, made it second-and-five. Although Campbell had only one catch at that point, there was little doubt as to Lancaster's preferred target in scoring territory, especially in a game of such import. Sure enough, Lancaster called for Campbell to run a comeback pattern to the quarterback's left. The pass was low, but in an area where only Campbell could make the catch. He came up with a sliding reception despite close coverage by Ottawa defensive back Joe Poirier. As CBC's Nobby Wirkowski observed: "Poirier was helpless."

Reed was stuffed for no gain on first-and-goal from the five, and the gun sounded to end the third quarter. The final quarter opened with the Roughriders in a passing situation. Everyone was focusing on Campbell — especially Lancaster and Poirier. The Ottawa defensive back, who had effectively shadowed Campbell for most of the game, had lined up to Lancaster's left. Upon seeing Campbell on the right, Poirier scurried over to that side of the field as Lancaster studied the defence.

Lancaster took the snap from Ted Urness and did a half-roll to the right. Campbell settled into a spot just inside the goal line, attracting the attention of three Ottawa defenders — Poirier, O'Billovich and Gene Gaines. Despite triple coverage, Lancaster fired the ball toward his ace receiver. Campbell leaped and made the catch, with Poirier closest to him, before falling to the turf. The ball came loose, but possession had been established. A touchdown was signalled. Saskatchewan was ahead.

"It was a great play by Campbell on a hook pattern," Poirier said following the game. "I had a piece of the ball, but he grabbed it away from me. By the time I recovered and snatched the ball away from him, it was too late." Yet again, a defence had been powerless to disrupt the timing of Campbell and Lancaster. "That one was kind of a lucky

Hugh Campbell *touchdown in triple coverage* |
Photo courtesy of *Vancouver Sun*

throw," Lancaster said. "Even I'd have to say that. I didn't think it was when I threw it, but after looking at it on film, it was pretty lucky. I didn't see all those black jerseys around him. It hit him right in the numbers but, man, it had to duck and dodge and dive to get in there. But he caught it. That's the main thing. We didn't throw as much as we probably thought we would, but we got our running game going and that's what hurt them."

Campbell continued running after the touchdown catch. He clapped his hands and rushed to the sideline, without engaging in any of the elaborate touchdown celebrations that have become so prevalent. "It wasn't false modesty or anything else," Campbell said. "That's just the way people were then. You didn't bring as much attention to yourself. It just wasn't in you. It wasn't a consideration. The thrill was still as big as ever. There wasn't the individual emphasis. It was just team, team, team."

Abendschan converted Campbell's major to put Saskatchewan ahead 21-14 — the same score by which the Roughriders had lost to Ottawa in the Grey Cup 15 years earlier.

In the second quarter, Ottawa had answered a Lancaster touchdown pass with a scoring bomb to Tucker. The Eastern Conference representative was not as fortunate after the Campbell major. Gaines returned the kickoff 40 yards, but two incompletions followed. On first down, Jackson attempted to go deep to running back Ron Stewart, but the play was disrupted by pressure from Ken Reed, Ron Atchison and Ed McQuarters. More pressure from Reed prevented Jackson from connecting with Tucker on the next play as well.

Saskatchewan assumed possession and kept running the football effectively. Six successive running plays produced 40 yards and continued to consume precious time before

George Reed pounds his way for extra yardage |
Photo courtesy of *Vancouver Sun*

George Reed's touchdown – not to be denied |
Photo courtesy of *Vancouver Sun*

Ford was forced to punt. Jackson proceeded to find Tucker for nine yards, but Wally Dempsey responded with a monstrous defensive play — flattening Jim Dillard for no gain on second-and-one. Once again, Cline was forced to punt from deep in Ottawa territory.

Again, a running attack was prescribed. After Ed Buchanan ran for six yards on first down, George Reed stormed for 10 yards. Upon being tackled, an unusually demonstrative Reed punched and kicked the turf, furious at himself for not gaining additional yardage. Nonetheless, Reed had moved the chains, positioning Saskatchewan on Ottawa's 31-yard line. Reed had casually shuffled back to the line of scrimmage, as was his custom, but that did not indicate fatigue. Knowing that, Lancaster called Reed's number for the 15th time in a span of 29 second-half plays. The Roughriders' quarterback also changed the blocking assignments at the line of scrimmage, calling for a play known as 31M.

Cross-blocks by Urness and Abendschan cleared a hole that was quickly accessed by Reed. Urness crossed in front of Abendschan, the left guard, and eliminated defensive tackle Ted Collins. Abendschan took one step to his right before surging ahead to neutralize middle linebacker Ken Lehmann. Reed hit the hole just to the left of Abendschan. With Lehmann out of the picture, the secondary was the last line of defence. Poirier dove for Reed but was unsuccessful as the bruising fullback stormed toward the goal line, high-stepping the final few yards.

"I was pissed off, because they had stopped me the play before, and they shouldn't have stopped me," Reed recalled. "I guess it was kind of, 'Well, you can't stop me this time.' I was a little bit perturbed at myself because I had gained 10 yards the first time and they had tripped me up. [The high-stepping] wasn't to try to show up anybody. I don't know whether I felt someone was nipping at my heels. It was just one of those things that happened." Lancaster felt the long run by Reed was inevitable. "We'd been having success running inside and I felt they were going to be in that [balanced] defence again, which is their basic defence," he told CBC. "We hadn't broken anything up through there yet and it was a matter of time before we were going to get something through. We just changed the blocking a little bit and the hole was there. When he gets through, that's it." And that was it. Reed's touchdown essentially put a dagger in the Eastern Riders. Reed described the feeling of crossing the goal line as a sense of: "Now we've put you away. The Grey Cup is ours. You have to bring all the champagne and beer from the Ottawa dressing room over to our dressing room."

Some 30 yards away, Abendschan savoured the scene. "I really felt good about that one," he said. "I didn't feel good about missing the field goals." Abendschan more than compensated for two earlier misses, and a third that was to follow. "The field was wet," he said. "It had been raining for a while. I was a straight-ahead kicker, so a lot of times when it's wet like that and you plant your left foot to bring your right foot through the kick, it'll give a little bit. I guess I could use that reason. That's the only negative I remember about the game, really."

The scoring concluded at 11:41 of the fourth quarter when Ford punted for a single to give Saskatchewan a 29-14 lead. This was in the era before the two-point conversion, so Ford's boot put Ottawa in a situation where it needed three scoring plays in slightly more

They say you never forget your first time | Photo courtesy of *Vancouver Sun*

than three minutes. His rouge was preceded by an interception from an unlikely source — defensive lineman Don Gerhardt, who foiled a trick play by settling under a wobbly pass from running back Ron Stewart. On that play, Ed McQuarters "materially assisted with pressure," according to the eloquent Sgambati.

Over the final 30 minutes, Saskatchewan dominated both lines of scrimmage. "The second half turned it," Jackson said. "They came out and they got the ball and George just started running at us. He'd pick up seven and eight yards. They were just crushing us. When we'd get the ball, we were two-and-out too often. The defence just got tired out."

The Saskatchewan offensive linemen — Ted Urness, Jack Abendschan, Al Benecick, Clyde Brock and Reg Whitehouse — routinely cleared holes for Reed and Buchanan. Meanwhile, the defensive line — a five-man front — harassed Jackson and played a key role in preventing a customarily potent Ottawa offence from crossing midfield for the entire second half. Along with the interception, Gerhardt sacked Jackson and pressured him throughout the afternoon. Shaw and Dempsey made immense contributions at their linebacking positions.

Dempsey and Ekstran led the Roughriders with seven tackles apiece. Bob Kosid added six stops. There was also the omnipresent Shaw. "That was probably the best game I ever played from '61 to '66," he said. Appropriately, the game ended on a tackle by Shaw — Cliff Shaw. "My brother went in for me at the end of the game and made the tackle, and I got credit for it," said Wayne Shaw, who was awarded the tackle by the official statisticians.

Cliff Shaw wrapped up Bo Scott on a sweep to the right in the waning seconds. After Scott was trapped for a loss of two, some of the 32,344 spectators — about 4,000 below capacity — assumed centre stage. "The fans have invaded the field!" Sgambati said as the Vancouver crowd reprised the premature ending to the 1960 Grey Cup, also held at Empire Stadium. "There's four seconds showing on the clock." And, after 56 years of waiting, one Grey Cup to show for the Roughriders' efforts.

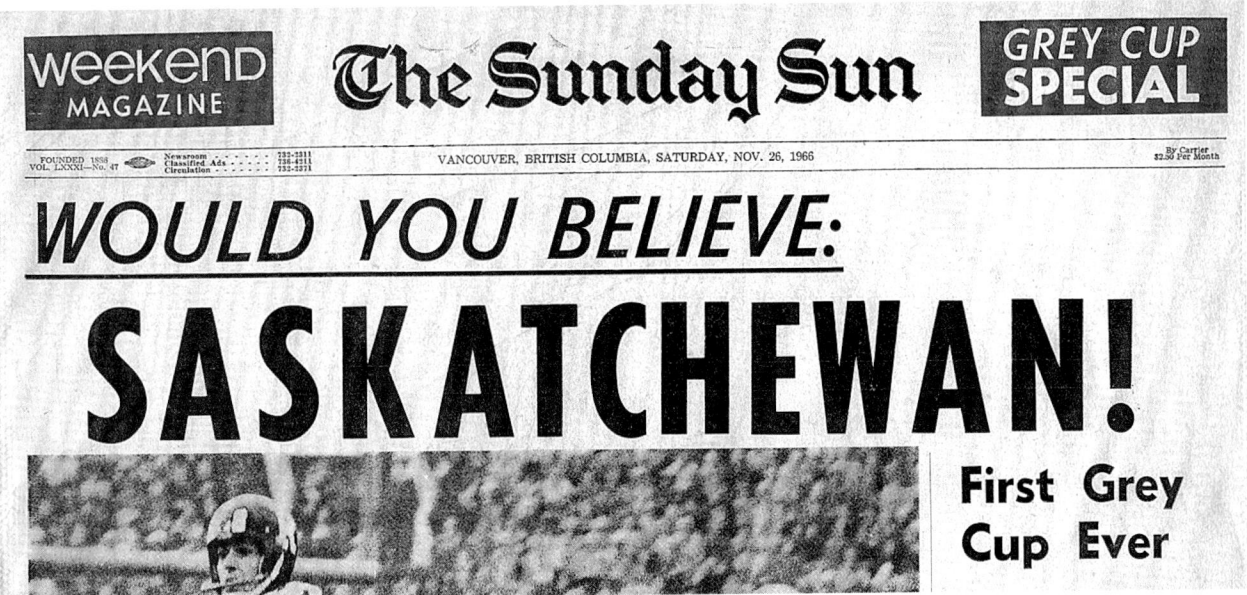

Believe it! | Courtesy of *Vancouver Sun*

CHAPTER **21**

"BEAUTIFUL SATISFACTION"

Larry Dumelie was reputedly a punishing hitter — as one fan who attended the 1966 Grey Cup could attest. The fan was among the revellers who swarmed the Empire Stadium turf with four seconds remaining in the game, with the Saskatchewan Roughriders leading Ottawa 29-14. The invasion was such that the game was called. "On the last play, Bo Scott ran the ball and we tackled him," remembered Dumelie, who made a beeline for the game ball after Scott placed it on the grass. "All the fans came on to the field. Two of them jumped me. One right on my back tried to take the ball away from me. I spun one away and the other guy was coming at me, so I cold-cocked him. It was probably one of our own fans. I don't know. But then I got away from them. I took off on the dead run to the dressing room because there were thousands of fans on the field by then. I figured that after that, there would be more than one person trying to get the ball."

Dumelie's defensive backfield cohort, Ted Dushinski, was a little slower getting to the dressing room. One Roughriders fan, wearing a First World War-style army helmet, grabbed one of Dushinski's legs and would not let go. Dushinski dragged the fan across the field and toward the locker room before finally escaping his clutches.

Meanwhile, John Haggett was looking for his friend, Gord Clark. Haggett and Clark had travelled to the game together, but sat on opposite sides of the stadium. Their Regina-bound

Larry Dumelie | Photo courtesy of SSHFM

train was leaving shortly after the game, so Haggett tried to rejoin his buddy as quickly as possible. As the final seconds ticked away, Haggett was among many fans who hopped barricades around the end zone. Some fans ran toward the players. Haggett, by contrast, planned to scurry across the end zone — nowhere near where the ball was being scrimmaged — to take the most direct route to Clark's seat. "It almost cost me my life," Haggett said. "I started running and noticed all these mickey bottles across the field. The people in the end-zone seats took great delight in throwing bottles at people. I was dodging missiles. Somehow, I got across the field without getting hit. And then — bang! — the gun went off and I looked on the field, and there was Gord. He was one of the guys hoisting Ron Lancaster on to his shoulders."

Most of the fans were filing out of the stadium in orderly fashion, but a surprise awaited them, too. The *Vancouver Sun* had prepared a souvenir edition. "Erwin Swangard — the managing editor at the *Sun* — decided he wanted to have a special rush edition published and sent by helicopter from the roof of the *Sun* to Empire Stadium to catch the crowd coming out," said Jim Taylor, one of Canada's pre-eminent sports columnists. "And for that special edition, he wanted the football writer's byline on the game story. So I sat in his office at the *Sun* and wrote a running-copy game story. Best game I never saw. There was, however, a happy ending. Some of the bundles weren't tied tightly enough to the helicopter and flew off as it ascended. Inside, I cheered."

Outwardly, so did the legion of Roughriders fans who finally had a championship to celebrate. "We were among the delirious fans who stormed on to the field," recalled

Fans showing their support as they hoist Rider lineman **Don Gerhardt** *on their shoulders* |
Photo courtesy of *Vancouver Sun*

Ron Lancaster *looks to pass while* **George Reed** *and* **Alan Ford** *are blocking, giving him plenty of time* |
Photo courtesy of *Vancouver Sun*

Regina's Neil Sawatzky, whose son Jeff became the Roughriders' official national-anthem singer some 40 years later. "Some tried tearing down the goal posts with hopes of getting a souvenir splinter to commemorate a great event in Roughrider history. Being true stubble-jumpers, we had the bright idea to rip clumps of turf out of the soggy field from the end zone where George Reed had scored so we could transplant the hallowed ground in our own backyard in Regina. Unfortunately, it never took. We either pampered it too much or it simply couldn't survive our winter."

Ed McQuarters survived the Grey Cup game. The aftermath was the dangerous part. "The worst injury I got all season was Garner Ekstran hitting me on the back after the game," McQuarters said of his defensive-line cohort. "I had a champagne bottle up to my mouth. I said, 'Everybody's having fun. I'm going to tip this champagne bottle up.' " That was a rarity for McQuarters, a non-drinker, but these were special circumstances. "As I tipped it up, he hit me on the back. *Bam*! The bottle hit my tooth and it chipped my tooth," McQuarters said. "Everybody was celebrating the win in the championship game. As an athlete, that's your pot of gold at the end of the rainbow. The pot of gold didn't have much gold in it, but that's the whole reason for doing it. All the pain and all the stuff you go through is worth it."

Ron Lancaster leaned back and let it all soak in. "The most gratifying feeling after you win is that you can actually sit down and relax, knowing that you don't have to prepare for another game," he said. "You know you got to the game that mattered and you know you won it. It was nice to just sit there and watch everybody celebrate."

For Hugh Campbell, the occasion was enhanced by the opportunity to watch a teammate and close friend enjoy the victory. "I remember what it meant to Ronnie," Gluey Hughie said. "It wasn't that long after he had been traded away from Ottawa so that Russ Jackson could play more. It was a deal where a guy who got let go by one team comes back and beats that team in the Grey Cup. He didn't talk about it like it meant much, but you could see him glow after the game. I felt like he was as happy as he could be right then."

Lancaster downplayed the significance of quarterbacking Saskatchewan to victory over his former team, but did not deny that the scenario provided additional satisfaction. "It's always nice to beat the people that you had played with, but not to the degree that most people think," Lancaster said 40 years later. "I was watching *60 Minutes* when Tiger Woods was talking to Ed Bradley about being competitive. Tiger kind of smiled and said, 'I'm competitive. If we were playing cards, I'd want to kick your butt.' Ed Bradley said, 'So you really want to win.' He said, 'No, no. There's a difference between winning and kicking your butt. I want to kick your butt.'

"That's probably what it is. Any athlete that I've ever met, he wants to win, and then when he wins, he wants to kick your butt so you don't forget it. So it's not a case of who you're playing against. It made it kind of nice, but a lot of those guys have been my friends for a long time, like Whit Tucker and Russ Jackson. We're still pretty darned good friends. One of them's going to lose and, the way I always looked at it, it might as well be them. They got us later [in 1969], but we got them in that game."

Ron Lancaster *getting ready to throw while* **Alan Ford** *and* **George Reed** *block* | Photo courtesy of *Vancouver Sun*

Lancaster finished with 10 completions in 20 attempts for 160 yards, with three touchdowns and no interceptions. The three touchdown tosses tied a Grey Cup record, established by Joe Krol of Toronto (in 1946) and equalled by Sam Etcheverry of Montreal (1954). Although George Reed had also enjoyed a fine game, rushing 23 times for 133 yards, it was unofficially decided that Lancaster was the game's top player. "There was no formal award, but I actually have a little plaque downstairs in a box that says I was the player-of-the-game in the 1966 Grey Cup as determined by the media, or however it was written," he said 40 years later. The Grey Cup reinstated the formal most-valuable-player award in 1967, following a four-year interruption.

The Roughriders' players were not preoccupied with individual accolades as the celebration raged. After eight unsuccessful trips to the Grey Cup, it was finally the Roughriders' turn. Even so, some members of the team adhered to tradition by experiencing disappointment at game's end. It was, however, a different kind of disappointment than the Roughriders had endured so many times before.

"We were sad the game ended," guard Al Benecick said. "Sometimes you can't wait until they end and you're glad it's over, but we were sad that one ended. We could have kept going and going and going. It was a wonderful feeling."

The same sentiment was not felt on the other side of Empire Stadium, where Ottawa lamented its fate during postgame interviews with CBC's Ernie Afaganis. "I actually didn't think they'd beat us," middle linebacker Ken Lehmann said. "Ronnie, he's the one who did it, really, because he called the automatics and did a real good job with it." Lehmann also noted that "the footing was bad out there. We couldn't get our running game going. You just can't depend on the long bomb when they're in a zone defence."

The Rough Riders were unfailingly cordial, and complimentary of Saskatchewan, in conversation with Afaganis. "We were beaten by a very fine team today — Eagle Keys' Saskatchewan Roughriders," head coach Frank Clair said. "All credit goes to them. They played well. They outplayed us. We had a few tough breaks." Clair added: "A great team like they are, they just outplayed us and they won it very honourably."

Russ Jackson, always the epitome of class, also commended the winning side.

Eagle Keys *focused on winning* |
Photo courtesy of *Vancouver Sun*

"We got the two long passes, but that's about all they gave us," Jackson told Afaganis. "We didn't move the ball very well and we couldn't come out of our own end when they put us back there. They kept us in there and that's how they won." Defensive back Gene Gaines was most gracious, telling CBC: "I'm glad that they were the ones that beat us, because they deserved to beat us. They were the better team today."

Head coach Eagle Keys was the first Roughrider to be interviewed by CBC. "Words can't describe how I feel," he told Afaganis. "This is the greatest thrill that I've ever had in my life. What more can you say?" Keys seldom said more than was necessary, nor did he reveal many emotions. He responded to his self-described greatest thrill with a slight smile. "We have a big party all lined up. It's been a long time ...," Keys went on to say. "I'd just like to say to the people of Saskatchewan, 'This is your Cup ... for this year.' "

Keys was then presented with the Grey Cup by outgoing CFL commissioner Sydney Halter. "For the first time ever, the name of the Regina Roughriders will be inscribed on it," Halter told Keys while using the city instead of the province to identify the victorious team. "It's a very, very happy occasion and my heartfelt congratulations." The ranks of the dignitaries included Regina mayor Henry Baker. "Hello, Regina and Saskatchewan," Baker said to Afaganis. "I hope you don't tear the city apart before we get home." Baker estimated that between 6,000 and 7,000 Saskatchewan residents were at the Grey Cup, including 5,000 from Regina. "We're very, very happy," Baker concluded. "We've made history today."

Hugh Campbell, who had made CFL history that season by catching a league-record 17 touchdown passes, was asked by Afaganis about being double-covered. "We had a lot of plays called anticipating this," Campbell said after catching three passes for 28 yards. "I had fun being a decoy ... I'd just say Ronnie made the right call at the right time and we beat an awfully good team."

But the Rough Riders were not as good as touted — at least not on Nov. 26, 1966. "They've got a great defensive ball club," George Reed told Afaganis. "They've got a great ball club altogether, but I think we were a little irritated all week. The press kind of built them up to be superhuman and we didn't have a chance. We just wanted to prove that we had a good football team, also. I think you saw two good football teams fighting it out and the better team of the day won."

Reed's backfield sidekick, Ed Buchanan, also noted that Saskatchewan's chances were widely discounted. "Just about every game we played this year, we were the underdog," Buchanan said on television after rushing 10 times for 54 yards and setting up a touchdown with a 23-yard reception. "I love being the underdog ... It fires us up a little bit. They always think of Saskatchewan as small and so on. They don't realize that we have just as good a team as anybody else, if not better. It's just like the Green Bay Packers. They're from a little small town and they're the champions. I think the people judge our team on the size of our town instead of the size of our team and the ability of our team, and we have a great team." The easygoing Buchanan concluded the interview by alluding to the anticipated bedlam in Regina. "I'm glad I'm not going back until tomorrow," he said, "because they'd probably kill us if we came back there tonight."

***Ed Buchanan** hugging the Grey Cup* |
Photo courtesy of Vancouver Sun

The Roughriders' long-awaited Grey Cup victory was truly intoxicating. "All the champagne had been in Ottawa's locker room, from what I've heard," linebacker Wally Dempsey said. "They were so sure that Ottawa was going to beat us that they stacked everything up over there. By the time it was close to the end of the game, I guess there was some heavy-duty shuffling going on because it was in the wrong locker room. Nobody thought we were going to win — absolutely nobody. That was the first time I drank champagne in a shower. Champagne was flowing all over the place."

Reg Whitehouse saw to that. Following the final game of his 15-year CFL career, Whitehouse played a key role in the rapid disappearance of four cases of champagne. "I stacked them up by the door," he recalled. "When all the fans walked past, I gave them a bottle." Whitehouse and his teammates also sipped champagne from the Cup. More than once, the trophy's bubbly contents were dumped over players' heads.

The Roughriders' head coach also ended up being soaked. "Coach Eagle Keys managed to escape for a while by hiding behind a covey of news people and well-wishers," Clancy Loranger wrote in the *Vancouver Province*, "but eventually he was discovered and carted off to a damp denouement." Keys' assistants, Jack Gotta and Jim Duncan, were likewise doused. Then it was the general manager's turn. "After they dumped Eagle in the shower, they wanted to throw Ken Preston in," said Barry Armstrong, a visitor to the dressing room who was the marketing manager for Molson at the time. "They had to allow him to change into a sweatsuit before they put him in."

Jack Abendschan was well ahead of the curve, having been saturated during the pregame player introductions when he took a tumble and landed on the soggy field. "I just slipped," Abendschan told reporters while sipping champagne. "I felt real cool — then, oops. Will I make the record books with that?" Dale West, who was burned for two first-half touchdown bombs to Whit Tucker, was also able to make light of his misfortunes. As he told reporters: "The official score of the game should be Saskatchewan 29, Dale West 14."

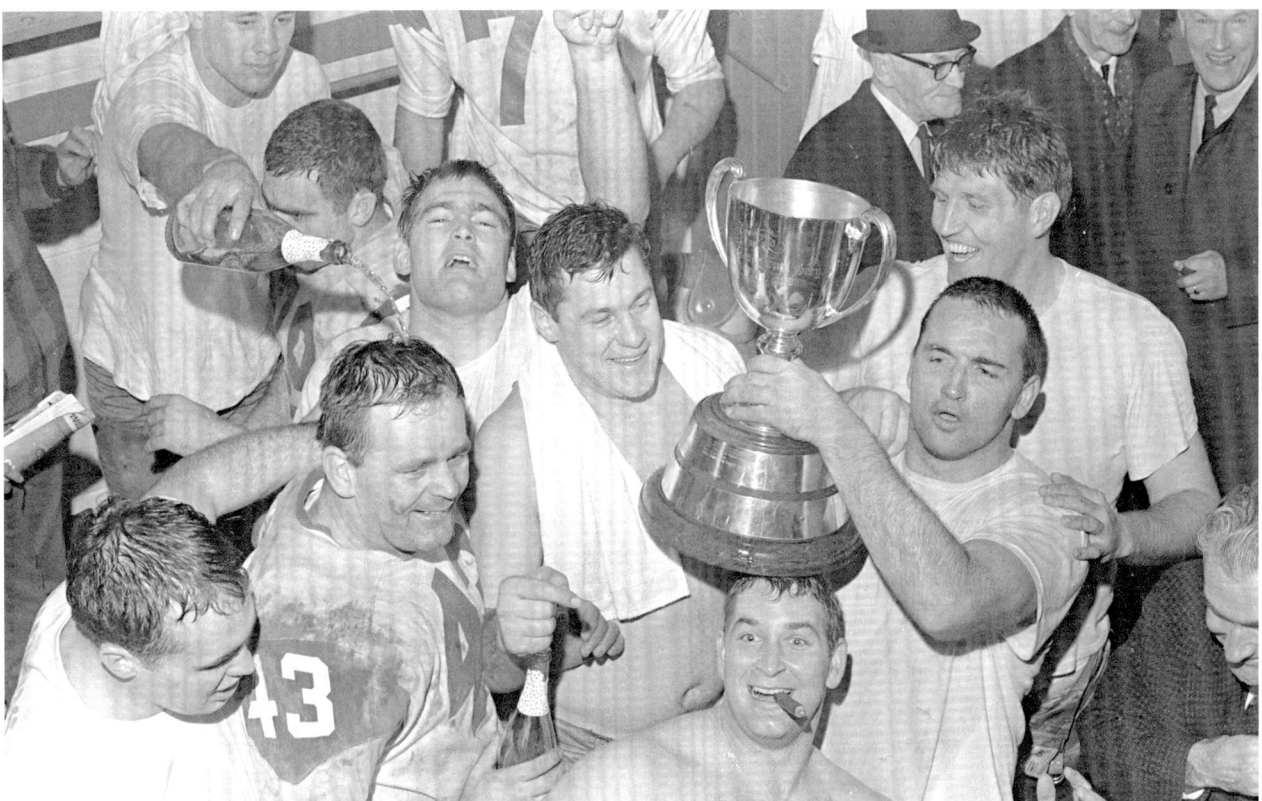

Linemen revel in their hard-earned victory | Photo courtesy of *Vancouver Sun*

During post-game interviews, Eagle Keys had been interrupted by tight end Jim Worden. "Quit bullshitting, Eagle, and get drinking," Worden suggested. As the Roughriders and their fans rejoiced, the Ottawa players quietly showered, got dressed and boarded a bus. "One of the quotes I always remember is from after the game when we were leaving the stadium," Rough Riders defensive back Bob O'Billovich said. "Some guys can have humour in the worst situations and other guys are pretty distraught after losing. I remember Whit Tucker was in the back of the bus and someone said something like, 'Well, it's too bad we lost.' He said, 'Well, I got my two.' I'll never forget that. That was a good line."

Saskatchewan had good lines on both sides of the ball. "Saskatchewan was taking big, wide line splits and our defensive front wasn't adjusting to the splits," O'Billovich reflected. "We kept splitting out with them. George Reed was coming through there like there was nobody there." The absence of Rough Riders assistant coach Bill Smyth, who had died unexpectedly as Ottawa prepared for the playoffs, was also noted. "Because coach Smyth wasn't there, there wasn't a defensive coach who was able to get our guys together and tell them what was happening and explain what we had to do to adjust," O'Billovich said. "That had a lot to do with the outcome, because George had a big second half running the ball."

The Rough Riders had peaked in the finale of the Eastern Conference championship, defeating the Hamilton Tiger-Cats 42-16 at Ivor Wynne Stadium to win the two-game, total-points set 72-17 — despite the trauma of losing Smyth. "To go down there and beat

Hugh Campbell and Ron Atchison – *Atch finally gets to celebrate after 15 years!* |
Photo courtesy of *Vancouver Sun*

them on their own field, it was a pretty emotional thing," O'Billovich said of the Hamilton series. "When we got to the Grey Cup, maybe we lost a little bit of the adrenalin that we had the week before. I think it was more to do with not having the coach there to help us than it had anything to do with your emotions and your feelings, because we were all professional athletes and you've got to do what you've got to do. We weren't really as well-prepared and as well-coached as we could have been if he had been there."

The only devastation in Saskatchewan's dressing room pertained to the tattered sweater (not to be confused with a football jersey) of venerable defensive lineman Ron Atchison. Teammates had kept threatening to destroy Atchison's green pullover, which they deemed to be an archaic eyesore. The Grey Cup victory provided the impetus for Atchison's colleagues to follow through on their oft-stated threats regarding the sweater.

"I told them they couldn't do that to me because I'm the only guy on the team who gets paid so low I can't afford a new one," Atchison told Denny Boyd of the *Vancouver Sun*. "But I don't mind trading this old sweater for today." Atchison was then asked if the fate of the sweater foreshadowed his future (or lack thereof?) as a player after 15 seasons of Canadian professional football. "You mean, am I going to retire?" Atchison retorted. "Hell no. If the team will just start paying me what I'm worth, I figure I have another four years left in me. I'm only 36 and when you live good and think good, you can play forever. I want to stick with this club and these coaches. We won this thing today, but the guy who got us here was Eagle Keys and he's the greatest coach I've ever played for. You can tell everybody that."

Gradually, the Saskatchewan players filed out of the dampened dressing room and made their way to the bus. Empire Stadium was almost vacant, but the celebration was only

The Shaw brothers celebrate with their family | Photo courtesy of the Shaw family

beginning. "They brought out the champagne at the hotel," defensive back Larry Dumelie said. "They had glasses and there was a fireplace. We were drinking the champagne and firing the glasses into the fire. We had all kinds of people there who probably didn't belong. Some of the guys I remember vividly. Jackie Parker was a good friend of Eagle's so I'm sure he was invited, but there were a lot of friends of the team as well as the fans. They didn't bar anybody. It was pretty wild."

The list of guests included Joe and Audrey Kosid, then of Chicago. "I'll tell you what was really special. Mom and Dad were there," said defensive back Bob Kosid, whose sister Janet was also in attendance. "After the game, the Grey Cup was passed around at the hotel. I had the opportunity of presenting it to my father, full of champagne. Oh gosh. He grew up in Saskatoon and he played a little football for the University of Saskatchewan and then World War II grabbed him. That was a special, special moment. I was like, 'This is the way it is in Hollywood. Don't pinch me.'"

Joe Kosid shared fond recollections of that occasion. "I remember drinking champagne from the Grey Cup, primarily," he said. "My son was a thoughtful young man and he hid a bottle of champagne away. When we arrived at the party, he dragged out the bottle and poured it in the Grey Cup and I drank from it. That was a big, big deal."

Ed Shaw was able to share in the celebration with two of his sons — linebackers Wayne and Cliff. "It was the first time he ever flew in an airplane," Wayne Shaw said. "All my brothers were at the Grey Cup. I have four brothers. I *had* four brothers. They're all gone now. After the game, my dad had a photographer come in and he arranged for a picture of Cliff and me and my dad with the Grey Cup. There's also a picture of Cliff and me and my dad and our three other brothers. It was a very proud moment."

At the same postgame party, CKCK Radio sportscaster John Badham chatted with former Roughriders president Bob Kramer. "He came up to me and said, 'We may have created a problem. People will expect us to win every year now,' " Badham remembered.

The victory was particularly gratifying for the Roughriders' elder statesmen — Reg Whitehouse and Ron Atchison. Both linemen had endured some of the darkest days in franchise history, such as the 1956 airplane crash that claimed teammates Mel Becket, Mario DeMarco, Gord Sturtridge and Ray Syrnyk. Three years later, Whitehouse and Atchison were part of the worst-ever Saskatchewan team, which won but one of 16 games.

As a contrast, there were the landmark events of 1966. "It was beautiful satisfaction," Atchison said. "It was something that you just longed to do and you finally had that fulfillment. It was a feeling of, 'Thank goodness. I thought this was never going to happen.' It was a joyful feeling. I had a good feeling — a wonderful feeling — right up until next year's training camp. It was like floating on air. Nothing could take away that nice feeling of, 'My goodness, we've finally won the Grey Cup.' "

Joanne and Reg Whitehouse with team president Don MacDonald | Photo courtesy *of Leader-Post*

Nobody revelled in the victory more than Whitehouse. "He celebrated enough for a few people," Alan Ford said. Whitehouse also celebrated the end of his playing career. After the game, he handed his cleats to Canadian football legend Annis Stukus. "My knees and my legs were giving out on me," Whitehouse said. "I didn't want to go out there and embarrass myself. I didn't want to play football anymore." He was, however, the last to quit socializing.

As the Grey Cup party wound down at the team's Burnaby hotel, Whitehouse informed team president Don MacDonald of his intent to take the trophy to downtown Vancouver. MacDonald and general manager Ken Preston eventually provided grudging consent. "My main objective was to give all those Saskatchewan fans that had travelled to Vancouver a chance to see the Cup and drink from it," Whitehouse told the *Leader-Post*'s Laurie Artiss. "It was all fun. I never stopped laughing all night. And I was hanging on to that thing too tight to have anybody get it away from me."

Whitehouse had been granted permission to take the Grey Cup on tour on the condition that he was accompanied by his wife, Joanne. "She had to be the bodyguard," Whitehouse said in a 1982 interview with John Chaput of the *Leader-Post*. "I'd promised I'd have it back by three in the morning. But when I got back to MacDonald's room at the Hotel Vancouver, the guard said no one was allowed in. 'But I've got the Grey Cup,' I said, and he goes, 'Well, I've heard everything now,' but he looked at the inscription — 'Hey, that IS the Grey Cup!' — and let me in."

In his travels that night, Whitehouse ran into CFL commissioner Sydney Halter. "Sir Sydney almost lost his Charles de Gaulle cool when he spotted the Grey Cup being mishandled and suggested Reg forthwith and posthaste deposit it in a safe place," Artiss wrote. "But Reggie had been striving too long not to want its company for the full night." Or considerably longer, as it turned out. "Reggie was here, there and everywhere," trainer Sandy Archer said. "He must have partied for four or five days when we got back to Regina."

CHAPTER **22** | # "WE ALL WON IT"

As the Saskatchewan Roughriders sipped, spilled and sprayed champagne, fans poured on to the streets of Regina. "On the way home, you couldn't drive more than two or three houses down the streets," recalled Gordon Currie, who had coached the Regina Rams to their first national junior football title only 15 days before the Roughriders' ice-breaking triumph in Vancouver. "Women were coming out of the houses and so were guys. They were dragging people out and kissing them and hugging them and they were going crazy. That's the biggest impression that I've ever seen, live, of people being really excited."

Downtown Regina was especially congested between 6 and 10 p.m. A police officer was required to direct traffic at the intersection of Broad Street and 11th Avenue. Despite his best efforts, thousands of vehicles crept along. One motorist said it took a half-hour to drive from Albert Street to Broad Street on 11th Avenue. "In one case, a young man was nearly completely out of the car, with one leg hanging down one side of the car," the *Leader-Post* reported. "Another car came up alongside and brushed the fellow's leg." Only superficial injuries resulted, police said. They ended up arresting 35 people, mostly for minor offences. There were two instances of vandalism — a broken store window and the rear-view mirror being torn off a car — but police could not confidently attribute those instances to the football-related frenzy.

Gordon Currie's *Rams won the "Little Grey Cup" by the same 29-14 score, 15 days earlier |*
Photo courtesy of *Leader-Post*

"In some ways, I wish I could have been there in Regina, because the way people were celebrating was something else," said George Reed, who flew back with his teammates the following day. Fans young and old took part in the festivities, including 15-year-old Thom Collegiate student Jim Hopson — a future Roughriders offensive lineman and president-CEO. "There was a party at the north end of Pasqua Street," Hopson said. "When the Riders won, we drove down Albert Street to be part of it. All the horns were blowing. It was a spontaneous celebration. People were hanging out of car windows. I was sitting with my girlfriend — she wasn't my girlfriend for much longer — and I was almost more interested in impressing her. I remember the sheer joy of the city. It was a big deal ... and it still is."

The city also prepared to welcome home the Roughriders players, who were to fly back from Vancouver nearly 24 hours after their 29-14 victory over the Ottawa Rough Riders. Naturally, Ron Lancaster was in for quite a reception, having thrown three touchdown passes. Lancaster's neighbours were responsible for some alterations in the giddy hours that followed the Grey Cup. "I remember waking up at our home on Emerald Park Road with the two snowmen that Ronnie [Lancaster Jr.] and I had built dressed as Saskatchewan Roughriders," recalled Lana Mueller, Lancaster's daughter. "Little green-and-white flags were strung between our trees, and the name of our street was changed to Lancaster Road. Of course, I didn't realize why — being only seven years old and thinking that Dad had only won another game." Well, he had, but ...

A surprise was also in store for defensive back Larry Dumelie. "My neighbours had decorated our house and had a big party waiting for us," he remembered. "They had great big lights on it and a big image of a football player with Number 26 on it and all kinds of decorations. It was quite impressive. I think it lasted until Christmas. It might still be up."

Back in Vancouver, some fans were frantically preparing to return to Regina. "One of the biggest laughs of the weekend came as our Grey Cup train was leaving," Gary Crone said. "After the game, we only had about two hours before our departure, so it was quite a scramble. Plus, there was a fair amount of celebrating going on — so much so that one of our fellow passengers stood on the platform and waved goodbye to us all as the train slowly pulled out of the station. Rumour has it he arrived back in Regina a few days late!

"After the win, my thoughts were that it would be a wild and tumultuous night on the train. Surprisingly enough, outside of a few party-hearty types, the rest of us succumbed to the tension of the day, and most people were fast asleep long before midnight. Things changed around noon the next day and the party was on, non-stop, until we arrived in Regina at a very early hour of the morning. As you can imagine, a trainload of people arriving at that time in the morning soon used up all of Regina's taxicabs. John Holash of Molson's and I were standing outside the station, vainly looking for some kind of transportation to get us to our homes in south Regina. Much to our surprise — and our relief — a city police cruiser rolled up and a voice yelled, 'Hey, John! Need a ride home?' My 1966 Grey Cup weekend ended with me being dropped off in my driveway in the early-morning hours — in a police car, no less."

Leader-Post correspondent Ray Guay was also on a train that departed Vancouver at 6 p.m., shortly after the game. Guay's assignment was to chronicle life on the train, to and from Saskatchewan, and the spirit of the event. "If at any time in the years to come you want to remind yourself of this first Grey Cup victory in a concrete manner, all you have to do is go to Jim Gates' barber shop in Lumsden," Guay wrote. "Hanging in there prominently will be one of the 20-yard markers, complete with signatures of many of his fellow travellers. Mr. Gates emulated thousands of others by heading towards the field in the closing minutes of the game. He was too late to get the big 'G' for 'Goal' or the 10-yard marker, and quite happily settled for the 20-yard plate.

"A more personal souvenir was carried back by a Regina woman. It was an autograph, signed for the benefit of the woman's young football-playing son. The inscription read, 'The best team won today. Best wishes, Frank Clair.' "

Given the demeanor of Reginans in the hours that followed the Roughriders' Grey Cup victory, local entertainers did not have to worry about warming up the crowd. The Club 62 Rhodesmen, for example, were playing at the YMCA on the evening of Nov. 26. Mick Grainger, Bill Rothecker, Gene Haas and Terry Malloy had selected that engagement to debut their rendition of the Rolling Stones' hit, "Satisfaction." It was an appropriate selection for a band that included someone named Mick.

"Our guitar player had acquired a new fuzz effects box to get that [signature] guitar riff sounding like it was Keith Richards himself playing with us that night," said Grainger, whose group performed at the YMCA one Saturday per month, taking turns with three other ensembles that represented CKCK Radio (620 on the AM dial, hence the Club 62 label).

"Heading to the dance, I came across honking cars racing along Albert Street, full of celebrating Rider fans. As I recall, the dance started normally enough, but then more and more people just kept coming as the night went on. It seemed that for the younger folks, the post-Grey Cup parties were moving into the Y. These Saturday night dances were held in the smaller East Hall at the YMCA. It got packed, sweaty and wild. I remember looking out over the surging and rapidly growing crowd with a touch of amazement and fear. How many more kids could they cram into the room without over-running the stage?

"There were lots of Rider cheers, general whoopin' and hollerin', and the odd disagreement that usually resulted in an intense but brief melee. It was too crowded for combatants to really square off, and this turned out to be quite an effective peacekeeping feature. Oh yes ... and there were lots of slurred bellows from the floor for replays of 'Satisfaction.' I don't know how many times we played that tune but we really got our money's worth out of the new fuzz box. Keith would have been proud and right at home. All in all, the 1966 Rider Grey Cup victory was one of the most memorable nights in my mercifully short musical career."

As memorable nights go, few in Regina's history can rival Nov. 27, 1966, when the Grey Cup appeared in Regina for the first time following a Saskatchewan victory. Leading up to the team's arrival, residents had been urged to turn on Christmas lights to enhance the city's attractiveness to the players as their aircraft approached Regina. "We had that fantastic reception by the city," Hugh Campbell said. "That was one of the most fantastic moments of my sporting life. When we got to the airport, it was just quiet. It was nighttime and there wasn't anybody there to greet us, which I thought was a little weird. I thought, 'Maybe they're all still in B.C., drinking or something.' As we left the airport, people were lined in the streets in front of all the houses and we weaved through a pre-designated path. There were people on their front lawns with signs. It was just the most fantastic greeting."

Fans had been urged to welcome home the team at the Regina Armoury in order to avoid an unprecedented and unmanageable torrent of humanity and traffic at the airport. Roughriders supporters began assembling at the Armoury at 6:30 p.m., three hours before the team surfaced. The 10,000-square-foot auditorium was packed with an estimated 6,000 to 8,000 fans two hours before the first sign of the Roughriders. The *Leader-Post* reported that at least six people fainted from the heat. St. John Ambulance also treated 12 others who "were just plain weak from the crush or sick to the stomach."

With those notable exceptions, the wait was worthwhile, even though people were shoulder-to-shoulder. Sitting was out of the question due to the scarcity of space. The Roughriders received a three-minute ovation when they entered the Armoury. Eagle Keys introduced the players, praising each one. Then the players stepped before the microphone, led by Ron Lancaster. "The only thing I can tell you is what you said all year: We had them all the way," Lancaster said to the crowd's approval. He was followed by George Reed, Hugh Campbell, Ed Buchanan and Ron Atchison. "Ever since I've been here, we've had great fans," Atchison said. "This year we had a great team." Afterward, Reg Whitehouse held the Grey

Ron Lancaster *hugging the Grey Cup* |
Photo courtesy of *Vancouver Sun*

Ron Lancaster *and* **Ron Lancaster Jr.**, *happy to see Dad* |
Photo courtesy of *Leader-Post*

Cup over his head and exclaimed: "This is the greatest moment of my life. All I want to do now is get home to sleep because I've been partying it up pretty good all night."

The dignitaries included Premier Ross Thatcher, Mayor Henry Baker and 75-year-old Lt.-Gov. Robert Leith (Dinny) Hanbidge. The latter had every reason to cherish the celebration. Hanbidge played for the Regina Rugby Club — which became the Roughriders — during the franchise's early years. Fifty-three years after Hanbidge's final game as a player, he was able to rejoice over a long-awaited title. So was team president Don MacDonald, who was in his 31st season on the executive.

At 36, Atchison was an elder statesman of another sort. "We were up on the stage at the Armoury," he said. "It was a beautiful feeling. You're happy for the people. The fans that we had here, you'd think that they'd played on the field. Our fans here are just so super. It's a wonderful feeling, but you can only stay up in the clouds for so long and then you've got to come down to earth."

The down-to-earth nature of the Roughriders' players still resonates with Mike O'Donnell, who was among the thousands of people who congested the Armoury. "It was chest to chest," recalled O'Donnell, who was 15 at the time. "We didn't move and we didn't care. There wasn't a person without a smile on their face." That included O'Donnell's father, Wilf. "I saw my father's joy," said O'Donnell, who became a Regina city councillor in 2007 after a 30-year career as an educator. "That's what I remember more than anything. We were pretty close to the stage — Row 3. I can remember seeing the players up on the stage and remember the humility from most of them. I remember looking at my father and seeing his sense of pride, and thinking how our team was successful. The players shared the championship with the community. It wasn't those guys who won it. We all won it.

"Before that, the Roughriders hadn't been to the Grey Cup since 1951 — the year I was born. My father had started a small grocery store about 1950. The next year, Glenn Dobbs was the Riders' quarterback. My father had always described Glenn Dobbs as a gentleman and someone to be looked up to. He was the only person I remember my father describing in that fashion. When we went to the Armoury, I thought of Glenn Dobbs and Ron Lancaster — quality people to be admired. Glenn Dobbs had been the face of the team — not necessarily in a playing sense, but in how he had carried the team. I looked at '66 and the face of the team was Ron Lancaster. He was not tall and statuesque, like Glenn Dobbs, but he was the face of the team. The ability level was similar. The humility was also part of it. I could tell you where Ron Lancaster had breakfast every Sunday morning because we would always sit right across from him. He would always say hello to the kids. He was a normal human being — a family guy. That's what I remember."

The losing team, meanwhile, made a long and indirect trek back to the nation's capital. The Ottawa Rough Riders flew from Vancouver to Seattle before changing planes and jetting to Chicago. From there, they boarded a chartered aircraft and embarked for Ottawa. They finally returned at 5:30 a.m., on Mon., Nov. 28, and were welcomed by 125 fans, many of whom were teenagers. Bob McKenzie of The Canadian Press reported that the Rough Riders' players were in disbelief over their fans' show of support, which included banners.

Fans clamoured for quarterback Russ Jackson, chanting "We Want Russ!" As McKenzie wrote: "When he finally stepped through the door, he was mobbed and kissed by a half-dozen shrieking girls." That evening, the city of Ottawa honoured the Rough Riders with a parade and a reception — although a reception of a different kind stood out for defensive back Bob O'Billovich.

In the second quarter of the Grey Cup, O'Billovich had stepped in front of a Ron Lancaster pass in the end zone. A seemingly certain interception turned into a Saskatchewan touchdown when the ball slipped through O'Billovich's outstretched hands and was cradled by the Roughriders' Alan Ford for a touchdown. "When we went to that dinner, Russ got up to speak," O'Billovich said. "They had us riding in different cars in a little parade to get down to Lansdowne Park. I was kidding the guys. I said, 'Yeah, they had me in a bulletproof car in case someone decided to take a shot at me.' I remember Russ getting up at the dinner and mentioning what I said. He went on to say what I said earlier: 'Hey, that's why you play the game, and on that particular day they were the better team and deserved to win the Grey Cup, so we've got to get ready for next year.' "

Saskatchewan had been next-year country until 1966. That thought occurred to a former prime minister. "John Diefenbaker spoke at the dinner," O'Billovich said. "He said, 'I was kind of twixt and between, being an old Saskatchewan guy, and being located in Ottawa all these years now. They hadn't had a Grey Cup for so long in Saskatchewan, it was like the great drought. The trees were looking for the dogs to pee on them. I have to admit that, down deep, I was kind of glad to see Saskatchewan finally win a Grey Cup because Ottawa had won before, so Ottawa didn't have as long a drought as Saskatchewan did.' I remember him saying that at dinner. That was kind of cute."

Both teams' homecomings were documented on the front page of the Nov. 28, 1966 edition of the *Leader-Post*. The banner headline read "WEST RIDERS BEST." Nearby, just beneath the print that proclaimed the single-copy price of 10 cents, was a front-page column by Laurie Artiss. "It was the end of an era that had been lasting and durable — until Nov. 26, 1966," Artiss wrote. "Dashed forever more is the poor-li'l-Rider routine. They've got money in the bank and the Grey Cup on the mantelpiece. No longer will the sad story of starvation and privation swell sentiment for the underprivileged. As champions of all they survey, Saskatchewan Roughriders will now instigate a new consideration. It will be respect for the best in the business, not merely for the guys who always try. And finally, they may emerge from the ranks of the under-rated. You know the gag among the football forecasters: pick Riders for last and figure out the rest. Altered thinking was even slow in coming this year, despite leading the West from flag to finish."

That edition of the newspaper included detailed analyses by the head coaches — Saskatchewan's Eagle Keys and Ottawa's Frank Clair. Keys and Clair had been commissioned to submit three articles in advance of the game, plus a postmortem.

"My worst fears came true in the Grey Cup game," Clair began. "We just didn't have the sharpness we needed to win the national football championship. While we were playing one of our poorer games, Saskatchewan Roughriders were playing an extremely good one. Now

THE LEADER-POST

VOL. LVII—No. 277   FIFTY-TWO PAGES   REGINA, SASKATCHEWAN, MONDAY, NOVEMBER 28, 1966   ★ ★ ★ ★ ★   SINGLE COPY

Saskatchewan humbles Ottawa . . .   *. . . to win first Grey C*

WEST RIDERS BEST

Sounds like a good name for a book

let me say right here that Saskatchewan might have beaten us even if we had played well. I give them a lot of credit for a tremendous effort and I think Eagle Keys did a great coaching job, particularly on defence. He had his club on Cloud 9."

The tone of Keys' article was different, as one would expect in light of the outcome. "You'll hear a lot about George Reed's great running, about Ron Lancaster's excellent quarterbacking, about the blocking and about the touchdown passes to Jim Worden, Hugh Campbell and Alan Ford, and I agree with every word of it," Keys wrote. "But I don't believe any of those things were really the major factor in our Grey Cup victory. I'm convinced we won it with our defence."

Another factor, according to Keys, was the plaudits Ottawa had received in the media as game day approached. "The publicity sure didn't hurt," he wrote. "The way folks were writing about the game, you'd have thought we didn't belong on the same field with Ottawa. That got to our fellows a bit. They have some pride in themselves, after all, and they didn't enjoy being downgraded that much. We had beaten some pretty good teams to get this far, you know.

"I curfewed them all week, just to make sure they kept their minds on business. We were here to do a big job and enjoying Grey Cup week had to come second. As it turned out, they enjoyed it a good deal more than anybody else in Vancouver."

Four days after the game, Laurie Artiss delivered a column headlined "Grey Cup Leftovers." Artiss punctuated the piece by publishing a letter he had received from Andy Currie, the supervisor of Western

Ken Reed *defensive stalwart* |
Photo courtesy of SSHFM

Conference officials. Currie paid tribute to Al Ritchie, who had died on Feb. 21, 1966 at age 75. The Silver Fox, as he was known, had coached the Roughriders to Grey Cup berths from 1929 to 1932, and was also renowned in local hockey circles.

"As I watched the great Saskatchewan victory on Saturday, I was filled with admiration for the game Eagle Keys and his team played, and with pride that I was once a Roughrider — a pride which must have been shared by many other Rider alumni all over the continent," Currie wrote. "Somewhere, I am sure there must have been a special viewing section for Al Ritchie to watch the triumph he was denied in life. What a fitting memorial to a man who gave the game so much — to a coach who had no equal as a conditioner of men. Al would have loved this Roughrider team — blind to the possibility of defeat, hungry for victory. And Eagle is his kind of coach."

Jim Proudfoot of the *Toronto Star* said the Roughriders' head coach showed astuteness in his handling of matters on and off the field. "Eagle Keys took a huge gamble this season, and won," Proudfoot wrote. "Just a few weeks ago, Keys was offered a new, long-term contract as coach of the Saskatchewan Roughriders. He turned it down, reasoning that he could negotiate much better terms as coach of the Grey Cup champions than he could then as coach of an aspiring club. He took the risk because he was absolutely confident. Make no mistake about it, either. This was very much an Eagle Keys triumph."

CHAPTER **23**

"NEXT-YEAR COUNTRY BECAME NOW"

In the works since 1910, the Saskatchewan party raged for several days — even months — after the Roughriders won the 1966 championship. "Everybody was partying and celebrating this great thing of winning the Grey Cup for the first time," remembered Nancy Barwell Kraft, whose late husband, Gord Barwell, caught a Ron Lancaster bomb for a 46-yard gain early in the CFL final. "It wasn't just a team thing. It was an entire community — a provincial event. It was such an exciting thing." That was especially true for the players, who were seemingly inexhaustible. "We just partied," defensive lineman Garner Ekstran said. "We just kept 'er going. We'd go to somebody's house or somebody's establishment." One of the unlikeliest hosts was head coach Eagle Keys, who welcomed the players shortly after the team returned from Vancouver.

"We had an all-nighter in his basement," Hugh Campbell recalled. "Up until that moment, he had always been the coach who you wouldn't think you'd ever be with in a social situation. After everybody else had left, and Eagle and I and Garner were the only ones there, Eagle and I had a long talk about coaching. He was my idol as far as going into coaching. He was somebody I thought I wanted to be like. For me, it was educational. His only criticism of me at that age was, 'Hughie, I don't know if you can put up with this if you don't drink a little more.' He said a lot of other things, too, that were more important."

Keys' words resonated with Campbell. "I always knew I wanted to coach and I always had planned to coach in high school," he reflected, "but it was the first time I ever considered whether I might be able to coach in professional ball."

While the players cherished the Grey Cup conquest, the veterans also had something to lament. Two long-time Roughriders linemen had retired shortly before Saskatchewan completed its lengthy march to a CFL title. Len Legault, for example, had toiled in the

Bill Clarke | Photo courtesy of Gord Heenan, Heenan Studios

trenches from 1957 to 1965 before calling it a career. Similarly, Bill Clarke was a universally respected member of the Roughriders from 1951 to 1964.

"We talked specifically about Bill and how nice it would have been for him to be there," defensive back Dale West said of the Hall of Fame lineman. "He was a renaissance man. You look at all the stuff he did after his playing career. He was a deputy minister [for the Province of Saskatchewan] and he was basically responsible for the lottery. He was an amazing man ... He was a real leader. It was a case of you listened. You didn't have any choice in the matter. He would straighten you out if you needed it — and God knows some of us needed it."

One fine evening, **and** well past that, one of the most memorable post-Grey Cup social gatherings was held at the residence of Scotty Livingstone, who celebrated the championship seasons of his two beloved football teams — the Roughriders and the junior Regina Rams. The teams' chief strategists did not require an introduction. Keys and Rams head coach Gordon Currie had become fast friends. "Scotty Livingstone used to be a good friend of Eagle's. Scotty thought that it would be a good idea for us to get together on a personal basis," said Currie, who was appointed the Rams' field boss in 1965 — the same year Keys became the Roughriders' head coach. "I used to spend a little time with Eagle

Eagle Keys |

Gordon Currie |

Scotty Livingstone |

and Jimmy Duncan and Jack Gotta, who were the assistant coaches, listening to them and trying to learn just by being in their presence."

Some of their discussions pertained to the X's and O's of football, but the conversations frequently concerned the handling of people and the team dynamic. "I took from them a lot of intangibles — things that you don't realize the importance of until you look at things in retrospect and start to figure out yourself what helps to constitute success consistently," Currie said. "Sure, I would have to say that I owe quite a bit from what I gleaned indirectly or directly from the presence of Eagle Keys and, to some extent, from his coaches — but especially from the Eagle. The way he portrayed himself as an individual commanded the respect of just about anyone who was in his presence. That, to me, was an indication of the greatness of who he was as an individual person. Maybe he wasn't royalty and maybe he did come from very common and simple beginnings, but that presence that he displayed was the thing that stood out above all other things. On top of that, he was a pretty sound-thinking person and a pretty intelligent guy."

Currie got to know Keys on a basis that few, if any, of his players did. A distance was almost always maintained between the coach and his players. But when Regina's two most notable football coaches convened, Keys was able to open up. "The way it appeared to me, he portrayed himself to be two different people at different times — during the football season and after the football season," Currie said. "During the football season, he was very businesslike and he was on top of everything and gave attention to all the detail that was necessary. Then, at the end of the season, he was so much more relaxed and was more of a fun-loving kind of a person.

"Eagle and his wife both doted on their children. They loved the heck out of them. He was a very soft-hearted person, but he very seldom showed that publicly. When you got to know him personally, you could see this softness, this genuine caring that he had for people. He cared about his football players, but he wasn't a hugging type of a coach. You wouldn't detect anything like that, yet he had great feelings for his players.

"He'd also get playing the spoons. He was quite an accomplished musician when he got a couple of spoons in his hands, which I guess was a trait that many Kentuckians possessed. It was almost like living with the history of the southern United States when you were in that man's presence. He had a presence. That was the thing, more than anything else, I detected. When he walked into the room, everything stopped. His presence just filled the room with something that you couldn't understand, but it was there. He had many different traits. That's what made him so very special in the eyes of everyone, even those who didn't get to know him very well."

Currie and Keys got to know one another even better during that memorable party at the Livingstones' domicile. "Everyone left about three o'clock in the morning, after all of the ping-pong tournaments and various activities that were going on," Currie said. "The ones who were left were Eagle and myself, evidently, along with Scotty and his wife, Betty. After the season, Eagle was not averse to becoming pretty playful. He insisted that he have somebody who would listen to him, and I became the scapegoat. We sat at the kitchen table. Scotty and Betty went to bed. Before they went, Scotty brought out a bottle of rum and put it in front of me, because that's what I drank, and he put a bottle of rye in front of the Eagle. We sat there and talked football.

"At about 8:30 in the morning, Betty got up and started making us bacon and eggs and we carried on during breakfast. By that time, Scotty had got up. Then we moved into the living room area and proceeded to enjoy each other's company. To tell the truth, some thought that it was a contest. I'll have to admit that if it was a contest, I lost. I was pretty proud of my abilities to sit and consume things that I had no business consuming, but I met my match. The Eagle, he was tougher than me.

"Eagle got homesick then. He had this soft spot in his makeup. He phoned his wife and, the next thing you know, his wife and his two kids came. His wife brought him a whole pack of sandwiches and he sat there and carried on. In the meantime, Jimmy Duncan came over to visit, to see if he was OK. I guess this would be getting on to 11 or 12 o'clock. By that time, I conceded and shook hands with the Eagle ... and walked home. I did not drive."

More than 40 years later, Currie still spoke reverentially about the marathon session with Keys. "We talked football, but we talked more so about the intangibles," Currie said. "We talked about having purpose. We talked about qualities that people have and what kinds of qualities are desirable and to what extent they're desirable and what impact they have upon not just ourselves, but upon all those with whom we're associated and how this relates to not just football, but to work, to life, to family life.

"We were all over the map. We were not so much trying to be philosophical, but to interpret what really mattered most in life and what really counted and what the true rewards were of winning a game or winning a championship. We talked about to what extent winning the Cup was of any meaning without other things being present — everything that, to me, was important. That's why I sat there and listened to this man, for whom I had great admiration and respect, and was virtually mesmerized in learning that we shared so many common thoughts and ideals.

"How many of us would have sat there all night to have been in the presence of this guy? I was going to say that he had a magic personality, but he was low key. That's the crazy part of it. He was a paradox. His whole makeup and being seemed to be that way. He was so interesting and intriguing. You just felt like you were in a godly presence of some kind. It's an honour for me to know a man of the stature of Eagle Keys. He's beyond being one of a kind. He's a treasure."

The provincial treasury helped to underwrite yet another football fete — honouring the Rams' and Roughriders' championship seasons. "The provincial government — Ross Thatcher's government, at that time — put on a dinner for both teams," said Currie, who had also won five consecutive provincial high school football championships and six successive city titles with Regina's Balfour Tech Redmen before beginning a successful 12-year run as the Rams' field boss. "We were very fortunate because they wouldn't have put on a dinner for the Rams, but because we had both won national championships, they had a dinner. They found it very difficult to understand how we could have won by identical scores. Both teams were honoured at the Hotel Saskatchewan and presented with engraved Bulova watches, with our names and the year and the championship. It was a very well-done dinner, with no holds barred. It was a real thrill for a guy who had done nothing but high school stuff before that."

At the banquet, held Dec. 3, Roughriders president Don MacDonald offered the crowd something extra for dessert. He announced that Keys had signed a five-year contract extension — an agreement unprecedented in franchise history.

"While we are delighted in having won the Grey Cup, it is not out of sentiment that we extended Eagle's contract for five years," Bill Clarke — not the ex-Roughrider, but the team's treasurer and a member of the management committee — told the *Leader-Post*. "We were prepared to offer him something like this during the season and prior to the playoffs. It didn't take a Grey Cup victory to realize Eagle is a smart, competent coach, that he provides outstanding preparation for games, and wears well in our community. In all these aspects, he exceeds any previous coach that we've had." The same applied to the length of contract. Until late in 1966, the Roughriders had never extended a head coach's contract for longer than two years. Keys had signed a two-year deal when he took over in 1965.

"The contract gives us a long-range plan," said Keys, whose first priority was to ask Jack Gotta and Jim Duncan to remain as assistant coaches. "They did an outstanding job and were instrumental in winning the Grey Cup. As the champions, everybody will be looking to knock us off."

Considerable energy was expended in the weeks that followed the Roughriders' momentous victory in the 1966 Grey Cup. "We came back to Regina and put in a whirlwind two weeks," George Reed said. "It was quite the scene. It was a good time, and it was a great time that following offseason. You come from a smaller city and people doubt whether you can do anything. When you do it, you can just see the pride of the people of Saskatchewan, the way it swelled up. That was one of the great things, too.

"Of course, you got to go to parties with the boys and then you had official functions, one after another. Everybody wanted to invite you over. You could almost kill yourself, but you tried to keep up with it. After two weeks, I had to get away for a while to kind of relax. I went back to my hometown of Seattle."

What was it about that 1966 Roughriders team? Record-wise, Saskatchewan would field better squads than the one that went 9-6-1 before knocking off Ottawa in the CFL final. "Football is a tough, tough game from June to November," Ron Lancaster explained. "Every team enters training camp thinking this is the year that they're going to win it. Things happen during the season. Injuries are going to hurt you. You don't make the plays when you need to, or whatever. But if you can get hot in late October and play well down the stretch in the last few league games and be in position to be in the playoffs and be playing your best football come November, you can win it all. That's what's crazy about the game.

"In that particular year, that's really what it was. It wasn't a case of where we were any better than the other teams. We just made plays at the right time and got hot down the stretch and in the playoffs we won. That carried us right to the end and allowed us to walk away as champions. That's what it was all about. Good, bad or indifferent, it doesn't matter. At the end of the season, we could sit back and say we won."

They couldn't say it often enough in the months to come. And the fans never tired of hearing it. "They'd waited a long time," Lancaster concluded. "It's like I've said many times: The year that the Saskatchewan Roughriders have dictates the rest of the season. Winter doesn't seem to be as cold. The moisture's better in the summer for the farmers and they have better crops. Everybody's in a better spirit. That's the impression I had when I got there. When we won it there, next-year country became now. That meant a lot to be able to live there and go through it and see it. We had the Grey Cup all over that province. Every little town, village, whatever, we were there and we had it there. The people were ecstatic."

Team captain Reg Whitehouse was never far away from the celebration. "He took the Grey Cup across the province," recalled his son, Timber. "I've got all his plaques that say he was the honorary mayor of this town or that town. I talked to one fellow who remembered Mom and Dad coming to a Craven ladies' tea one afternoon. He held the Grey Cup and met my dad. He connected with the community and the people. I heard it over and over and over."

CHAPTER 24 | "I NEVER LIKED FOOTBALL"

Ironically, the Saskatchewan Roughriders' highest-ranking paid employee had one of the lowest profiles. Despite the instrumental role he had played in assembling a champion, general manager Ken Preston's name rarely appeared in the newspaper during the 1966 CFL season. Preston was equally inconspicuous during the telecast of the 1966 Grey Cup game. "Ken kept himself out of the limelight," said Alan Ford, who was the Roughriders' GM from 1989 to 1999. "He was more the administrator." In that respect, Preston was a stark contrast to more flamboyant Roughriders GMs. "He definitely wasn't a Roy Shivers or an Eric Tillman," said Tom Shepherd, the team's auditor in 1966. "They're out front. Ken very seldom would be out front — maybe in some moments of crisis or something. With the day-to-day operations, he always left that to the coach. He had that typical Saskatchewan attitude of just doing his work. He was very behind the scenes — very, very low key."

The same can be said of the appointment of head coach Eagle Keys, who succeeded Bob Shaw in 1965. "There wasn't a lot of fanfare when they hired Eagle," Shepherd said. "Losing Bob Shaw, I was all upset because I liked him as a coach. Hiring Eagle, it was, 'He couldn't even win in Edmonton,' but Ken picks Eagle and he was sensational. He was perfect for Ronnie and these guys. You've got to give Preston a lot of credit."

Shepherd also credited Preston for timely player moves. "He had a very good ability for getting that one or two players every year in the fall," the former Roughriders president said. "Hughie Campbell came in late one year. So did Ed McQuarters. Those were the one or two players each year that made a difference. It wasn't that he was out scouting all the time. He wasn't a bird-dog like Roy Shivers. Roy goes and evaluates them all. Ken obviously had a network, but he didn't talk about it."

Not even at the Preston residence. "He never brought the job home with him," said Rich Preston, Ken's youngest son. "We'd ask him questions. Ron Lancaster and George Reed and Hugh Campbell and those guys were our idols. He'd give us one-word answers. He would never expound on anything. He'd never say, 'Hey, we've got this good player coming in …' He would always say, 'It's about the players. They deserve the adulation.' "

When reporters sought interviews, Preston was available but rarely expansive. Neither was the number of reporters. Alan Ford observed that "there wasn't the constant barrage of media." Nowadays, players and coaches are often encircled by reporters after practices and games. "The communication is so much more instant," Ford said. "The pressure is just continuous. In those days, at least it wasn't quite as much about other people writing about you or radio people. It was more about you and your team. That made it possibly a little bit less onerous for Ken."

While there were fewer reporters, there were also fewer colleagues. Preston ran the business from a small office. "For most of the years he was the GM, it was just him and the secretary," Rich Preston noted. The current Roughriders operation has grown to the extent that the football personnel is housed at Mosaic Stadium, whereas the business side is located a few blocks away on Albert Street. "Ken was kept busy," Ford said. "In those days, too, it wasn't a slam dunk that every team was getting through financially. There were lots of struggles, but a lot of it was kept behind closed doors. From the middle '70s on, that became a bigger issue of not only the Roughriders, but also the league. That's another item that he didn't really have to deal with as much in the public as other people in his position."

Alan Ford *holding his 1966 touchdown ball* | Photo courtesy of *Leader-Post*

Upon catching a touchdown pass in the 1966 Grey Cup, Ford's immediate reaction had been to flip the ball to the nearest official — as was the custom for players of that era. Ford did not think twice about the football until the following May. "I got a phone call and it was a guy coming through Regina from Vancouver," Ford recalled. "He said, 'Hey, I got the ball that you caught for your touchdown. It was kicked into the end zone on the convert. Would you like to buy it?' I said, 'Sure.' He said he'd bring it by. I had seen a Grey Cup ball, so I knew it had the stencil and what it looked like on the side. Sure enough, he had a Grey Cup ball." But there was a catch. Ford had to pay $50 for the ball. "I was rich then," Ford said with a chuckle. "Ken Preston was paying me all that money. I had the Grey Cup money, too. I think the Grey Cup money was $2,400, to go all the way through and win the whole thing. That was about a third of my contract, you know."

Ford displayed his sure hands by catching that football, thrown by Ron Lancaster, for the Roughriders' second touchdown in the 1966 CFL final. The ball proved to be equally elusive once it was in his possession for a second time. "I got it autographed by all the guys on the team," Ford said. "A number of years later, I went down to find the ball in my rumpus room and it wasn't on the little trophy case. I happened to find out that my son [Rob] and a bunch of his buddies were over in the church parking lot playing football with it, so a few of the autographs got scraped off. You can read a few of them. I'm sure I could read some other ones if I took a magnifying glass and blew it up a bit. It's a nice memento."

This was, of course, merely one of the game balls. There was also the football that defensive back Larry Dumelie retrieved after the final play of the 1966 Grey Cup. "I got it and brought it to the dressing room and gave it to the equipment manager and said, 'Hang on to it and we'll decide who gets the ball,' " Dumelie said. Dale Laird, who was in his first season as the equipment manager, felt that members of the community-owned team's hierarchy were best-suited to determine what became of the ball. "I was pretty green at the time," Laird said. "When we got back to Regina, I phoned Ken Preston and said, 'I've got the ball. Larry Dumelie saved it. What do I do with it?' Ken said to bring it into the office, so I did. They presented it to Don MacDonald, who was the president at the time. I never saw it again. I took a lot of flak for that from the players. They thought I had pulled a fast one on Larry Dumelie, but it wasn't that way at all. When Larry came back [in 2003] to be inducted into the Plaza of Honor, I talked to him about that. I apologized to him. I told him I wished I had given the ball back to him and let him decide what to do with it." Dumelie responded: "Don't worry about it."

Opposing offences had every reason to worry about Ed McQuarters. He was virtually unstoppable in his first full season with the Roughriders, terrorizing quarterbacks and ball-carriers with his combination of speed, quickness and power. McQuarters, who had joined the Roughriders in September of 1966 after being released by the NFL's St. Louis Cardinals, was named the CFL's outstanding defensive player in 1967 — one year after playing an instrumental role in Saskatchewan's first championship season.

Considering the individual and team successes, it should have been an enjoyable time for McQuarters. There was only one problem. "I never liked playing football," he said. Playing against him was not particularly enjoyable, either. But how could someone perform so well while barely tolerating the experience? "I can't explain it," McQuarters said. "All I know is in my gut, and in my soul, I had an obligation to do as best as I could at all times. I had an obligation to my father, to my mother, to all my siblings, to my relatives and, most important, to my family — my two boys and my wife. So no matter how bad I felt and how much I wanted to complain about things, I had to suck it up and go. That's the way I've done it all my life."

Ed McQuarters *pressuring the passer |*
Photo courtesy of John Solilo, Solilo Studios

Health-related matters played a significant role in turning a game into a chore. Travelling, for example, became a hardship because McQuarters frequently encountered airsickness. "On road trips, I admired how the guys seem like they're having fun and enjoying themselves," he said. "I'm not afraid of flying, but I get airsick really easily. I get motion sickness really easily. In fact, if you and I get in a car and you drive to Saskatoon, I'll be sick before we get there. But if I drive, I'm OK. When somebody else is driving, I get sick. My stomach hurts. My head hurts. I just get out of synch. I feel awful. That's one reason why I never liked football, because of the travelling aspect. Everybody was having fun, and I'm just sitting there."

The condition went undiagnosed throughout McQuarters' playing career, which concluded in 1974. "It took until I was out of football to understand why I felt physically the way I did — even emotionally, psychologically and mentally, too," he said. "I had high blood pressure — extremely high blood pressure, but I didn't know it." As a player, McQuarters was able to keep the blood pressure under control because of the active lifestyle of a pro football player. "Coffee contributed to my high blood pressure, and I drank coffee all the time at the office," he said. "It took me a while to get off the coffee, plus I smoked at the time. That didn't help either. We could smoke and get out there and perform. You could do that when you're in shape and you're out there all the time. People always asked me, 'Ed, how do you smoke and play?' I responded, 'I don't know, but I do it.' ... Socially, it was OK and acceptable at that time. When my doctor and I agreed that these things were no good, I got off the coffee. I finally got off the cigarettes, too, and started feeling better."

High blood pressure actually worked to the benefit of defensive lineman Don Gerhardt —
at least in one respect. He faced the prospect of joining the United States Army and being
sent to Vietnam before the results of a medical eliminated that possibility. "A number of
the guys I played with in college, none of them got drafted, but when they would find their
draft number was close, they'd enlist," recalled Gerhardt, who attended Concordia College
in Moorhead, Minn., before joining the Roughriders in 1966. "I was classified 4F. It was a
physical disqualification. I was in fabulous shape, standing there in my undies, in this long
line with other guys who weren't weightlifters or in shape or anything, and I was 4F and
they weren't 4F. It was really kind of weird.

"The doctors in Regina followed me for two years because every time I'd take a physical
[in Minnesota] for the army, I'd have high blood pressure. The doctors thought it was just an
emotional thing for me. I was ready to enlist, but my blood pressure hung high. They would
watch my blood pressure before the games and everything and it would be just fine, so it was
really interesting. I think I was getting all uptight when I was going down to the draft board.
It was a real different kind of pressure and something to try to live with." Gerhardt had some
misgivings about not being sent to Vietnam when, in many respects, he was considerably
healthier than those who served. "That bothered me some, but the docs said, 'We're not
going to take you,' so I didn't argue," he said. "I was ready to go, but whatever. That's a long
time ago."

Ron Lancaster had closer ties to that war. "My youngest brother, Bill, was in Vietnam,"
the Roughriders' quarterback reflected. "We're not going to sit down and write letters. That's
just not us. So he could keep up with the football season, we had the *Leader-Post* sent over
to him from the first day of camp to the Grey Cup. A lot of people in his battalion and the
people he was with knew the Saskatchewan Roughriders better than they knew any team in
North America. He would read the paper and they would pass it around. All his friends were
all interested in how the Roughriders were doing. It was amazing. We got a lot of publicity
over that. We did that for him every year he was over there. He said it was great. It was
something to look forward to."

Saskatchewan kept moving forward after the Grey Cup season of 1966. The Roughriders
followed up on their championship effort by posting a 12-4-0 slate in 1967. The 12 victories
were the most in franchise history to that point. Saskatchewan and Calgary had identical
records in 1967, with the latter getting the nod for first place based upon points for and
against. Calgary received a bye into the Western Conference final, while Saskatchewan
downed the visiting Eskimos 21-5 in their first-round playoff game. The Roughriders
went on to collide with Calgary in the best-of-three conference final — a gruelling affair.
Saskatchewan lost the opener 15-11 in Calgary before winning 11-9 at Taylor Field and 17-13
on the road to advance to the Grey Cup for the second successive year. However, the nature
of the conference final left Saskatchewan rather spent for the Grey Cup. The second game, in
particular, exacted a physical toll due to icy conditions in Regina.

"When I got in the dressing room after the game, it took about 15 minutes to stop shaking to death," Stampeders linebacker Wayne Harris said. "Ohhh, it was cold."

To offset the precarious footing, Ron Atchison, the 37-year-old Roughriders defensive tackle, decided to improvise. "After the rainstorm, it froze, so the field was just a piece of ice," he said. "They sanded down the middle of it. I went to our waterboy and asked him to help me out. He had to go back to the exhibition grounds — and that wasn't just going next door — and get my Hush Puppies. When I had to put my Hush Puppies on and they had sanded the middle of the field because it was ice, I had very good traction. I was looking pretty damn good and I made plays that I could never have made with cleats." After the game, Atchison changed into his street clothes, with one exception. He wore the Hush Puppies on the way home.

George Reed *builds up a head of steam* |
Photo courtesy of *Leader-Post*

Saskatchewan won the deciding game of the 1967 conference final on the strength of a courageous performance by George Reed. "I looked like a mummy," he recalled. "If you had walked into the dressing room, you would have seen both shoulders taped and my ribs taped. From my knees all the way down to my ankles was completely taped." Even so, Saskatchewan held a 14-6 lead after 30 minutes. As Reed put it: "Eagle's favourite speech at halftime was, 'Three things are going to happen. Urness, you're going to centre the ball to Lancaster. Lancaster, you're going to give the ball to Reed, and we're going to run.'" And run they did. Reed carried the ball 35 times for 201 yards. "George has never, *ever* run any better," Eagle Keys said after the Roughriders' 17-13 victory.

The 1967 Grey Cup proved to be a letdown for the Roughriders, who lost 24-1 to the Hamilton Tiger-Cats in Ottawa. The Roughriders were banged up, having played five games in 21 days. Tight end Jim Worden and guard Al Benecick, who had missed most of the season with injuries, were not as physically dominant as they were in 1966. Reed, Garner Ekstran and Ed Buchanan played hurt in the 1967 CFL final.

The Roughriders' preparations for the Grey Cup were hampered by a slippery practice field. Such are the risks of holding a championship game on Dec. 2. "You'd be amazed the way our skating has improved after a few days of practising on ice down here," Eagle Keys said after the loss to Hamilton. "Now that we've lost the Grey Cup, we may challenge for the Stanley Cup. Let me put it this way: I'd have appreciated a better chance to prepare. But you're not going to win many football games by scoring one point."

Saskatchewan squandered one golden opportunity to score six points. Shortly after Hamilton opened the scoring with a touchdown run by quarterback Joe Zuger, Buchanan lined up in the slot and outran Barrie Hansen on a deep route. "Buchanan was wide open and Ronnie threw him a perfect pass," Reed recalled. "He dropped the pass. It would have been a sure touchdown. I think that would have picked us up. I'm not putting the blame on Ed, but he dropped the ball. That seemed to turn the game around right there." Keys also pointed to that play following the game. "It's interesting to imagine how things might have gone if Buchanan had got his hands on that first bomb. A play like that can change the complexion of a game." Lancaster, by contrast, felt the play did not have a significant impact. "Had he caught that pass, we would have lost 24-8," the Roughriders' quarterback told reporters.

Although Buchanan is remembered for the dropped pass, he was the only Roughrider to make more than one reception in that game. His four catches netted a game-high 99 yards. "He'll always be held [responsible] for the one in Ottawa, unfortunately," Bob Kosid lamented. "Somebody's got to take you there. He did a heck of a job ... Ed Buchanan's name has never really been mentioned in the same way you might say George Reed or Hughie Campbell. Yet, his contribution meant a great deal." That was evident in 1966, when Buchanan had a 73-yard touchdown run in the second game of the Western Conference final against Winnipeg. He followed that with a strong performance in the 1966 Grey Cup victory. Unfortunately, those contributions have been overshadowed — at least in the opinion of some Roughriders followers — by one infamous play in 1967.

"Unfortunately, Buke took a back seat to George during his time with the Riders, but he didn't mind," Ed McQuarters said. "He accepted that role with class, style, and a personality. He had all the athletic attributes — size, strength, speed, agility and intelligence. Aside from his obvious football skills, he was very personable, fun-loving and quick-witted. He loved to laugh and joke around. He and Gord Barwell were in competition often to see who could concoct the best pranks on players. You always knew where you stood with him. He was a straight shooter. There was no two-faced bull from Buke. During the 1960s, he contributed to the success of the Riders as much as anyone — but from the shadows of the man, George Reed."

Despite the lopsided result of the 1967 Grey Cup, an estimated 3,000 fans welcomed home the Roughriders at Exhibition Stadium. "Unfortunately, we met a real good Hamilton team," Keys told the gathering. "And unfortunately there were some things we had wanted to do but didn't do and some things we almost did. That sounds terrible. I'll just be quiet and introduce the players ..."

CHAPTER 25 | # "I SPOKE MY MIND"

Within two weeks of the 1967 Grey Cup, George Reed decried what he described as the discriminatory attitudes of some Reginans. The *Toronto Telegram* interviewed Reed and several other Canadian Football Leaguers after Hamilton receiver Ted Watkins told the CBC that he faced discrimination while playing for Ottawa. "I have had many problems in Ottawa which made me feel like I was in Mississippi somewhere," Watkins told the *Public Eye* television program. The Canadian Press sought reaction from other black players in the CFL, including Ottawa defensive back Gene Gaines. "Anyone who tries to tell me there is no prejudice or racial discrimination is trying to kid himself and others," Gaines told the wire service.

When the topic was broached with Reed, he responded with the typical straight-ahead, hard-charging approach that served him and the Roughriders so well on the football field. "There is flagrant discrimination against Negroes in Regina," Reed was quoted as saying in the *Telegram* article. "I have come face to face with more racial problems in my five years in Regina than I ever had living in a suburb of Seattle. In the beginning I couldn't find anyone who would rent me an apartment."

That problem had already been documented by the *Leader-Post*'s John Robertson in the Aug. 4, 1963 edition, when he wrote about the difficulties three black Roughriders players — running backs Reed, Ed Buchanan and Billy Gray — had encountered in finding a place to live. Robertson reported that Buchanan was "turned down flat when he applied to rent a furnished apartment. Earlier, so was George Reed, for the same reason. I don't know how you feel about it, but this makes me a little sick inside." Robertson implored fans to provide Reed, Buchanan and Gray with assistance in finding apartments, concluding that "I am embarrassed for a few of my bigoted fellow Reginans."

Reed eventually found a home, but the surroundings were not always comfortable, as he emphasized in the *Telegram's* story. "My five-year-old son, who never knew what discrimination was, is suddenly called names he doesn't understand. My wife has become so defensive that when she leaves the house she's like a coiled cobra that's ready to strike at anybody. Regina is like living in the heart of Alabama as far as I'm concerned. Sure, people give you the glad hand and pretend your colour doesn't make any difference because you're a big football hero. The hell it doesn't. Those same people won't sit down and have a beer with you once the season's over. People talk about racial discrimination here and point to the south. Well, I hope what Ted Watkins said makes them open their eyes and realize what's going on in Regina and do something about it now."

Once those comments hit the news-stands in Toronto, they reverberated far away in Saskatchewan. *Leader-Post* sports editor Laurie Artiss was quick to contact Reed and ask him about the *Telegram's* story. Reed did not take the easy way out and claim he had been misquoted or quoted out of context. Instead, he stood behind and reiterated his statements.

"I feel quite bitter about this thing, not only because I've been confronted with it, but that most people don't even believe it exists," Reed told Artiss. "I've had people tell me they're not prejudiced and then they'll express views and say things you don't even hear in the south. It's like fighting a battle. At least if you knew what to expect, you could accept it. The first time I visited Texas, I knew some places were off-limits to me because I was a Negro. I didn't like it, but I accepted it. Up here, where there's not supposed to be discrimination, I have run into the same thing."

Reed went on to acknowledge that the nature of his off-field vocation could have contributed to the problem. As one who worked in marketing and public relations with Molson's Brewery, Reed was often in social situations where alcohol was being consumed. As Artiss noted, liquor consumption "often has a way of removing inhibitions, politeness and proper conduct." Reed did not disagree. "Somebody gets filled up with false courage and suddenly starts calling me 'Darky' or 'Nigger,'" he told Artiss. "They never say 'Negro' and I'm proud of being a Negro. It's funny. This never comes from the so-called upper class. It always comes from what you might say is the middle-class person."

Reed emphasized that the discrimination never emanated from the Roughriders' dressing room. "There is none among the players on the team," Reed told Artiss for the Dec. 15, 1967 edition of the *Leader-Post*. "We kid around a lot, but we're a pretty close-knit group." Reed also commended his other employer, Molson's, as an "excellent company." When first employed by Molson's early in 1966, Reed had resided in Saskatoon, but said he had not encountered any prejudice in that city. Reed asserted in an interview for this book that he was not citing the conduct of all Reginans, noting his appreciation for being named the president of Massey School's Home and School Association. That said, Reed did note — as he did in the *Telegram* — that Canadians were routinely blind to the existence of racism. "Everybody closes their eyes in Canada and then they don't understand how we can talk about racial discrimination in this country," Reed told the now-defunct *Telegram*. "It's time those people took a close look at the Negro in Canada." As Reed told Artiss: "That is the crux of the problem and sums up my feelings. People don't even want to believe there is discrimination here because there aren't very many Negroes that live around here. Anything I've put up with have been racial slurs, but what about the average Negro trying to work in this country? I'm doing well financially, but others of my race in this country certainly don't have the same employment opportunity or economic equality."

In addition to reporting and expanding on Reed's comments to the *Telegram*, Laurie Artiss weighed in with his sentiments regarding the issue of racism. "I bow to no man in my respect for George Reed," Artiss began. "While attempting to remain aloof from emotions in the reporting business, I've glowed inwardly as he churned up 5,000 yards of real estate in recent seasons. I've winced when he has fumbled a football. I've been pleased that his exploits with the Saskatchewan Roughriders have carried him to honours as the nation's outstanding player in 1965 and the only unanimous All-Canadian choice this season. I've looked on in wonder and amazement at his ability to provide a peak performance, despite the punishment he takes. He elicits admiration when you can observe the pain he often plays with, and this is for the inward man, not for the outward ability."

Artiss went on to respectfully disagree with some of Reed's sentiments. "It is conscientiously and with objectivity ... that I say I don't agree with George Reed in some of his statements about racial discrimination in Regina ... Certainly, there are degrees of discrimination here, just as there are anywhere else in this country or on this continent. George has to be overstating a case — and being overly sensitive — to say there is 'flagrant discrimination against Negroes in Regina' or likening it to 'the heart of Alabama.' He is correct, however, when he objects to his five-year-old son being called names by neighbourhood youngsters, his wife, Angie, sometimes being placed on the defensive, or he, himself, having to absorb personal slights by the bigoted and the unthinking."

Artiss offered another perspective on the matter of housing. "George has stated the difficulty of being accepted for apartment accommodation, and I'm not certain how much of this can be directly attributed to colour. I'm not certain George knows, either. It is a fact many players have had this problem, particularly those who are single, or who don't bring families with them. Many wish furnished apartments, which are far from plentiful, and apartment owners are not usually crazy about the idea of renting to anybody for a few months. Then there is the belief (not without some justification) that football players can act in an irresponsible manner. Call it prejudice, but it is directed at football players in general.

"There is also the matter of crank phone calls, at any time of day or night, that Reed has received. Other members of the football team are not immune to them, however, and I've received the odd one myself, including the kind of kook who calls and then doesn't say anything. It only proves some people are not receiving the psychoanalysis they require, and that Reed's callers have a persistent and devious dedication. His home has an unlisted number. Since George is hesitant, understandably, in stating specific instances, it is difficult to determine to what extent, or how often, he has been confronted with the colour question. It is possible he is interpreting discrimination when it may be the price he has to pay for football fame and being in the public eye. That he is confronted with any indignity to his race at all, however, is shameful in this country, in this province and in this city."

More than 40 years later, Reed is still outspoken about the issue of racism. "It was really a big deal then, and it's still a deal with me because there is a way that human beings should be treated," he said in an interview for this book. He emphasized that most of the problems he encountered were in the mid-1960s. "It was difficult at first," Reed said. "The first couple of years, I couldn't get an apartment in Regina. It was tempting at times to pack up and go back [to Washington state]. Then something happened and all of a sudden I didn't have a colour because I won the Schenley in '65 [as the CFL's most outstanding player] and that was the greatest thing since sliced bread.

"It was difficult walking into certain places that everybody didn't know who George Reed was. I'd get treated one way and then, all of a sudden, somebody would recognize me and it was a total different way that I was treated. That probably was as hard to take as anything because I hadn't changed colours. I just had become a pretty good football player. It bothered me, and it bothered me the way other ones were treated. Whether the league wants to admit it or not, I still say there was a quota system on black players back in those days. If you go back and check the rosters, outside of Hamilton, you tell me which team had more than four blacks at one time on a football team. In those early years, we had three to four players and that's all there was. You can almost go through and check everybody's roster in Western Canada and it was almost the same way. If you had more than one [black player] show up for training camp, they were stacked at the same position and one was going to win and the other two or so were going to lose and go home."

How difficult was it to live in a community where he detected that mindset? "It was very difficult, because a lot of people thought that because I was from the States, I should have been used to it," Reed responded. "But I grew up in Washington and there might have been 20 blacks in my high school. When I went to Washington State, I think there were two blacks on the football team, but you never felt anything. The closest that I came to it was when we went to play the University of Houston. Me and another guy had to stay at Texas Southern University, which is a black university, because they had nowhere for us to stay. After that, the coach [Jim Sutherland] said, 'The University of Texas wants to play us the next year,' and the only way he would go was if all his players would stay together.

"When I was in high school, it might be different now, but I never had a problem and I never had to face anything. I just seemed to be one of the ordinary guys mixed in with everybody else. At the university, it was basically the same way, so it was a little strange and a little tough when I first got [to Regina], but through it all you looked at it and said, 'Some day, some things have got to change,' so you just keep going ahead. I think when the time was right, I spoke my mind."

Reed understood the times, as difficult as they were to accept. When possible, he made the best of the situation. For example, when Reed and his black teammates with Washington State were required to stay at Texas Southern, he extracted a positive aspect from the injustice. "It didn't bother me as much because the coach had to give me extra money to stay there," Reed said. "Of course, we got invited to go to parties and the other guys were locked up. That was a lot of fun that way but, yeah, it was difficult.

"I think we were down there for two or three days and you'd go to practice. They'd all get on a bus and go back. You'd get in a cab and away you'd go. That was the tough part about it, but I think what made it all good was when [coach Sutherland] made the statement that it would never happen again and 'if my whole football team can't stay together, then we will not play.' The next year when we went to Austin, Texas to play the University of Texas, someone said, 'I don't know whether you can stay.' They said, 'Well, if he can't stay with the football team, we'll forfeit the game. We'll just get back on the plane and go back to Washington State.' Of course, they got that settled down quickly and I stayed with the team and we got beat by the University of Texas 14-13, but it was a great game. I never had any other problems with that."

Instead of evading the problems, Reed confronted them directly. That explained his candor with the *Telegram* and with Artiss. "You become bullheaded or someone has to say something or someone has to do something," he said. "A lot of times, if you do something, people will follow by example or they will take a different look. After playing in '65, I decided that I was going to move to Regina full-time and if I was going to move there full-time, then I've got to be ready to face the thing head-on. If I can help change people's minds or the way in which people look at you, that's what I was going to do.

"As you grew with it and because we were so tight on the football team, it was never any question on the football team. The players were always with me. We decided, 'OK, I've got 31 other guys who are with me.' There were a lot of other people who were good people. I'm not trying to say that everybody in town wasn't good people. We had a lot of good people in town. You have to try to say something. A lot of things that I said and a lot of things I worked with were for other people because George Reed, after '65, didn't have any problems … I just felt that I had to try to do something. I had to say something. I just couldn't let it all hide, because things were different for me. I just couldn't sit back and idly let that pass by. That's why I said a lot of things and that's why I got involved, whether it was at Massey School or with different charities. I got involved to try to change the perception."

Reed got so involved that he was eventually affiliated with 47 different community groups — at once! Those tireless contributions, combined with his exploits on the football field, were recognized in 1976 when he was the inaugural recipient of the CFL's Tom Pate Memorial Award, which recognizes exemplary conduct on and off the field. Two years later, Reed's attributes were celebrated when he received the Order of Canada.

By then, the issues that prompted Reed to speak out had largely disappeared. That helps to explain why he remained a full-time resident of Regina until 1984, when he was transferred to Calgary by Molson's, and why he returned in 2009 to become a corporate event host for the Saskatchewan Gaming Corporation. "I'm not blaming the city today," Reed emphasized. "I'm saying the way it was and I'm happy to say that things have progressed for the better."

Defensive tackle Ed McQuarters had encountered racism while he was with the St. Louis Cardinals. He does not deny that there were also episodes of racism in Regina, but they were isolated in comparison to the situations Reed underlined. "I personally have never, ever experienced racist behaviour or attitude on the Saskatchewan Roughriders, past or present," said McQuarters, who settled in Regina shortly after joining the Roughriders.

"The only racist experience of note that I have experienced in the Regina community was when my family and I were looking to buy a house in 1967. We found a house. I was looking forward to moving in as soon as the bank cleared the credit check by the realtor. Later I found out that the realtor had asked residents in that neighbourhood if it would be all right if 'that black family' moved into the neighbourhood. The folks in the neighbourhood said no. The realtor came back to us and said the previous owner of the house could not get the financing for another house he was wanting to buy, so that house we wanted was taken off the market. We rented another house just two blocks from there. The next month the original house we wanted to buy was sold."

Oddly enough, **Bob Kosid** (who is white) had more interaction with black players in Saskatchewan than he did in the United States. "I played in the Southeast Conference. It was all white," said Kosid, who was a Roughriders defensive back from 1964 to 1972 following a stellar career at the University of Kentucky. "There wasn't a black guy in any school — be it LSU, Alabama, Georgia — and look at their teams today ... I never had any contact with a black person."

Kosid had three black teamates on the 1966 Roughriders — Reed, McQuarters and Ed Buchanan. One time, the irrepressible Buchanan emerged from the shower covered in white talcum powder and joked: "Can I join you boys now?!" Kosid remembered one instance where Buchanan was asked why he dated white women in Regina. "Bobby, look around you," he replied. "How many black women do you know in Regina?" To which Kosid responded: "You've got a point there."

Ted Watkins — whose comments to the CBC were the catalyst for this discussion of race — had played against Saskatchewan in two consecutive Grey Cups — in 1966 with Ottawa and in 1967 in Hamilton. He caught a 72-yard touchdown pass in the latter game — his last in the CFL. Watkins died in Stockton, Calif., after being shot four times by the manager of a liquor store following a struggle on June 2, 1968. An Associated Press report said Watkins, who was 27, was shot after attempting to rob the store. (Clifton Watkins, Ted's brother, was tried and acquitted in 1969 on a charge of armed robbery. John Campbell, foreman of the jury, told the *Stockton Record* after the six-week trial that he and his fellow jurors believed the Watkins brothers "went into that store to buy a bottle of wine — that's all" and that there was no intent to commit robbery.)

The AP story referred to Watkins as a "leading Black Power advocate in Canada." The story also mentioned Watkins' address to a business group in Toronto, in which he said: "The racial problem isn't as bad in Canada as it is in the United States. But it's here, and I'm going to live in Canada and do my best to solve the problem."

Those plans changed, though, after Watkins spoke out to the CBC. "His television interview, which he claimed only showed the more sensational aspects of his talk, brought some violent reaction," Bob Scott wrote in the *Ottawa Citizen* shortly after Watkins' death. "It included numerous phone calls — he had his phone number changed several times — informing him he wasn't wanted in Burlington, where he resided. These calls eventually led to the decision to move his wife and family to the United States."

Coincidentally, Alan Ford was in Stockton, Calif., at the time Watkins was killed. The news of the fatal shooting hit home, being that Watkins and Ford were football teammates in 1962 at the University of the Pacific in Stockton. Ford and his wife, Sally, often returned to Stockton in the offseason.

"I remember the night Ted was killed," Ford recalled. "It was a real shocker. I was playing hockey at the time. Sally was at home. A news report came on saying that a Canadian Football League player had been shot and killed in a liquor store in Stockton. No names were given." The report alarmed Sally Ford. "Obviously, her first thought was that it might be me. There were a few CFL players from around that area, but you always worry." Sally was worried until the moment her husband walked in the door. "She just said, 'Wow, I'm glad it wasn't you.' Good thing I wasn't out too late."

Ford remains perplexed by the fate of Ted Watkins. "The way it always struck me is, 'It doesn't make sense,' " he reflected. "I knew him very well. He was a good football player and a good teammate. To me, he was a pretty good guy."

CHAPTER 26

"WELL, THIS IS IT, ATCH"

Exceptional moves contributed to Hugh Campbell's phenomenal success as a receiver. But late in the 1967 season, there were rumours of a move that Roughriders fans would not enjoy. The Nov. 11 edition of the *Canadian Football News* devoted its front page to a story about Gluey Hughie. The bold headline read: TRADE RUMORS STARTING ABOUT HUGHIE CAMPBELL. It was merely conjecture, but a story was built around the Roughriders possibly trading Campbell to Edmonton for a fellow flanker, Randy Kerbow.

"The rumour is apparently not true," Andy Hardy wrote in the *News*, "but it caused one wag to mutter: 'If I were Edmonton, I'd trade Kerbow and the OTHER HALF of the team to get Campbell.' That shows the high regard people still have for Campbell out West. But respect for the Washington State grad is slipping. It will slide even further if 1968 turns out to be another bad year." Hardy observed that "the slope-shouldered, 185-pound flanker has undoubtedly had a poor year by Campbell standards." After making 66 receptions for 1,109 yards and a league-record 17 touchdown catches in 1966, Campbell's production had dropped to 42 catches, 710 yards and eight majors.

"After a little more than three seasons in the CFL, defensive backs began catching up to his tricky moves," Hardy wrote. "They realized they could allow him certain liberties and still use their superior speed to recover. Until this year, Campbell would latch on to his share of aerials even though two men were on him. He is still double-teamed, but he is not catching as many as before."

Campbell moved on after the 1967 season, on his own initiative. At 26, he decided to retire as a player and accept an assistant-coaching position at his alma mater, Washington State University. The WSU job opened up when one of its assistant coaches died. Campbell was not given assurances beyond one year, but he took the position. "An opportunity to coach at one's alma mater is an attraction one does not want to pass up," the *Leader-Post's* Laurie Artiss wrote when the announcement was made in February of 1968. "Campbell will probably make a fine coach. He will approach the task with the same dedication and thoroughness he applied to playing. For one who didn't necessarily have the build of a football player, Campbell had to study, learn, practise and hone his skills much more than others blessed with more natural attributes. He is a class individual who doesn't smoke, drink or even emit cuss words, which may or may not be a handicap in the frustrating and ulcerous world of coaching. As a player, he certainly geared all his thinking toward a day that he had a coaching opportunity." One of the catalysts had been a late-night conversation with Eagle Keys in the head coach's basement, following the 1966 Grey Cup.

Even without Campbell, the Roughriders' regular-season performance improved in 1968. Under coach-of-the-year Eagle Keys, Saskatchewan posted a 12-3-1 record — tying its single-season franchise best for victories, established when the team went 12-4-0 in 1967. The Roughriders earned a bye into the best-of-three conference final, only to be swept by the Stampeders, who won 32-0 and 25-12. "We never seem to be worth a damn when we're favoured," Roughriders defensive back Bob Kosid said after the 32-0 drubbing. "We only seem to come up big when we're underdogs ... the 1966 Grey Cup ... last year's final ... and how many people picked us to finish first this year?"

The Roughriders were without several familiar faces in 1968. Defensive back/punt returner Gene Wlasiuk and centre Galen Wahlmeier had concluded their playing careers. Guard Jack Abendschan had joined the American Football League's Denver Broncos, only to return to Saskatchewan during the season. Garner Ekstran was traded to the B.C. Lions after a contract dispute with Roughriders general manager Ken Preston. Ekstran had been named an all-Canadian linebacker in 1967, after previously earning league all-star honours as a defensive end in both 1962 and 1963.

"I had played out my option in 1967," Ekstran said. "I was not under contract for 1968. We were $500 apart and I offered to split the difference and Preston wouldn't do it. There was an unwritten rule that nobody played out their option. Eagle kept saying, 'Sign the damn thing. I won't let you play for anyone else.' I told Eagle that if I'm not worth $250, screw it. He said, 'You're not playing for anyone else.' I said, 'Fine, I'm done.' " Ekstran was promptly traded to the Lions, with whom he spent his final half-season in the CFL. "I don't want anyone to get the impression that I was down on the Riders," Ekstran emphasized. "My blood's still green. I don't want anyone to be saying, 'He's carrying a grudge.' "

Ekstran was able to enjoy a successful career in professional football even though, judging by his appearance at a young age, he was hardly suited for the sport. "From the time that I was eight or 10 years old — and I was a midget — I told everybody whether they asked or not that I was going to play pro ball," said Ekstran, a graduate of Burlington Edison High School in Bow, Wash. "They all laughed at me, of course. I went into high school in the ninth grade at 5-foot-4 and 95 pounds. But I wore a size-12 shoe, so I knew I was going to grow into something."

He eventually played college football at Washington State University, where his teammates included three future Roughriders — receiver Hugh Campbell, fullback George Reed and linebacker Wally Dempsey. "I was extremely lucky in college," Ekstran said. "I had a line coach [Laurie Neimi] who I still feel is the best line coach I've ever seen, and he taught only fundamentals. He always said, 'We can give you any kind of play to block or defence to line up with, but if you don't know your fundamentals, you can't play the game. If you do and there's somebody ahead of you, knock them on their butt.'" Ekstran routinely did just that, sometimes incurring the wrath of opponents. Even so, Ekstran disputed any suggestion that he was a mean player, noting: "I just got even a lot."

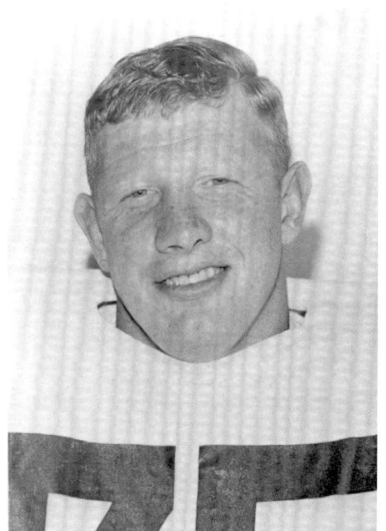

Garner Ekstran |

Ekstran's playing weight was sometimes an even 200 pounds, making him light for a defensive end or a linebacker. "The only time I ever felt like I was at a weight disadvantage was when I walked into a hotel and I was smaller than the ball boy," he said. "I never felt disadvantaged at all. To me, size is so over-rated." Ekstran, by contrast, was under-rated. Despite repeatedly earning all-star recognition, Ekstran was often overshadowed. Other players may have garnered more headlines, but nobody derived greater enjoyment from the game than Ekstran. "I would have paid to play," he said. "It was just a great environment. I loved it — and I don't know of anybody who didn't. It was just a great bunch of guys. We had fun and when it was time to play the game, we played."

Ekstran played more than 40 years ago, and has yet to fill the void created by his departure from football. "I don't think you do," he said. "I have a lot of very good friends, but none of them will ever take the place of my teammates. I would imagine people in the military who have gone through wars have the same kind of bonding as we do as a team. It's very hard for anybody else to understand that kind of bonding."

Venerable defensive lineman Ron Atchison resolved to wade into the on-field wars for an 18th season with the Roughriders in 1969. "I never quit until they fired me," the six-time all-star said with a laugh. "I wanted to play some more. After spring training [in 1969], I thought I was slowing down, and I was a little concerned. After the training camp, Eagle Keys said, 'Atch, I'd like to see you in my office.' Well, I felt about the same way when my mom died. I just thought, 'Well, this is it, Atch. He's calling me in to tell me,' because they don't call you in if you've made it.

"I remember how bad I felt. Eagle softened the blow as much as anybody could. He said, 'Atch, you're at an age where you should retire. I don't want to cut you.' So he let me announce that I'd retired. If I didn't announce my own retirement, he'd have had to cut me.

I was devastated. I told Eagle, 'I was hoping to get a couple of more years in.' He said, 'Atch, you've worked hard.' He gave me the old story, but he said, 'We've got a little something for you.' I said, 'Yeah, I can imagine. *Very* little.' I got the whole year's salary and they lined me up a job with Saskatchewan Government Insurance, doing promotion and advertising. I was a goodwill ambassador for the insurance company."

According to Atchison, a whole year's salary amounted to $15,000. "You worked beside football," he said. "I think in my last two years, I didn't work. Up until then, I worked. I went to practice after work and played the games. I was a carpenter. It never bothered me. I felt good about it."

The same sentiments applied to a halftime tribute to Atchison, held on a Sunday afternoon in late September. In advance, the *Leader-Post* devoted a full page to Atchison's career. The stories were headlined "SaskATCHewan." The page included a tribute from former *Leader-Post* scribe John Robertson, who wrote: "I might have suggested that he was the only pro football player who loved the game so much he'd play for nothing. How was I to know that Ken Preston was to take my suggestion literally when he and Atch sat down to talk contract?"

The man of the hour was choked with emotion on Ron Atchison Day. "Standing here, knowing it is for the last time ... well, it makes the right words hard to find," Atchison told the crowd of 16,828. The tributes had actually begun the night before, when the Roughriders' board of directors held a dinner in his honour.

For the fourth consecutive season under head coach Eagle Keys, the Roughriders improved their regular-season record. After going 8-7-1 in 1965, Saskatchewan posted records of 9-6-1 (1966), 12-4-0 (1967), 12-3-1 (1968) and 13-3-0 (1969). The 13 victories represented an all-time high for the franchise, and enabled Saskatchewan to finish atop the Western Conference for a second straight season.

The 1969 Roughriders' high-powered offence easily led the West in points scored, with 392. Eleven touchdowns were scored by Hugh Campbell, who had returned after a one-year hiatus. Clearly, his skills had not diminished during the respite. Gluey Hughie's mastery of his position was especially evident on Sept. 1, 1969, when the B.C. Lions visited Taylor Field. Two touchdown catches by Campbell helped Saskatchewan win 32-14. The following day, the *Leader-Post*'s game story was headlined "Hughie's Haven no place for Leos."

Hughie's Haven was a popular label for the cramped Taylor Field end zones, which were surrounded by Styrofoam-covered fences. Campbell crashed into the padded fence while making both of his touchdown catches against B.C., burning Lions defensive back Craig Murray each time. One month earlier, Murray had been injured after slamming into the fence while attempting to cover Campbell.

Campbell revisited Hughie's Haven in 2003, when the Edmonton Eskimos were preparing to face the Montreal Alouettes in the second Regina-based Grey Cup. At the time, Campbell was the Eskimos' president and chief executive officer, but he was more than happy to take a few minutes to reflect on the 1960s while providing this author with a guided tour of the

Haven. "I've always loved this spot," Campbell said while walking toward the north end zone. "I've always felt that it was a sacred spot."

Upon arriving in the end zone, Campbell talked animatedly about his former territory. "There were stands all the way across the back line. There was a fence that was about waist-high in the back of the end zone, and it was the back of the end zone. The back line and the fence were one and the same. And the fence was about this high." Gluey Hughie indicated his waist. "Then there was a place where people could walk around from one side of the stadium to the other, right behind that [short fence], and then there was a higher fence keeping the [young fans in the] Knothole Gang from running on to the field."

Campbell walked over to the sideline in the northwest corner of Hughie's Haven. "One particular time, Ronnie threw me a pass against B.C. As I caught the ball, I hit the fence and went over the fence. Then I hit the wire [on the taller fence] and cut my helmet. You could see through it. My helmet was destroyed on the play."

Hugh Campbell *beats another Edmonton defender |*
Photo courtesy of *Leader-Post*

Campbell himself emerged unscathed — unlike Craig Murray, who had been injured in an Aug. 3, 1969 game. "He hit the fence with his face, right where I'd hit it just below my waist," Campbell said. "He was diving and he just broke his nose all over his face. After that, the legend of the fence just got bigger, and then Ronnie would throw more and more passes to me near the back of the fence. The defensive backs would shy away from going there. I can remember that when we played B.C. the next time, Ronnie threw one right at the fence. I was sliding feet first and caught it and then crunched into the fence. The defensive back was kind of just standing there." The fence itself would not be standing there for much longer, either. "It wasn't a skill," Campbell said of catching passes there. "It was just a weird circumstance. The next year, they fixed it."

After earning top spot again in 1969, the Roughriders vowed to make amends for the disappointment of one year earlier. Mission accomplished. Saskatchewan defeated Calgary 17-11 and 36-13 to sweep the best-of-three Western final and advance to the 1969 Grey Cup.

The victories over Calgary proved to be expensive. Gord Barwell, the Roughriders' primary deep threat, suffered a shoulder separation and was unable to play in the Grey Cup against the Ottawa Rough Riders. Tight end Jim Worden, who sustained rib injuries, was also sidelined. Two other members of the 1966 Saskatchewan team that had defeated Ottawa — defensive lineman Ron Atchison and defensive back Dale West — had retired before the 1969 season. As well, veteran guard Al Benecick was traded to Edmonton.

Turnover was also a factor with the Eastern Riders. Ottawa quarterback Russ Jackson made it clear that the 1969 season would be his swan song. The Grey Cup just happened to be a rematch of the 1966 final, in which Ron Lancaster and the Roughriders defeated Ottawa 29-14. The 1966 result was not on Jackson's mind as he prepared for the 1969 final. "That was my last game," Jackson said. "I just wanted to go out and win it. It didn't matter who we were playing. We had won the Grey Cup in '68 against Calgary, and then we went back in '69 to try to win back-to-back. That was the big thing for us."

Jackson helped Ottawa defeat Saskatchewan 29-11, throwing four touchdown passes in his finale. Saskatchewan's lone major came on a 28-yard pass from Ron Lancaster to Alan Ford, who had also scored a touchdown in the 1966 Grey Cup. The connection in 1969 helped Saskatchewan assume an early 9-0 lead, but the Eastern Conference champions handled most of the scoring from that point forward. "In '69, we just got an ass-whipping," George Reed remembered.

Jackson was named the game's most valuable player, collecting 103 votes — 10 more than diminutive running back Ron Stewart, who had caught touchdown passes of 80 and 32 yards. "People say, 'You had one win and one loss against Ronnie,' " Jackson said in reference to Lancaster, a former quarterbacking cohort in Ottawa. "It wasn't Ronnie. It was the Saskatchewan Roughriders." Despite the outcome, Roughriders head coach Eagle Keys managed a chuckle. "Jackson was great," Keys said. "I wish he had retired last year."

Lancaster also marvelled at Jackson's brilliance, along with the storybook ending to his career. "What a way to go," the Roughriders quarterback told Ron Campbell of the *Leader-Post*. "Very few of us in professional sports ever get the opportunity to step out of the game as Russ Jackson did today. Usually we are asked to quit or are just cast aside. Here he has done everything. It couldn't have been better for him. He has done everything and he has earned this day. I know it is next-year country out west, but we'll be back."

The same could not be said of Campbell, who retired — again — following the 1969 season to become the head coach at Whitworth College in Spokane, Wash., where he would resuscitate an ailing program and transform it into a perennial power. He was only 28 years old, and very much in his prime, when his CFL playing career concluded. In five-plus seasons with Saskatchewan, Campbell had compiled some staggering statistics — 321 receptions, 5,425 yards and 60 touchdown catches.

"I'm not going to lie and say I didn't miss it, but I felt it was a good time to get on," Campbell told Ian Hamilton of the *Leader-Post* in 2003. "And Eagle felt that way, too. I had talked to him about it and I think he'd had enough of me." Opposing defensive backs, no doubt, felt that way.

Following the 1969 season, George Reed also pondered the notion of leaving Saskatchewan. The Denver Broncos courted him in hopes that he would spend the 1970 campaign in the National Football League. After serious contemplation, Reed declined the Broncos' offer.

"I wanted to go where I could have some insurance," Reed recalled. "They were willing to give me a one-year, no-cut contract and I wanted a three-year, no-cut contract. We came to about a year and a half or two years, and I said, 'Naah.' At that time, I was working with Molson's. Between Molson's and my football money, I might have been making $5,000 more playing down there, and I just didn't see any reason to go."

This was hardly the first time Reed had received overtures from the United States. "It really started in '64," Reed said. "San Francisco tried to sign me. Cleveland tried to sign me, but why in the hell would I go to Cleveland with Jim Brown there? I had about nine or 10 different offers to go play."

Reed countered family tradition by not playing in the NFL. Two of his brothers, Smith and Frank, played for the New York Giants and Atlanta Falcons, respectively. Smith was a halfback. Frank played cornerback. Reed's brother-in-law, Jerry LeVias, was a receiver with the Houston Oilers and San Diego Chargers. Reed's cousin, Mel Farr, was the featured running back with the Detroit Lions. Another cousin, Miller Farr, was a defensive back with the Chargers, Oilers, Lions, Broncos and St. Louis Cardinals. Not only that, Reed's half-brother — defensive back Clancy Williams — was a first-round draft pick of the Los Angeles Rams in 1965. Williams played with the Rams until 1972. Despite so many family ties to the NFL, George Reed opted to remain in Canada.

"Some of the offers were tempting, but how much was it worth to really move around?" he said. "The money was not like it is today. Guys go down there even for a trial and they get $250,000 or $300,000. We were talking a difference of maybe $5,000. You're talking of me playing down there because I wanted to play in the National Football League. All I wanted to do was try to make a living from the game and play the game that I love.

"I had brothers and cousins who played in the National Football League and I'd go down there and see them. I'd go with them for a day and we'd leave home at seven o'clock in the morning and get home at six or seven o'clock in the evening. Everything was football. You couldn't leave. You couldn't even go to the university in the evening unless you got permission from the football team. I just didn't want to get into that. I saw what went on. If I had to spend that much time around it and be told what I could do, I wanted some further compensation.

"I enjoyed working for Molson's and then going in at four o'clock for practice. From four until nine, that was it, and then I didn't have to worry about that until the next day. I didn't have to sit in meetings. I think it helped me along the way because it took my mind off the game when I worked all day."

CHAPTER **27** # "NOT A CHANCE"

The Roughriders' best season — playoffs excepted — had one of the worst endings. Saskatchewan breezed through the 1970 CFL regular season while overcoming injuries to George Reed and Ron Lancaster. Reed suffered a fractured leg bone that forced him to spend time on the injury list for the only time in his illustrious career. The resilient Reed rushed for 821 yards even though he played half a season with the injured leg. Lancaster, despite being hampered by a sore throwing arm that resulted from a buildup of scar tissue, was named the league's most outstanding player. It was fourth-time lucky for Lancaster, who had been the runner-up in 1966, 1968 and 1969.

Ken Reed |

Lancaster led the Roughriders to the Western Conference final — and another meeting with Calgary. Calgary's 9-7-0 record paled in comparison to Saskatchewan's franchise-best 14-2-0, but regular-season performance was seldom a barometer when the Roughriders and Stampeders squared off in the playoffs. The 1970 postseason would not be any different, as was evident when Calgary opened the best-of-three series with a 28-11 victory. The Stampeders were also poised to win Game 2, and the series, when they marched deep into Saskatchewan territory while trailing 4-3 with just under two minutes remaining. Despite being within range for a go-ahead field goal, Calgary opted to pass. Quarterback Jerry Keeling was sandwiched by Wayne Shaw and Ken Reed. The ball was jarred loose. Ed McQuarters scooped up the fumble, reminiscent of Game 2 of the 1966 Western final in Winnipeg, and ran 87 yards to paydirt. He crossed the goal line with 39 seconds remaining. The Roughriders won 11-3 to force Game 3.

It was a costly victory. Lancaster suffered cracked ribs and a bruised muscle in his back on a hit by defensive lineman Dick Suderman. Therefore, with a Grey Cup berth at stake, Saskatchewan had to start Gary Lane at Taylor Field. Complicating matters, the Roughriders and Stampeders played in frigid conditions, with the wind chill dropping temperatures below minus-30. It was so cold that the national anthem was not played. The Roughriders and their fans felt a chill from other sources as well.

Late in the third quarter of a tight game, Lane swept around the left end from the Calgary 12-yard line. Lane felt he had crossed the goal line. The officials had a different view, and the final say. They ruled Lane had stepped out of bounds at the one-yard line. Nonetheless, it was an advantageous situation for the Roughriders, who were first-and-goal. Lane fumbled on first down, but Saskatchewan recovered the ball. On second-and-goal from the two-yard line, the Roughriders intended to hand off to Reed, but he slipped on the treacherous turf. Lane improvised by spinning to the left and lunging toward the end zone. One official signalled a Roughriders touchdown, but he was over-ruled. "We were in the end zone twice from the waist up and they didn't allow the touchdown," Reed lamented. The possession ended with Lane fumbling on third down.

Despite those setbacks, the Roughriders were leading 14-12 in the waning seconds. Calgary began its final possession on Saskatchewan's 42-yard line. On first down, Keeling flipped a screen pass to Hugh McKinnis, who gained 16 yards. Had the Roughriders allowed McKinnis to advance a little further — say, another 10 or 15 yards — before being tackled, time may have expired. Instead, three seconds remained. Calgary had time for one more play. Larry Robinson was called upon to attempt a 32-yard field goal into a wind that was gusting up to 60 kilometres per hour.

"I didn't think there was a chance," Robinson reflected. "I tried kicking into the wind from there before the game and never even got one to the goal line. When I did kick it, I thought it was going to make the goal line but go wide. Then a gust hit it and, whew, it went through." In shocking fashion, Robinson had made amends for a missed field goal that had allowed the Roughriders to win "The Little Miracle of Taylor Field" in 1963.

"The best team we ever had was in 1970," centre Ted Urness said. "[Calgary] never should have won it." Those sentiments are echoed by Eagle Keys. "We didn't think he had a chance in the world to make the thing," he said of Robinson. "It was like somebody took the ball and dropped it over the goal posts. We felt like we should have won that one and gone to the Grey Cup again." Following the game, Lane was adamant that he had scored. "They took it away from us twice," he told the *Leader-Post*. "I stepped into the end zone inside the flag on that run ... I know I did." That was in reference to the run from the 12-yard line. When asked about his dive toward the end zone on second-and-two, Lane responded: "I made it. I was lying across the goal line when the whistle stopped play. They ruled me out again."

Ironically, Lane would not always refer to the officials as "they." He went on to enjoy a long and successful career as an NFL official. He was a side judge, and later a referee himself, during an officiating career that lasted from 1982 to 1999. He also worked in two Super Bowls (1989 and 1999). In 2003, a heart attack claimed Lane at age 60. He had retired as an NFL official prior to the 2000 season, when he failed a physical due to a heart problem.

Shortly after the 1970 season, Eagle Keys resigned to become head coach of the B.C. Lions, with whom he worked alongside executive general manager and former Edmonton teammate Jackie Parker. "We'd improved every year since I got there, from 1965 until 1970," Keys said. "I just felt that there's always a time to leave. It was nothing personal. You get to a point where you have a chance to do something else and you do it." The Roughriders offered Keys a long-term contract extension, but that did not deter him from leaving. Keys had one season remaining on his existing pact, but the Roughriders' brass gave the Lions permission to negotiate.

Along with Keys, the list of departees included Ken Reed and Ted Urness, whose association continued through their farm-machinery business. Reed was normally unheralded, although he was named a Western all-star defensive end in 1969. Urness was an all-Canadian centre from 1965 to 1970, and the West's outstanding lineman in 1968. "When Eagle was gone, I was gone," Urness said. "He was sure my idea of a head coach. He couldn't really take Saskatchewan much further than he did. He had an opportunity for bigger money."

Ted Urness |

Urness, who left football at age 33, played his final game against a future Hall of Fame defensive lineman "John Helton retired me," he said with a chuckle. "I got tired of lying on my back and yelling at Ronnie to look out ... I say that with the highest respect for Helton. He was an excellent football player. He was young and I was old. I wanted to leave the game on my terms. I didn't want people to say I was over the hill. There were a lot of opportunities and I wanted to get another career going."

After the Roughriders' first-place finish in 1970, Ed McQuarters spent plenty of time in the basement. His major offseason project was home renovation. "I wanted to finish our basement so that the boys, Eddie and Mike, would have a bit more room to play during the long, cold winter months," McQuarters remembered. "Also, it was about my time to host a Rider after-game party in the upcoming season, so I had two good reasons to get the basement finished during that 1970 offseason. I figured I could do it myself. I would come home from the office [at SaskPower] every day, have a bite to eat, then go down to the basement until about one or two in the morning. On the weekends I would work down there just about 24 hours. So, less than three weeks later, I was about 75-per-cent finished.

The bar area panelling still had to be done. Panel board nails don't bend. When I mis-hit them with the hammer, they would fly all over the place. On a couple of occasions, I thought that I should put on some goggles, but I didn't. I was pretty tired and wanted to get the basement done. There was a corner in the basement bar area that I couldn't quite get my big butt into. So I had to half-back into that area, bend over, and twist my body to get a good hit on the heads of those nails. I couldn't hold the nails with one hand and hit them with the other hand because of my awkward position.

"I did manage to get one of those nails started into the panel board — just enough where I could hit it properly, I thought. I managed to tap the nail a second time. The third hit was a hard one, but I mis-hit it. It ricocheted off the floor with bullet-like speed and hit me in my left eye. It stuck there on its side because of those little screw-like ridges. Instantly, a tear from that eye dripped on the floor. I pulled that nail out of my eye, looked at it, swore at it, then put it back into the hole it was in. Then I said to it, 'I'll be back to get you all the way into that panel board.' I went upstairs and looked at my eye in the mirror. The lens of my eye was now egg-shaped. There was no pain, just a numb feeling. A few minutes later, my vision had become blurred in that eye. I cleaned up a little and drove myself to the hospital, and on the way the sight in the eye became more blurred. Suddenly, I had a feeling that I would never see out of that eye again."

Two interns at the hospital confirmed the severity of the injury. One of the interns called McQuarters' doctor and asked for instructions. They then put a salve in the injured eye, covered it with gauze and applied an eye patch. He was given prescription drugs to stop the pain and to curb infection, and was instructed to call his physician in the morning.

"I got back home, went down in the basement and finished pounding that nail into the panel board," McQuarters said. "I used my wife's red lipstick to mark that one nail because I wanted to see it, and swore at it all the time. However, over time the lipstick faded. I managed to sleep that night, but the next day there was mild pain in that eye. It had a cloudy look to it, and my vision was more blurred. I called in sick to the office for two days because the pain was getting worse. My doctor finally was able to get me in to see a specialist two days after the accident. The specialist examined me for only five minutes. Then he announced that the eye had to be removed. I said, 'No, I want to try to keep it even though I can't see out of it.' He said, 'OK, but I'll see you later in the operating room, Ed.' I could still see light, but no shapes or colours. He cautioned me that infection was well-established and that's where the pain was coming from.

"For the next two weeks I suffered the extreme pain, hoping the infection would go down and I would be able to keep my eye. My co-workers were telling me that I looked awful and that I should go to a doctor. I didn't tell them what the problem was. I was losing weight because I couldn't eat or sleep. The pain was almost unbearable. I went to my doctor on two occasions. On both occasions, somehow I talked him into putting the telephone receiver down. He was calling the hospital to book an emergency operation for the removal of my eye. I wanted to keep my eye."

By the third week, the pain had become intolerable. "I called my doctor, and he got me in to see a different eye specialist," McQuarters said. "That second specialist looked at my eye for about 10 seconds and said, 'Ed, you're going to the hospital right now. The infection in there is so bad that it has moved over to the nerves in your good eye.' I got to the hospital and was begging everyone — practically yelling — to remove my eye. The pain was simply indescribable. I do remember a nurse who gave me a shot on one of my butt cheeks. I was putting up such a fuss, so she jammed that needle into me real hard. It really hurt! All this was happening in the late morning.

"In the early afternoon, I woke up from the anaesthetic, heavily bandaged over my left eye. Immediately I could feel the relief. The pain in my eye and in my head was gone. Then I thought, 'Well, Ed, you tried to keep your eye. But sometimes you have to let things go for your own good.' Before the operation, the specialist said I was well on my way to going totally blind due to all the infection in the bad eye."

The eye was removed on June 16, 1971. After a week, McQuarters had regained the ability to focus with his good eye, although there was still some blurriness. Each day, McQuarters' wife, Bunny, would visit and tell her husband about the volume of letters and get-well cards that were arriving at their home. By this time, the Roughriders had begun their 1971 training camp under newly appointed head coach Dave Skrien. In those days, the Roughriders practised in the infield at Regina Exhibition Track, located on the exhibition grounds — near McQuarters' hospital room. "I would open my window so that I could hear the sounds coming from the Riders' practices," he said. "I knew they were thinking about me because I was thinking about them. Sandy Archer brought me a huge fruit basket and said it was from the players, coaches and management. They were in training camp in two-a-day practices, but a few players took the time to come and visit me twice."

When McQuarters was discharged from the hospital, his wife asked him to visit the basement. He was expecting to see the carpeting that had been installed, but a surprise was in store, courtesy of his colleagues at SaskPower. "The entire public relations male staff had finished the basement for me," McQuarters said. "They even added some enhancements that I never thought about. It was wonderful. We had a basement-warming party when I was able to return to work. Those folks are simply outstanding, even today."

McQuarters applied the same description to the people who offered encouragement and best wishes. "While I was convalescing at home from the hospital, it took me a whole week to personally answer every one of the 500 cards and letters I received from all across Canada, and some from the U.S.A.," he said. "I didn't care about my stationery and postage-stamp bill. I figured those people were thinking about me during a very serious and emotional time in my life. I owed them a reply of 'Thanks!' "

Throughout the ordeal, McQuarters maintained his desire to return to the football field. In early July, he dropped in to visit his teammates, and soon resumed practising. He returned to the lineup on Aug. 27, 1971 — only 72 days after the left eye had been removed — when Saskatchewan opposed Ottawa. A Taylor Field crowd of 16,980 gave him an extended standing ovation. "It was a humbling experience," he said. "After my first defensive play

I knew that I could still play the game." So did the opposition. A robust performance by McQuarters helped Saskatchewan win, 42-21.

Saskatchewan had a 2-4-0 record when McQuarters returned to the lineup in 1971. With No. 61 at his familiar left defensive tackle spot, the Roughriders went 7-2-1 over their final 10 regular-season games. Despite missing six games and one eye, McQuarters was named the Roughriders' outstanding lineman in 1971. The recognition was hardly new. Neither was the Roughriders' matchup with Calgary in the Western Conference final. For the fifth consecutive year, Saskatchewan and Calgary met in a best-of-three series, with the winner to advance to the Grey Cup.

In most years, there was little to choose between the Stampeders and Roughriders. The 1971 season was no exception. Both finished with 9-6-1 records, with the Stampeders getting the nod for first place. "It was always great playing against a team like that," said linebacker Wayne Harris, whose Stampeders won the 1971 Grey Cup after defeating Saskatchewan 30-21 and 23-21 in the playoffs. "When you do win, you feel like you accomplished something. We were playing about five or six games against each other every year with the playoff system the way it was."

Ed McQuarters | Photo courtesy of *Leader-Post* archives

Perhaps more than anyone, Harris — who excelled for the Stampeders from 1961 to 1972 — collided with George Reed. Game after game, year after year, Harris and Reed slammed into one another. "George was a super football player — one of the best that has ever played in the CFL," Harris said. "George was a quiet guy. He'd just get up and go to the huddle. You'd wonder how he was going to come back, but he did. He missed very few games, even though he took a lot of hard hits.

"We didn't talk to one another very often on the field. It's like we hated them and they hated us, so we didn't speak, but we didn't do anything dirty. Everything was above board. They were just a very competitive team. That was the way football was designed. It reached its peak at that time. You had a lot of respect for the players and the opponents that you played against. It was played in a sportsmanlike way."

Harris also had more than a passing familiarity with Roughriders quarterback Ron Lancaster. "He was very smart," Harris said. "You knew that they were going to come up with something new in every game. He hated to lose. He wouldn't say too much. He'd just give you a dirty look if you did something wrong, or something he felt was wrong. Then he'd go back to the huddle and come back swinging again."

CHAPTER 28 | # "WE'RE HITCHHIKING"

The Roughriders had a chance meeting with "The Golden Jet" — in an airport, appropriately enough. "Bobby Hull was a Rider fan," defensive back Bob Kosid recalled. "We were in the Toronto airport and Bobby was besieged by autograph-seekers. He saw me and pointed over at me and said, 'Go and get that guy's autograph. He's a great football player.' I thought, 'What a gentleman.' "

Throughout the 1960s and into the 1970s, Hull was one of the National Hockey League's pre-eminent players while unleashing slapshots on behalf of the Chicago Blackhawks. "Bobby Hull came to a couple of our games during his offseason when he was a Blackhawk," Kosid said. "He was just absolutely amazed at the parties and the camaraderie. He'd show up in Regina. Half the football team probably wouldn't recognize him for what he was, because they were all from the States."

Kosid had a first-hand appreciation for Hull. "I grew up in Chicago," said the Brandon-born Kosid, who spent much of his childhood south of the border. "I can remember going to the Stadium and watching a young Bobby Hull and a young Stan Mikita." Kosid and his teammates eventually befriended Hull. "He sent me a picture and a hockey stick, all autographed by the Blackhawks," Kosid recalled. "I've been told that if I had kept that stick, it would probably be worth a fortune, but I had to use it one day in a street hockey game. But I've got the picture of Bobby Hull on my wall."

Hull became a Roughriders fan largely due to the influence of Blackhawks teammate Gerry Pinder, who was born in Saskatoon. "I was a fan of Ron Lancaster and the bunch that played pretty well and won the Grey Cup back then," Hull reminisced. "I just loved football and I loved the way they played. Lancaster was a great field general and ran the game the way it should have been run with the talent that he had. They were an exciting team."

Pinder and Hull were spotted occasionally at Roughriders games. "I expect that the folks were certainly cognizant that I was there, but they didn't go out of their way to take the emphasis away from their Roughies," said Hull, whose son Bart had a brief stint as a fullback with the 1994 Roughriders. "Sure, Gerry and I were asked for autographs, but I don't think I was much of a deterrent to the game on the field. I know I went to a Winnipeg game in 1972 when I went to Winnipeg to help form the World Hockey Association. The quarterback was Don Jonas and he was having a rough time. The fans started to holler that they wanted me to go out there and pitch the ball, which I didn't appreciate and I'm sure Jonas didn't, either."

Hull had left the Blackhawks in 1972 to sign with the Winnipeg Jets of the fledgling World Hockey Association. During the Jets' infancy, the Roughriders visited Winnipeg to oppose the Blue Bombers in the Western Conference final. Winnipeg (with a 10-6-0 record) had earned a bye to the 1972 final by virtue of its first-place finish. Saskatchewan had claimed third spot at 8-8-0, registering its fewest victories since the 8-7-1 campaign of 1965.

For more than half the game, the Western final did not appear to be much of a contest. A field goal by Don Jonas six minutes into the third quarter gave Winnipeg a 24-7 lead. However, the Bombers would not score again. A touchdown pass from Ron Lancaster to Alan Ford, a Jack Abendschan field goal, and a scoring run by George Reed — part of his 156-yard rushing performance — enabled Saskatchewan to create a 24-24 tie before a disbelieving audience at Winnipeg Stadium. Jonas did not help the Bombers' cause by serving up four interceptions.

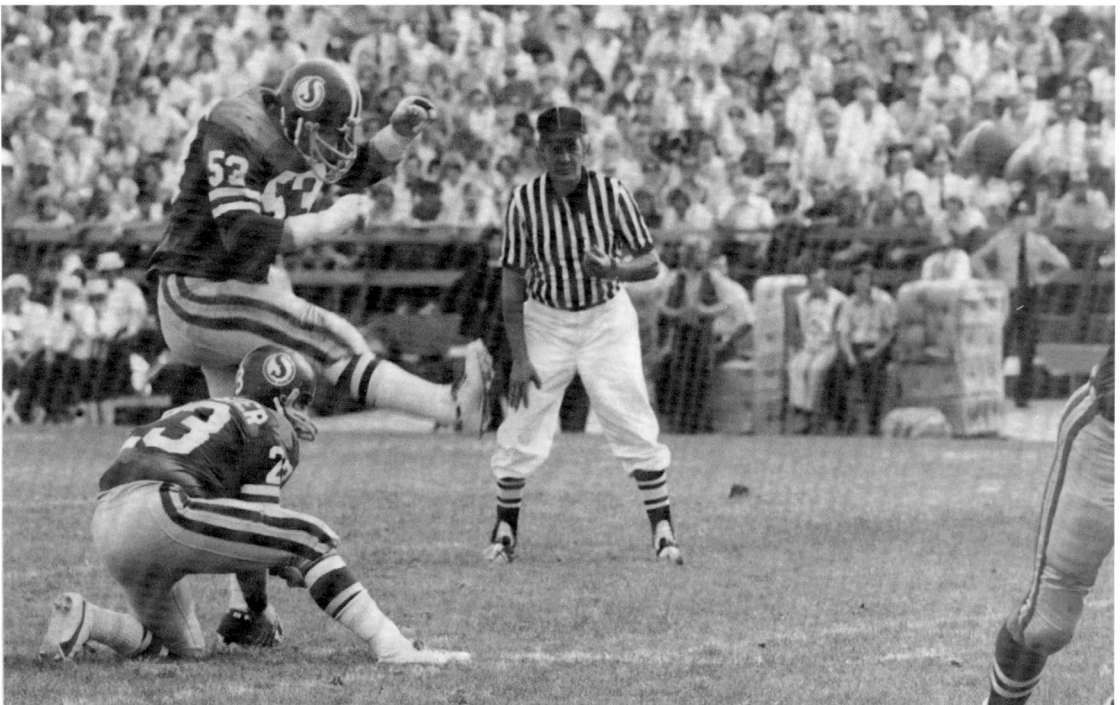

Jack Abendschan *was one of the last of a dying breed, a position player who also kicks (and straight ahead, not soccer-style)* | Photo by Wyatt Photography. Photo courtesy of SSHFM

With six seconds left, the Roughriders were on the Bombers' 25-yard line. Abendschan was called upon to attempt a 32-yard field goal which, if successful, would propel Saskatchewan into the Grey Cup. The kick was errant but, knowing that a single point would still win the game for Saskatchewan, Winnipeg's Mike Law booted the ball out of the end zone. Lancaster, who had pinned the ball for Abendschan, retrieved Law's kick and punted the ball back into the end zone. Winnipeg's Paul Williams fielded the ball and kicked it back again. Saskatchewan's Charlie Collins settled under the ball and was immediately felled. Flags flew. Winnipeg was called for no yards, enabling Abendschan to attempt another field goal — again from the 32. The veteran guard was unerring on his second attempt, giving Saskatchewan a 27-24 victory.

"I'm glad we won the Grey Cup [in 1966] and I'll always remember that, but I still think the best game we ever played was the Winnipeg game in 1972," said Abendschan, a seven-time all-star guard.

The Roughriders' next game was also decided by a last-play field goal. This time the decision went the other way. As time expired, Ian Sunter kicked a 34-yarder to give Hamilton a 13-10 Grey Cup victory at Ivor Wynne Stadium. For the third time since the landmark Grey Cup conquest in 1966, the Roughriders had been unsuccessful in their bid to bring a second championship to Saskatchewan.

"In '72, we got cheated out of the game," George Reed said. "I will always say that. They gave Dave Fleming a touchdown. He caught the ball and he was out of bounds." Reed was referring to Fleming's 16-yard, first-quarter touchdown reception from Chuck Ealey. Fleming made the catch near the sideline and the officials signalled a touchdown. Fleming's major, plus a field goal by Sunter, put Hamilton ahead 10-0 after the first quarter. Saskatchewan responded with 10 points of its own, courtesy of Ron Lancaster's touchdown pass to Tom Campana and an Abendschan field goal, but other opportunities to score were not seized. Saskatchewan finished the game with 24 first downs — one more than Hamilton. On Saskatchewan's final possession, Lancaster completed two passes to Campana and one to Bob Pearce, but the Roughriders could not advance any further than Hamilton's 48-yard line.

After a punt by Pearce, Hamilton scrimmaged the ball on its 15-yard line. Ealey proceeded to complete three consecutive passes to Tony Gabriel, who gained a total of 54 yards on his only catches of the day. Ealey's fourth completion of the drive was a 13-yarder to Garney Henley on second-and-eight. Henley made a spectacular reception while falling backwards, putting the Tiger-Cats in position for Sunter's Cup-winning kick.

"We got back into the locker room after the game and the team just broke down," defensive back Ted Dushinski said. "We all cried. We couldn't believe it." The disbelief endured. "That one hurts because that's the one we should have won," said Reed, who did not get any disagreement from his quarterback. "In '72 in Hamilton, we couldn't stop them on that last drive and [Sunter] kicked the field goal," Lancaster said 35 years later in his capacity as a Tiger-Cats special advisor. "It was a great setting. It's a sold-out stadium. You're standing there and the scoreboard's in the background and the ball's in the air going through the uprights with no time showing on the clock. It's over. It's just one of those things. We just didn't play well enough to win. We should have won, but we didn't."

In 1973, a former Roughrider made the big time, or at least the big leagues. Jim McKean, who had punted for Saskatchewan in six games during the 1966 regular season, was forced to end his pro football career shortly thereafter due to a ruptured kidney. The Montreal native remained actively involved in sports by taking up umpiring. By 1973, he had advanced to baseball's Class AAA ranks. One day, McKean was in Pawtucket, R.I, when he was approached by American League supervisor of umpires Dick Butler. "He said, 'Jimmy, do you know where you're going tomorrow?' " McKean recalled. "I said, 'Yeah, I'm going to Richmond or Rochester.' He said, 'No, you're going to Fenway Park. The game's tomorrow at one o'clock.' I never came back from there. I started at second base in Fenway Park and that was it."

McKean had started his CFL career with the Montreal Alouettes; in 1966 he was dealt to the Roughriders, who were looking for a punter. "I billeted at a house," McKean remembered. "Another thing I remember is people used to sit on the sideline at Taylor Field. They just sort of sat on the grass. I thought Regina was a great place. It was a great football town. You could equate it, in those days, to Green Bay. I enjoyed my short time there."

McKean especially enjoyed his time in baseball. He umpired in three World Series, three all-star games and five American League Championship Series. He was involved in more no-hitters (seven) than any umpire in major-league history but, oddly enough, was not behind the plate in any of them. In 1988, he was voted the big leagues' umpire-of-the-year. He called his final game in 2002 before becoming an umpire supervisor for Major League Baseball. "I've had a great run," McKean said from his home base in St. Petersburg, Fla. "It has been very exciting for a local Canadian kid."

As the 1970s progressed, some of the Roughriders' stalwarts from the 1966 championship season began to leave the game. Henry Dorsch wrapped up his playing career in 1971. Wayne Shaw, Bob Kosid, Wally Dempsey and Bruce Bennett played their final games in 1972. By 1973, Gord Barwell — a 10th-year Roughrider at age 29 — was limping and poised for retirement. The rigours of the game also affected Ed McQuarters, who signed off in 1974. "After two major knee operations, three broken fingers, developing a bad neck, hip and shoulder, and playing on really bad feet, I'd had enough," said McQuarters, a 1988 inductee into the Canadian Football Hall of Fame. "Plus, my depth perception was thrown off with the loss of my eye ... I tried to play some softball once in a celebrity game. Forget it! I didn't have a clue where that white ball was in the air. But I did slightly tip it once. Interestingly, no one knew what was going on with me in that game. They just thought that I was a bad softball player."

By the mid-1970s, George Reed was establishing CFL and pro football records every time he carried the football. The 1973 season featured Reed's all-out assault on the record book. In back-to-back games, he eclipsed Jim Brown's pro football marks for rushing touchdowns and yardage gained along the ground. The touchdown record was set Aug. 8, 1973 at Taylor Field, when Reed rushed for three Saskatchewan majors in a 38-19 victory over the B.C. Lions.

George Reed honoured for his record-setting career by then-Premier Allan Blakeney and
Lt.-Gov. Dinny Hanbidge, who was an early-era Rider himself | Photo courtesy of Leader-Post

Reed finished the game with 107 career touchdowns — one more than Brown. "George has
something special," Lions head coach Eagle Keys told Bob Hughes of the Leader-Post. "When he
gets near the goal line, his nose starts twitchin' and there's no way you're gonna stop him. All
the great ones have it."

Upon scoring the record-breaking touchdown, Reed handed the ball to the nearest official
and jogged toward the sideline, refraining from any celebration. "I didn't have the energy to
do that type of thing," he said. "Someone told me, 'If you do anything special, act like you've
been there before and don't give people a reason to look at it.' Another thing that I learned
when I was playing is that some guys got some pretty good hits on me at times, but they
never knew when they had hurt me because everything was always the same way. Whether
I was feeling great or if I was hurt, I got up the same way and walked back to the huddle.
They never knew. I was never one to throw the football. I always felt, 'Give the football to the
official and sit down and rest and get ready to go again,' because I knew I had to go again."

Reed did it again the following week, in an 18-12 victory over Ottawa. With 40 seconds
remaining in the game, Reed broke Brown's career mark of 12,312 rushing yards — finishing
the contest with 12,313. Reed also scored both Saskatchewan touchdowns, putting him three
ahead of Brown on the all-time list. While Reed was surpassing Brown, the Aug. 13, 1973
edition of Sports Illustrated was on the news-stands. That issue included a profile of Reed,
headlined: "Running At A Record Pace." The story, written by Joe Marshall, included a

quotation from Minnesota Vikings head coach Bud Grant — a former Winnipeg field boss: "George Reed would have been a superstar here just as he is in Canada."

The Ordinary Superstar — 1972 Heisman Trophy winner Johnny Rodgers — was paid $100,000 by the Montreal Alouettes in the mid-1970s. Lancaster and Reed were receiving less than half of that amount, despite being Canadian football royalty. "They get me every time my contract comes up for negotiating," Lancaster told Douglas Sagi for a story that appeared in the *Canadian* magazine. "I keep telling myself that they are not going to do it to me this time, but they do. I don't get what I want, but I'm still here. Maybe if I had an agent negotiating for me, I wouldn't be here. And maybe I'd be the best-paid quarterback in Canada." Sagi wrote that "Lancaster has the feeling the Roughrider fans may be getting tired of their team, the same faces, the same victories. Winning can become boring." For example, the Roughriders had drawn only 9,373 fans for the 1973 Western semifinal against the B.C. Lions. "And the weather was really great, too," Lancaster told Sagi. "It was 20 above and the sun was shining. Maybe they're tired of old Ronnie and old George. If they are, maybe they should trade us."

In 1975, Lancaster eclipsed a landmark pro football record by completing a five-yard pass to Steve Mazurak during a 20-14 victory in Winnipeg. That connection gave Lancaster 40,242 career passing yards — three more than Johnny Unitas, who held the previous pro football mark. Blue Bombers fans recognized Lancaster's feat with a standing ovation.

"If you play a long time, you'll break some records," Lancaster noted. "It was nice that some of them were his, just because of what I thought of him. I still think he was the best." Lancaster had felt that way since the 1950s, when Unitas burst into prominence with the Baltimore Colts. "I started following the Colts because of him," Lancaster said.

Like Unitas, Lancaster grew up in the Pittsburgh area — Lancaster in Clairton, Unitas in nearby Mount Washington. Both quarterbacks also blossomed in their second pro football stop. Unitas had a stint with the Pittsburgh Steelers before finding a home in Baltimore. Lancaster spent three seasons with Ottawa before being traded to Saskatchewan in 1963. And both quarterbacks — renowned for their cerebral approach to the game — had a telepathic relationship with a receiver who compensated for a lack of abundant physical tools by relying upon intelligence, technique, dedication and an uncanny ability to catch the football. Lancaster sparkled in collaboration with Hugh Campbell, as did Unitas with Raymond Berry.

Asked if he idolized Unitas, Lancaster responded: "That would be about right. I really thought a lot of him." Those sentiments were reinforced in May of 1975, when Unitas was invited to Regina to speak at the Optimist Club of Regina's sports dinner. "I was supposed to go to a dinner somewhere else — I don't remember where — when they told me he was coming," Lancaster said. "They asked me if I wanted to be a head-table guest and spend the day with him. Well, heck yeah! I called and cancelled the other dinner. I met Unitas in the morning. We had lunch. We spent the afternoon going places and then I sat beside him at the dinner. He was just a great guy to talk to. He was everything you expect. He could walk in anywhere and feel at home. He was very down to earth. You know what was great? After

George Reed, Johnny Unitas, Ron Lancaster — *three pro football legends share stories* |
Photo courtesy of *Leader-Post*

the dinner, he went upstairs to the suite where the Optimist members who worked the dinner were. He talked to those guys until three o'clock in the morning, and he had to catch a plane at seven. He told stories and laughed and seemed to have a great time. It was just nice because you always want to meet somebody like that, and he was everything I was expecting or hoping for. He was a great person. I just wanted to meet him, and it was well worth it. That was a great day."

Early in the 1970s, the Edmonton Eskimos replaced the Calgary Stampeders as Saskatchewan's perennial playoff opponent. Saskatchewan paid visits to Edmonton four consecutive years, beginning in 1972. The Roughriders won the 1972 Western Conference semifinal in the Alberta capital before losing to the Eskimos in the 1973, 1974 and 1975 conference finals. Despite the latter defeat, Ron Lancaster and George Reed still attended the 1975 Grey Cup, along with their wives. Lancaster and Reed were in the crowd at Calgary's McMahon Stadium, where Edmonton defeated the Montreal Alouettes 9-8.

"Remember how cold it was?" Lancaster began. "Bev [Lancaster] and Angie [Reed] stayed at the hotel. George and I went to the game and it is *cold*, and we're freezing. I said, 'George, we're getting out of here at halftime.' I had to do an interview at halftime so I said, 'As soon as I do this interview, we're going to go.' He said, 'You bet.' You couldn't drive to that game. You had to take buses or something. There were no cars allowed. So there's George and I out on the road by McMahon Stadium, hitchhiking. A guy stopped and picked us up. We said, 'We were at the game, but it was too damn cold, so we had to get out of there.' He drives us right down to the hotel. We thanked him and he goes on his way. He had no problem at all. I don't know if the guy believed it, but there was George Reed and Ron Lancaster, hitchhiking from the game because we were frozen. How could you believe that? But hey, it was fun."

Chapter 29

"I CAME, I PLAYED, I STAYED"

The year 1976 began on an auspicious note for the Roughriders when George Reed signed a two-year contract extension in January. At 36, he was coming off one of his finest seasons. In 1975, he had carried the football a career-high 323 times — a short-lived CFL record — for 1,454 yards and 11 touchdowns. The yardage total was his third-highest in a professional football career that dated back to 1963.

Little did the Roughriders or their fans suspect that Reed would make another announcement prior to the 1976 season. On the final day of May, Reed held a media conference to reveal that he had decided to retire. "The time has come, I guess," he told reporters. "My mental preparation for the season hasn't been right. It hasn't been what it should be by this time in the year. When that happens, you know it's time to step down." The decision had been made May 19, when Reed was in Saskatoon. "I woke up in the morning, after tossing and turning a lot, and something told me to hang it up," he said. The words of Jim Duncan had been proven true. Duncan, who was an assistant coach with the Grey Cup-winning team in 1966, had told Reed: "You'll wake up one day and know it's time to quit." Reed made the announcement a week after being named the inaugural winner of the CFL's Tom Pate Memorial Award, which recognizes outstanding sportsmanship and community involvement. Ron Lancaster won the award the following year.

Reed left the game with rushing totals of 3,243 carries, 16,116 yards and 134 touchdowns, plus three majors on receptions. He owned pro football records in all three of those rushing categories. In addition, Reed had rushed for more than 1,000 yards in 11 of his 13 seasons as a Roughrider. The numbers were only part of the legacy. Off the field, Reed had immersed himself in community activities. In 1974, the George Reed Foundation for the Handicapped was established. He was also the honorary chairman of the Muscular

Dystrophy Association and Easter Seals, along with being an honorary head coach with Special Olympics. As well, Reed served as president of the CFL Players' Association — playing a vital role in the strengthening of that group — and the Saskatchewan Sports Hall of Fame and Museum. "I just felt there were some things that needed to be done," Reed said. "I was kind of a workaholic, anyway. Different organizations needed help and I felt that I could help, so you devote some time."

The Roughriders managed to enjoy a successful 1976 season without some notable alumni from the Grey Cup team of 10 years earlier. Along with Reed, offensive linemen Jack Abendschan and Clyde Brock played their final games in 1975, and Alan Ford could not complete the following season due to injury. In Reed's absence, Steve Molnar became Saskatchewan's leading rusher. The challenge was to find a backfield mate for Molnar. The list of cohorts included Pete Van Valkenburg, Keith Barnette, Robert Holmes, John Washington and Molly McGee. At one point, a knee injury to Molnar forced Saskatchewan to go with a single running back. Even so, the Roughriders' offence remained productive, thanks largely to the fact that Ron Lancaster was enjoying one of his finest seasons.

Although Reed had retired, he played a major role in the sporting calendar for 1976. The seven days leading up to an Oct. 24 home game against Winnipeg were designated George Reed Week. The festivities included a testimonial dinner, held Oct. 20 at the Saskatchewan Centre of the Arts (now the Conexus Arts Centre). The event attracted a capacity crowd of 850, including a lengthy list of dignitaries and prominent people in Reed's life.

One of the guest speakers was John Suzick, who had coached Reed back home in Renton, Wash. "In high school, there were athletes who were every bit as good as George Reed, but there were none who worked harder," Suzick told the audience. "George was always something special ... He always took time to come back to Renton, after he went to college, to speak to the kids on the team. The biggest thing about George Reed was his presence. By that, I mean just his being there affected those around him."

Eagle Keys, the Roughriders' head coach from 1965 to 1970, also paid tribute to Reed. "All I would do was stand on the sidelines and say, 'C'mon, George,'" Keys said, adding that he "just felt fortunate being a coach in the era of someone as great as George Reed." Reed was so great, in fact, that Keys felt compelled to try his hand at rhyming: "Only God knows if He'll plant another seed, to produce a football player as good as George Reed."

Typically, Lancaster ran the show. As master of ceremonies, he fired off a succession of one-liners throughout the evening, but concluded on a serious note. "I've known this guy a long time and I played with him through all his career," said Lancaster who, like Reed, had arrived in Saskatchewan in 1963. "We've been through some good times and bad, but with George you always knew you were in it together. I could never hope to find a better friend." The last word belonged to Reed, who punctuated the gala by saying: "I came, I played, I stayed." George Reed Week was capped by a special ceremony at halftime of the Winnipeg game. There were 22,508 eyewitnesses at Taylor Field. Reed received a standing ovation, along with several gifts — including a grandfather clock and a 1977 Cadillac. Roughriders

*Former teammates **Tim Roth** (66), **Gary Brandt** (54) and **Alan Ford** (21) present **George Reed** with a grandfather clock upon his retirement* | Photo courtesy of *Leader-Post*

general manager Ken Preston also announced that Reed's No. 34 jersey would be retired. Reed then handed over his uniform to the Canadian Football Hall of Fame.

There was only one downside to the afternoon for people with loyalties to the Roughriders. Winnipeg won 21-19, jeopardizing the Roughriders' hopes of finishing first in the Western Conference for the first time since 1970.

At one point, it appeared likely that Winnipeg would overtake Saskatchewan for first place on the final day of the 1976 regular season. The Roughriders needed a victory over a non-playoff team — Calgary — to secure top spot, but the Stampeders were a stubborn adversary, jumping to a 24-0 second-quarter lead. By halftime, the Stampeders were ahead 27-8.

The Roughriders dominated the second half, but would it be enough? Saskatchewan began its final possession with 2:13 remaining in the fourth quarter. Calgary was leading 31-26. The goal line was 79 yards away. Nine plays later, Saskatchewan was situated on the Stampeders' four-yard line. One play remained. With first place on the line, Lancaster looked to his favourite receiver, Rhett Dawson, in the end zone. Pressure prevented Lancaster from actually seeing Dawson, but the Roughriders' quarterback threw to a spot. Dawson, a Hugh Campbell clone in many ways, was there. The pass was perfect. "I just remember squeezing that ball as tight as I could," Dawson recalled. "What a great moment."

And what a comeback. Lancaster was renowned for his improbable rallies, but he might have outdone himself on Nov. 7, 1976 in Calgary. "Likely, he has never been the architect of such a miraculous kind of comeback as he was here," the *Leader-Post's* Bob Hughes wrote from Calgary. After the game, Hughes interviewed veteran Stampeders centre Basil Bark. "I didn't come down in yesterday's rain," Bark said. "I've played too many times against them to know better than to let yourself think you've ever got them. You have to step on their throats and keep your foot there. You know, even when we had them 24-0 they didn't look like they were down or beaten. They just looked mad. I've played a long time against Ronnie. I know Ronnie. You don't take anything for granted with him. You know that sooner or later he's going to come after you, and you'd better be ready."

With top spot secured, the Roughriders readied themselves for the Western Conference final, having earned a first-round playoff bye. As it turned out, Saskatchewan would once again face Edmonton for the privilege of representing the West in the Grey Cup. But the 1976 showdown had a different twist. After visiting Edmonton in the previous four post-seasons, Saskatchewan would finally be at home to oppose the Eskimos while participating in its 11th consecutive Western Conference final. In friendly surroundings, the Roughriders prevailed 23-13 on the strength of a powerful ground attack. Steve Molnar's career-high 144 rushing yards were supplemented by Molly McGee's 100. Saskatchewan salted away the game when Bob Richardson made a one-handed catch of a Lancaster pass for a 25-yard touchdown. "It wasn't a pass," Lancaster said, "it was a catch." Either way, the Roughriders would soon be catching a plane for Toronto.

Lancaster's preparations for the 1976 Grey Cup matchup against Ottawa were interrupted by an important engagement — the Schenley Awards. As the day of the big game loomed, Lancaster was honoured as the league's most outstanding player. At 38, he was the oldest player to receive the award, but he seemed to be immune to the aging process. Following the retirement of George Reed, Lancaster registered career highs in passing attempts (494), completions (297) and yards (3,869) while throwing 25 touchdown passes. Lancaster's presence, along with a stingy defence, created the widespread expectation that Saskatchewan would capture its second Grey Cup.

Ottawa had other ideas, assuming an early lead at Exhibition Stadium in Toronto. The Roughriders' sluggish start prompted one so-called fan to telephone the Lancaster residence. "I remember that Saskatchewan was down 10-0 in the first quarter," Ron Lancaster Jr. said. "I answered the phone and this guy on the other end of the line was ripping [Ron Sr.]. The next thing you know, Saskatchewan was ahead at halftime. The same guy phoned and apologized. He said, 'I'm very sorry. He's having a hell of a game.' "

A 51-yard field goal by Bob Macoritti gave Saskatchewan a 20-10 third-quarter lead. However, the Western champions did not hit the scoreboard again. Their offence was hampered by a rib injury to McGee, who was knocked out of the game in the first half. Complicating matters, the Roughriders had opted against dressing a second import running back (Robert Holmes), instead activating inside receiver Tom Campana as the designated import. Campana had missed the Western final with an ankle injury.

That ill-fated decision backfired on the Roughriders and their head coach, John Payne. Late in the fourth quarter, after stuffing Ottawa on third-and-goal from the one-yard line, back-to-back runs by Campana gained insufficient yardage. Saskatchewan was forced to punt from its end zone. Ottawa began its final series on Saskatchewan's 35-yard line and made the most of the advantageous field position.

With Saskatchewan clinging to a 20-16 lead, Ottawa quarterback Tom Clements called a play in the huddle: "Fake 34, Tight End Flag." The tight end was future Hall of Famer Tony Gabriel, whom everyone in the stadium expected to get the ball. Sure enough, he did. The only surprising element of the play was the lack of attention Gabriel received from a Saskatchewan defence that had performed so admirably for most of the season.

For starters, Gabriel was not impeded as he began to run his pattern. The lack of a pass rush gave Clements plenty of time to watch the play develop. Gabriel made a quick move toward the middle of the field, forcing Roughriders safety Ted Provost to take a step in that direction, before cutting back toward the right corner of the end zone. "I could see Tom Clements eyeball to eyeball, because there was nobody in between us," Gabriel recalled.

Ron Lancaster and **Alan Ford** *played together and later coached together* | Photo courtesy of *Vancouver Sun*

"When the ball was in the air, my eyes were six feet wide, because I wasn't going to drop this. I watched it all the way into my hands." Touchdown, Ottawa. Letdown, Saskatchewan.

"Everybody in the world knew they'd be going to Gabriel," Lancaster said after the game. "They've run the play 64 times, and then they make it work." Once again, Gabriel had scorched Saskatchewan in the latter stages of a Grey Cup.

When interviewed after the 1976 Grey Cup, Provost said: "One damn play and it ruins the whole season." On that day, and long thereafter, the veteran safety was widely tagged as the goat. "Poor Ted Provost still takes a heck of a riding or is still being blamed for something that wasn't his fault," Lancaster reflected. "We had so many chances to win that football game."

Provost, a two-time all-star, was inducted into the Roughriders' Plaza of Honor in 2008.

One of the spectators at Exhibition Stadium on Nov. 28, 1976 was the recently retired George Reed, who stood on the sideline with the Roughriders. His presence, along with the outcome, prompted the inevitable, unanswerable question: How would events have unfolded if Reed had followed through on his initial plan to play that season? "I thought if I had been there, I could have added something to the game, but I had no regrets about my decision," he said. "I had said that, once I made a decision, I was going to stick with it. Probably the only person who could have got me to come back earlier in the year would have been Ron if he had asked me, but he didn't and I'm thankful that he didn't. You look back at it and you say, 'A couple of times that they needed a couple of yards that might have changed the course of the game, I think I could probably have got those couple of yards.' That goes in your mind but it's not a regret, no."

Bob O'Billovich's Grey Cup regrets were eased on that chilly November day in Toronto. In 1976, O'Billovich was a first-year assistant coach with Ottawa. Ten years earlier, O'Billovich had played in his first Grey Cup, only to lament Saskatchewan's 29-14 victory over Ottawa. Ottawa went on to win Grey Cups in 1968 and 1969, but O'Billovich was not part of those celebrations. He retired prior to the 1968 season after a contract dispute with Rough Riders general manager Red O'Quinn. "I just felt, 'Well, maybe it's time for me to get out if you're not going to be remunerated according to what you're worth,' so that's what I did," O'Billovich recalled. In 1976, he was finally able to celebrate a CFL championship. "I missed it as a player. That was my first one as a coach," said O'Billovich, who was the Toronto Argonauts' head coach when they won the title in 1983. "It was a great experience."

The Roughriders' glory years ended in 1976. Lancaster was the last remaining player from the team that had captured the 1966 Grey Cup. "The thing that hits you right away is that it's the only one we won," Lancaster reflected. "As good as our football club was for a number of years and only winning one ... The best part of '66 was just the idea of winning. It was our first one. That was the whole name of the game. They had never won in that province before and it was a great place to be. The other side of the coin is that we didn't win enough of them. That's the sad part."

Still, Lancaster preferred not to dwell on the ones that got away, especially in 1972 and 1976. "You try not to," he said, at the same time conceding it is easier said than done. "The main reason is, you never forget the ones you lost. You've got to sit down sometimes when you're alone and think about some of the times you won when you shouldn't have won. You never, ever forget the games that got away from you. It's one of the sad things of life. People have a tendency to maybe remember unpleasant things. We had such a great time together as a group. We played together for a long time. Eagle Keys put this team together and he kept it together. Just remember the good times, because we had a lot of them."

And a lot of victories — 117 of them, to go with 55 losses and four ties, from 1966 to 1976. "I didn't realize that maybe we were the winningest team for a 10-year period and still only won one Grey Cup," Lancaster said at a 40th-anniversary reunion of the 1966 Roughriders. "They said there were all these seasons in Saskatchewan — the wind blew in the winter, the spring and the summer, and Lancaster would blow playoff games in the fall. But, looking back on it, it was a great place to play and these guys were great to play with."

CHAPTER **30** | # "YEAH, THAT WAS A GOOD DAY"

Tony Gabriel's Grey Cup-winning touchdown catch initiated a protracted drought. After losing to Gabriel and the Ottawa Rough Riders in the 1976 CFL final, the Roughriders did not participate in another playoff game until 1988. "Nineteen seventy-six was our last hurrah," Ron Lancaster said. "'That was a bunch of guys who had been together for a while and you could see it falling apart. It was time for them to move on and go on with life. Once '76 was over, our football team didn't really resemble the football team that we had played together on in the early '70s." The drought was a drastic turnaround for the Roughriders, who, beginning in 1962, had qualified for the playoffs in 15 consecutive seasons.

The 1977 Roughriders were in playoff contention until the final day of the regular season, but ended up finishing fourth in the five-team Western Conference at 8-8-0. After posting that same record in 1972, the Roughriders were able to make the playoffs and advance to the Grey Cup, but the circumstances were different five years later. By 1977, only Lancaster remained from the group of players who had captured Saskatchewan's first-ever Grey Cup.

However, another link to 1966 remained. The 1977 season was Ken Preston's last as the Roughriders' general manager. In understated fashion, Preston had assembled a perennially competitive team during the most successful era in franchise history. But after 20 years at the helm, Preston announced in December of 1977 that he was stepping down. The connection to 1966 was maintained by the appointment of Henry Dorsch as Preston's successor — although the latter would remain involved with the team for one year as a management consultant.

"When Preston does leave the club, his contributions to football in this city, this province and to the league will not leave with him," Bob Hughes wrote in the *Leader-Post* on Dec. 13, 1977. "He has had one of the most amazing, yet largely unrecognized, careers in professional sport of anyone, anywhere. The man turned the Roughriders into the winningest pro football team in North America, was among the first to recognize the value of having Canadian talent, and was the backbone of the Roughriders' incredible rise from an also-ran to a team which made the playoffs for 15 straight seasons. If there is one man in management who is responsible for the success the Roughriders have had in the last 20 years, it is Ken Preston. When he took over as general manager in 1958, season-ticket sales were at the 6,470 mark. Now they are over 16,000."

Long-time Roughriders trainer Sandy Archer was an obliging target on May 17, 1978, at the Don Powell Memorial Sports Celebrity Roast, held in memory of the former Roughriders assistant coach. "I've often wondered why Sandy has been with the team for so long, and then I figured it out," master of ceremonies Ron Lancaster said. "Usually when you've been with a team for 25 years, they give you a gold watch. Well, the Riders won't spring for one, and Sandy won't quit until he gets one."

Lancaster was just getting started. "Sandy used to play Spin The Bottle when he was a teenager, and the deal was that if the bottle pointed to someone you didn't want to kiss, you had to give the person 25 cents," he said. "Well, Sandy paid for his parents' home by the time he was 15." *Leader-Post* sports editor Bob Hughes also chimed in. "It takes him so long to get to injured players on the field that they sometimes recover from their injuries before he gets there," Hughes said.

Archer, who was born in Moose Jaw, spent five years in the Canadian Army medical corps as an operating-room technician before working in the physiotherapy department of the Department of Veterans' Affairs from 1946 to 1948. For the next nine years, he was a physiotherapist at Regina's Medical Arts Building, where he often treated the Roughriders' players. Archer's involvement in sports intensified in 1951, when he joined the Roughriders and the Regina Pats junior hockey team as the trainer. His tenure with the Pats lasted until 1965. He spent 30 years with the Roughriders.

"Sandy was unbelievable," Dale West said. "He could work anything for you. He could tape anything. Ron Atchison used to say, 'If I can hurt it, Sandy can tape it.' " Bob Kosid, who played alongside West in the defensive backfield when Saskatchewan won the 1966 Grey Cup, also marvelled at Archer's techniques. "We called him the Medicine Man," Kosid said. "He had this black satchel. It didn't matter what you needed. He had a pill in there for you." Archer, who was also known as the Wizard of Gauze, is the subject of some tales of the tape. "A day after one game, Sandy treated my knee," defensive lineman Garner Ekstran recounted. "Then I went to see Eagle Keys in his office. I had to crawl up the stairs on my hands and knees because I couldn't walk. We had four days until our next game and Sandy said, 'He's not going to play.' Eagle said, 'He'll play.' Sandy taped me up and I played." But some of Archer's best work was done without the assistance of medication or tape. "Sandy was as much the club psychologist as he was the trainer," Alan Ford said. "He was a master of getting players back on the field. I would have missed a ton of games if not for him."

George Reed was always quick to voice his appreciation of Archer. "In about six different seasons, I would have missed four or five games if it hadn't been for Sandy," said the Hall of Fame fullback, who speculated that his career may have been extended up to two years because of Archer. "I had a lot of faith in that man. I never found him trying to mislead me. He always told me if I would risk further injury by playing. When I had my dislocated toe, for instance, he told me there would be pain, but that I couldn't damage it any further." With that in mind, Reed persisted in playing. "The dislocated toe might have been one of the most painful things I had," he said. "For the first two or three times I took shots in it, I couldn't stand the needle. I said, 'If I can't play without the needle, I won't play.' I think I played several more games on it. It was, 'We'll just tape it up and away we go.' It was important to be ready to go on to the battlefield with the guys. That's how much I thought about the guys. I thought that if I didn't play, I would let down the other 31 guys on the football team."

Hugh Campbell, Sandy Archer *and* ***George Reed*** |
Photo courtesy of SSHFM

Archer's efforts also elicited praise from Lancaster. "He knew his business. He knew what your injury was and the rehabilitation for it. I think his main strength was that he was sort of a father confessor," he told Bob Hughes in 1981. "He always had time for everybody. The babysitting part of it was important. Even when a guy was hurt and couldn't practise or play, Sandy would make sure he would find something for him to do so the guy would feel he was still a part of the team. Sandy became a friend to everybody who was here. It didn't matter who you were or how long you were here. He was also a practical joker. You never knew what he would do next. He kept everybody loose and you need that. All you can say is he did a lot for this club in a lot of ways."

Archer was especially proud of an unofficial club within a club. "I used to have a team of my own, which I called the 100-Per-Centers — guys who would play regardless of injuries or regardless of the score," he said. "They would play every game. We must have had 12 or 15 or

18 guys with that kind of attitude and it permeated. If a guy got a little injured and he was thinking of missing a practice, they would get on him so bad that he'd be out there practising. They would put it to him. Eagle was like that. If there were guys in the training room when Eagle walked in, they just scattered. Eagle had that little half-smile and he'd say, 'What the hell are you doing in here?' They were tough and that lasted for 10 years. I can remember Ted Dushinski, Garner Ekstran, Bob Kosid, Clyde Brock, Reggie Whitehouse, Ted Urness, George Reed, Ron Lancaster ... They were all tough. They weren't going to miss a game."

Lancaster was in peak form to begin the 1978 regular season. During the first half of the opener in Hamilton, an unerring Lancaster dissected the Tiger-Cats defence while helping Saskatchewan assume a 20-3 halftime lead. The momentum was arrested, however, when second-year Roughriders head coach Jim Eddy replaced Lancaster with rookie Larry Dick to begin the third quarter. Eddy felt that Dick, who was touted as the Roughriders' quarterback of the future, could use some playing time.

Mistake. Hamilton stormed back and eventually won 27-23. Lancaster was fuming. At season's end, he said: "After that game, that was the beginning of the end for me. It destroyed all the work and the planning of the offseason. I really had looked forward to the year, but that just seemed to take everything out of me." Eddy was fired when the 1978 Roughriders' record dropped to 0-6-0 and replaced by assistant coach Walt Posadowski. Saskatchewan went 4-5-1 under Posadowski, but an overall slate of 4-11-1 put the Roughriders in the Western Conference basement for the first time since 1960.

There was one positive note to the season. Lancaster concluded his playing career by engineering his 50th successful fourth-quarter comeback in a Roughriders uniform. The finale was a stark and welcome contrast to the sad events of Oct. 22, 1978, when Lancaster played his final game at Taylor Field. Dick, the heir apparent, started the game against Winnipeg, only to be replaced by Lancaster with the Roughriders clinging to a 6-4 fourth-quarter lead. Lancaster, who was thrown in cold, was unable to enliven the Saskatchewan offence. Winnipeg ended up winning 13-7 and intercepting Lancaster twice. A segment of the crowd responded by booing Lancaster. That behaviour was greeted by outrage, but the damage was done. The unimaginable had happened.

Ron Lancaster |
Photo courtesy of the Willie Jacobs family

"This is a guy who has given almost half his life to the Saskatchewan Roughriders," an indignant Bob Hughes wrote in the *Leader-Post*. "This is a guy who came in here when they were nothing, when they were down, when they seemed to run out of life, and he made them into a dynasty feared throughout the Canadian Football League. This is a guy who has turned down chances to go play elsewhere, where the money would have been bigger, turned it all down so he could stay here because it was a good place to raise a family, and he did believe in Roughrider tradition. Hell, he was Roughrider tradition. And yesterday, they booed him. It was sad, and it was unfair, and people around Western Canada, who watched it and heard it on television, could not believe it."

Neither could Lancaster. "He was really disappointed with the fans at Taylor Field," Ron Lancaster Jr., said of the Winnipeg game. "Initially he was upset, but he realized it was only one section of fans, not the entire stadium. It bothered him because he felt he was a Saskatchewan guy."

Thankfully, Lancaster's next appearance in Green and White would be unbelievable for other reasons. The Roughriders' 1978 season came to an end Oct. 29 at Commonwealth Stadium in Edmonton. Before the game, some Edmonton Eskimos fans had put up a banner which read: "Thank you, Ron, for all the good years." Nonetheless, Dick made his second straight start at quarterback, with considerably better results. Even so, the Roughriders trailed 26-20 early in the fourth quarter. At that point, the crowd began to chant for

Joey Walters *makes a one-handed leaping touchdown catch* | Photo courtesy of *StarPhoenix*

Lancaster. Posadowski obliged by sending No. 23 into the game. Many of the 42,673 spectators responded by giving Lancaster a standing ovation. As Lancaster stepped on to the field, he accepted a handshake from Eskimos cornerback Larry Highbaugh. It was a remarkable and appropriate contrast to the events of seven days earlier.

There was also a notable difference in the outcome. Lancaster's second series of the game began after Ken McEachern recovered a Jim Germany fumble at the Eskimos' nine-yard line. Lancaster promptly hit Joey Walters for a touchdown pass — the last scoring toss of the quarterback's career — to create a 26-26 tie. Bob Macoritti's convert gave the Roughriders a 27-26 lead and put them ahead to stay. How did the Eskimos' fans respond? With another ovation. The Commonwealth Stadium scoreboard read "WOW!" The fire truck that customarily circled the field after Eskimos touchdowns did a lap to salute Lancaster, sirens blaring. A "Hoo-ray Ronnie" sign was affixed to the side of the fire truck.

"We still feared him, because you never knew," Eskimos equipment manager Dwayne Mandrusiak recalled. "It was like, 'Oh my God, here he comes,' right to the end. You couldn't have scripted it any better. It's like the old saying: 'Good things happen to good people.' He ended on a high and let it go. It was weird, because you almost had to cheer for him. Even though you hated the fact that he beat you, you cheered for him."

Lancaster was not finished after the go-ahead touchdown. On the Roughriders' next possession, he drove the team 55 yards for another major — which came when he scored from one yard away on a quarterback sneak, behind left guard Roger Aldag, on a third-down gamble. Lancaster waved the field-goal unit off the field before scoring. Saskatchewan won 36-26 on the strength of Lancaster's Hollywood ending. "If Ronnie had sat down and written the script himself, he couldn't have written it any better," Walters said. Lancaster concurred, noting: "That last game was kind of a storybook, wasn't it?"

Lancaster was moved by the recollection of that final game for the rest of his life. "That was outstanding," he reflected almost 30 years later. "That's something I'll never forget. I got a standing ovation from the Eskimos' fans going into the game and even after we won. It was kind of funny, because we sure didn't get a very good ovation the week before in Taylor Field when we played Winnipeg and I didn't play very well. But against Edmonton, it was a heck of a way to end a career. You thought we were the home team. It surprised the heck out of me. It was something you don't expect to get in another team's park. They weren't always the greatest fans in the world toward the opposition — they didn't like Saskatchewan a heck of a lot — but it was nice."

Fittingly, Hugh Campbell was there to witness the occasion. Although Lancaster accepted postgame congratulations from Campbell, Gluey Hughie did not share in the merriment. Campbell, who had combined with Lancaster to form a lethal pass-catch combination in the 1960s, was in his second season as the Eskimos' head coach. Earlier, he had coached Brian O'Hara — the recipient of Lancaster's final completion, for a 21-yard gain — at Whitworth College. On this day, however, Campbell was not overjoyed at watching Lancaster and O'Hara help to engineer a victory. "Hughie wasn't too happy," said Lancaster, who retired with CFL-record totals of 6,233 passes attempted, 3,384 completions, 50,535 aerial yards and 333 touchdown passes. "He said if they were going to lose, they were going to lose, but he didn't think it was real good for his fans to back the other team's quarterback in their stadium. I thought it was pretty good."

More than "pretty good," in the view of Ron Lancaster Jr. "He was so happy with that," he said. "That made him as happy as any Grey Cup victory. That's my point of view. If I had to talk for him, it's real simple. It would be, 'Edmonton sent me out the right way ... Play the game and close it and roll the credits.' He said, 'That's the best way I could go out.' "

The same could not be said of Lancaster's farewell season as a whole. "When the game ended, no one was really happy with the season," The Little General said. "You tried to forget it. It was tough. But, yeah, that was a good day."

In the same edition of the *Leader-Post* that documented Lancaster's final game, Bob Hughes reported that the legendary quarterback would soon become the team's next head coach. A formal announcement was made the day Hughes broke the story.

"Life is like a book," Lancaster said at a media conference. "This is just another chapter. This is the beginning of a new era. The time was here for me to retire as a player. It breaks the final link with the old way. I'm the only one left from that era."

Henry Dorsch and Ron Lancaster — *two former teammates become the Rider brain trust* | Photo courtesy of *Leader-Post*

Another legend from that era, George Reed, made news in 1978 when he became a member of the Order of Canada — the country's highest civilian honour. The decoration was especially noteworthy considering that Reed was born in the United States. "It was a tremendous honour," remembered Reed, who hails from Renton, Wash. "I was fortunate to get it. It was one of those things, I guess, where I qualified by helping out others. I'm sure football played a part in it, but when they read it out to me, it was for all the community work and the work outside of football. Football brought you here and football did a lot of things for you, but there is also a lot outside of football that they count."

And there was a lot outside of football. At one point during his time in Regina, Reed was associated with 47 community or charitable groups. "You just try to help," he said. "As they say sometimes, if you want somebody to do something, find a person that's busy."

Early in 1979, former Roughriders general manager Ken Preston was honoured with a testimonial dinner. Preston's wife, Dorothy, and four children — Bill, Doug, Rich and Donna — were on hand for the special occasion. Preston received a truckload of gifts, including a grandfather clock, a trip for two from Air Canada, several plaques and trays, a gold watch, a mounted football and a painting. "For all the players and the people around the CFL to say nice things, that was a proud moment for the whole family," Bill Preston recalled.

On behalf of the Roughriders' players, receiver Steve Mazurak presented Preston with a gold watch (engraved "for a job too well done" in reference to Preston's tight-fisted tendencies) and a chain. Mazurak was a natural choice to make the presentation, being that he had played high school football with Rich Preston at Sheldon-Williams Collegiate. Rich Preston was the quarterback. Mazurak was a favourite target. "I have never heard anyone say a bad word about any of them," Mazurak said of the Preston family when interviewed at the dinner. "I am a father and I would hope that my children will be the same — that they will be able to be a friend to everyone."

Preston, who preferred not to be the centre of attention, was floored by the tributes. "I can't believe it is happening," he said. "It's been terrific. But if we have been successful, the triumph is not mine alone. When we would go on the road, people always used to ask how we do it, how we survive in Regina. I told them it was because we had so many people dedicated to raising funds and keeping the club going. There were only two years when I was involved that the football operation alone showed a small profit. But because of our fans and the people who raised funds, we were able to have a reserve of $600,000."

More than 600 people packed a Hotel Saskatchewan ballroom for the occasion. They saluted Preston with three standing ovations and extended countless handshakes. "But the real measure of the man's worth to football here is beyond all that," Hughes wrote. "Twenty years after people said the Saskatchewan Roughriders could not possibly survive, the Saskatchewan Roughriders are still here. That is Ken Preston's legacy."

Another Roughriders legend was saluted in 1979. On June 30, George Reed was elected to the Canadian Football Hall of Fame. One year earlier, another member of the 1966 Roughriders — defensive lineman Ron Atchison — had entered the Hall. After the inductions of Atchison and Reed, it was clear that the Roughriders' next Hall of Famer would be Lancaster when he became eligible in 1982. But Lancaster was not one to rest on his laurels. As a first-year head coach of a team that had been in decline for two seasons, he had other priorities.

One of Lancaster's most formidable challenges would be to replace himself. Larry Dick was viewed as a project, so the Roughriders acquired Tom Clements from Ottawa. Clements was available because of his stated intention to try the NFL. His stint with the Roughriders turned out to be mercifully brief. Near midseason, the winless Roughriders dealt a bruised, battered Clements to the Hamilton Tiger-Cats for Lawrie Skolrood, who could play offensive line or tight end.

Clements' struggles in Saskatchewan were not of his own making. Lancaster identified the need to re-tool an aging offensive line. Lancaster opted for an infusion of youth along the offensive line, which included Roger Aldag and Bob Poley, but the growing pains were excruciating (particularly for Clements, who was acutely familiar with the brand-new artificial turf at an expanded Taylor Field). The 1979 Roughriders did not win a game until Oct. 14 — Lancaster's 41st birthday — when they upended the visiting Eskimos 26-25. That was a rare setback for the Eskimos, who went on to win their second of five consecutive Grey Cups under head coach Hugh Campbell.

Saskatchewan, meanwhile, finished with a 2-14-0 record for two successive seasons under Lancaster. The 1980 edition, while still dismal record-wise, was more competitive than the 1979 Roughriders — scoring 284 points (90 more than the season before). A developing offensive line provided improved pass protection. Instead of a carousel of quarterbacks that included Clements, Dick, Craig Juntunen, Lloyd Patterson, Danny Sanders and Tom Rosantz, the Roughriders finished the 1980 campaign with two veteran signal-callers — John Hufnagel and Joe Barnes. Lancaster also made the decision to move Joey Walters, who had caught The Little General's final touchdown pass, from wide receiver to slotback late in the 1980 season.

The Roughriders' brass recognized that progress was being made under Lancaster. He was offered, and accepted, a contract extension. The announcement was made. Lancaster then experienced a change of heart and resigned, ending a contractual association with the Roughriders that dated back to 1963. "I think I had kind of been around there long enough," Lancaster said. "I was part of that scene for a long time."

Lancaster also discussed the situation in 2006 during an interview with Rawlco Radio's Wray Morrison. "Quarterbacks are stubborn and I've never been accused of not being stubborn," Lancaster said. "I should have left after playing and went to Edmonton and coached with Hugh Campbell. He wanted me to come up there and be an assistant coach with him for a while. I needed to do that and get away from the scene in Regina and see how things are done in other places and learn a little more about coaching. Being stubborn and thinking that I could handle it, I tried to do it. It just didn't work for me there and it's not a big deal because I still enjoyed it."

Jim Spavital, who had succeeded Henry Dorsch as general manager following the 1979 season, hired Joe Faragalli to replace Lancaster. Under Faragalli, the 1981 Roughriders posted a 9-7-0 record — the team's only winning season during an 11-year playoff drought — and regularly packed Taylor Field. Barnes and Hufnagel complemented each other so effectively that the Roughriders' quarterbacking tandem was nicknamed J.J. Barnagel by the *Leader-Post's* John Chaput. Walters caught 91 passes for a franchise-record 1,715 yards while scoring 14 touchdowns in his first full season as an inside receiver. The offensive line, assembled and nurtured by Lancaster, was widely perceived as the CFL's best. Faragalli received many accolades, such as the coach-of-the-year award, for his fine work in 1981. Veteran guard Roger Aldag lauded Faragalli, but also noted "that was more or less Ronnie's team."

CHAPTER **31**

"I HAVE RUN THE GOOD RACE"

Gord Barwell's life and livelihood changed in the 1970s. A Roughriders receiver since 1964, Barwell concluded his CFL playing career in 1973. The following year, he and his wife, Nancy, attended an Athletes In Action conference in Chicago. "It was there that we got our eyes opened to what Christianity was really all about," Nancy Barwell Kraft recalled. "It just added new meaning and depth and dimension to our life and our marriage, and it went from there. We ended up going to work full time with Athletes In Action."

The Barwell family — including son Jay and daughter Jody — moved from Regina to Toronto in 1977. Gord soon began working closely with hockey player Paul Henderson, who became a national sporting icon by scoring the winning goal in the eighth and deciding game of the 1972 Canada-Russia Summit Series. Henderson had embraced Christianity in the early 1970s, as did Barwell. "He was one of my great buddies," Henderson said. "The common bond is that we loved the Lord. We were really interested in telling other people that the Lord loves them also. Neither one of us was what you would call a straight arrow before we became Christians. We understood what we'd been saved from." Barwell and Henderson also shared an abundance of laughs. "I loved his sense of humour," Henderson said. "We'd go for dinner and I'd turn around and there would be a grape sticking out of one of his nostrils. You never answered the phone when he was around. Anytime we were doing anything with football players, something would happen. He'd say, 'The phone's for you. Go pick up the phone.' Of course, it was filled with shaving lotion and the side of the player's head would all be covered with shaving lotion. Life's too short not to have a sense of humour."

Barwell pulled one of his patented pranks in the early 1970s, shortly before the Roughriders embarked on their first road trip of the season. "It was when he had the Mr. Big & Tall Shop," Nancy said, referring to a Regina clothier. "He told two or three different rookies that they should come in and he'd get them all dressed so they'd look good for the road. One by one, they all came in and he sold them exactly the same outfit. I think that was back in the days when there were the plaid leisure suits. So they arrive at the airport to go on their first big road trip and there they all are, dressed in the same jackets. I'm sure they got even somehow, but he just thought that was the greatest."

Anyone who associated with Barwell can recite a litany of stories about his practical jokes, or the revenge that was exacted. "[Equipment manager] Dale Laird and I were rooming together," trainer Sandy Archer began. "Barwell said he was going out with so-and-so, so we got his room key and went up to his room and we did the phone, and we sprayed Tough Skin — that sticky stuff — all over his toilet seat. We plugged the sinks up with tape so the water would spray all over the place. We got one of those ice pails and taped it up over the door so that when he opened the door, it would get him. Barwell came in and — bang! — this water pail got him. He laughed about it, because he knew how many times he'd gotten the other guys. We got him with everything — the toilet seat, the sink, the phone, the ice. He was a great guy, Barwell."

Nancy had the same appraisal of Gord when they met as 16-year-olds at a high school track and field competition in Saskatoon. "I borrowed his sweatpants and it was love at first whiff," she recalled. "We were high school sweethearts." Gord went to City Park High School. Nancy graduated from Nutana. After graduating from City Park, Barwell spent one season with the junior Saskatoon Hilltops — suffering a broken ankle — before making the Roughriders' roster the next year. He did not turn 20 until Sept. 6 of his rookie season.

Barwell's speed allowed him to make a rapid transition to professional football. As a second-year Roughrider in 1965, Barwell caught a 102-yard touchdown pass from Ron Lancaster. That was the longest completion in franchise history until Kent Austin found Jeff Fairholm for a 107-yard touchdown in 1990. Barwell retired from football in 1973 with 259 receptions for 4,314 yards and 32 touchdowns, averaging 16.7 yards per catch. He peaked at an eye-popping 25.1 yards per reception in 1967, when he caught 30 passes for 753 yards, including a

Gord Barwell *the player* |
Photo courtesy of *Leader-Post* archives

Gord Barwell *the broadcaster* |
Photo courtesy of SSHFM

long gain of 88. Injuries eventually affected Barwell's blazing speed, so he became a full-time clothier.

Barwell was able to remain actively involved with sports because of a ministry he had established with Henderson, in association with Athletes In Action and Campus Crusade For Christ. "He changed lives," said Henderson, the founder and president of The Leadership Group ministry. "He had a big impact on a lot of players' lives. Kids still come up to me and say, 'You spoke at my high school back in the early 1980s.' " Barwell also became a fixture at hockey arenas, given his son Jay's interest in the sport. "I'd be away for three or four weeks at a time at hockey schools and then I'd come home," Jay remembered. "We sat around and talked for four or five hours, but we talked as man to man. It was a defining moment. Part of it is you miss each other, but we discussed life as men. It was a really neat moment where you translated from simply father and son to friend."

As a defenceman, Jay Barwell progressed to the point where he played for the Ontario Hockey League's Guelph Platers from 1983 to 1985. "A favourite moment would be knowing that I played a good game and he would just have this subdued smile," Jay recalled. "He'd give me the high-five. Any encouragement you get from your father is a good thing, but coming from a guy I respected as an athlete, when he gave me that 'good game' kind of thing, that was always huge for me. If he affirmed that it was a good game, then it was a good game. That was really positive."

The perpetually positive Barwell family experienced a shock in the fall of 1987, when Gord was diagnosed with a malignant brain tumour. He underwent six hours of surgery and most of the growth was removed. Radiation treatment was prescribed and appeared to be successful. A CAT scan revealed that the remaining part of the tumour was barely detectable. "There are so many people out there praying for me," Barwell said during his illness. "I can already feel God's hand at work within me."

However, by the spring of 1988, doctors discovered that the cancer had spread to the other side of Barwell's brain, and the tumour was inoperable. "I remember sitting one afternoon by myself in his hospital room and I was watching him," Jay said. "He had no chance, so we really couldn't communicate at this point. It was just this powerful moment where I realized there were no regrets. We were always affectionate. As a family, we

Gord Barwell | Photo courtesy of *Leader-Post* archives

always told each other we loved each other. We'd had great times together. There are things you always would have liked to have fixed, but that's just life. For the most part, it was awesome. Sitting there, I realized that if I wanted to do anything about lost opportunities, the chance was gone. And to sit there and realize 'no regrets' ... There were no I-love-yous not said. If you've got to go, this is a pretty good way to go. The slate is clean."

Gord Barwell died on April 21, 1988. He was 43 years old. John Robertson, who worked for the *Leader-Post* when Barwell debuted with the Roughriders in 1964, paid tribute to Barwell and his family in the *Toronto Star*. "Nancy Barwell redefined the meaning of the word 'courage' for me, as I watched her keep a 24-hour vigil at her dying husband's bedside ... answering endless phone calls ... welcoming hordes of sympathetic visitors ... exchanging the same heartfelt expressions of sympathy over and over again, with such genuine warmth and affection that she made each visitor feel as if she were hearing their words for the first time," Robertson wrote. "Losing track of all time except for the few precious days her husband has left ... sitting alone with him through the lonely quiet of the night ... remembering ... and telling herself that it was okay to cry now."

Remarkably, Nancy Barwell was comforting the people who sought to comfort her. "One question I never asked was: 'Why? Why me?' " she reflected. "Why not me? Just because Gord lived a pretty good life and loved the Lord and was serving people doesn't mean these things can't happen. Illness, sickness and death are the result of man's failure way back at the beginning of time. Just because you're a Christian doesn't mean that you're not going to have tough times. What it means is that you've got somebody to take you through the tough times. That's the strength that you get from that relationship. I was thankful for the years we had. I would have liked to have had a lot more, but that was one question that I didn't deal with."

Like Nancy Barwell, Henderson did not struggle to reconcile a loving God with the early death of a devout Christian. "It's a fact of life," Henderson said. "Jesus died at 33. There was John the Baptist. Look at all of Jesus's friends. There's nothing in the Bible that's going to promise you a long life. John 16:33 says, 'In this world, you will have trouble.' A lot of things don't make any sense to me, especially with people who are young and vibrant and love the Lord. And having good ministries, you would think, 'Goodness gracious, you'd want to leave these guys around for a while.' Of course, in my economy, I would have left Jesus around here for 100 years. This side of heaven, there's a lot more questions than there are answers."

A memorial service for Barwell was held at Regina's First Baptist Church the week after he died. A pamphlet distributed at the service included a photo of Barwell, accompanied by the words: "I have run the good race." In the handout, Barwell's loved ones shared their thoughts. Jay Barwell, then 22, wrote the following message to his father:

Dad, it's through teary eyes and a broken heart that I sit down to write this letter. And as I write I can't help but cry again and again, "I Love You!" You are my father, and I say that with great pride and admiration. You are, and always have been, a man of integrity, a man of honour and a man of love. You are and always will be my hero, my idol, the best father and role model a boy could ever ask for.

Oh, Dad! It's so tough to let go. How do I say goodbye to the greatest friend I have ever had? My big buddy, I want you to know I appreciate the many years and hours of support you've given me. No matter what I was doing or how trivial the task, I could always be sure that my greatest fan would be there — hoping and rooting for me. Dad, these are fond memories, memories that have shaped my life, memories that will live with me forever.

Nancy remarried 10½ years after Gord Barwell's death, exchanging vows with Gerry Kraft (who lost his first wife to cancer) and moving to Tsawassen, B.C. Kraft is the head of a mission organization, Outreach Canada, that works with churches nationally and internationally. Nancy is also heavily involved in Outreach Canada. In both marriages, she has been able to share her faith. Gord is often in her thoughts. "When that's your first love and you marry and have children and spend over 27 years together, probably not many days go by that you don't think of something or other that has to do with him," Nancy said. "You're happily married again, but that's just part of your life." Nancy is a grandmother of four. Jody has a son and a daughter. Jay has two sons, one of whom is named Tanner Gordon Barwell. "I look at my life now and think of all those years not lived," said Jay, whose full name is Gordon Jay Barwell. "Would it have been great to have him around as a friend and a counsellor? Absolutely. Would it have been great for him to have watched his grandkids grow up? Absolutely. But the years we had were awesome years, so we'll take all the good out of them that we can and live with the rest."

Paul Dudley seldom commanded headlines — until he was killed. Despite being the second-leading rusher and receiver on the 1966 Roughriders, Dudley was often overshadowed by cohorts such as Ron Lancaster, George Reed and Hugh Campbell. Even so, Dudley left an indelible impression in his one full season with the Roughriders. "He was tough, but extremely personable," trainer Sandy Archer said. "He was quite a guy." Dudley did not suit up for the Roughriders in a CFL game after 1966. His name would not resurface in the media until March of 1987, when news circulated that he had been stabbed to death in Las Vegas.

"When I learned of Paul's death, I was shocked," Les Anderson, a close friend of Dudley's, said from Prince Albert. "I felt a deep hole inside of me. How could this happen to such a great guy that had no enemies, just friends?" Included in that circle were Anderson and two other men who shared an apartment with Dudley in Regina. "Paul was a real caring, sharing and fun-loving person," Anderson said. "He enjoyed movies, bowling and bar-hopping, as he knew so many people in Regina. He was a Roughrider on the team that won the province the Grey Cup. He had

Paul Dudley |

friends that he had never met and when he did meet them, he was so polite and cordial. You just can't imagine how proud we were to be associating with him.

"Paul loved playing jokes, and even today, if you look at the official picture of that winning team, you will see Paul standing in the back row, a head taller than everyone else. Just to prove he was taller than Ed Buchanan, he grabbed the belts of Ed on his left and Ron Lancaster on his right and lifted himself up as the picture was taken."

The laughs and good times are part of Dudley's legacy. "Paul left a good, positive impression on anyone he met, and Lorraine [Anderson's wife] and I shall never forget him," Anderson said. "He left two beautiful daughters here in Riderville that he would have been very proud of." Dudley died shortly before his eldest daughter, Deanne Newkirk, graduated from high school. Her parents separated in the early 1970s. "I had intentions [in 1987] to begin to correspond with him and get to know him a bit better," said Newkirk, who had hoped to invite Dudley to her high school graduation. "But, unfortunately, that was not to be. So [younger sister] Renee and I would like to learn more about Paul as well."

Numbers tell part of Dudley's story. In 1966, he rushed 120 times for 584 yards and one touchdown; he also caught 32 passes (which placed him second on the team to Hugh Campbell's 66) for 442 yards, adding two more majors. Dudley also returned a team-high 23 kickoffs (averaging 23.6 yards per runback) and even threw a 28-yard touchdown pass to Campbell on a halfback option. Dudley did not play in the 1966 championship game, due to a severely bruised kidney, but Ron Lancaster noted that "he did a lot to help get us to the Grey Cup."

Jack Gotta | Photo courtesy of SSHFM

A second Grey Cup victory for the Roughriders seemed inconceivable through most of the 1980s, during which *Leader-Post* columnist Bob Hughes coined the term "Reign Of Error." The Roughriders had missed the playoffs for 11 consecutive seasons — enduring losing records in 10 — after qualifying for the postseason from 1962 through 1976. The Roughriders' brain trust had hoped to revive the team by hiring head coach Jack Gotta and general manager Bill Quinter after the 1984 season. Gotta had been an assistant coach with the 1966 Roughriders, who had defeated the Ottawa Rough Riders 29-14 to win the Grey Cup. Quinter played for Ottawa in 1966.

The Roughriders continued to languish under Gotta and Quinter, who were fired after the 1986 season. "We were reluctant to let them go, but if you want to win, you have to put your best foot forward," said Ted Urness, who was a member of the Roughriders' executive at the time. The executive also included Bill Baker, who had been a fearsome defensive lineman with Saskatchewan and the B.C. Lions from 1968 to 1978. "We said, 'Now what are we going to do?' " Urness said. "We bounced it around the table. I ended up saying, 'Why don't you do it, Bill?' You could have heard a pin drop, but then everyone got on it. Two days later, he agreed to do it. I give Bill full marks for getting the team together."

Baker's first major hiring was that of John Gregory as head coach. The on-field results were not distinctly different during Gregory's first season as Saskatchewan's field boss, but the team's talent level was improving. Quarterbacks Kent Austin and Tom Burgess arrived in 1987, as did wide receiver Don Narcisse, linebacker Dan Rashovich, running back Tim McCray and cornerback Harry Skipper. Bobby Jurasin blossomed as a sophomore, registering 22 quarterback sacks. Placekicker Dave Ridgway, who had been traded after clashing with Gotta, returned without missing a season, via a dispersal draft after the Montreal Alouettes folded in the spring of 1987. The Roughriders weren't in robust financial shape, either, so a telethon was held. Ron Lancaster and George Reed quickly answered the call to help out. The Rider Nation responded, as per tradition.

Baker continued to bolster the team in 1988. Jeff Fairholm, who was drafted second overall, gave Saskatchewan a speedy inside receiver to complement the bruising Ray Elgaard. Baker also added veterans such as defensive linemen Rick Klassen and Vince Goldsmith, fullback Milson Jones, defensive halfback Richie Hall and offensive lineman Bob Poley. The latter was back in Green and White after a three-year intermission with the Calgary Stampeders. Poley was reunited with his close friend, guard Roger Aldag. Poley and Aldag were part of the young and inexperienced offensive line that head coach Ron Lancaster had put in place in 1979.

"Eleven Years Is Enough," an allusion to the Roughriders' protracted playoff drought, became a rallying cry — and even a jingle — in 1988. The Roughriders posted an 11-7-0 record and finished second in the West Division. In the Roughriders' first playoff game since 1976, they lost 42-18 to the B.C. Lions in the West semifinal. Following the season, Baker resigned to become the CFL's president and chief operating officer. He was succeeded as general manager by his assistant, Alan Ford — one of the heroes of the 1966 Grey Cup.

CHAPTER 32

"A GREAT PARENT"

Alan Ford *proudly displays his 1966 Grey Cup ring won as a player and 1989 ring won as general manager* | Photo courtesy of *Leader-Post*

Alan Ford celebrated a happy anniversary on Nov. 26, 1989. Twenty-three years to the day after the Roughriders' first Grey Cup championship, he rejoiced over another title. Ford, who had caught a key touchdown pass in the 1966 Grey Cup, was the first-year general manager of the second Saskatchewan team to win the championship. The Roughriders captured the long-awaited second title at Toronto's SkyDome, defeating the Hamilton Tiger-Cats 43-40 in a classic match. Dave Ridgway kicked the game-winning field goal from 35 yards away with two seconds remaining in the fourth quarter.

Courtesy of The Kick, as it came to be known, Ford was the first person to have his name engraved twice on the Cup as a Roughrider. "As a player, you don't really realize what a great feeling and what a great accomplishment it is until you get away from the game," Ford said. "We were winning so many games [in the 1960s]. You just looked at our team and thought that after '66 we were going to be there a number of times. Who would have thought we'd never win again? That just doesn't make sense. All the time as a player, I don't think I appreciated the accomplishment of how tough it is to win that final game. I developed more appreciation for it when I was the general manager, because I knew how hard it was to get there."

The road to the 1989 Grey Cup was laden with potholes. After a 4-1 start, Saskatchewan lost eight of its final 13 regular-season games. Injuries contributed to the decline. At one point, the Roughriders were so hobbled that their third-string quarterback, Jeff Bentrim, was deployed as a slotback and kickoff returner. Jeff Treftlin, who was already undersized in his capacity as a reserve defensive back, was thrust into duty as a linebacker. By playoff time, however, the Roughriders were close to fielding their best team. Even so, it was an unheralded player — Brian Walling — who made the difference in the West Division semifinal. Late in the game, Walling ran for a 50-yard touchdown to snap a 26-26 tie. Saskatchewan defeated the host Calgary Stampeders 33-26, winning a playoff game for the first time since 1976. Next stop: Edmonton, where the Eskimos were prohibitively favoured after winning a league-record 16 regular-season games and losing only twice. That was immaterial to the Roughriders, who engineered one of the CFL's all-time upsets, winning 32-21 at Commonwealth Stadium to advance to the 1989 Grey Cup.

In that game, as in the 1966 West final, a fumble return was a crucial play for Saskatchewan. Ed McQuarters had scored on such a play during the fourth quarter in Winnipeg in 1966. Twenty-three years later in Edmonton, Eddie Lowe's jarring hit on

Kent Austin *with Gary Hoffman during the 1989 Grey Cup* | Photo courtesy of *Leader-Post*

Eskimos quarterback Tracy Ham dislodged the football, which was scooped up by Dave Albright and returned 62 yards to paydirt early in the second quarter.

Seven days later, Kent Austin emulated Ron Lancaster by throwing three touchdown passes to pilot Saskatchewan to a Grey Cup victory. Lancaster was at the 1989 final, working in the CBC booth alongside play-by-play man Don Wittman. "It was kind of neat," said Lancaster, whose son-in-law (Larry Mueller) was Roughriders assistant general manager in 1989. "It was great to do it, because of the fact that it was such a great game — one of the best games ever played. It may be the best Grey Cup ever played. I can still remember Tony Champion's great catch in the end zone [for the Tiger-Cats]. Naturally, you remember the field goal. You were there for the first Grey Cup, and being there for the second one was kind of unique."

With 44 seconds remaining, Champion had made a spectacular, nine-yard touchdown catch to pull Hamilton even at 40-40. Playing despite injured ribs, Champion caught the pass while falling backward. Following the play, Roughriders fans had a reason to wonder if Champion would be remembered in the same context as Ian Sunter and Tony Gabriel — players whose late-game Grey Cup heroics had come at Saskatchewan's expense. Austin had other ideas. Three consecutive clutch completions — one to Ray Elgaard, followed by two to Mark Guy — put the Roughriders in position for Ridgway's climactic kick.

Afterwards, comparisons between the 1966 and 1989 Roughriders were inevitable, and not just because of Ford's presence. "They weren't supposed to win. We weren't supposed to win," Ted Urness said. Like Ford, Urness was a part of the Roughriders' first two championship editions. The erstwhile centre was a member of the executive when Saskatchewan won in 1989. But, for Urness, there was a more important tie to the 1989 edition. His son, Mark, was an offensive lineman with the team. "We enjoyed that," said Ted Urness, who had been enshrined in the Canadian Football Hall of Fame earlier in 1989. "It was quite a thing. I've got an '89 Grey Cup ring. I bought one, because they were available to us [on the executive]. There's quite a difference between the rings. One looks like a wedding band and the other one is like a billboard."

Urness was a bridge between the victorious 1966 and 1989 teams. Al Bruno was involved in both games, but with different results. Bruno was a losing coach each time — as an assistant coach with the 1966 Ottawa Rough Riders and as head coach of the 1989 Tiger-Cats. Running back Tim McCray had a less-obvious connection to the Roughriders' two Grey Cup conquests. McCray, who led the 1989 Roughriders in all-purpose yardage while being named the team's most outstanding player that season, was coached in high school by Bruce Bennett — Saskatchewan's starting safety in 1966. "Timmy McCray was a great young man and a great football player," said Bennett, who coached McCray at Ware County High School in Waycross, Ga. "I really enjoyed coaching him. I was tickled to death to hear he made the Grey Cup. It gave you a warm feeling to think that somebody you had worked with had won the same championship."

Bennett's former defensive-backfield cohort, Dale West, was able to enjoy the homecomings of both Grey Cup-winning teams. In 1966, West and his teammates were onstage at the Regina Armoury when an estimated 6,000 to 8,000 fans greeted the Roughriders upon their return from Vancouver. In 1989, West savoured the victory as a fan, much like he had enjoyed watching Glenn Dobbs and the Roughriders win the West final in 1951. West was among a reported 15,000 people who occupied Taylor Field's west grandstand when offensive linemen Roger Aldag and Bob Poley — the two remaining holdovers from the Ron Lancaster era — carried the Cup into the stadium after the team returned from Toronto on Nov. 27, 1989. "That took me back to my experiences in 1966," West said. "I knew exactly what the feeling was."

The experiences of 1966 were also revisited in June of 1990, when the Canadian Football Hall of Fame announced that Eagle Keys and Ken Preston were among that year's five inductees. Keys was the Roughriders' head coach from 1965 to 1970. Preston had served as Saskatchewan's general manager from 1958 to 1977. Although there were several successes during their tenures, the team's fortunes peaked in 1966 when Saskatchewan won its first-ever Grey Cup. It was appropriate, then, that Keys and Preston were to enter the Hall together. "This is quite an honour," Keys told the *Leader-Post*'s Darrell Davis. "Ken Preston deserves it, too."

The celebration of Preston's induction was tempered by his health situation. "At that time he had Alzheimer's and he was struggling," said Bill Preston, Ken's eldest son. "I had to go to Hamilton for the announcement that he had been accepted. That was a pretty proud moment for our family and me, especially. I don't know if he really realized he had gotten that honour." Rich Preston, a former Roughriders waterboy who went on to play in the World Hockey Association and National Hockey League, represented his ailing father that autumn at the Hall of Fame induction ceremony in Hamilton.

"That was really tough," Rich Preston remembered. "It was a real honour to do it, but it was difficult because I was saying, 'Hey, my dad should be here, not me. Why couldn't it have been a couple of years earlier? Why did they wait so long?' " The onset of Alzheimer's had been a puzzle to Preston's family. After a period of uncertainty, the condition was diagnosed at the Mayo Clinic in Rochester, Minn. When diagnosed, the condition was not advanced. Preston was able to live at home and drive a car. Eventually, his condition worsened to the extent that he entered a special-care facility. "He was really distraught because he didn't want to lose his independence," Bill Preston said. "That was a fairly common reaction." Even so, Ken Preston would settle into the facility. "He seemed to be OK," Bill said. "He didn't seem to be unhappy."

Ken Preston died on Aug. 2, 1991, at age 73. Tributes poured in from friends, admirers and members of the football fraternity, who lauded his contributions to the most successful era in Roughriders history. Under Preston, the Roughriders not only survived, but thrived. "Ken Preston epitomizes everything that's good about the Saskatchewan Roughriders," then-Roughriders president Phil Kershaw said when Preston died.

The day of Preston's funeral was especially memorable for his youngest son. Rich Preston had flown to Regina for the service. His wife, Laura, was back in Chicago, in the final stages of pregnancy. Rich was hoping to return from the funeral in time for the birth of the couple's third child. "The night of the funeral — Aug. 8 — Laura phoned," Rich recalled. "She was at the hospital. Her sister drove in from Milwaukee to be the midwife. It was just before midnight when I got the call. I'm on the phone and there are probably 20 people in the living-room area. I'm getting the blow-by-blow of the delivery over the phone: 'The head's coming out ... It's a boy!' " Thomas Preston had arrived. "That's one of the things I'll never forget," Rich said. "We were burying one person and bringing another into the world. It was pretty special."

Ken Preston presided over a special era in the team's history. "In a small city, a lot of people — most of them in their 70s or 80s — to this day will hear my name and say, 'Are you any relation to ...?' " reflected Bill Preston, a longtime veterinarian in Regina. "I don't think a lot of people really knew him, but they knew of him." Bill adheres to that description to some extent, despite being Ken Preston's elder son. "I never really got to know him as a person," Bill said. "He didn't spend a lot of time around the dinner table talking to us. A lot of kids get to know their parents more when they're grown up and can ask adult questions. I never did. My impression is of him being a very private person. If it wasn't for my mom, I don't think he would have had any social life."

Ken Preston | Photo courtesy of SSHFM

Preston's wife, Dorothy, was stricken with cancer in the late 1960s. She battled the disease until it claimed her life in 1984. "She was basically the one who held everything together, even though she was so sick," Bill said. Rich Preston added: "She was a saint. Dad wasn't a real talker. Mom was the exact opposite. She was a great person — someone who was really outgoing. She was the yin with the yang."

Bill and Rich remember their mother as a catalyst for social activity. In that realm, Ken Preston occasionally revealed a less-serious side. "I'd hear him when he was playing bridge and he would start doing his imitation of Steve Owen, after a few drinks and a few cigars and that sort of thing," Bill said. "You had to keep your door open just enough to listen to what they were saying."

Preston was more at ease on the golf course. "That helped him get away from work," Bill said. "He was a pretty good golfer and he had a good group of friends who he would golf and play bridge with. I remember him saying just before he retired that he was really looking forward to retiring because he could get out on the golf course more often. This was in the spring. In the fall, we had another conversation and he said, 'I thought I would enjoy getting out on the golf course as much as I want to, but I don't enjoy it as much. It's like I have to go out there. When I was working all week, golf was something I would enjoy more, because I would look forward to it.' "

Bill Preston looked forward to the day when he could talk to his father on an adult-to-adult basis. "I really wanted to sit down with my parents and talk about how they did things during our childhood, but it was never like that," he said. "He didn't open up to anybody, including us. I wish we could have gone to the bar and sat around without him having the pressure of having to uphold his persona."

Although such a session never materialized, Bill Preston does not hold that against his father — of whom he is proud. "He was a great parent," Bill said. "I didn't want for anything. We had a roof over our heads. It was a good environment. We were brought up right and we all turned out well."

Preston's children emulated him by becoming heavily involved in sports. After retiring as an NHL player, Rich Preston went on to become the head coach of the Western Hockey League's Regina Pats and an assistant coach with three big-league teams — the Chicago Blackhawks, Calgary Flames and San Jose Sharks. Like Bill, Rich was a star high school quarterback with the Sheldon-Williams Spartans before attending college in the United States. Rich played hockey at the University of Denver. Bill accepted an athletic scholarship to Washington State University, but soon decided to forego football to concentrate on his studies in animal science. He then attended veterinary school at the University of Saskatchewan, graduating in 1974. "I imagine, looking back, that he was proud of my accomplishments," Bill said.

The paternal pride was evident when Bill Preston was playing for a Regina minor football team that won a city championship. "We'd had a pretty successful year, so he showed me some deke moves in the backyard," said Bill, whose father played for the Roughriders in the 1940s. "That was pretty cool. Back then, you didn't have as much coaching as players do now, so you went on natural ability. That was about the only time he gave me individual coaching advice. I can't remember any other time like that in my childhood, other than the time he showed me football moves in the backyard. I regret that, but I don't hold it against him. Being a parent back then was a lot harder than it is now. It was a different era."

Rich Preston saw a softer side of his father. "Being the youngest boy, it was pretty easy for me," Rich said. "I've got three boys now, too, and the youngest one can get away with murder. It's the same with me — you're always the hardest on the oldest. I thought my dad and I were pretty close, but I can see where Bill's coming from. He told us stories afterwards, in front of the campfire, and we'd say, 'You're kidding me.' He wasn't a real conversationalist, let's put it that way."

Nonetheless, Rich Preston enlisted his father's assistance in handling contractual matters. Ken Preston negotiated his youngest son's first three pro hockey contracts. Rich played in the World Hockey Association with the Houston Aeros — Gordie Howe was a linemate — and Winnipeg Jets before joining the National Hockey League's Blackhawks. "I can imagine him and Bob Pulford talking," Rich said of the notoriously tight-fisted Blackhawks GM. "I'm surprised I wasn't playing for free. They were the tightest GMs ever. I said, 'Dad, you've got to go the other way now.'" Rich Preston's first contract included a $25,000 signing bonus. "I kept track of the money I borrowed from my dad while I was in college," Rich said. "After I got the signing bonus, I took $2,000 and said, 'Dad, here's what I owe you for four years.'"

Preston's children feel indebted for several reasons. As youngsters, they shared their father's love of sports, and even helped him build two of the family's houses, along with a cottage. Doug Preston applied those skills by making a career out of construction. Rich Preston, to cite another example, has spent most of a lifetime in hockey as a player or a coach. "I've been around dressing rooms my whole life," Rich said. "It was a dream come true. When I was a waterboy with the Riders, I had a great initiation to team sports and what teammates are all about. I love dressing rooms. They're like a shrine to me. It's a sanctuary. It's where you can go to get away from it all. You close the door and it's just you and the players. It was like that with the Riders, and it's still that way."

Within a month of Ken Preston's death, there was more bad news for the Roughriders community. Ed Buchanan, a fleet halfback for the Roughriders from 1963 to 1967, died of amyotrophic lateral sclerosis — Lou Gehrig's disease — in a San Diego hospital on Aug. 31, 1991. Before his death at 51, Buchanan had been suffering from ALS for 2½ years and had been paralysed for 18 months. Late in 1990, Dorothy Laing of Calgary wrote a letter to the *Leader-Post* on behalf of the Buchanan family, thanking Roughriders fans for their many messages of support. "His spirits are good and because of his belief in God, he is somehow able to withstand the discomfort of his illness," Laing wrote. "He is still able to move his head and talk. He still has his wonderful sense of humour and often cheers his visitors up — instead of them cheering him up!"

One of the visitors was one-time Roughriders teammate Clyde Brock. "It was just a sad thing," said the former offensive tackle, who lived in San Diego when Buchanan was stricken. "I wouldn't just go by myself. There would be a group of us — three or four guys." The NFL Alumni Association chipped in to help out Buchanan, even though he had not played in that league. "He would just sit up in his room, so we got him a TV and stuff like that," said Brock, who was with the Dallas Cowboys and San Francisco 49ers before joining the Roughriders in 1964. "We didn't really get together and talk about old times. He was pretty sick."

That was a stark contrast to Buchanan's demeanor when he played for the Roughriders. The easygoing Buchanan was always in good humour during his time in Saskatchewan.

"He was the prince of the locker room," George Reed told the *Calgary Herald* in 1990. "I'll always remember his sense of humour. He had a great zest for life." That was reflected in a Canadian Press article on an ailing Buchanan, published in October of 1990. "His mind is sharp, but his nervous system is deteriorating," read an excerpt from the story. "He knows exactly what is happening to him, but not why. All he can do is pray and tell jokes to staff at the centre."

By the 1990s, **Ron Lancaster** was eliciting widespread praise for his work on CBC's football telecasts as an analyst alongside Don Wittman. Lancaster had moved into television shortly after concluding a two-year stint as the Roughriders' head coach. His analytical skills served him — and his audience — exceptionally well. "What's my appeal? I don't know," Lancaster said in a 1990 interview with Allan Maki of the *Calgary Herald*. "I've never understood that. I don't think I'm any different off the air than I am on it. After every game, I go home and ask my wife Bev if she understood what I was saying, because if she does then everybody does. She doesn't understand football at all."

Lancaster had the knack of boiling down the intricacies of football and explaining them to the audience in a folksy, easily comprehensible manner. "He will explain a game the same way on television as he would in your basement having a beer," Maki wrote. "He's Don Cherry without the act; John Madden without the telestrator; Don Meredith without the song. He is all of this and still himself. And he makes every football game a little more fun to watch. So why does 51-year-old Ron Lancaster want to get back into coaching?"

Lancaster was not lobbying for or craving another head-coaching job, but he was open to considering opportunities if they arose. "The television was fun," Lancaster said. "I really enjoyed that. It was like watching game film live. It was like stealing. It was fun because I got to talk to all the coaches that I'd never, ever got to talk to before. We'd go in to do games and I'd get to talk to all these guys, like Mike Riley, Jack Gotta, Don Matthews and Hugh Campbell. We'd go in the day before the game and have a chance to sit down and talk with them about things and tell stories. I enjoyed every bit of that."

With CBC, his contributions were not restricted to football. He was the network's basketball analyst at the 1988 Summer Olympics

Ron Lancaster *as a CBC broadcaster* | Photo courtesy of CBC

in Seoul, South Korea, working alongside Wittman. Lancaster referred to that assignment as "a fantastic experience" — one of the highlights of his career. "I never thought I'd get a chance to see the Olympics, let alone televise them," Lancaster told Ed Willes of the *Leader-Post* before departing for Seoul.

After 10 years with CBC, Lancaster was prepared to remain at the network. "I had two appointments to talk to CBC and get the contract signed for the next year and they cancelled both meetings," he recalled. "I don't remember why." At the time, Edmonton general manager Hugh Campbell was looking for a head coach. Campbell, a star receiver with the Roughriders in the 1960s, contacted his close friend and former quarterback about filling the vacancy. "If I had gone to that meeting and signed those contracts, then I would have never gone to Edmonton," he said. "I would have stayed in television. But the meetings were cancelled and I wasn't under contract." So Lancaster thought: "Why not? Let's give it a shot." In February of 1991, Ron Lancaster was named the Eskimos' head coach. The Little General and Gluey Hughie were together again.

Although it was a natural association, some Roughriders fans found it difficult to digest the notion of Lancaster wearing green and gold — considering Saskatchewan's long-standing rivalry with the Eskimos. "One day, I was standing in line at a drug store in Edmonton," Lancaster recalled in May of 2008. "A guy walked by me and said, 'Hey, traitor.' There were a lot of Rider fans in Edmonton. I guess when you're associated with that team as long as I was, I'm only looked on as a Rider. I'm not looked on as an Ottawa Rough Rider or an Edmonton Eskimo or a Hamilton Tiger-Cat. I'm a Saskatchewan Roughrider."

CHAPTER 33 | # "JUST ME AND DAD"

Long after the 1966 Grey Cup, Roughriders progeny were establishing their own names in athletic circles. One of them was a chip off the old Brock. Clyde Brock's son, Matt, played on the defensive line in the NFL from 1989 to 1996 with the New York Jets and Green Bay Packers. Jay Barwell — whose father, Gord, was a Roughriders receiver — played defence for two seasons with the Ontario Hockey League's Guelph Platers. Dale West's son, Tim, excelled on the offensive line with the University of Saskatchewan Huskies. Ed McQuarters Jr., became a CFLer, having stints as an offensive lineman with the Roughriders and Winnipeg in the 1980s. Mark Urness was the first third-generation Roughrider, following his grandfather (Al) and father (Ted). Rich Preston, Ken's son, enjoyed a long and successful career as a professional hockey player and coach. Ron Lancaster's sons, Ron and Bob, ended up coaching football, as did Hugh Campbell's son, Rick. Lancaster's grandson, Marc Mueller, quarterbacked the Sheldon-Williams Spartans to the 2006 Regina and Saskatchewan 4A high school football titles before joining the University of Regina Rams. Lancaster Jr. was a quarterback with the junior Rams in 1982.

Georgette Reed, meanwhile, would reach Olympian heights. Her famous father shared in the journey. George Reed travelled to Montreal in the spring of 1992 to watch Georgette qualify in the shot put for that year's Summer Olympic Games in Barcelona. "He was proud of me. I was proud of him," Georgette recalled. "I felt like I did something pretty special, as far as something that could be accomplished by a father and daughter."

Georgette is one of George and Angie Reed's three children. The elation over Georgette's trip to Barcelona was shared by her mother, brother (Keith) and sister (Vicki), but only George was able to attend the 1992 Olympic trials. "It was just me and Dad," Georgette said.

"My dad and I are like buddies. It was cool to realize that dream and to have my dad there to watch that event." The official selection of Georgette Reed to the Olympic team was made later that week.

"What stands out is she was trying to accomplish something and she was working very hard towards it," George said, proudly. "I was able to sit in the stands and watch, and give a few tips to her about certain things she was doing. I've got my chest poked out because I'm watching one of my children accomplish some things that very few people get a chance to accomplish."

While specializing in shot put and discus, Georgette competed in a succession of major events — including the Olympics (at which she finished 17th in the shot put), Commonwealth Games, Pan American Games and world championships. She also participated in the 1997 Francophone Games, winning a silver medal in the shot put and a bronze medal in discus. The accomplishments were especially noteworthy in light of the fact that track and field was not the first sport she seriously pursued. Georgette was a competitive swimmer for 14 years. Her prowess in the pool led to a swimming scholarship from Washington State University — her father's alma mater — in 1986. A year later, a serious shoulder injury ended Georgette's swimming career.

Like her father, Georgette was not deterred or derailed by injuries. She made a quick and seamless transition into track and field and, by the fall of 1987, was a member of the Washington State track team. Georgette proved to be a natural at her new sport, winning 17 Canadian titles (15 in shot put, two in discus) and repeatedly shattering Washington State's shot-put record. Despite a string of accomplishments, Georgette was far from satisfied, and her versatility had yet to be entirely tapped. From shot put and discus, she branched off to bobsleigh and nearly made the Olympics in that discipline. Following a long, diversified and decorated career as a competitive athlete, Georgette became the head track and field coach at the University of Alberta in Edmonton. She credited the paternal influence for her accomplishments in various sports.

"My dad was definitely known for his tenacity and the way that he played the game," Georgette said. "I think I picked up on that in my career and made sure that no matter what it was that I was doing, I was going to do it to the best of my ability.

Georgette Reed *is proud of her father* |
Photo courtesy of *Leader-Post*

I think a little bit of the stubbornness got me to keep trying to do the very best that I could and never give up. That helped me get right to the Olympic Games."

Georgette noted that her father's good name was also beneficial while she was growing up in Regina. "It was interesting," she said when asked about life as the daughter of a legend. "I didn't really know any different. You'd just go out there and do what you do. A lot of times I was a brat, or whatever, and people thought I acted the way that I did because my dad was George Reed. They didn't realize I was actually a little brat. I probably got a lot of latitude. It kind of gave me an opportunity to grow and to figure out who I was and go off and do some of the things I wanted to do." The opportunities unfolded "with people at least letting you get your foot in the door to do some things. I had to handle it from there."

As a standout football player, George was accustomed to the scrutiny. Georgette does not cite any instances of the attention marring family outings. "In Regina, it was fine," she said. "People knew who we were, but we never got harassed. It's not like you see now for a lot of stars or celebrities who go out. Now they get totally mauled. We were quite fortunate. People were used to seeing him around. He was always trying to do things and help out. He always believed a lot in community and he still does. He still goes out and does things for people. I'm proud of the way that he has lived his life and the things that he has done. He has really set a nice benchmark for me and others like me to follow."

Georgette said her father set the benchmark by "the way that he treated people. He didn't do anything halfway. If you were going to do something, you had to do it the very best that you could. He instilled in me that you should have pride in whatever you do, whether you're sweeping floors or selling cars or running multi-million-dollar businesses. It's not what you do that makes you important or makes you special. It's how you do it."

George Reed | Photo courtesy of *Leader-Post* archives

Georgette has always appreciated how her father does things, but wonders if some members of the public have misconceptions. "Sometimes people didn't understand him," she observed. "He doesn't really say a lot, but when he does say something, it's important. He doesn't mince words. He doesn't ramble on. He's very straightforward. He's very transparent. He's not a person who just talks to listen to himself talk. He's not a person who needs pomp and ceremony. He's actually a pretty humble, pretty simple guy. I think sometimes people thought he might have been arrogant or something, because he was quiet, but he's very unassuming, very straightforward and down to earth. He really wants to do the right thing. He really cares about people."

Cliff Shaw was 22 years old, and looked even younger, when he was interviewed by CBC's Ernie Afaganis after the Roughriders' 1966 Grey Cup victory. "When I see the film, he looks like he's 15 years of age, and he's all excited because he got in the Grey Cup and made two or three tackles," said his older brother, Wayne. Cliff Shaw had been a reserve for most of the game, but in the game's waning minutes he was deployed at linebacker, replacing Wayne. Cliff registered the game's final tackle. Although Wayne Shaw had enjoyed one of the finest games of his 12-year career, it was the younger Shaw who appeared on television after the victory.

Cliff Shaw |

"It looks like you've been playing in a mud bath," Afaganis told a beaming Cliff Shaw, who had been toiling in soggy conditions at Vancouver's Empire Stadium. Shaw responded: "Beautiful! I've never had a better mud bath in all my life." As a rookie in 1966, Cliff Shaw registered what turned out to be his only career interception, and his only two fumble returns as a CFLer. Wayne Shaw said "it was really special" to win the Grey Cup alongside his brother, but cited pangs of regret. In five seasons with the Roughriders, Cliff Shaw did not become a prominent player, although he did contribute at middle linebacker, corner linebacker, centre and guard when called upon. "In some ways, Cliff was a better football player than I was, in that he played more positions," said Wayne Shaw, who played until 1972. "I always assumed he would be the guy who took over for me when I retired. Then he hurt his back and he ended up in Calgary for a little while. He also ended up in Winnipeg, and then he had to have a spinal fusion on his back." Throughout his football career and beyond, Cliff Shaw approached life in easygoing fashion. "The difference between Cliff and me is that I was always really uptight and serious," Wayne Shaw said. "Somehow, they had me convinced I was going to get cut if I didn't go out there real hard. Cliff probably had more fun in his five years than I did in my 12, because he was always joking around. One time,

Cliff told everybody he was making more than George Reed and Ronnie Lancaster. George and Ronnie got sort of restless about that until Cliff told them that in terms of minutes played, he got paid a lot better than they did."

After football, Cliff Shaw settled in Davidson — not too far from the old family farm — and sold insurance and real estate. Shaw and his wife, Vanna Gay, operated Cliff Shaw Agencies until he died on June 15, 1993. "He was only 49 years of age," Wayne Shaw lamented. "I never really got over that yet, to tell you the truth. Anyway, that's just one of those things ..." Vanna Gay continued to run the family business with her oldest son, Jason Shaw. Cliff and Vanna Gay had another son (Ryan) and a daughter (Corla Gay). Cliff's death was one of many misfortunes that befell the Shaw family. "My brothers all died," Wayne said in reference to Cliff, Doug, Dennis and Al. "It makes me sad and I miss them very much."

One of the joys of Wayne Shaw's life also happened to be his livelihood. He operated a used book store — A Book Hunter (Wayne Shaw) — in Saskatoon until January 2009, after which he bought and sold select publications out of his home. "I started in Winnipeg in 1980 in a used book store and I've been doing it pretty much ever since then," he said. "I just love books. When I was a kid on the farm, my dad read all the time. Then I went to Notre Dame College and Father Athol Murray loved old books. I could retire, but do you know how many retired guys become bored and boring idiots? A lot of retired guys came to my book store — not to buy books, but to talk football or for me to entertain them. I'll bet you over the last 10 years, I've had 20 or 30 retired guys tell me they golf every day. It's not because they like golfing. It's just to put in time. I don't get it at all. Most people are too serious. There are very few really good golfers in the world, but most people take it too seriously and get all frustrated. I'd rather go for a nice walk in the country."

Ron Lancaster |
Photo courtesy of *Leader-Post*

Hugh Campbell *celebrates an Eskimos Grey Cup victory* |
Photo courtesy of *Edmonton Journal*

Ron Lancaster's 27-year wait for another Grey Cup ended on Nov. 28, 1993, when he coached the Edmonton Eskimos to a 33-23 victory over the Winnipeg Blue Bombers in Calgary. "He just stood in the background," Eskimos equipment manager Dwayne Mandrusiak remembered. "He said, 'They won it. Let them have their moment.' He told everybody that. It was amazing. I've dealt with coaches who are the first guy up on the podium, and he's like, 'It's their moment. Let them shine.' "

Lancaster had previously won Grey Cups as a player in 1960 with Ottawa and in 1966 with Saskatchewan, when his fourth-quarter touchdown pass to Hugh Campbell proved to be the winning score as Saskatchewan defeated Ottawa 29-14. Lancaster and Campbell shared another championship with the Eskimos in 1993. It must surely have taken them back 27 years ... or did it? "Not really, because he was a general manager and I was a coach," Lancaster said. "It made it great to be able to win one again with him. But, again, it was more fun for the players. The game belongs to the players. It was great that we had the opportunity to go through things together, but it's not the same as playing."

The significance of Al Benecick's playing career was acknowledged in 1996 when he was inducted into the Canadian Football Hall of Fame. Benecick had been out of football for nearly 30 years when his accomplishments — such as three-time recognition as an All-Canadian guard — duly impressed the selection committee.

After Benecick's playing career, he coached in Edmonton before moving to Ottawa and then Florida. "I stayed down there [in Florida] for a number of years," said Benecick, a native New Yorker. "I was in the real-estate business. It got too hot for me, especially in the summertime. I could hardly walk on the pavement. So I put two and two together and thought, 'Where did I have the most fun? Where are the people the nicest?' So I came back to Canada and I'm happy I did. I stayed here because there's a comfort zone. When I first came here, people were nice. Cars stopped. It was, 'Come over for a meal.' It was how things used to be in New York."

Benecick moved back to Regina in the mid-1980s and spent 15 years working for the Saskatchewan Property Management Corporation while living in a downtown apartment. "I had work. I had a home here. I had good times here and the people were nice," Benecick said. "A lot of people say, 'What the hell do you stay here for? You've got New York and you've got everything.' These are good places to visit — not the greatest places to live. When I get homesick or I want to get away — the winters get cold here — I'll go to Florida or Mexico, but I enjoy coming back.

"The summers here are pretty neat. I stay because things are convenient. I don't have a car. I use a bicycle, or else a bus in inclement weather. It's only a block or two for shopping. The university's close by. The hospital's close by. The doctor's close by. Everything I want is close by. I'm comfortable here. Regina's a great place. A lot of people say, 'Where the hell is that?' I enjoy hearing that. We'll keep it that way."

In the mid-1990s, **Benecick** travelled to Vancouver, where he had helped the Roughriders win the Grey Cup in 1966. One side trip took him to the Pacific National Exhibition grounds, where Empire Stadium once stood. "It was a parking lot," Benecick recalled. "I rode around there on my bike. The place was locked up and there was a guard there. I said, 'Would you mind if I just went in and walked around?' So he opened it up and I walked around. It was a parking area and they were storing construction. It just wasn't what it used to be."

The stadium had been built for the 1954 Empire Games (later known as the Commonwealth Games). It was the site of the Miracle Mile — site of the historic sub-four-minute mile run by Roger Bannister and John Landy in 1954 — and later for concerts featuring Elvis Presley and The Beatles. By the time Benecick paid a return visit, the surroundings did not bear any resemblance to 1966, but he was moved by just being there. "It was just the memory of the Grey Cup, going back and reminiscing," he said. "I could stand there and hear the band playing and I could see the soil, the mud. In my mind, the stadium is still there and the fans are still there. The players are still there. Everything's still there, even though it's gone. That's quite a place."

The demolition permit for Empire Stadium had been issued in January of 1993. The PNE and Vancouver civic officials, faced with a choice between renovating or demolishing the stadium, opted for the latter. The site — part of Vancouver's Hastings Park — soon became an expanse of concrete. That was a temporary condition. Elements of the Hastings Park Restoration Concept Plan were completed in 1997. Part of the blueprint called for 4.5 hectares (11 acres) of land to be redeveloped, and so it was that Empire Fields opened in September of 2001. The complex includes several soccer pitches and softball diamonds, along with an oval running track.

Like Benecick, **Ed McQuarters** ended his vocational career in the 1990s. He had worked in various capacities at SaskPower — public affairs, special projects, community relations and quality improvement — before being named the Crown corporation's diversity co-ordinator in 1995. Three years later, McQuarters was dismissed due to what he termed a disagreement over a harassment policy he played a key role in formulating as part of a nine-person diversity committee. McQuarters said he would not comply with a senior manager's insistence that he delete one component the committee considered essential to the policy.

In the months to follow, McQuarters attended 10 job interviews and seriously considered taking two positions, but his heart was not in the process. "After 30 years at SaskPower and eight with the Riders, I'd had enough." Even so, McQuarters remained involved with work-related issues. He created a website — *http://users.accesscomm.ca/ediversity/* — to promote a respectful work environment. "That's why I did the website — to nicely and politely vent to the world about my 30 years at SaskPower," he said. "It's general and it talks about what happens in the workplace. It has nothing to do with ethnicity. It could happen to anybody, and it does. These kinds of horrible things happen to people in the workplace." But the good things stand out when McQuarters assesses his life, particularly the time spent in Regina. "I've enjoyed every minute of it, except for the other stuff I've been telling you about," he concluded. "I wouldn't trade it for the world."

CHAPTER **34** **"DIGGER"**

Bob O'Billovich was framed — as he realized upon meeting with Roughriders general manager Alan Ford in 1998. O'Billovich and Ford are forever linked as the result of a second-quarter play in the 1966 Grey Cup. In that game, O'Billovich stepped in front of Ford and was in position to make an interception, only to have the ball glance off his hands and toward Ford. The Roughriders' receiver cradled the ball while falling to the ground for a key touchdown.

"I remember when I took the job with Saskatchewan for a couple of years," O'Billovich said. "Al hired me to be their personnel guy when Dan Rambo went to the Denver Broncos. I went into his office and he had a big picture of that play in his office. The ball is coming through my hands and he's down on the ground. I laughed when I saw it. I said, 'I knew that play was going to do me some good somewhere along the way. You felt like you owed me this, huh?' It got me a job, I guess."

Alan Ford put his job on the line during the winter of 1999. Although the Roughriders had appeared in the 1989 and 1997 Grey Cups with Ford as the general manager, the team's fortunes were waning. In 1998, the Roughriders missed the playoffs for the third time in four seasons. Ford vowed to step down if Saskatchewan was again excluded from the postseason. The 1999 edition proceeded to win three games. A tearful Ford announced his resignation shortly before the season concluded.

"So much of my life is tied to the Saskatchewan Roughriders," Ford reflected. "It was very emotional for me at that press conference. I probably got through it OK until I saw my family. My two girls [Jill and Tracy] were there with [his wife] Sally. It was tough for us because they had been with me for the whole thing. I knew in the back of my mind that it was eventually going to happen. That's the nature of the business. It's the nature as a player and the nature as a coach and certainly the nature as a manager. It didn't matter whether I called it or not. It was going to happen. I knew we had to play really well for me to continue as GM. That was the bottom line. It wasn't like it was a surprise."

Upon announcing his resignation, Ford did not clean out his desk. He remained in the office until Dec. 31, 1999, helping to ease the transition to a new GM. Ford's successor, Roy Shivers, was hired in late December of that year. "Al sat in the office every day, looking after everything, even though he was gone ... every day!" marvelled Tom Shepherd, a former Roughriders president who wept at Ford's press conference. "He was there until Dec. 31 at five o'clock looking after everything, and the club and the executive had complete faith in him. He was doing whatever it took with players and running the administration. You tell me another person in the world who would do that. He didn't want to leave the organization for two or three months before they hired a new general manager."

Even after Ford vacated his office, he was a regular at Taylor Field — as a Roughriders season-ticket holder. "I don't know of anybody who has given more to the Saskatchewan Roughriders than Al Ford — not just as a paid employee, but with all the other stuff he does," Shepherd said. "Whenever they need anything or the league needs anything, these people always call Al. He's taken for granted, but he bleeds green. He goes to every game and he lives and dies with the Roughriders."

Ford's final two years with the Roughriders were difficult, but two other seasons resonate. He helped the Roughriders win a Grey Cup as a player and a general manager. "Al has been that stabilizing force and that unsung hero in both instances," said Shepherd, who was the Roughriders' auditor

Tom Shepherd (left) with **Alan Ford** | Photo courtesy of *Leader-Post*

in 1966 and the team's president in 1989. "He's a guy who is always doing his job. He's not the superstar, but the guy that you can't win without. That's what Al Ford's all about. I see his legacy being every bit as great as Ken Preston's. They're the type of people who just cared. Al made all kinds of sacrifices for this club — financially, personally, and in all kinds of other things, when the time was needed. He always looked after the money for the club like it was his own, the same as Ken Preston."

Preston's name was often mentioned when the 1966 Roughriders gathered at a reunion 40 years later. "Ken Preston comes up in discussions about being cheap," Ford said at the time. "We laugh at it, but it's really a sign of respect. When the '89 team comes back after 40 years, they'll be talking about Ford and how cheap he was — and I hope they are."

The 1999 season ended on a joyous note for one of Ford's former teammates. Ron Lancaster coached Hamilton to a 32-21 Grey Cup victory over Calgary in Vancouver — where Lancaster had won his first two Grey Cups. The 1999 victory was additionally significant for Lancaster because his eldest son, Ron Jr. (or R.D., as he was known in coaching circles), was the Tiger-Cats' offensive co-ordinator. "That was exciting," the senior Lancaster recalled. "That was really fun, because he never had the opportunity to play, and the only way he was going to get a Grey Cup ring was to get it as a coach. He was in a few of them, but the biggest thing was one of them was with me. That was nice."

In 1999, Ron Lancaster won his fourth Grey Cup, with his fourth different team. He was a quarterback with the victorious Ottawa Rough Riders (1960) and Saskatchewan Roughriders (1966) before winning as a head coach with Edmonton (1993) and Hamilton (1999). "I always hear people say the last one's the best," Lancaster said. "I think they're all the same. It is so hard to do. Each one, at that particular time, is the biggest thing that can happen to you."

George Reed and his family experienced some worrisome times in 2001, after the legendary fullback underwent surgery to remove a brain aneurysm. After experiencing blurry eyesight, Reed called an ambulance. He soon underwent surgery, from which he made a full recovery.

"It was a huge scare because usually when you hear of an aneurysm, it's something that's fatal," said his daughter, Georgette Reed. "It really threw me for a loop. It was scary at first, but he came through it like he does with everything. We were really fortunate to have him still be around. He just approached it like he did with anything else and made sure that he was diligent in his recovery to make sure he could get over it."

Get over it, he did. "My wife would say I'm not 100 per cent, but I came out good," Reed remarked. "The important thing is that it happened and I recognized it and I got some help. I called Emergency and they did all these tests and then they made the decision on me. They said, 'You can not have the surgery and this or that can happen, or you can have the surgery but in some ways you're taking a chance.' Two weeks later, they had me on the operating table. The recovery was probably as great [a challenge] as anything. Now, all of a sudden, you're changing. It's just trying to get stronger and trying to bring everything back. Once you realized what had to be done, you proceeded along those lines."

Reed, then a car salesman in Calgary, was off work for approximately three months while he recuperated. The health scare reminded Reed and his family that tomorrow is not assured. He had some time to ponder his mortality between diagnosis and surgery. "You're sitting there for two weeks, thinking, 'Is this thing going to be successful?' " he recalled. "One of the great things was the doctor was straightforward. He wasn't sugarcoating anything. He laid all the things out for me and said, 'It's up to you,' and walked out of the room. He said, 'Here's the facts. You've got these two or three options. This is what I recommend. Let me know what you think.'

"When you're hit between the eyes with something like that, you know where you're at. They told me that the doctor who did the surgery was one of the great specialists in Canada, so I had no fear. I had to be at the hospital at seven o'clock that morning. They told me to put the gown on and they gave me the stuff to put me to sleep. The next thing I know, I got up and my head was all wrapped up, like it had a big towel on it. I wasn't laying around. I was still moving around. Four or five days later, they said, 'You can go home under these conditions.' I took it very easy and took my walks like they wanted me to do."

Lifestyle changes were required. "You have to slow down and you can't just dive into everything the way you did," Reed said. "I wasn't going to be bullheaded. A lot of times before, I would have something happen to me and I'd say, 'I can't stay down. I've got to get up and get going.' The first week [after leaving the hospital] was probably the scariest and the loneliest because, all of a sudden, your whole life has come to a halt. They would say, 'There are some things that you can do. There are some things that you can't do. We strongly recommend that you follow what we have prescribed.' The other thing you looked at is, 'Am I going to be able to drive a car?' "

Reed was required to take a driver's test, which he passed. "There was some uncertainty, but I had some good support," he said. "At the time, I was working for McKay Pontiac Buick. They helped me out. It wasn't like I was left out by myself. Of course, my wife was great. When you have those types of things happen, it makes you realize what you appreciate. I think it also helps you heal."

For Ron Lancaster, it was supposed to be a routine medical examination. Dye was injected into one of his arms for a test at McMaster University Medical Centre, in Hamilton. Little did Lancaster, or anyone, suspect that the dye would trigger an allergic reaction. Very quickly, Lancaster began to swell up and encounter difficulty breathing. His body shut down. The jolt had dislodged some plaque in a coronary artery, disrupting the flow of blood to his heart.

"It happened on a Monday, and I didn't remember anything until Wednesday night," Lancaster said while rewinding four years to March 29, 2004. "I had no idea — nothing. I wasn't there. I didn't know where I was. So I was lucky that somebody was there." That somebody was a cardiologist, who was just around the corner. "He fixed it all up and, next thing you know, I was back to normal," Lancaster continued. "Right place, right time."

Just like that, the 65-year-old Lancaster — the Hamilton Tiger-Cats' general manager at the time — became an ex-smoker. "I was in intensive care for four days," he said. "[A doctor] said, 'Now you've gone through the hardest part. You went four days without a cigarette.' I never had another one ... It's a heck of a way to have to do things. Everything I've done, I've done the hard way, anyway. I never usually listen to advice. I always have to go and make the mistakes when other people said, 'Don't do that.' "

Unfortunately, Lancaster was not finished with hospitals in 2004. In September of that year, he underwent surgery to remove a cancerous tumour from his bladder. His prostate was also removed. Two serious health matters within a few months provided cause for contemplation. "It changes the way you think about things," said Lancaster, who received a clean bill of health following the procedures. "You are normal. You are human. You're

Ron Lancaster *as Hamilton Tiger-Cats head coach* |
Photo courtesy of *Leader-Post*

not indestructible. It's like playing football. Everybody always says you can never worry about getting injured, because if you thought you were going to be injured, you'd never be able to play. You always thought it would be someone else. It's the same thing with your health until somebody knocks the hell out of you and you get a little bit lucky at the right time, which I did. It was a little bit scary. When you think about it, it makes you change. I don't like to dwell on it. I just keep going."

Lana Mueller, the eldest of Lancaster's three children, noticed a difference in her father after the health scares of 2004. "He was quite concerned that he had lost two days and he was never going to get them back," she said in the spring of 2008. "The best thing that came out of it was he quit smoking. This put enough of a scare into him to quit. He lost two younger brothers to cancer. The fact that he walked out of the hospital when his brothers didn't kind of set him back."

Lancaster announced in August of 2008 that he was again battling cancer. Media reports at the time revealed, correctly, that he had lung cancer. But only a few people knew that cancer was also discovered in his brain.

Lancaster's fans remember the touchdown passes, the comebacks, the victories — and the Ronnie and George Show. Although Lana Mueller shares some of those recollections, she will always be most appreciative of a "very good father." Like Georgette Reed, Lana grew up in Regina as the daughter of a celebrity. "Most of [the fans] didn't realize he had a daughter," Lana said. "They knew Ronnie and they knew Bobby because of their involvement in sports. I kind of went through it without much of a hassle."

The families were often seen at the Regina airport when the Roughriders' players departed and arrived. "Nothing was enclosed, so the players had to walk across the tarmac," Mueller recalled. "They had the big windows at one end and we were all there. All the families were there. I'm sure the airport authority people were thinking, 'Oh my God. The Riders are leaving today.' There was just bedlam in the airport with the kids. There were little kids running in all directions. There would be all these little fingerprint smudges along the windows, where the kids were all looking out to say goodbye to their dads. It was cute, but it was just bedlam.

"Usually, one of the wives of the players would have the families over. We'd all go over there and play, and the moms would have coffee. The wives also had listening parties. In those days, a lot of the games weren't on TV. A lot of times, it was pot luck. The wives would be downstairs, listening to the game."

Occasionally, people who approached the Lancaster residence on Emerald Park Road were in for a surprise. "There was a big park in front of our house," Mueller said. "Ron Wood lived just across from us. He said to Dad that anytime he needed someone to throw the ball to, he would go out and throw with him. Dad would be out there, warming up his arm and getting ready for the season with the neighbours. People would drive by, not realizing, and he'd be out there in the middle of the park."

That is the extent to which Lancaster was visible in Regina. He was an ordinary citizen of extraordinary accomplishment. "Mom and Dad believed that we needed to get involved in the community," Mueller said. "We were members of the Wascana Winter Club, where we took skating lessons and Mom and Dad curled. Dad had season tickets to the Regina Pats games. He enjoyed going on the hockey trips with my brothers when their teams were in tournaments. He didn't get to see a lot of their football because that was in the same season. He coached baseball when he had the time. When he was at Central Collegiate, he helped with the track and field and coached basketball. It was fun growing up."

At the Lancaster household, the responsibilities were well-defined. "Mom ran the household. Dad played football," Ron Lancaster Jr. said. "Mom ran the finances and the whole bit. I think Mom said to Dad, 'You can run the finances for one month and you can go to the grocery store.' Dad came home with cookies and cake for the kids and we loved it. Mom said, 'Did you pay the bills?' He said, 'What bills?' She held court at home. You knew you were in trouble when she'd say, 'I had to call your father.' She was the rock. She handled everything."

Ron and Bev Lancaster were married 50 years. "Bev is probably what you would call — and I guess it's proper to say it — an old-fashioned wife," The Little General told Rawlco Radio's Wray Morrison in 2006. "We're from the old school. She was ready to make the commitment to whatever we wanted to do. She knew sports was my life. She never had any qualms about living in Ottawa, moving to Saskatchewan, moving to Ontario. It was just pick up and go. She's really the reason the kids turned out to be pretty good people, because she was the one who did most of the raising of the kids. I was always involved in football and never had the time to put in. Sometimes, looking back on things, it's kind of a little bit that I missed, but she did a great job of raising the kids."

As families, the Reeds and Lancasters were known to collaborate on mini-vacations. Until cable television arrived in 1978, Reginans had access to only two English-language television stations — CTV and CBC — which made it difficult to follow American sports. "I remember the Reeds and us going to Bismarck, North Dakota," Lana Mueller said. "We'd leave on Boxing Day and come back on the second of January so Dad and George could watch their bowl games."

The images of both legendary Roughriders are now prominently displayed on the west side of Mosaic Stadium. The giant, black-and-white photos were unveiled shortly after Taylor

Field was renamed in 2006. Mueller has grown accustomed to seeing the photo of her father, given the frequency with which she visits the stadium.

The photo serves as one reminder to Lana Mueller of her father's legend, which led to his 1982 induction into the Canadian Football Hall of Fame. Lancaster was enshrined in his first year of eligibility. Mueller marvelled at the ceremonies that revolved around someone she called Dad. "You go down there and you see all these other people and you know who they are," she said. "Really and truly, you'd look around and say, 'This guy did this,' or 'I know that guy's name.' It never really hit me that that's what people would think of him.

Ron Lancaster outside Mosaic Stadium in 2006 in front of his picture which is displayed on the west side |
Photo courtesy of *Leader-Post*

"It's like when Brock University gave him the honorary doctor's degree. They asked if he would accept it. Dad said, 'Geez, I don't know.' Dad just started laughing. It wasn't anything that he thought he was deserving of. Then he phones my mom and she starts laughing. Then they phone here and they phone my brothers and we all laugh. My mom said to my dad, 'Geez, Ron, I thought they only gave that to famous people.'"

Other family members referred to Lancaster as Digger — a nickname not commonly known to the general public. "Dad and I were watching a Notre Dame college basketball game when I was in high school," recalled Ron Lancaster Jr., a former quarterback with the Rams and Campbell Tartans. "I'm a Notre Dame basketball fan. They showed Digger Phelps, who was Notre Dame's coach, and he was being very animated on the sidelines. Dad goes, 'He's grandstanding. He's playing to the camera.' I said, 'I'll start calling you Digger, then.' It was him and I in the basement in Regina. I said, 'I'm going to start calling you Digger unless you take it back.' He wouldn't take it back, so that's how he became Digger. I always called him Coach, but everyone else always called him Dig or Digs or Digger. I did not envision that sticking. At the same time, he loved to be called that by us. That says it all."

CHAPTER 35

"THEY NEVER REALLY LEAVE YOU"

In his final months, Ted Dushinski sounded a sombre warning. "Quit smoking and get a damned check-up — just go out there and do it," Dushinski stated in April of 2005 — nearly two years after he was diagnosed with lung cancer.

When Dushinski played for the Roughriders, their dressing room was located at Regina Exhibition Track, where the team practised in the infield of the horse racing complex. Following games at Taylor Field, the team would board a bus for the short commute to the exhibition grounds. It was routine for players to light up as soon as they got on the bus. "Yeah, even the guys who *didn't* smoke," Dushinski said with a chuckle. "It was stupid, really." Dushinski smoked a pack and a half per day for 30-plus years. He quit smoking the day a tumour was discovered in his left lung. The cancer would spread to his left hip and behind one of his retinas. There was also a small tumour on his stomach wall at the time of the interview. "I'm blaming it, I guess, on my smoking," Dushinski said at age 61.

During Dushinski's playing career, which lasted from 1965 to 1977, it was not unusual for professional athletes to smoke. "I thought I'd live forever," he said. "Smoking didn't bother me. I ran every day, and did this and that Ron Lancaster and George Reed and I, we were the smokers in the group. [Attitudes about] cigarettes were different back then. It didn't seem to bother us that much."

Despite the sad subject matter, Dushinski was upbeat during a half-hour conversation. "The first six months were the roughest," he said. "You think of everything. Now that I've lived with it for damn near two years, it's sort of second nature. It sort of runs off your back. You do all you can do and say, 'Hey, don't let it get you down.' You try to forget about it, but you can't shake it. You get down in the dumps once in a while. You sort of get feeling sorry for yourself and then you say, 'To hell with that.' "

Dushinski credited his attitude and his survival to his wife, singer Susan Jacks. The couple had moved from Nashville to Vancouver in December of 2004. "We sort of grew apart there for about three or four years," Dushinski said. "Since I've come down with this, we've sort of grown back together. If it wasn't for her, I would have been gone a long time ago. She has been a real trouper. She has been great — unbelievable. She has taken me to every chemo-treatment. Every time I have to go to the hospital, she has taken me. She has done everything for me."

Ted Dushinski and Susan Jacks were well-known long before they knew each other. Dushinski, a two-time Western Conference all-star defensive back with the Roughriders, was wrapping up his playing career with the B.C. Lions when he was introduced to Jacks. She was responsible for hits of a different sort. As a member of the Poppy Family (which also included her first husband, Terry Jacks), Susan was a fixture on the charts. A 1969 recording, "Which Way You Goin', Billy?" became the No. 1 song in Canada, and was second on the *Billboard* charts. Worldwide sales exceeded 2.5 million. The Poppy Family dissolved when Terry and Susan Jacks' marriage ended in 1973.

Four years later, Dushinski and Susan Jacks were introduced. "Actually, we didn't like each other," she recalled. "Well, I shouldn't say we didn't like each other, but he was the big football hero and I thought he was full of himself, and he wasn't. And he thought I was full of

Ted Dushinski | Photo courtesy of SSHFM

myself, and I wasn't. Then it was, 'I guess he's OK ... I guess she's OK.' I guess we were both very spirited and we found that part of each other very attractive."

Dushinski and Jacks were married in 1980. Five years later, they moved to Tennessee, where Dushinski worked with a trucking company and Jacks concentrated on songwriting. Eventually, there was a distance between them, although they remained married. "We're not under the same roof anymore, but we don't live far apart," Dushinski said in 1999. "It's one of those growing-apart things, but we're better friends than ever. We're buddies now. It's a lot better than when we were under the same roof."

"We had stayed such good friends," Jacks remembered. "Of course, we have a son [Thaddeus] who adores both of us and we adore him. Ted and I had grown apart. It's hard to explain because we stayed so close. We celebrated birthdays and went out for dinner together. We both looked at it like, 'You go through this life once and when people mean something to you in your lives, you don't just throw that away,' because maybe we weren't the best living together, but we knew that we cared about each other." That was obvious when Dushinski was afflicted with cancer. "I think he knew that he needed me there to help him go through it and I knew that I needed to be there to help him go through it," Jacks said. "There were just no questions asked. It was an automatic thing."

The following year, Dushinski and Jacks returned to Vancouver. The bout with cancer, as sad as it was, put Dushinski and Jacks under the same roof once again. "We spent more time relating to each other on a whole different level — on a better level and a much closer level," Jacks said.

The move back to Canada also made it more convenient for Dushinski's family members in Calgary to visit him. Dushinski had sufficient health-care coverage in the United States, and the Canadian medical system also served him well. "He amazed the doctors with his fight, because he was only supposed to have eight months to maybe a year," Jacks marvelled.

During Dushinski's bout with cancer, Jacks put her musical career on hold to care for her husband. "I didn't really do anything else during that time," she recalled. "I got more out of that as far as a life lesson. Ted was on constant chemo, except for the last few months. Up until then, it was every week, constant. I would go to every one and meet all these people. There is such a connection that all those people had who were fighting for their lives. They didn't even have to say anything. They just looked at each other. It was amazing. There would be a nod or just a slight smile because they knew what each other was going through. I was privileged to be a part of that. I learned so much from it. The human survival instinct is so strong, but I don't think you always get that close to it. I'll take that with me for the rest of my life."

Even amid the sad circumstances, the couple extracted the most from their final months together. "There he was, faced with something that he'd never been faced with before," Jacks said. "He was quite private and he was very unemotional [beforehand]. We cried more and laughed more through that whole ordeal than we ever did. It was a real experience. Ultimately, it was wonderful for Ted. He used to

Susan Jacks | Photo courtesy of *Leader-Post* archives

say that, 'None of us get out of here alive.' He just made the best of it. He handled it in an admirable way." As did his wife. "When we came up here, I got a little place," she continued. "It was down in Point Roberts. It was on the ocean and he loved the ocean. I wanted some place that was just beautiful and quiet and tranquil and some place that he would love to be. He adored it there. Even when he was in a wheelchair, I would wheel him out and he would say, 'It doesn't get much better than this, does it?' "

Dushinski's spirits were also buoyed by a final trip to Saskatchewan, in June of 2005. Roughriders president and chief executive officer Jim Hopson — a former offensive lineman who was a teammate of Dushinski's from 1973 to 1975 — invited his friend to Regina for a game. "It was fabulous," Jacks remembered. "He got off that plane after being in Regina and he was ecstatic. I could see it in his eyes and in his face. Big grin. He had such a fabulous time. The Lions also had lunches for him and they also treated him well. He was such a lovable guy — really a nice, nice person. All the guys really liked him, so they gave us some tickets to go to the games. It was just wonderful."

The couple's spirits also brightened when Dushinski was chosen as a defensive back on the Roughriders' all-century team. The fans, who voted for the team, remembered the 33 interceptions he made in 157 regular-season games with Saskatchewan. The Saskatoon Hilltops product added five more interceptions in 25 playoff games.

"You should have seen his face when he was voted on to the dream team," Jacks said. "That was shortly before he died. I don't mean to get too graphic, but by this time the cancer had also gone to his brain, so he was a little bit out of it at times and wasn't cognizant of everything that was going on. He was in the hospital and I took [a copy of the all-century team] in and I showed it to him. He just all of a sudden lit up. Oh my gosh. This was such a wonderful gift for him and he absolutely knew what it meant. He just held on to the paper. He had it on his chest and he didn't want me to take it off. It was really very touching. He was so honoured by that."

Shortly thereafter, Dushinski was moved to a hospice. Jacks was constantly at her husband's bedside, as was Thaddeus (who had flown to Vancouver from Nashville to be with his father) and Dushinski's sister, June. Ted Dushinski died on Oct. 24, 2005.

Jacks was left to adjust to life without her husband of 25 years. "It probably took me about a year and a half just to get over it," she said. "I lost someone I loved. Aside from that, I went through an experience. I basically walked hand in hand with him. I was holding his hand when he passed away. It was amazing, but it wore me out. I was so tired. My whole focus was on Ted for almost 2½ years. You don't realize how emotionally draining it is. I would do it again in a heartbeat because it was almost a gift to me. I know that sounds really corny, but there's so much that you learn. Life is so short and there's so many things that you need to learn to cherish. Something like this takes you to a whole different dimension."

Yet, in some ways, life felt the same after Dushinski's death. "Sometimes, I can't believe that he's really gone," Jacks concluded. "It just feels like his spirit is here with me.

"We learned so much more about sharing life together because it wasn't just a cliché for us. There was a time limit here and we both knew it — although I think sometimes Ted didn't want to know it, but I think he knew in his heart. When people are very close to you, maybe that's part of the plan — that they never really leave you. They're always a part of your life, even in your heart somewhere or in your memories."

Barely a month after Dushinski died, Hugh Campbell celebrated his 10th (and last) CFL title. Campbell — then the Eskimos' chief executive officer — watched his team defeat Montreal 38-35 in overtime at BC Place Stadium on Nov. 27, 2005. The victory provided a form of symmetry, being that Campbell had also experienced his first Grey Cup victory in Vancouver. On Nov. 26, 1966, Campbell caught the go-ahead touchdown pass as the Roughriders defeated the Ottawa Rough Riders 29-14 at Empire Stadium.

Campbell watched the 2005 championship game and thought: "The first one was on a moist field and this one is indoors and you're warm and comfortable." It was Campbell's 32nd season in the league, and his teams had reached the Grey Cup on 17 occasions. "I thought that it has been a lot of years and a lot of time," he reflected.

Campbell had won a Grey Cup as a player (in 1966), head coach (1978 to 1982, inclusive, with Edmonton) and executive (in 1987, 1993, 2003 and 2005 with the Eskimos). The 2005 classic was a different experience. "I was more relaxed during it and after it than I had ever been before," he said. "In all the time as a coach, you felt like you had escaped. I did. I never felt the joy of winning that I should have because it was always like, 'How are we going to do next year?' My thought was almost like, 'It's too bad we didn't lose so that next year when we win it, we'll think it's good.'

"I don't mean to be negative. I've read books from other people who have had some winning streaks — John Wooden, Red Auerbach — and somewhere in those books there's the same type of comment. You kind of feel relieved that the season's over and you did what you're supposed to do, instead of thinking that the season's over and you had a heck of a great year. But at the last one in Vancouver — and it's probably a sign of old age — I felt a real warm glow."

Campbell's string of successes was recognized in 2000. He was elected to the Canadian Football Hall of Fame as a builder. That completed the collection for Campbell, who was also inducted into the Roughriders' Plaza of Honor, along with the halls of fame at Los Gatos (Calif.) High School and Washington State University.

"It has been a long road and it goes by quickly, and it has been fun," Campbell said. "It was just as fun to win [in 2005] as it was before. As they say, it's the path. I had a lot of good years and a lot of fun. Even in years when we didn't get to the Grey Cup, there were worthy and high-character organizations that I've been with — with Saskatchewan and Edmonton — where the fans really care. It's not the end result. It's the fun along the way."

At 65, Campbell stepped down a year after his 10th CFL championship. The news was announced at the Eskimos' annual dinner. There was one surprise guest. Unbeknownst to Campbell, Ron Lancaster had flown into Edmonton for the occasion. "I just don't like to see him go," Lancaster told Vicki Hall of the *Edmonton Journal*. "I don't like the idea of him retiring. I still think he has a lot to offer the Canadian Football League and the Edmonton Eskimos. I just think he should have stayed a little longer."

CHAPTER 36 | # "AUSTIN IS NOW A GOD"

In 2006, Reg Whitehouse reflected on the most tragic development in Roughriders history — the plane crash of 50 years earlier. Four of Whitehouse's teammates — Mel Becket, Mario DeMarco, Gord Sturtridge and Ray Syrnyk — were among 62 people killed when the aircraft in which they were passengers crashed into Mount Slesse, near Chilliwack, B.C. Becket, DeMarco, Sturtridge and Syrnyk were returning from the East-West Shrine All-Star Game, played at Empire Stadium. Whitehouse had also participated in the all-star game, but was not on the doomed Trans-Canada Airlines flight. His wife, Joanne, was to have made the trip but, acting on a premonition, the Roughriders lineman cancelled her reservation and travelled to Vancouver by himself.

A half-century later, Whitehouse and his wife, Joanne, dealt with unavoidable reminders of the crash. "I can see Mount Slesse from where I'm sitting," Reg said in a 2006 interview from his home in Chilliwack. Joanne said looking at the mountain produced "the shivers ... it gives me the creeps," adding that "it brings you back to reality."

After Reg retired from football in 1966, the Whitehouses remained in Regina until 1970, at which point they moved to Montreal. While back in his hometown, Reg re-established ties with football while also working as the national sales manager for Northern Electric. He was an assistant coach with his former Quebec Junior Football League team, the Notre Dame de Grace Maple Leafs, before assuming the head-coaching reins with the Verdun Invictus. After a brief stint in Quebec, the Whitehouses moved to Cranbrook, where Reg started a lighting and electrical consulting business. They relocated to Richmond, B.C., in the mid-1980s before spending their final years in Chilliwack. Joanne Whitehouse died on Oct. 22, 2007, at age 72, following a lengthy illness. Reg died on Aug. 6 of the following year at age 75, apparently of a stroke. "It was extremely hard on him when Mom passed," said the Whitehouses' son, Timber. "They had been together every day for more than 50 years. He struggled. I think he was heartbroken as much as anything."

Regina-born Joanne Baird, who was Miss Grey Cup in 1953, exchanged vows with Reg Whitehouse on May 29 of the following year. "People said that Dad had the ideal life," Timber reflected. "He had the Grey Cup in one arm and Miss Grey Cup in the other. He had it all."

Whitehouse had earned a long-awaited Grey Cup title in 1966. Offensive-line cohort Galen Wahlmeier, who made his debut with the Roughriders in 1957, had also paid his dues, weathering some of the team's worst years. However, Wahlmeier's name does not appear on the championship trophy — even though he played in all 16 CFL regular-season games with the 1966 Roughriders.

In the regular-season finale, Wahlmeier suffered stretched ligaments in his left knee. The injury forced him to miss all three playoff games, including the 29-14 Grey Cup victory over Ottawa on Nov. 26, 1966. Wahlmeier watched that game on the sideline while leaning on crutches.

"It was a mixed bag, but also very exciting from the standpoint that we won," Wahlmeier said from his home in White Bear, Sask., as the 1966 Roughriders prepared for a 40th-anniversary reunion. "I never did get to play in the game, so my name didn't appear on the Grey Cup. Only those on the roster got their names on the Cup." Wahlmeier did not learn of this until several years later, while serving as mayor of Estevan. "The Grey Cup was brought to Estevan and I started looking for my name," he said. "That's when I discovered that it wasn't on it. There was not too much happiness, I tell you."

Even so, as the reunion approached, Wahlmeier was able to make light of the omission. When informed that the Grey Cup would be present, he quipped: "I'll have to bring my own engraver."

In 2007, the Roughriders lost two members of their 1966 championship team — tight end Jim Worden and trainer Sandy Archer.

Worden died of a heart attack on Feb. 25 in Wellington, Ohio, at age 64. Failing health had prevented him from attending the Roughriders' reunion the previous year. In his final months, Worden had been bedridden for all but an hour per day. Shortly before the 40th-anniversary reunion of the 1966 Roughriders, an apologetic Worden telephoned Alan Ford — one of the event's organizers — and conveyed his regrets about being unable to attend, explaining that his health situation was prohibitive. "It was his type of attitude that made the team champions," Ron Lancaster said after learning that Worden, a fellow graduate of Wittenberg College, had died. "Even though everyone has to go sometime, it was a sad day to hear about the passing of The Hog."

"The Hog … ," Garner Ekstran added. "It really needs to be brought out how great a ballplayer he was. God only made a very few great tight ends, and we were lucky to have one of the best that ever played. I don't know of a better one. He was as good a blocker as the guards, the tackles or the centre, and he'd go downfield and catch passes."

Archer had overcome heart problems — including a heart attack that had forced the first of his two bypass surgeries in 1978 — and lived to the age of 86. He died April 14, 2007. After first encountering illness, Archer had shared the trainer's duties with Ivan Gutfriend, who took over full time for the 1980 season. "I still follow the techniques that Sandy taught me about taping," Gutfriend, the Roughriders' athletic therapist for 30-plus years, told Darrell Davis in 2007. "I didn't have to go through Steps A to Z, because Sandy had tried them all, so he knows how to tape an ankle. He would keep up with all the latest techniques, but the one thing I learned from him was to have fun with your job. He always had fun with the players and they had fun with him." George Reed was always quick to commend the work of Sandy Archer, noting that the venerable trainer had added a year or two to Reed's career.

Due to Reed's excellence and longevity, many of his career records were thought to be unbreakable — most notably his standards of 16,116 rushing yards and 137 touchdowns. However, Mike Pringle retired following the 2004 season with 16,425 rushing yards — most of which were gained on behalf of the Baltimore Stallions/Montreal Alouettes — and was also tied with Reed in career touchdowns. Enter Milt Stegall.

Winnipeg's **Milt Stegall** *is congratulated by* **George Reed** *for surpassing his long-standing record of* *137 touchdowns* | Photo courtesy of *Leader-Post*

Stegall tied Reed's touchdown record in the opening game of the 2007 season, but the Winnipeg Blue Bombers' slotback went scoreless in his next three games. As a July 27, 2007 game against the Hamilton Tiger-Cats loomed, Reed was interviewed by George Johnson of the *Calgary Herald.* "I've had my time," Reed said. "He'll have his."

What if Reed's time with the Roughriders had been extended for another season or two? He retired after rushing for 1,454 yards — the third-highest total of his illustrious career — in 1975. In those days, regular-season schedules were 16 games. "They play two extra games now," Reed said. "Over the course of my career, that'd translate into an additional year and a half of playing time ... If I'd had the two games or played another season, maybe they'd still be chasing me. But maybe doesn't matter. My body wasn't beat up at the time. But I was tired mentally. There were things the [players' association] was going through. It was just time."

And it was time for Stegall to break the record, according to Reed. "I owned or had a part of the record a good long time," he told Johnson. "I'm always asked, 'You're losing a record like that. How can you possibly be happy?' But I just say, 'Take a look at who's going to take it.' When good things happen to good people, how can you not be happy?"

On the day Johnson's column appeared, quarterback Kevin Glenn flipped the ball to Stegall for a one-yard, record-breaking major to help the Blue Bombers defeat the visiting Hamilton Tiger-Cats 36-18.

After 63 years of marriage, Bob Shaw spent the fall of 2007 adjusting to life as a widower. His spouse, Mary, had died in August of that year. "My wife took great care of me," Bob Shaw said in his 86th year. "She was a super coach's wife. She raised two great kids and I'm happy about that. It was beautiful. I think that's why I'm lasting so long. I wasn't a boozer and a drinker. I put stuff away and I'm living comfortably." Shaw is also comfortable with his legacy in Saskatchewan, where he was the head coach in 1963 and 1964. "When you build something and they go on and are successful, you've got to appreciate what they did," he reflected. "I was extremely pleased that they won in '66."

After leaving Saskatchewan, Shaw coached the Toronto Argonauts from 1965 to 1968. Then the NFL beckoned, leading to stints as an assistant coach with the New Orleans Saints, Chicago Bears and Buffalo Bills. In 1976, Shaw resurfaced as a CFL head coach with the Hamilton Tiger-Cats, with whom he earned coach-of-the-year honours. Shaw remained Hamilton's head coach in 1977 before spending the next two seasons as general manager. Shaw then retired from football — at least for a while — but remained involved in sports as a baseball scout. He was hired by George Steinbrenner to scout Ohio for the New York Yankees.

As much as Shaw enjoyed scouting, football was still in his blood. In his mid-60s, he returned to coaching — running the football program at Otterbein University (his alma mater) for three years. Shaw retired from football, for the final time, in 1987. Twenty years later, still in good health and robust voice, Shaw was delighted to reminisce when contacted in Westerville, Ohio. He took the phone call in his residence on the appropriately named Old Coach Road.

Kent Austin returns in 2007 to help the Riders win their first Grey Cup since he won as a player in 1989 | Photo courtesy of *Leader-Post*

The Roughriders rode a new coach — Kent Austin — into the 2007 CFL playoffs. Austin had been the first major hiring by general manager Eric Tillman, who succeeded the fired Roy Shivers midway through the 2006 campaign. Shortly after that season, Tillman decided not to retain Danny Barrett for an eighth year as the Roughriders' field boss. Austin, a close friend of Tillman's who had enjoyed success as the Argonauts' offensive co-ordinator, was the obvious choice to take over from Barrett.

As a first-time head coach, Austin guided Saskatchewan to a 12-6 regular-season record, and to its first home playoff game since 1988. In the West Division semifinal, the Roughriders outlasted the visiting Stampeders 26-24 before upending the host B.C. Lions 26-17 with a Grey Cup berth at stake.

In the midst of a hectic week of preparations for a Grey Cup showdown with Winnipeg, plans were made to transport young cancer victims to Toronto for the big game. There had been a similar act of compassion in 1966, when a group of disabled Saskatchewan fans — the Rider Roller Rooters — were flown to Vancouver for the Grey Cup.

The initiative of 2007 originally revolved around 24-year-old Chris Knox, who was terminally ill with brain cancer. Following the West final, various businesses and individuals donated money to help Knox and his loved ones attend the Grey Cup. Knox left for Toronto two days before the game aboard a provincial-government jet, in the company of newly elected Saskatchewan Premier Brad Wall. The money donated to assist Knox also helped to send 10 other pediatric cancer patients to the game. The excursion was dubbed the "Rider Pride Ride For Cancer."

With the exception of Knox, who was too ill to leave his room, the cancer patients arrived at the Rogers Centre just as the Roughriders were completing their final practice — a walk-through — before the Grey Cup. After the brief workout, Saskatchewan quarterback Kerry Joseph presented his practice jersey to 14-year-old cancer patient Matthew Epp (who died in January of 2009).

Two days before meeting Epp, Joseph had been named the CFL's most outstanding player — joining George Reed (1965) and Ron Lancaster (1970, 1976) as the only Roughriders to win that award.

On Nov. 25, 2007, Joseph joined Lancaster and Austin as the Roughriders' only Grey Cup-winning quarterbacks. The Roughriders defeated the Blue Bombers 23-19 in the very same stadium where Saskatchewan had won its second Grey Cup 18 years earlier. In a sloppily played game, the outcome was in question until just under a minute remained, when cornerback James Johnson intercepted quarterback Ryan Dinwiddie — substituting for an injured Kevin Glenn — to extinguish a Blue Bombers rally. Johnson, who had returned his first of three interceptions for the Roughriders' opening touchdown, was named the Grey Cup's most valuable player.

Austin had also captured an MVP award in 1989 after passing for 474 yards and three touchdowns in a 43-40 victory over the Hamilton Tiger-Cats. By winning a second Cup as a Roughrider, Austin found himself in select company. The exclusive group consisted of Richie Hall (who played defensive halfback in 1989 and was the defensive co-ordinator in 2007), Ted Urness (who was the starting centre in 1966 and a member of the executive when Saskatchewan celebrated its second title 23 years later), Alan Ford (who scored a touchdown in the 1966 final and was the general manager of the 1989 edition) and Tom Shepherd (auditor in 1966; president in 1989). Athletic therapist Ivan Gutfriend and equipment manager Norm Fong were also with the Riders' championship teams in 1989 and 2007.

After the 2007 game, Austin discussed the significance of the feat. "You can't play or coach in Saskatchewan without understanding what it means," he said. "You have to be there and spend time there as a player or coach to truly understand the level that it's at. We get that. We understand that as a team. The culture of Saskatchewan is tied so closely to the Roughriders."

Gene Makowsky's ties are closer than most. The affable offensive lineman, who was born in Saskatoon, became a year-round Reginan after establishing himself with the Roughriders. He was a throwback to previous Grey Cups in that, as a long-serving lineman, he was a sentimental favourite. The 1966 championship was especially sweet for Ron Atchison and Reg Whitehouse. In 1989, veterans Roger Aldag and Bob Poley finally sipped champagne from Earl Grey's grail. In 2007, Makowsky — in his 13th year as a Roughrider — experienced his first championship celebration.

"I don't think anything unites this province or brings this province together like the Riders," Makowsky said. "I don't think anything is even close. Even outside the province, it's

Gene Makowsky *celebrates 2007 Grey Cup win in Toronto* |
Photo courtesy of Joe Bryksa, Canwest News Service

a phenomenon the way this franchise and the people of Saskatchewan are almost one. To describe it is tough. It's like they say: 'If you've experienced it, no explanation is necessary. If you haven't, no explanation will suffice.' For a guy like me, it's an honour to be part of this province, for one, but also the franchise and to see how close it is to the people of the province.

"It has been around since 1910 and it's the only pro sport. It's a big deal and the grassroots football here is something else. They play six-man football in places you wouldn't believe that have it and they travel for three hours to play against other teams. People come from Prince Albert to watch our games. The football culture here is so entrenched and it has been that way for a long time. It rises and falls a bit with the fortunes of the Riders, but there's always a good part of the population that really cares. It matters a lot to them."

In typically modest fashion, Makowsky deflected the credit in the giddy aftermath of the 2007 Grey Cup. There was, however, one departure from tradition. The soft-spoken Makowsky is seldom inclined toward bold proclamations, but he made an exception when asked about the head coach. "Austin is now a god," Makowsky told Steve Simmons of the *Toronto Sun*, adding: "He's maybe the all-time MVP of this franchise."

Makowsky was asked the following spring about the interview with Simmons. "I was on a bit of a high there," he said with a laugh. "I think I was asked, 'To the people of Saskatchewan, what was he like?' At that particular point, he probably was in that category. He has been very involved in two Grey Cup wins. He was a big difference-maker in 2007, and in the late '80s and early '90s, he could throw touchdowns at will, it seemed. He's a once-in-a-generation type of person."

"Once in a generation" describes the frequency of Saskatchewan's Grey Cup victories since the landmark conquest in 1966. In each of the three championship seasons, the Roughriders were not the odds-on favourite to win it all. In 1966, the Ottawa Rough Riders were widely expected to defeat Saskatchewan, which nonetheless prevailed 29-14. In 1989, the Edmonton Eskimos posted a 16-2 record before being upset by the visitors from Saskatchewan — a 9-9 unit — in the West Division final. The 2007 Roughriders won the Grey Cup after defeating the B.C. Lions, who had won a franchise-record 14 games during the regular season, in the West final.

"We weren't the early favourites in 2007, that's for sure," Roughriders president-CEO Jim Hopson said. "I think you do see a parallel. In 1966, the team was getting better, but I don't think anybody saw them as a dominant team. They turned out to be a dominant team for the next 10 years, right through '76, but they were a young team in '66. Ronnie Lancaster was a young quarterback who Ottawa had discarded. In '89, that one sort of came out of nowhere, with a 9-and-9 record, and kept playing better and better. In 2007, we had all the changes. We were very optimistic and excited, but I don't think a lot of the sports writers and fans were picking us to be in the Grey Cup, and we got there."

On Nov. 26 — 41 years to the day after the 1966 victory — Alan Ford was providing radio commentary for CBC when the 2007 Roughriders marched on to the Taylor Field turf with the Grey Cup. Unlike approximately 8,000 fans who endured a wind chill of minus-36°C to welcome home the team, Ford was in the comparative comfort of a studio, watching the proceedings on a video monitor. "There wasn't as much snow as in 1989, but it was a heck of a lot colder in 2007," Ford noted.

After chartering back to Regina, the 2007 Roughriders took a bus to the stadium. Gene Makowsky and defensive halfback Eddie Davis carried the Cup on to the field, followed by teammates, management types, family members and Roughriders staffers. The fans' response was much warmer than the conditions. "That was crazy," Austin told Murray McCormick of the *Leader-Post*. "I wouldn't have been able to stand out there for 20 seconds."

But the fans persevered. "I remember what Kent Austin told me when we were getting on the buses, because he had been a part of it before," Roughriders general manager Eric Tillman remembered. "He said, 'You're not going to believe what you're about to see when we get to the stadium.' We get there and it's 100 below zero. The wind is blowing. It's the coldest I had ever been in my life — until the Grey Cup parade — and those people have been sitting there for an hour, waiting for us. They're screaming and yelling. That's why you want to be here. That's why you want to be a part of it." The Roughriders' first-ever Grey Cup victory parade was held the next day. The procession began 15 minutes earlier than planned due to the minus-30 wind chill. Fifteen half-ton trucks carried the Roughriders and the Grey Cup south on Albert Street for two kilometres, completing the journey at the Legislative Building. The initial blueprint called for an outdoor ceremony, but Premier Brad Wall invited the throng — consisting of approximately 1,000 people — inside the Legislative Building. "One of the best parts of this job is I get to make decisions," Wall said. "The best decision was to move this celebration inside."

The rotunda was congested with humanity. Even in the balcony, the crowd was three or four deep. The loudest cheers were reserved for Austin. "Now we're going to accomplish something that's never been done," said the victorious head coach, to whom the crowd responded by yelling "Repeat! Repeat!"

The excitement of Roughriders fans was tempered, to say the least, on Jan. 16, 2008. Kent Austin announced he was stepping down to become the offensive co-ordinator at his alma mater, the University of Mississippi. Despite the frigid mid-winter conditions, Austin departed with nothing but warm feelings about Saskatchewan and the Roughriders' 2007 season. "It was my most special year in football — of any year, as a player or a coach," he reflected. "If you weren't on the inside, it's hard to explain how magical it was."

CHAPTER **37** | # "THE ICONS"

Kent Austin | Photo courtesy of *Leader-Post*

The year 1963 turned out to be pivotal in Saskatchewan Roughriders history. Kent Austin, Ron Lancaster, George Reed and Hugh Campbell all arrived in '63, albeit in different ways. Austin was born June 25, 1963, shortly before Lancaster was traded to Saskatchewan by the Ottawa Rough Riders. Reed was at his first training camp with the Green and White. In September of that year, Campbell landed in Regina after being released by the San Francisco 49ers.

Like Campbell, Austin became a Roughrider at midseason after being cut by an NFL team — the St. Louis Cardinals, with whom he had spent the 1986 season. When Austin touched down in Regina, he had never heard of Canadian football icons named Ron Lancaster and George Reed. How soon would that change? "First day," Austin said with a chuckle from Oxford, Miss., in June of 2008. "You cannot play there without knowing who those guys are. I learned who they were very quickly. They're two of the greatest players who ever played for the organization — the greatest quarterback who ever played for the organization. Then I found out how long he played and thought,

'You've got to be kidding.' That's a long time to play football." And especially to play it well, as did Lancaster and Reed. "They embody everything that's great about Saskatchewan," Austin said.

Austin, a Rider great in his own right, enlivened a Saskatchewan air attack that had been largely dormant since Lancaster retired as a player. Austin emulated The Little General by throwing three touchdown passes in a Grey Cup — the Roughriders' 43-40 victory over the Hamilton Tiger-Cats in 1989 (23 years to the day after the 1966 conquest). Over the next four years, Austin broke many of Lancaster's single-season Roughriders passing records, peaking in 1992 with 35 touchdown passes and 6,225 aerial yards. By then, Lancaster and Austin were well-acquainted. The two would chat, for example, when Lancaster was a football analyst with CBC.

Austin quickly developed an appreciation for Lancaster's varied contributions to the CFL, lauding him as "an unbelievable ambassador for that great league." The same applies to George Reed. "Class guy. Down to earth. Nice human being," Austin said. "Everything that you already know." Austin was frequently reminded of Lancaster and Reed while serving as the Roughriders' head coach in 2007. Each day, Austin saw giant images of the Canadian football legends displayed on the west side of Mosaic Stadium. "You couldn't miss them," Austin recalled.

Austin reaffirmed his status as a Roughriders legend in one storybook season as the team's field boss. Along the way, he was in frequent contact with Lancaster. "He called when I got the job to congratulate me," Austin said in June of 2008. "He called when I won my first game. He called when we won our first playoff game. He called when we won the Grey Cup. He's so considerate. He's very, very thoughtful. He has never failed to do those things with me. That shows you the quality of individual that he is."

The quality of Austin as an individual, and as a coach, elicited plaudits from those who played for him in 2007. "He brought intensity to the team and you just didn't want to let him down, because he had that high of a level of expectations," offensive lineman Gene Makowsky said. "He just had smart things to say. I can't remember a time when I rolled my eyes or I didn't really buy in. He really made you think. With everything he said, it was, 'Yeah, OK, I agree with that,' and, 'That's a good point.' It wasn't just football. It was kind of about life. The guys had a ton of respect for him and wanted to play for him."

Austin's reputation was already well-established when he accepted the Roughriders' head-coaching position. "From his playing days, coming in you have a respect for him and what he did in the league and how good he was," Makowsky said. "He's just one of those guys who you respect right away and you want to play for. You hold him in high regard, kind of like a guy you look up to. You're immediately impressed with him. There's few people in life who are like that, but he's definitely like that."

Receiver Matt Dominguez quickly detected the difference in the organization when Eric Tillman took over as general manager midway through the 2006 season. Tillman would soon appoint Austin as head coach. "We didn't have a terrible team before Kent and Eric came," Dominguez said. "We were 9-and-9. We were a mediocre, underachieving group. What they did was change the culture. They made people professionals. When you do that, and you change that culture and you change that mentality, that's all it really took. We were already good. With the way that Kent projected himself when he walked into a room, you knew that he knew what he was talking about, cared what he was talking about, and expected you to do the same. When you have somebody like that, people want to follow."

Already accomplished as a quarterback, Austin ascended to iconic status — as Gene Makowsky emphasized after the 2007 Grey Cup while exclaiming that "Austin is now a god" and touting him as possibly "the all-time MVP of this franchise." That assessment put Austin in a stratosphere with Ron Lancaster and George Reed.

"I think as time goes on and there's that perspective, he'll be right up there," Makowsky said of Austin. "He was here a short time but accomplished so much. People wonder what he could have done if he had stayed a little longer. He was part of two of the first three Grey Cups. This game is all about winning and he did a lot of that while he was here. As this generation grows up, they'll talk about the old days of Kent Austin and I think he'll be right up there."

For all their accomplishments, Reed and Lancaster were associated with only one championship team in Saskatchewan — the 1966 Roughriders. Austin was a highly visible component of two Grey Cup winners. If the sole criteria is championships won, Austin is more comparable to Alan Ford, who won as a player (in 1966) and general manager (1989), than to Lancaster or Reed.

Jim Hopson | Photo courtesy of *Leader-Post*

Yet, photos of Lancaster and Reed are affixed to the stadium, and Austin is honoured only by having a nearby parking lot named after him. The difference relates to longevity. Lancaster and Reed spent 16 and 13 years, respectively, as Roughriders players. They were year-round residents of Regina. Austin and his family were exemplary citizens when he was the Roughriders' head coach, but he held that position for barely 13 months. As a player and coach, Austin spent a combined eight seasons as a Roughrider.

"Kent has that aura of winning the Grey Cup as a quarterback and a coach," Roughriders president-CEO Jim Hopson said. "I don't know if Kent would have had to have had a 10-year career here as a coach [to rival Lancaster and Reed]. If it would have been five years and if he had won another championship or two, I think he would have been at that level of greatness that we hold Ronnie and George to."

Hopson can speak of Lancaster and Reed from first-hand experience, as a former teammate. "They symbolize so much of what's good and special about the Saskatchewan Roughriders," said Hopson, who was a Roughriders offensive lineman from 1973 to 1976. "They both played a tremendously long time here at a very high level, but they also lived here. They were part of the community. They coached, they taught, they worked, they raised their kids, and they really came to be the role models and the mentors in that locker room.

"When I had my shot at the Roughriders in '73, I was in awe of those guys. To sit in the locker room — my locker was directly across from Ronnie — it sounds so corny, but literally you want to pinch yourself. I'd be sitting there looking at Ronnie and thinking, 'I'm on the same team as Ronnie Lancaster.' George and Ronnie were well-established vets. I was a dumb-ass rookie from the [junior] Regina Rams, just trying to make the team. They weren't mean to me, but they were veterans. When I'd do something stupid, like blow a block or step on George's foot, George would say, 'Rookie, watch where you're going!'

"You just lived for the day that they would accept you. It just kind of happens. You prove yourself and you're around. Then, one day, George says, 'Some of the guys are coming over for beer. Do you want to come by?' And you go, 'I'm going to George Reed's house!' It's true. It really is. You look up to these guys."

Lancaster and Hopson were teammates for four years. Hopson's first three seasons with the Roughriders were Reed's final three. Although Hopson closely observed only a fraction of their careers, he was able to grasp the essence of what made Lancaster and Reed exceptional. "I'd be hard-pressed to think of anybody more competitive or anybody who wanted to win more than those two guys," Hopson recalled. "It didn't matter, with Ronnie in particular, whether it was racquetball or baseball, he was going to beat you. In football, he just had an unbelievable will to win and was willing to pay the price."

Long before Hopson arrived, people across the CFL marvelled at Reed's tolerance for pain. In his mid-30s, long past the best-before date for most running backs, Reed remained an elite ball-carrier and enjoyed some of his best seasons. "I watched George literally, totally sell out and sit down at his locker after a game and pass out from exhaustion," Hopson said. "He'd tell everybody to leave him alone and that he was fine."

The Roughriders believed they would be fine as long as Lancaster and Reed were around. "We always felt with Ronnie and George that we were in a game," Hopson said. "We were down by 21 sometimes and we never got beat. We just ran out of time. Ronnie just needed one more chance. Ronnie and George really came to stand for the organization. We've had some great players since and we have some great players right now. There's the Roger Aldags, the Gene Makowskys and the Kent Austins. It's not like we haven't had other great players, and we will continue to, but Ronnie and George played at a very special time. The team had a very good run for a very long time. They were the unofficial and official leaders of that team. To those of us who played with them, they're pretty special guys."

Gene Makowsky grew up hearing all about Ronnie and George. "They were big stars. That's what I remember," said Makowsky, who was two years old when Reed played his final game and five when Lancaster signed off. "I never saw them play live, but they're the icons of the franchise, really. Those two guys are as big as it gets when it comes to the Riders. That's my image of them. I heard Ron Lancaster speak at the [2007 University of Saskatchewan Huskies'] Dogs' Breakfast in Saskatoon. I was so fired up. I wanted to get playing right then. He had three or four standing ovations. That just showed how much those guys mean to the province."

Unlike Makowsky — and more like Austin — Matt Dominguez was not aware of Lancaster or Reed until arriving in Saskatchewan in 2003. "Ever since I've been here, those are the guys you always hear about," said Dominguez, a native Texan. "It was a joke around the locker room until 2007 that these guys have been immortalized because, at their time, they were predominant winners, but they only had one Grey Cup. They had one more Grey Cup than me until 2007. From my experience, living here year-round, that was the biggest thing they did in the community. They were here every day and people saw them every day. You have great players that you get to interact with every day. I met a guy who said that Lancaster was his teacher and George Reed lived up the street from him. When you have players who are playing at a high level in your community, everywhere you go, it means that much more — as opposed to the guys who are here six months and gone for six months. There's kind of a disconnect."

The Roughriders' connection with the past is obvious as soon as one approaches Mosaic Stadium from the west side and sees the giant images of Lancaster and Reed. "Several guys have said, 'Who are those dudes?' " Dominguez said in reference to newly arriving American players. "It came to mind, too, that haven't we had any players beyond '66 who warrant being on the stadium? George Reed and Ron Lancaster are the last great players we've had here? The young guys open my eyes to it. At the same time, they transcended just playing football and being football players. I think that's why they mean so much."

As much as Dominguez appreciates the accomplishments of Lancaster, Reed and their cohorts, he has always been a strong proponent of accentuating the present. That became much easier when Saskatchewan defeated the Winnipeg Blue Bombers to win the 2007 CFL title. "Since we won that Grey Cup, I hear a whole lot less about '66 and '89," Dominguez observed. "Beforehand, it was, 'I remember in 1966 ...,' and, 'I remember in 1989 when we won the Grey Cup ... ' You don't hear anything about that anymore because we've got a Grey Cup now. Instead of looking in the past, now you can look to the future. You take the past for what it is, but if you keep dwelling on the past, you're not enjoying what you have now."

Dominguez has enjoyed the best of both eras. While underlining the importance of not living in the past, the veteran receiver paid homage to the legends who preceded him. In 2005, for example, Dominguez learned that Reed was visiting Regina. Seizing the opportunity, Dominguez invited Reed over for a visit. Reed was obliging, so Dominguez quickly headed over to the Hotel Saskatchewan to pick up the famous fullback. "I've had George Reed at my house twice," Dominguez noted. "We were talking about the CFL Players'

Association agreement and things of that nature because that's what he handled back in the day. We didn't even talk about X's and O's. We were just talking about state-of-the-CFL type of things."

Reed is proud of his contributions to the CFLPA, but feels his involvement in the union may have impeded him from contributing to the league at the front-office level. "That's the area I would have wanted to work in," he said. "However, I think that some of the things I did with the players' association also counted against me. So be it. I thought the things that I did were very important for not only the players who were playing then, to start getting them on the right track, but also for the ones who came later. I have never really thought about it that much after that ... I was told one time by one person who was on the management side — I won't mention his name — that it would take me a long time to get on the management side after the walkout the players had in 1974 [when job action during training camp resulted in the players emerging with a greatly enhanced collective bargaining agreement]. He said it would be a while before I would be able to convince him that I could cross over the waters and be on their side."

Reed was a two-term president of the CFLPA (1972-80 and 1986-93) while also working at Molson Breweries for most of that time. Early in 1992, he was among 125 employees cut by Molson, ending an association with the brewery that dated back to 1966. In the mid-1990s, Reed was hired by McKay Pontiac Buick (now Shaganappi Pontiac Buick GMC) in Calgary, and remained with the dealership until being hired as a corporate event host for

Kind of says it all! George and Ronnie in the Hall of Fame | Photo courtesy of Joseph Dojack

the Saskatchewan Gaming Corporation. In 2009, George and Angie Reed became year-round Reginans for the first time in 25 years. "I don't know if I ever want to retire," he said. "I've been too busy to really shut it down."

Even while selling cars, Reed welcomed people who associated him more closely with football than with automobiles. "I got a lot of interesting reactions," he said. "A lot of interesting people didn't even come to buy a car, but they knew I was there. One family drove in from Winnipeg just for an autograph and to take some pictures with me. Then they turned around and got in the car and drove back. I had a couple of guys drive down from Edmonton for the same reason. Probably my biggest fan out of Regina came in with all his Club 34 stuff [from Reed's charity work] and his green car. They couldn't believe it at the dealership that this guy was that way. A lot of people came in for an autograph or a picture."

Oftentimes, they also mentioned Lancaster, given the extent to which the two football careers are intertwined. "They will always look at him as The Little General," Reed said. "He was the glue that kept us together, whether it was going between management and the players. On the football field, all the guys had respect for him because he ran the football team. That's why we were so successful. I think he will always be remembered and endeared to the people probably because of his size as much as what he did on the football field."

When they both resided in Regina, there was seldom much distance between Lancaster and Reed, or their families. They lived in Whitmore Park, in the city's south end. Their children attended Campbell Collegiate. Football-wise, Lancaster and Reed are inextricably linked, and the closeness extended to their friendship. "George and I were probably a lot closer than people realized, but not as close as a lot of people thought," Lancaster said. "I had a lot of respect for him. I'm sure he felt the same way. He was the kind of guy — and I know he felt the same way — that if I called him and needed something, he'd be there. If he had needed something, I would have been there."

Lancaster and Reed had a shared philosophy regarding being accessible to the fans. In 1996, for example, a fan walked up to Lancaster — who was then the head coach of the Edmonton Eskimos — following a Grey Cup week practice at Ivor Wynne Stadium in Hamilton. The fan told Lancaster that meeting him represented the attainment of a lifelong goal. Lancaster proceeded to sign an autograph for the admirer, and also spent several minutes chatting with him. After the amicable meeting, Lancaster shook hands with the fan and headed to the dressing room. The fan walked away, beaming. It was a quintessential only-in-the-CFL moment.

"It would never happen at the Super Bowl or the World Series," Lancaster said. "That's the one thing about this league. The players are always accessible." Lancaster, for example, responded to every piece of correspondence from a fan, a practice Reed also maintains. "My whole career, I answered all the letters and everything that I got — all of them — and sent pictures," Lancaster said.

Lancaster could relate to the lot of the fan. Once upon a time, he was a teenaged signature-seeker at a major-league baseball game in Pittsburgh. "We played in a Pony League game and we won an award," he remembered. "We ended up at Forbes Field on the third-base line, right by the Milwaukee Braves' dugout. They had to come up out of the dugout to go and bat. We were right there when they came up out of the dugout. We got down there early and collected autographs. I had Del Crandall and Warren Spahn and Lew Burdette and Eddie Mathews and Johnny Logan and Hank Aaron and Jim Pendleton and all those guys, but Joe Adcock wouldn't sign my book. I never liked him after that. Everybody else signed it, and he wouldn't sign it. I thought, 'I wonder why he wouldn't sign any autographs?' Maybe he was just having a bad day or was sick or whatever, but he wouldn't sign it, yet all those other guys did.

"I always felt that if somebody's going to come and ask you, sign it. It won't hurt you. Most times, people are really nice about it. They don't come and say, 'Here, sign this!' What does it take? Thirty seconds? The other thing I used to tell players — and I never did get this across to many of them when I was coaching — was 'try to sign your name so people can read it, because there's going to come a day when they're not going to be able to read it.' Some guys are only there for a year and some are there forever, but you have no idea who that person is because you can't read the name. I said, 'Why don't you write it so people can read it? It might take a couple of seconds longer. They're asking for your autograph for a reason. At least make it legible for them. You know what? It doesn't happen."

Lancaster's signature, so frequently and cordially provided, remains as clear as the imprint he left upon the CFL. "I have made a career in the Canadian Football League — a league that I didn't even grow up watching," Lancaster reflected 4½ months before his death. "The only game I had really seen would have been around ninth grade and it would have been around 1953. I came in the house on a Saturday afternoon and there was a football game on television. I was getting a drink of water and I stopped to look at the TV and it was a Canadian game out of Montreal. I looked at it and saw something about kicking the ball into the end zone and getting a point. I said, 'This is a stupid game,' and I left. A few years later, I came up here to play football and ended up being part of the league for 50 years and enjoyed every bit of it. When you're part of something for so long, it's like family. In a lot of ways, that's what this is — a family."

CHAPTER 38 | "I'M GOING TO MISS HIM"

George Reed's phone rang while he was en route to a meeting in Calgary just after 9 a.m., on Sept. 18, 2008. "I was at a stop light," he recalled. "Somebody from a radio station called my cell phone and asked if I had heard the news. I said, 'What are you talking about?' Then he told me that Ronnie had passed away.'" That morning, Ron Lancaster had died suddenly at age 69. "Next to losing my mother, that was the toughest shock," Reed said. "It knocked everything out of me. It was so bad that I had to find a place to pull over. I was shaking and everything else. I was devastated. I could hardly talk."

But talk he did, throughout that dismal day, as the football player most closely associated with Lancaster remembered his legendary teammate and great friend. By the afternoon, Reed had done nearly 20 interviews, while fielding assorted inquiries from friends and fans.

Reed had last spoken with Lancaster the previous month, after news circulated that The Little General was confronting cancer for the second time. "In fact, I was just getting ready to e-mail him and make some kind of joke and go from there," Reed said. "I guess I waited a day too late." Reed made that comment during a conference call in which Hugh Campbell also participated. "It's just something that's stunning," a shaken Campbell said a few hours after his close friend had died. "I knew of his illness, but I thought we had a lot more time than this."

So did everybody. Lancaster's tone was upbeat on Aug. 6, 2008, when he released a statement regarding his diagnosis via the Hamilton Tiger-Cats, on whose radio broadcasts he had served as an analyst early in the 2008 CFL season. "As much as I love the game of football, there are some things more important than what happens on the field of play,"

George and Ronnie, Ronnie and George — *that's the way it was!* | Photos courtesy of Ken Solilo, Solilo Studios

Lancaster said. "[Four] years ago, I survived a battle with [bladder] cancer, and now we have another battle on our hands. In July, I was given the news from my doctors that another form of cancer has appeared. Over the last few weeks I have begun radiation and chemotherapy treatments and therefore I will not be around the office and out in the community as much as I have been in the past. The goal is to get this taken care of and move forward just like I did [four] years ago. We will approach this the same way and I thank you all in advance for your kindness as I am on my path to recovery."

Lancaster was acutely aware that the path would include some detours. The public was advised, through media reports, that Lancaster had been diagnosed with lung cancer. But only those closest to him knew the full extent of his illness. "He told me, 'You know, D, it's in my brain. Yeah, it's going to be a little bit tough,' " recalled Edmonton Eskimos equipment manager Dwayne Mandrusiak, one of Lancaster's closest friends. "I said, 'What did they say?' He said, 'It's not good. It's going to be tough.' I asked if there was anything I could do. He said, 'Don't worry about it. I'll be fine.' "

Mandrusiak was able to visit Lancaster in late July — shortly after the diagnosis — when the Eskimos travelled east for games against the Tiger-Cats and Toronto Argonauts. On July 25, Lancaster was joined in a golf foursome by Mandrusiak, Neil Lumsden and Dan Kepley. "It was hot out," Mandrusiak recounted. "He looked pretty pale. We got a bunch of water and some Gatorade for him and we started playing. Even then, if he didn't hit a great shot, he'd be so mad at himself. For the 18 holes, we didn't talk once about him being sick. We didn't talk about treatment. We bullshitted about stories from the past. We laughed our asses off. At the end, I knew he was having fun because when we got to the 17th hole, he said, 'You know what? What are the odds of them cancelling the game tonight and us playing another 18?' I said, 'I'd love that.' He said, 'So would I.'

"That's the last time I saw him, but I talked to him a few times after. I'd call his house. I knew he was getting treatment on a certain day and I'd wait a couple of days or whatever, especially with the stuff he was getting. I'd call and ask how he was doing and he'd say, 'I'm a little tired, but I'm good. Things are going great.' "

Lancaster also conveyed that impression on Labour Day, when the Tiger-Cats played host to Toronto. He cheerfully circulated at Ivor Wynne Stadium, holding court with his many friends. "He looked good," TSN's Brian Williams said. "He had lost his hair, but he looked healthy and was laughing and talking." Lancaster's demeanor was the same while he golfed with Damon Allen, Rob Hitchcock and Danny McManus the weekend before his death. Another golf date had been planned around festivities for the Canadian Football Hall of Fame enshrinements in Hamilton. With induction

George Reed blocking for Ronnie | Photo courtesy of *Leader-Post*

weekend looming, Lancaster began to experience discomfort. He was admitted to hospital on the evening of Sept. 16 and felt much better the following day. The next morning — Sept. 18 — Lancaster was preparing to go home when he was stricken with sudden respiratory failure, which caused cardiac arrest. He fell back on to his hospital bed and was gone. In an instant, a remarkable life had ended, one month shy of its 70th year.

"It was very fast," said Lancaster's daughter, Lana Mueller. "All he ever said to me was he didn't want to get sick. Well, he got his wish. He was pretty healthy right to the end. He was going to the office daily and enjoying life. And when it is all said and done, is that not how we all want to go?" Lancaster's son, Ron Jr., echoed those sentiments. "All we ask is that we don't suffer. He never suffered," a proud son said. "If this would have happened 10 years from now, we would have said the same thing: 'It happened too early.' "

The devastating news quickly reverberated. "I was looking for him to beat this," Reed said that morning. "That's the type of guy he is. I just felt that, 'If anybody can do it, he can do it, and we'll be laughing later on this year together.' " Another close friend, former *Leader-Post* sports editor and columnist Bob Hughes, described Sept. 18 as "one of the saddest days of my life." As a cub reporter, Hughes had met Lancaster in 1965 while the Roughriders quarterback was coaching the Central Gophers high school boys basketball team. Hughes was often called upon to write about Lancaster, and a strong friendship developed. "I can think of no other athlete in the history of professional sports anywhere who affected as many people in as many wonderful ways as Ron Lancaster did in as many capacities," Hughes said. "I loved the man and will always cherish that he was my very dear friend."

Although Lancaster had first made an imprint as the Roughriders' quarterback, the messages of appreciation and condolence emanated from far beyond Saskatchewan. Lancaster had also been part of Grey Cup champions with the Ottawa Rough Riders (as a quarterback, 1960), Edmonton Eskimos (head coach, 1993) and Hamilton Tiger-Cats (head coach, 1999). Many CFL fans were introduced to Lancaster during the decade he spent with CBC as a television analyst.

"His contribution in every way to the CFL is unparalleled," Hugh Campbell said. "He has had such a huge effect, both face to face with the fans as well as with the players, and also with people who have never met him ... The combination of all of those things is really unmatched in the amount of fans that he has personally reached."

Ron Lancaster *with the Grey Cup in 1966* | Photo courtesy of *Vancouver Sun*

Lancaster's impact was such that a statement was released by the office of Prime Minister Stephen Harper, who saluted "a Saskatchewan and Canadian sports icon." Also from the political realm, Saskatchewan Premier Brad Wall reflected the sentiments of many fans who grew up watching Lancaster play. "That's who you were when you were playing a pickup game of football in the playground," said Wall, who was born in 1965 — Lancaster's third season with the Roughriders. "Everyone wants to be George Reed and Ron Lancaster. It's a sad day for the province. If you think about it, his best qualities are Saskatchewan's best qualities. He had a big heart. He punched above his weight. It also helps guys like me who are height-challenged to get inspiration from that. He had a real competitive edge. We don't talk about that a lot in Saskatchewan, but we compete hard.

"And he gave back. Just a couple of years ago, I watched him speak at the Huskies' Dogs' Breakfast in Saskatoon. He always gave back. Those are the best qualities of the province. That's the first time that I have ever heard the biographical talk. When he was done, I said, 'I could listen to him tell stories for eight hours.' The best one was the jersey story, where the equipment manager threw him Number 23 [after Lancaster was traded to Saskatchewan in 1963]. He had always been 16, and he said, 'I would like 16.' The equipment manager said, 'Don't worry, you're not going to be here for very long, so just take what I give you.' And now, 23 is iconic."

The reactions quickly turned from shock to appreciation as tributes poured in. By the end of a long day — Sept. 18, 2008 — the stories were more anecdotal than mournful. Many of the reminiscences had little to do with the Roughriders, pertaining instead to Lancaster and his family as citizens. Jan Beadnell told a story about minor football games that included Lancaster's youngest child, Bob. "Frequently, when there were no other volunteers, Ron was on the 'chain gang,' working the yardsticks as well as cheering on the Cats," Beadnell recalled. Paul Harasen, who was a teammate of Bob Lancaster in minor hockey, remembers his friend's famous father volunteering to open and close the players' gate on the bench. Other people remembered having Lancaster as a physical-education teacher or coach at Central Collegiate.

"He had time for everybody and everybody had equal importance in his mind," Hugh Campbell said. "He treated all the people who I saw him deal with at the same level as far as his interest in their story. He had time to stop and talk to a stranger in an airport or at a hockey rink. He also had time to talk to fans and be interested. He was genuinely interested in their story of why they came to the game or what they saw him do years ago. He had a great feel for putting himself in the other person's shoes and realizing that they had an equal reason to be on this earth as he and the rest of us did."

Lancaster was a minority of one in that he did not regard himself as a big deal. That mindset was in effect Sept. 22, when a memorial gathering was held at Bay Gardens Funeral Home in Hamilton. It was not a funeral, per se, and it did not include a formal eulogy. "What struck me was how long it took in line to get to say hello," recalled TSN's Brian Williams, a former colleague at CBC. "It was not a service. It was just a visitation. Ron Jr., Bobby, Lana, Bev and the grandchildren were all there. It took me from 2:10 to 3:50 — nearly two hours — to go from when I lined up to when I got to Ron Jr. It was sort of happy. All the old warriors were there. It was a nice gathering of a lot of nice people. It wasn't sad. It was more of a celebration, and that's what Ron would want. And it should have been a celebration, because if there was ever a life to celebrate in this country, east and west, it's Ron Lancaster's."

And that life *was* celebrated. "He was a Canadian hero," Williams said. "Think about it. I don't think it's an exaggeration to say that. He should be celebrated. And when the Prime Minister of Canada issues a statement upon his death, let me ask you: How many times has that been done for a non-hockey player? Some people come and stay for opportunity. He stayed because he loved it. He loved this country. He loved the States and was very proud, but he loved Canada. Ron Lancaster believed that being pro-Canadian and pro-American were not mutually exclusive, and I think we can all learn from that."

Ron Lancaster — *Abe Jarrioch remembers on Sept. 18, 2008* |
Photo courtesy of *Leader-Post*

Shortly after learning of Lancaster's death, CBC's Peter Mansbridge posted an item on his blog, noting that he had admired The Little General since 1960. Back then, Lancaster was a rookie quarterback and defensive back with the Ottawa Rough Riders. Mansbridge was 12 years old and living in the nation's capital. He instantly became a fan while carrying Lancaster's helmet back to the dorm after a training-camp workout.

Three years later, Lancaster was traded to Saskatchewan — and Mansbridge changed his loyalties just as quickly. "I was devastated," *The National*'s chief correspondent said. "I chose right then and there that I was going to cheer for Saskatchewan. To heck with Ottawa." Later in the 1960s, Mansbridge was living in Churchill, Man., working for TransAir. "The only way you could get a Roughrider football game — because there was no live television there then — was to go out on to the tundra somewhere and try to find a high spot at night and go down the dial, trying to find a Regina radio station or any kind of Saskatchewan radio station which was broadcasting Rider games," Mansbridge said. "I'd go out in the middle of nowhere in my little Chevy 2, tuning in a Rider game."

Mansbridge proceeded to join the CBC, working in various bureaus. In 1976, he was hired as *The National*'s correspondent in Regina. "This was a huge deal for me because Ron Lancaster was still playing, and it was very much his heyday," Mansbridge recalled. "For the first time ever, I got to actually go to Taylor Field and watch a game. I can remember doing a piece on George Reed and getting an interview with Ron Lancaster. It was a big deal, and the last thing I would tell him was that I had carried his helmet, but I was pretty nervous about it and I remained that way over the years."

The feeling of awe was not diminished after Lancaster joined CBC's football coverage team as an analyst, thereby becoming Mansbridge's corporate cohort. "We became friends because of his work for the CBC, and Don Wittman was a really good friend of mine, so I'd see them quite often," Mansbridge continued. "Whenever I'd see him, it would be like I was 12 again. It was pretty exciting to see him and I'd get nervous about it and the whole bit, because he had been such a key part of my life as a youngster growing up, and then still as a young adult. It meant an awful lot to me. I lived and died with Rider games.

"By the time we sort of got to know each other, he seemed to be as interested in talking to me because of what I do as the other way around. But to me, he was still Ronnie Lancaster. He was Number 16 or Number 23. He was always going to be that for me." In the line of duty, Mansbridge has met and interviewed prime ministers, presidents and other world dignitaries. "The Queen ... the Pope ...," Mansbridge added. "Those were always great moments, but it wasn't like being near Ron Lancaster."

Dwayne Mandrusiak became closer to Lancaster than he could have imagined. Mandrusiak, the Edmonton Eskimos' equipment manager, was hired by the organization in the early 1970s. "If we were ahead by six and they had the ball with a minute left, in your mind you knew you were going to lose," Mandrusiak said. "Most times, you hate guys on other teams, but I always liked how he played."

Lancaster and Mandrusiak hit it off instantly in 1991, when Hugh Campbell appointed Lancaster the Eskimos' head coach. "When he came here, he talked to me like he had known me forever," Mandrusiak said. "In the equipment area, most guys will only talk to you when they want something, so when he did what he did, I thought, 'That's a pretty neat deal.' " Nearly 20 years separated Lancaster and Mandrusiak, but the age difference was irrelevant. "We clicked right away," Mandrusiak said. "It was amazing. He did so much for me. He was like my best friend, but also like my father if you needed help. I could talk about anything with him and he would just figure it out. I miss picking the phone up and calling him and just seeing how he is ... He was just a common guy. That was the amazing part. For being as famous as he was — and, really, he's a Canadian icon — he was as average a guy as I've ever met.

"You looked at the guy, with the way he was and the way he played, and it was almost like he was too good to be true. He really stepped to the plate when my father passed away [in 1992]. He was the first face I saw when I was doing the eulogy for my father, because he was sitting right near the front."

The friendship endured after Lancaster left the Eskimos following the 1997 season to join the Tiger-Cats. "He wrote this letter, which I will have for the rest of my life," Mandrusiak said. "It was from his heart and it was amazing. Those days when you're down, you just read it. It had absolutely nothing to do with football. He just wrote about the respect that he had for me and the respect that he had for what we did together. Because he was gone from Edmonton, that was irrelevant. We weren't friends because of football. We were friends because we were friends. We talked all the time." Mandrusiak dearly misses the conversations, but a tangible connection with his great friend is never far away. "The letter is in my drawer," he concluded, "next to my bed."

Grandson **Marc Mueller** *sharing his grandpa's legacy* |
Photo courtesy of Mueller/Lancaster families

Lancaster and his grandson, Marc Mueller, talked on a daily basis. Mueller phoned his grandfather at 4 p.m., virtually without fail. "Four o'clock's pretty tough on me, but that's the way it's going to be, I guess," Mueller lamented. Until September of 2008, there might have been a day or two each year in which they did not converse, even though Mueller resides in Regina and Lancaster was based in the Hamilton area. "It was before I'd go to practice," said Mueller, who joined the University of Regina Rams after quarterbacking the Sheldon-Williams Spartans to the 2006 Regina and Saskatchewan 4A high school football titles. "I'd tell him about practice and about the game plan and he'd say, 'That sounds good,' or, 'You should maybe try some of this.' Again, he'd tell me not to throw off the back foot, which was a pretty big constant."

Mueller frequently prevailed upon Lancaster's expertise. "Whenever I sent him a game tape, he would tell me the same two things," Mueller said. "He would say, 'Your drops are too slow, and you're throwing way too much off your back foot.' From Grade 7 on, it was the exact same thing.

"And then they showed highlights of him one day on TSN. It might have been when [Montreal Alouettes quarterback] Anthony Calvillo went over 50,000 yards. They showed 15 of his [Lancaster's] throws. Every single one was off of his back foot. Not two or three — every single one. So I immediately called him. I said, 'You're all over me for throwing off my back foot — which I don't think I do, by the way, but that's beside the point. I saw highlights of you and every single pass was off your back foot, and most of it was while you were backing up.' He said, 'It worked, didn't it? Were they completed passes?' I said, 'Yeah.' He said, 'Well, then, what's your problem?' We had a pretty good chuckle about that."

Mueller's outgoing manner and absorption with football are reminiscent of Lancaster, as is his manner of speaking. "I like to talk, so people say that I either look like him, or a couple of guys say I got my bowl-cut brush-cut from him," Mueller remarked. "I always thought I got it from The Beatles or something like that, but I guess I got it from him. I get people saying all the time that, 'You carry yourself on and off the field like your grandpa would be proud of, and like he did.' That's just how I turned out. I grew up around him and I guess that's how it rubs off. That's the way it was.

"To me, he was just Grandpa, and I'm going to miss him."

To others, he was Digger, The Little General, Ronnie, Coach, or Dad. So many labels were applied to a diminutive giant of Canadian football during nearly a half-century of involvement with the league. Lancaster neither began nor finished his CFL career in Saskatchewan, yet it was while wearing the Green and White that his legend was established.

"I think back to what he said one time: He owes his career to the people of Saskatchewan," Ron Lancaster Jr. said. "I can speak for Bobby and Lana in the fact that he loved his time in Saskatchewan, and we are very, very fortunate to have been a part of his life. We are as proud of him as he would be of us."

The family celebrated a proud moment on Nov. 20, 2008, when Ron Lancaster was posthumously honoured with the Commissioner's Award. Mark Cohon presented the award to Ron Jr., at the CFL Player Awards in Montreal.

"Ron Lancaster did it all in our league, and everything he did was marked by hard work and high ideals, extraordinary talent and a common touch," Cohon said three days in advance of the 2008 Grey Cup, while also honouring recently deceased friends of the CFL such as Bob Ackles, Ralph Sazio, Jake Gaudaur, Earl Lunsford, Don Wittman, Don Chevrier and Leif Pettersen. "Unique in that he contributed to our league in so many different ways, he is typical of the friends who left us this year, role models and mentors who were often as humble as they were highly accomplished, men who have left us all a legacy on which to build."

Lancaster was not one to build himself up. On numerous occasions, he could not comprehend the fuss. Yet he was gracious with those who flocked to him — and appreciative of the country that adopted him.

"He said that during his life he made two big plays," Ron Jr. concluded. "One was marrying his wife, Bev, and the second was coming to Canada. I think that says it all."

EPILOGUE

Eagle Keys has never courted attention, but nonetheless received it in abundance when the 1966 Roughriders reconvened. The first formal function of a 40th-anniversary reunion was held on a Thursday evening in the Telegraph Room at Casino Regina. Without any fanfare, Keys entered the room and settled into a chair, just to the right of the entrance. One by one, or in small groups, those who played for Keys made their way over to renew acquaintances with their former head coach. Long-retired from football, and from a post-coaching career at IPSCO in Vancouver, the 82-year-old Keys chatted amiably with everyone who approached him. There once was a time when Keys provided entertainment at social gatherings by playing the spoons. On this occasion, he sat back and savoured it all.

Not far away, Ron Lancaster was holding court, as only he could. The Little General was involved in a series of animated discussions with ex-teammates and long-time friends. The fun continued for four days — July 6-9, 2006 — as most of the 1966 Roughriders reconnected. "It couldn't have been done better," Lancaster said of the reunion. "It was just an outstanding four days, especially when you count the number of people who came back for it. That, number

Ron Lancaster and **Ron Atchison** at the 40th reunion |
Photo courtesy of *Leader-Post*

one, is a surprise. We had five who had passed away. Everyone who was there really enjoyed it. [The Roughriders] did it right. I don't know of anybody who did not have fun ... and it was great that Eagle could get back there."

Almost everyone did. It was a walk around the block for Regina residents Sandy Archer, Ron Atchison, Al Benecick, Dale West, Henry Dorsch, Dale Laird, Ed McQuarters, Alan Ford, Ken Reed and Gene Wlasiuk. Wayne Shaw and Ted Urness made the trip from Saskatoon. Galen Wahlmeier came in from White Bear, Sask. Longer journeys were made by Don Bahnuik and Hugh Campbell (both from Edmonton), George Reed (Calgary), Tom Beynon (Waterloo, Ont.), Gil Petmanis (Oshawa, Ont.), Jack Abendschan (Abilene, Tex.), Bruce Bennett (Lake Wales, Fla.), Clyde Brock (Lake Oswego, Ore.), Wally Dempsey (Sacramento, Calif.), Bob Kosid (Hamilton), Larry Dumelie (Osgoode, Ont.), Garner Ekstran (Bow, Wash.) and Don Gerhardt (Golden Valley, Minn.). Some of them were still active in football. Abendschan was coaching the offensive line and tight ends at McMurry University in Abilene. Likewise, Bennett was coaching at Lake Wales High School. Campbell was the Edmonton Eskimos' chief executive officer.

Archer retired after his long and successful career with the Roughriders. Atchison and Laird went into carpentry. Benecick spent 15 years with the Saskatchewan Property Management Corporation, retiring about five years before the reunion. West, who enjoyed a lengthy career as a teacher and principal, went on to become the program co-ordinator with the Saskatchewan Sports Hall of Fame before being elected to the Regina Public School Board. Dorsch spent 25 years with the Public Service Commission before retiring in December of 2005. Ford was semi-retired at the time of the 2006 gathering, working as a sales representative for Intergold. Ken Reed remained active in business circles as the operator of Reed Leisure Products. Wlasiuk was a wine representative until his retirement.

Urness retired in 1997 after spending five years as chairman/CEO of the Saskatchewan Liquor Board, plus 22 years in the farm and industrial equipment business. Also in Saskatoon, Shaw operated a used-book store — A Book Hunter. Wahlmeier, a former school teacher, kept enhancing the lives of young people by helping out at boys' and girls' camps at Kenosee during the summer. The mayor of Estevan from 1976 to 1982, Wahlmeier also served as a board member with the Southeast Saskatchewan Association for Culture, Recreation and Sport.

Bahnuik became a financial and insurance adviser. Brock lived in San Diego for nearly 30 years, working for medical-supply and trucking companies, before moving up the coast to Oregon. Dempsey settled in California, running Dempsey Construction in Sacramento. Dumelie journeyed to the reunion from the Ottawa area, where he owns a 100-acre farm. Kosid, based in Hamilton, took a break from his job as the loading dock foreman for Northam, an office management company. Gerhardt was the CEO of Medical Alley/MNBIO — a health care and life science trade association — when the 1966 Roughriders reconvened. Ekstran was as busy as ever as the Western Canadian territory sales manager for Miller Ag-Bag, which sells agricultural products. Based in his birthplace of Bow, Wash., he often returns to Regina for business reasons. The reunion was a pleasure trip.

Ron Cobbledick and Don Thompson also enjoyed the festivities. Although they did not play in a game for the 1966 Roughriders, they were members of the team's taxi squad that season. Cobbledick previously played linebacker with the Luther Lions and Regina Rams. Thompson, a running back who graduated from Central Collegiate, was on the taxi squad in 1965 and 1966 after attending Bemidji State University in Minnesota. Cobbledick, like Thompson, became a respected educator.

Petmanis was not located until the reunion was six weeks away. When reached by the author in Oshawa, Ont., the former receiver was emotional. "If I have to hitchhike, I'll get there," Petmanis, then 65, said in late May of 2006. "If I get the info, I will be there, and I'll make myself younger ... Oh God, I get nostalgic. I'm starting to cry. This is the first time I've heard from anyone in a long, long time ... This is shocking. I never thought I'd hear anything like that. You tell them that if they send me the brochures and letters, I will be there." His contact information was promptly passed on to Jim Hopson, who took it from there. Petmanis, a Roughrider for only one year, had a grand time.

In most cases, those who attended the reunion did not have to be introduced to one another. Susan Jacks was a notable exception. She knew of everyone, but was meeting many of the 1966 Roughriders for the first time. The previous October, her husband — Ted Dushinski — had died of cancer at age 62. "She said she had to come to this reunion," Lancaster said. "She had heard so many stories from Ted about the people he had played with in Saskatchewan that she had to meet them to see if they were the way she had them pictured. She hadn't met a whole lot of us. She really enjoyed it."

Even so, it was also an emotional time. "For the 1966 reunion, I represented him on the field," Jacks recalled. "All those guys absolutely embraced me because they all loved Ted. I felt like I was one of them." That sentiment was strengthened when the Roughriders played host to the Calgary Stampeders on Day 3 of the reunion. "I went out on the field and they started to play the national anthem and I was in tears," Jacks said. "I just felt this rush of Ted being there and getting ready for the game."

For Jacks, the entire weekend was a rush — an experience that resonated with her long after the 1966 champions had dispersed. "I'd met some of the guys before, but Ted was always there," Jacks said. "Whatever that feeling was between them, I could see it, but I never really felt it pass through me until the '66 reunion. I even had so many of them send me e-mails after that, almost embracing me as one of the team. I was so touched by that. I don't know if I turned the page, but it helped me soak up some of the things. When I went to the reunion, I felt the relationship Ted had with the guys. They didn't have Ted there to direct it to, so it was directed to me in honour of him. It was fabulous. I feel like I could see those guys at any time. I can carry Ted's honour with me. I'm honoured by him and, to me, that's pretty special.

"We all have our own thing that we do. Mine is music, and I have a lot of people that I'm close to in the music industry. Ted got to know them, but he never got to feel what I got to feel. What I felt at the reunion was pretty amazing. All the ladies had a luncheon and we were all supposed to introduce ourselves. I totally lost it because all of a sudden it would flood back to me about little stories he told about the wives. I knew how much all these people meant to him. It was overwhelming."

Bob Kosid and his son, Rob, cherished a reunion within a reunion. Both Robert Kosids arrived in Regina on Day 1 of the 40th-anniversary gathering, at which point they saw each other for the first time in just over a year. The younger Kosid, a lieutenant-colonel in the United States Marine Corps, had returned home to Oceanside, Calif., on March 24, 2006, following a fourth deployment in Iraq. His father travelled to the reunion from Hamilton.

"My Grey Cup is coming home ... and coming here," Rob Kosid said in the lounge at the Hotel Saskatchewan Radisson Plaza, shortly after embracing his father. Rob marked the occasion by giving a present to the former Roughriders defensive back. "When my dad retired from football, he gave me his football helmet," Rob said. "To reciprocate, I brought him the floppy hat I wore in Iraq. I also brought an indelible marker. I'm going to ask all his teammates to sign the helmet this weekend."

Rob had received his invitation to the reunion via e-mail in January of 2006 while stationed at a base near the Jordan/Syria border. For the reunion, the Roughriders covered the costs for each player and one guest. Bob Kosid — with the encouragement of his second wife, Wendy — invited Rob as his guest. "I was floored, absolutely," said Rob Kosid, then 41. "We were living in plywood shacks. I said, 'I'm going to Regina!' They all knew my old man played ball up here and that I have an affinity for all things Canadian. I said, 'I'm going back to the town I grew up in.' " Upon returning to Regina, Rob sat in the hotel lounge, surrounded by the likes of Roughriders luminaries Larry Dumelie, Eagle Keys and Bill Baker. "These were my first heroes," Rob said with a smile.

Rob Kosid was involved in a few "skirmishes," but accentuated the positive experiences. He worked to develop and fortify the Iraqi army and also contributed to the restoration of schools while away from his wife (Michelle), daughter (Sarah) and son (Cameron). Barely two months after rejoining his home team in California, Rob was reunited with his father in Regina. "It's difficult to put into words," Rob said. "It's like you've been anticipating a movie — something you've been waiting to see for a long time — and now you're in the first five minutes and it's really good so far. I've been thinking about this day for a long time."

Tom Beynon had spent a considerable period appreciating the generosity of another former Roughriders offensive lineman. Jack Abendschan had played an instrumental role in enabling Beynon to attend law school at the University of Saskatchewan while playing for the Roughriders. At one point, it appeared that Beynon would have to quit football during the 1966 season to attend law school in Ontario, but the scenario changed due to Abendschan's intervention. Beynon went on to enjoy a lengthy and successful career in law. As the reunion approached, Beynon made this author aware of Abendschan's contributions. Beynon composed and e-mailed a story that he headlined "Thanks, Jack Abendschan. Thanks, Saskatchewan." Beynon's story was excerpted in the *Leader-Post* and the e-mail was promptly forwarded to Abendschan. Only then was the seven-time all-star made aware of the extent to which he had impacted Beynon's life and career. "A lot of times when we do things with people, we don't know the significance that what we say or what we do is going to have on that person," Abendschan said after reading the e-mail.

Tom Beynon (left) and Jack Abendschan renew old friendships at 40th reunion | Photo courtesy of *Leader-Post*

Beynon and Abendschan were reunited in Casino Regina's Telegraph Room on July 6, 2006. It is impossible to say how Beynon's legal career would have unfolded if not for Abendschan's assistance. "If he hadn't done that, I would have been, I'm sure, an able lawyer in Kitchener-Waterloo, but I would never have done what I did in the world marketplace," Beynon reflected. "It gave me a whole air of confidence and it introduced me to people I probably wouldn't have otherwise met. I would have never practised law with the people I did. I would have never travelled the world. I've had privileges and I'm grateful to so many people, but if Jack hadn't done what he did, I probably would have finished law school at [the University of] Western Ontario and come back to Kitchener-Waterloo and practised law."

At the reunion, Beynon applied a hug the moment he saw Abendschan. On this occasion, the two former offensive linemen had no qualms about holding.

Another erstwhile Roughriders offensive lineman enabled the reunion to become reality. "I felt very strongly that it needed to happen," said Roughriders president and chief executive officer Jim Hopson, who played for the team from 1973 to 1976. "A lot of that is because I'm an alumnus. I understand what it would mean to the guys. I understood what it would mean to the province, too. It was 40 years. I thought, 'This isn't going to happen again. If we don't celebrate it now, by the time we get to the 50th anniversary in 2016, a lot of them are going to be gone.' I knew if we were going to do it, we had to do it now, for a whole bunch of reasons.

I thought, 'What better way to capture that special feeling we have for the Riders in this province and who better to demonstrate that than that '66 team?' Part of it was feeling it was the right thing to do for those guys, for that team, and I also felt it would be a really good way to build up the image of the team and capture what we're about and who we're about. It was a great marketing opportunity. There were a lot of reasons.

"I know that with the joy that I saw in those guys when they were here and even since, it was a big deal to them and worth the trouble. I saw it in a lot of the fans, too, who really, really appreciated it. It was a lot of work. We did it in a hurry. But it was the absolute right thing to do. If you want to be a great organization, you have to remember where you come from and honour and respect those people."

Hopson emphasized that he was not solely responsible for the reunion. He quickly enlisted Alan Ford to assist with the organization. Ford was typically dutiful and thorough as he immersed himself in reuniting as many of his former teammates as possible.

Contacting the players and making travel arrangements was one part of the equation for Hopson, Ford and others who brought together the 1966 Roughriders. Planning the schedule was another. On Thursday night, there was the social at Casino Regina. The next afternoon, the players enjoyed a golf outing, followed by an evening social in Mosaic Stadium's Green and White Lounge. Saturday's festivities were highly public. The 1966 Roughriders signed autographs at the Saskatchewan Sports Hall of Fame and Museum before being honoured at an evening game against the Calgary Stampeders.

Chris Jaster, then 22, attended the autograph session, arriving 90 minutes in advance of the players. Even at that early juncture, the lineup stretched from the front door, down the steps, down the east side of the sidewalk and about three-quarters of the way down the block on Cornwall Street. Jaster ended up getting the signatures of every player but one — Hugh Campbell, who was en route to Regina from Edmonton following an Eskimos game — on a commemorative calendar. "By the time I left, I realized that I had just encountered greatness and a team that may never be forgotten," Jaster said.

Following the Stampeders' 53-36 victory, many of the players returned to the Hotel Saskatchewan to resume socializing. "After the game, we started hearing the same stories as when we played," Ron Lancaster recalled. "Hell, I thought these guys had played a game. It just was a fun time." That non-scheduled gathering is among Ford's fondest memories of the reunion weekend. "We were sitting around in the bar of the hotel," he said. "Eagle was there, and George and Ronnie and Kosid and Dorsch. It kind of reminded me of the social function after the season when we were players. It was just recalling the memories of a season then, compared to in the reunion recalling the moments of careers."

And the time whizzed by. "All of a sudden, it was 2:30 in the morning," Ford marvelled. "I never stay up that late. The people came by and said, 'Hey, um, we're closing. It's time to go.' I was thinking, 'What the hell? We just got here!' " That was merely one occasion where 2006 felt like 1966. "The other one was at the Hall of Fame," Ford said. "We're all sitting in the autograph line, going back and forth with one guy who's at the front of the line yelling at somebody. It was almost like sitting in a bus as a player and guys yelling from the front row of the bus to the back row of the bus. We had the chatter going all the time about who's signing slowly. It's kind of the same sort of chatter you had in those days when you're taking the bus from the hotel to pre-game practice or wherever else we would have gone."

The players who toiled for the 2006 Roughriders were preoccupied with the Calgary game, but many of them took time to associate with and appreciate the alumni from 40 years earlier. "At the time, we had some cynical players who ended up playing on different teams," receiver Matt Dominguez recalled. "It was, 'What about the Edmonton teams that have 15 Grey Cup rings? Are they going to celebrate those teams?' It's just different. There's not any other professional team, so those are the only championship teams you can hang your hat on. Forty years later, for those guys to come back, it was nostalgic for a lot of people. There were older fans who remember back in the time when those legends were playing."

Despite being one of the Roughriders' elder statesmen, Gene Makowsky is too young to have watched any of the heroes of 1966, except on film. With that in mind, the veteran offensive lineman seized the opportunity to get to know his forerunners. "It was pretty cool," Makowsky said. "A lot of the guys came out and that was nice. I just shook hands with a few of the guys. I didn't have a lot of time to chat a whole lot, but it was cool. The bad thing about it is, I saw how sore they were, with the bad knees and the bad backs and that type of thing, so that was something that struck me as well. But after 40 years, they're still remembered for that and that group is still special. They really got along well from the times I saw them together. That's something that I hope will happen with myself and my experience."

As much as the reunion was a celebration, there were bittersweet moments. The 1966 Roughriders took time to honour five players who had passed away — receiver Gord Barwell, running backs Ed Buchanan and Paul Dudley, defensive back Ted Dushinski and linebacker Cliff Shaw — with many of their family members in attendance. General manager Ken Preston, president Don MacDonald and equipment manager Hinckley Archer were also remembered. The notable absentees included assistant coaches Jack Gotta (health reasons) and Jim Duncan (who sent his regrets from Calabash, N.C., while overlooking a golf course from his backyard). Reg Whitehouse was invited but, for reasons that were never entirely clear, did not attend the reunion. Tight end Jim Worden wanted to be there, but illness made that impossible.

"Along the way, the conversation I had with Jim Worden came back to me," Alan Ford said. "Here's a guy who couldn't care less about these kinds of things [in the 1960s], yet when I talked to him, his voice was like if he had enough strength, he was going to do everything he could — even if it killed him — to get to this reunion. That was not like the Jim Worden I knew. He was a black-and-white guy who didn't care about all that stuff. To hear him call and kind of apologize for not being able to come because he just can't come out of the house, holy smokes ...

"It just made me appreciate the whole reunion a lot more. If there was any way possible, he would have been there. When he was healthy, he probably wouldn't have come. He would have said, 'I'm not coming back, anyway. Half those guys, I didn't know that well, anyhow,' but for him to kind of say that, those things in life, they pass you by, and sometimes you don't take advantage of them. It's different than a high school reunion or a college reunion. Those are good, too, but when you go through something we went through as a team and became the first ever to win the Cup for Saskatchewan, you had to be there."

The reunion wrapped up with a Sunday morning breakfast — another bittersweet occasion. "It was the last time that we were all together," Ford said. "Eagle and Ronnie and George were there. That was a pretty special moment. When you're there at the breakfast, you know it's over. You're not going to see many of these guys again who don't live here. By the time it's the next big time, there's going to be a bunch of them who won't be around. I think there was a lot of that feeling at the breakfast.

"During the time, when the guys came in and there were all these events, it was, 'What's the next event? Let's go.' All of a sudden, it's the breakfast and some of the guys have already left and people are getting up to leave because they've got to catch a flight to get out. You're thinking, 'Look around the room, because you're not going to see this many people again. A lot of these people won't be around very much longer.' There were a lot of different emotions for most of the players on that weekend."

There would be other Grey Cups for Roughriders fans to celebrate. The season after the 1966 reunion, Saskatchewan snapped an 18-year championship drought by capturing the third title in franchise history. The champions of 1989 and 2007 are noteworthy in their own right, considering the infrequency with which Saskatchewan has ruled Canadian football.

Until November of 2007, for example, Saskatchewan had won as many Grey Cups as Sarnia. Such a notion would be difficult for fans in Edmonton, especially, to digest. A reunion of one championship edition would be a preposterous suggestion in the Alberta capital, where the Eskimos have captured as many as five titles in succession.

Bob Poley and **Roger Aldag** *with Riders' second Grey Cup in 1989* |
Photo courtesy of *Leader-Post*

In Saskatchewan, by contrast, the championship teams are easily isolated and forever immortalized. The victories of 1989 and 2007 showcased stars such as Kent Austin, Richie Hall, Roger Aldag, Bob Poley, Gene Makowsky, Jeremy O'Day, Kerry Joseph, James Johnson, John Chick, Reggie Hunt, Ray Elgaard, Bobby Jurasin, Don Narcisse, Glen Suitor, Eddie Lowe and Dave Ridgway. But those players, and others, could not say that they were part of the first group to bring home a Grey Cup to Saskatchewan — 56 long years after the franchise's inception, and after eight previous losses in the national final.

"There is still the feeling today about how important that team was, not just to the community but to ourselves," Larry Dumelie, a defensive back with the 1966 Roughriders, reflected 40 years later. "It was such a huge task to win the Grey Cup up to that point. Since then, it has still been pretty tough for teams to win the Grey Cup. It seems like a tougher job than most.

"Having won that really made us feel special. Of course, the fans have made us feel special ever since."

ACKNOWLEDGEMENTS

So here we are, having reached the end zone. This project — which began as a dream — took nearly four years to complete, from the first interview to the time of publication. Granted, that is a fraction of the time that elapsed before the Roughriders finally won their first Grey Cup, but ...

This initiative began as an exploration of the 1966 season for publication in the *Leader-Post*, and ended up extending so much further, while becoming an obsession. There is so much more to that team than originally meets the eye. The same can be said of the book-writing process, particularly for a first-time author. Thankfully, I had plenty of wonderful people on my side.

My great friend Mark Anderson deserves commendation. Mark is the principal at Luther College High School in Regina. He interrupted a gargantuan writing exercise of his own — his doctoral thesis in Educational Administration — to read the manuscript and provide an assortment of suggestions. I felt sheepish about asking, given the myriad demands upon his time, but he cordially consented. To use a baseball analogy, Mark was the closer. Once the book received his assent, I knew it was ready to go. Mark is like a brother and a father to me, and I cannot thank him enough for everything he has done to enhance my life. That includes the blessing that is godfatherhood. Mark's son, Eric, always provided laughter when I needed a break from an imposing project.

This project would not have been possible without the selfless assistance of *Leader-Post* colleague Nick Miliokas, who repeatedly pored over every word of the manuscript and offered invaluable advice as far as structure and tone. You're a saint, Nick.

Another key contributor was my wife, Chryssoula Filippakopoulous. She has personally inspected the aforementioned sentence to ensure that one of the toughest challenges — the act of correctly spelling her name — was met.

I presented Chryssoula with more challenges than you can imagine. I am work-addicted at the best of times, and suddenly I wanted to add a book to the pile. More than once, I begged her: "Please let me get to 2009. Then you'll have a real husband." A considerable portion of my leisure time was dedicated to this project. Some of the precious time spent with my wife was devoted to this book. Chryssoula, who is a graduate of the Ryerson journalism school and a former ace reporter at the *Moose Jaw Times-Herald*, was remarkably patient throughout this protracted process.

We do not have children. Chryssoula understood that this book was my baby, and contributed mightily to its nurturing by simply allowing me to see this through. Nobody made more sacrifices than my wife, who even transported some of my 1966 files to Mexico in her carry-on luggage so that I could write this "baby" during an alleged vacation. The same thing happened when we went to New York three months later. Of the first 30 chapters, 23 were written during supposed vacations. Overnight, as my wife attempted to sleep, I would write ... and write ... and write. Chryssoula ended up finding Mr. Write. To my astonishment, she endures this.

Leader-Post editor-in-chief Janice Dockham was somewhat alarmed that I would write a book during vacation time. But Janice understands how passionate I am about this project and, without her, this book would not have been possible. She even understood when the *Leader-Post*'s microfilm machine needed to be repeatedly repaired — not at inconsiderable expense — because of my assaults upon the device during the research process. And, uh, I may have done a little extra photocopying ...

Kevin Blevins, a *Leader-Post* deputy editor, embraced the 1966 project from its infancy. I pitched it to Blevs early in 2006, as the Roughriders were beginning preparations for a 40th-anniversary reunion. Not only did he provide his blessing to a five-part newspaper series on the 1966 Roughriders, he also ensured that each day's kickoff story appeared prominently on the front page of the newspaper.

Early in the research process, it occurred to me that there was the potential for a spinoff into a book. Of course, everyone who has ever sat before a typewriter or computer thinks that he or she can write a book. There is, however, the matter of finding a publisher. I was blessed to be able to collaborate with one of the best — Dan Marce of PrintWest. As a lifelong fan of and contributor to the Roughriders, Dan understands football in Saskatchewan and shares my appreciation for the 1966 Roughriders. His unwavering assistance has been a gift. Dan's love of the Roughriders began in 1951, when Glenn Dobbs was the quarterback. Fittingly, the book begins with a flashback to 1951.

All of the aforementioned served as proofreaders. Any errors that appear in this book are my own.

Now, where does one begin in thanking those who were affiliated with the 1966 Roughriders? Every single person who was contacted for an interview willingly and instantaneously consented. Many of these people were interviewed on several occasions. Oh, if only I had a dollar for every time I warbled, "Sorry to bother you again, but ..."

Given the unfailing and unconditional co-operation of everyone I approached, it is with some hesitancy that I single out a few individuals, but some people went well beyond the call of duty.

Ron Lancaster punctuated each of our many conversations with a genial, "If there's anything else you need, just give me a call." So I called. Or I sent him e-mails. His cordial assistance and the unwavering precision with which he recalled events of more than 40 years ago absolutely floored me. In another sense, so did the news of his death on

Sept. 18, 2008. The first rough draft of the manuscript had been completed six weeks earlier. An additional chapter — 38 — was written in tribute.

How can one mention Ronnie without segueing into George Reed? He answered questions just like he ran the football — straight-ahead, without shying away from anything. I had interviewed George only once prior to writing this book. Getting to know this amazing man ranks as a career highlight. One day, he patiently gave me over an hour of his time when I telephoned him at Shaganappi Pontiac Buick GMC in Calgary. During the conversation, I overheard someone paging him. I can only hope that I did not cost him a commission.

Ed McQuarters has been a huge proponent of this project since its incubation. As mentioned in the prologue, his willingness to tell his life story was the catalyst for this book. Most people involved with the Roughriders' first championship edition refer to McQuarters as the difference-maker in 1966. He was certainly a difference-maker for me.

Alan Ford's congeniality and co-operative nature never cease to amaze. He even lent me his 1966 game ball for a day. He has answered more phone messages than anyone during the preparatory stages of this book. This classy gentleman is richly deserving of his two Grey Cup rings and the accompanying plaudits.

Ford was a valuable member of the Roughriders in 1966 (as a player) and 1989 (as the general manager). The Roughriders' first two championship teams have been enshrined in the Saskatchewan Sports Hall of Fame and Museum. If you ask me, Hall of Fame employees Sheila Kelly and Jacqueline Campbell are also worthy of enshrinement. They cordially opened up their files of printed and photographed material pertaining to the 1966 Roughriders and the key individuals on that team. The Hall is an invaluable and under-rated resource for a researcher or a sports fan.

Although a handful of people have been highlighted, profuse thanks goes to everyone else who was interviewed. They are, in alphabetical order: Jack Abendschan, Les Anderson, Sandy Archer, Barry Armstrong, Laurie Artiss, Ron Atchison, Kent Austin, John Badham, Don Bahnuik, Peter Barry, Jay Barwell, Nancy Barwell Kraft, Al Benecick, Bruce Bennett, Tom Beynon, Rob Bresciani, Clyde Brock, Hugh Campbell, Gary Crone, Gordon Currie, Roger Currie, Matt Dominguez, Henry Dorsch, Larry Dumelie, Jim Duncan, Bess Eisler, Richard Eisler, Garner Ekstran, Don Gerhardt, Mick Grainger, Ray Guay, John Haggett, Lorne Harasen, Paul Harasen, Wayne Harris, Paul Henderson, Jim Hopson, Bobby Hull, Susan Jacks, Russ Jackson, Eagle Keys, Bob Kosid, Joe Kosid, Robert Kosid Jr., Dale Laird, Bill Lancaster, Ron Lancaster Jr., John Lynch, Gene Makowsky, Dwayne Mandrusiak, Peter Mansbridge, Ian McKay, Jim McKean, Ed McQuarters, Ed McQuarters Jr., Rodger Milliken, Lana Mueller, Marc Mueller, Deanne Newkirk, Bob O'Billovich, Mike O'Donnell, Bob Pelling, Gil Petmanis, Ken Ploen, Bill Preston, Rich Preston, Wally Read, Georgette Reed, Ken Reed, Tim Roth, Neil Sawatzky, Bob Shaw, Wayne Shaw, Tom Shepherd, Marge Smith, Jim Taylor, Don Thompson, Eric Tillman, Frank Tripucka, Randy Tripucka, Ted Urness, Galen Wahlmeier, Brad Wall, Dale West, Joanne Whitehouse, Reg Whitehouse, Timber Whitehouse, Brian Williams, Gene Wlasiuk and Roy Wright.

Rhett Dawson, Glenn Dobbs, Ted Dushinski, Tony Gabriel, Larry Robinson and Joey Walters — all of whom were interviewed before research for this book began — were also valuable resources. They were interviewed for other purposes anywhere from four to 20 years ago. Their contributions are appreciated.

Assistance in various forms was also provided by Colleen Anderson, Roy Antal, Brenda Atchison, Mitchell Blair, Bob Boehm, Will Chabun, John Chaput, Scott Clark, Duane Cook, Randy Deck, Bob Florence, Don Healy, Bob Hughes, Shadia Ismail, Dave Jamieson, Chris Jaster, Wayne Koenig, Jean Lancaster Angotti, Delailah Little, Sue Marshall, Ashley Martin, Ryan Maurer, Kevin Mitchell, Wray Morrison, Jack Morrow, Larry Mueller, Barb Pacholik, Michael Petrie, Bruce Pierce, Jana G. Pruden, Joshua Sawka, Bryan Schlosser, Phyllis Schwann, Vanna Gay Shaw, Elaine Shein, Laura Vanstone Steadman, Sheri Trapp, Tom Valcke, Bev Wake, Ryan Whippler and Dan Yates.

And let's not forget CBC Saskatchewan's Costa Maragos, a very kind soul who dubbed me the entire 1966 Grey Cup telecast (including all the pregame and postgame coverage, plus some classically corny commercials).

Thanks as well to Sharon J. Maier and May P. Chan of the Regina Public Library's Prairie History Room, and Dana Turgeon and Krista Bradley of the City of Regina Archives.

When the words needed jazzing up, I often derived the necessary inspiration from Brian Delp. Brian is the host of *Jazz After Hours*, on radio station WBGO (from Newark, N.J.). A considerable portion of this book was written overnight while listening to WBGO on iTunes. Who could have imagined such technology in 1966?

I also wish to thank my colleagues in the sports department of the *Leader-Post* — Darrell Davis, Ian Hamilton, Murray McCormick, Tim Switzer and Greg Harder. The obsession with 1966 occasionally diverted me from matters of greater urgency. Their understanding and professionalism is appreciated. The same applies to Deputy Editor (Nights) David Ramsay, who tolerated the "work" days when I tinkered with this book. I am so blessed to work with everyone at the *Leader-Post*. Thanks to them, it isn't work.

Speaking of colleagues, a huge shout-out must go to Jana G. Pruden and Barb Pacholik — two top-notch *Leader-Post* news reporters who have written two books on Saskatchewan crime stories (*Sour Milk* and *Paper Cows*). I benefited from their prior experience as authors. On many an occasion, Barb asked me how the book-writing process was going, and always offered encouragement. Ditto for Jana, whose pep talks and perspective were invaluable. More often than I should admit, I lumbered over to Jana's desk and warbled something unintelligible on days when the writing was stalled, laboured or seemingly in another language. The enormity of the project intimidated me at the outset. Jana's advice: "Don't try to write it all in one day. Set a goal each day and attain that." Instead of trying to tackle 140,000 words in one sitting, I reminded myself of Jana's words. Profuse thanks to Jana and Barb.

Thanks to you as well for taking the time to read this book. I hope you found it to be worth your time and expense.

And thanks, Mom.

BIBLIOGRAPHY

Andrews, Garry, and Calder, Bob. *Rider Pride*. Saskatoon: Western Producer Prairie Books, 1984.

Chaput, John. *Saskatchewan Sports Legends*. Markham, Ont.: Johnson Gorman Publishers, 2005.

Coleman, Jim. *Fifty Years of Canadian Sport from the Man Who Saw It All* (edited by Jim Taylor). Madeira Park, B.C.: Harbour Publishing Co. Ltd., 2005.

Gifford, Frank, with Richmond, Peter. *The Glory Game*. New York: HarperCollins, 2008.

Kelly, Graham. *Green Grit*. Toronto: HarperCollins Publishers Ltd., 2001.

Meggyesy, Dave. *Out Of Their League*. Berkeley, Calif.: Ramparts Press Inc., 1970.

Neal, Roy (editor). *50 Years Of Progress: Regina, Queen City of the Plains*, 1903-1953. Western Printers Association Ltd., 1953.

Phillips, Curt. *Saskatchewan Roughriders Player Reference*, 1960-1996. Self-published, 1997.

Smith, Martin. "No Ordinary Black Man," from *The Nation* (magazine), Oct. 28, 1968.

Staubach, Roger, with Blair, Sam, and St. John, Bob. *First Down, Lifetime To Go*. Waco, Texas: Key-Word, 1974.

Sullivan, Jack. *The Grey Cup Story*. Don Mills, Ont.: Greywood Publishing Ltd., 1971.

Yuen, Edward. *92 Years of Roughrider Football*. Regina: Self-published, 2002.